*Second Edition*

# A Beginner's Guide to VAX/VMS Utilities and Applications

Property of Maureen J. Clancy

## Digital Press Users Series

*Paul C. Anagnostopoulos*
**VAX/VMS: Writing Real Programs in DCL**

*Philip E. Bourne*
**UNIX for VMS Users**

*James F. Peters III and Patrick Holmay*
**An Introduction to VAX/VMS**

*Ronald M. Sawey and Troy T. Stokes*
**A Beginner's Guide to VAX/VMS Utilities and Applications**, *Second Edition*

*Christine M. Gianone*
**Using MS-DOS KERMIT: Connecting Your PC to the Electronic World** *Second Edition*

*Second Edition*

# A Beginner's Guide to **VAX/VMS Utilities and Applications**

Ronald M. Sawey
Troy T. Stokes

**Digital Press**

Digital Press ™ is an imprint of Butterworth-Heinemann, Publisher for Digital Equipment Corporation.



Recognizing the importance of preserving what has been written, it is the policy of Butterworth-Heinemann to have the books it publishes printed on acid-free paper, and we exert our best efforts to that end.



**Library of Congress Cataloging-in-Publication Data**

Sawey, Ronald M.
A beginner's guide to VAX/VMS utilities and applications/
Ronald M. Sawey, Troy T. Stokes—2nd ed.
p. cm.
Includes bibliographical references and index.
ISBN 1-55558-066-1
1. Operating systems (computers) 2. VAX/VMS
I. Stokes, Troy T. II. Title.
QA76. 76.063S36 1991
005.4'449—dc20 91-30994
CIP

The publisher offers discounts on bulk orders of this book.
For information, please write:

Manager of Special Sales
Digital Press
Butterworth-Heinemann
313 Washington St.
Newton, MA 02158

Order number EY-F589E-DP

10 9 8 7 6 5 4 3 2

Printed in the United States of America

# Contents

# Preface

This book is designed to help beginners who may or may not have had any previous experience with computers. Many of these will be students in high school or colleges or universities where computer literacy and other fundamental courses are taught on a VAX/VMS system. Another class of users will be newcomers to commercial VAX/VMS sites who are enrolled in company-sponsored short courses designed to enable them to become knowledgeable VAX/VMS beginners in a short period of time. All these users will have their way paved for them by instructors or supervisors. The authors ask the indulgence of these readers in disregarding a large number of notes directed at those users who are working without support or supervision. We want this book to be useful for this category of beginners, too.

It cannot be emphasized too strongly that this book is a hands-on product to enable beginners to use a handful of applications quickly. It is not a reference manual or a text for advanced courses. Nor does it discuss philosophical or societal questions about computers.

To date, this book has been used in various revisions by more than 7,000 students. Many of these have been candidates for teaching certificates. These students often have an intense interest in word processing and text formatting. When this book has been used in introductory computer literacy courses, supplemental readings about the social changes occasioned by computers have been required by the individual instructors.

This text was used in its initial draft form by students at Southwest Texas State University in Fall 1986, shortly after two VAX 8600s were installed for student computing. It was written because no elementary introductory material was otherwise available. We surmise that the lack of such resources is connected with the fact that VAX computers were initially created to serve the needs of expert users such as scientists, engineers, and programmers. Now, of course, the VAX is in widespread use among many classes of users. Beginning computer literacy courses that rely on VAX/VMS systems are far from uncommon.

A word about language: Sometimes the term *user* is contrasted with *programmer* to indicate two different functions people carry out with computers. But we ask our readers not to imagine too deep a chasm between the two functions. Bear in mind that when you customize the way the VAX computer works for you by adapting your `LOGIN.COM` file, you are doing a kind of programming. The same principle applies when you customize your `MSKERMIT.INI` file for use on an MS-DOS microcomputer.

Both authors concede a bias in favor of computer literacy courses that rely substantially on use of the mainframe or minicomputer. With communications programs providing electronic mail on one computer as well as networking among computers all over the world, new users are invited to see the entry into computing as an entry to a new kind of community. This perception is often lost in a strictly microcomputer environment.

In that connection, we want to hear from you about how to improve this book. Our software illustrations are accurate for current versions, but we want to know when later versions cause revisions to become necessary. Please write us at the physical address:

Ronald M. Sawey
Department of Computer Science
Southwest Texas State University
San Marcos, TX 78666

You may also use the BITNET electronic address: RS01@SWTEXAS.

In closing, we both gratefully acknowledge the contributions of the following colleagues and friends: A. E. Borm, J. Slomka, T. Sumbera, C. Hazlewood, and Bo Threadgill.

*Ronald M. Sawey*
*Troy T. Stokes*

# Introduction

The VAX family of computer systems covers a wide range of equipment, from free-standing workstations to clustered mainframe processors linked in giant networks. Readers of this book will confront a variety of computer components, peripheral equipment, and applications programs that will differ from one VAX installation to another. However, all these computer systems share a similar internal design and run one of two operating systems (we will be discussing one of these, VMS). The VAX computers that use the VMS operating system all basically function alike.

Because the VMS operating system is designed to support a complex range of powerful equipment, VMS may seem more unapproachable to first-time users than microcomputer operating systems. With a little instruction and some hands-on experience, however, beginning users can learn to be comfortable with VMS.

This book is designed to help you confidently perform simple and useful tasks on a VAX/VMS system, no matter which particular equipment you are using. Once over this initial hurdle of making the computer work for you in some simple ways, you should then feel empowered to pursue more complicated applications of the programs we discuss. You should be able to proceed on your own, using the Quick Reference summaries and the detailed readings and documentation we suggest.

To make the VAX/VMS computer system easier for beginners to master, this book contains material set up on your VAX/VMS system in a directory of files called TEXTFILES. The files in this directory can be entered using a text editor and the listings provided in Appendixes C and I. There is also a less painful way. Simply order the MS-DOS diskette containing this material from Digital Press. This instructional diskette also contains material for creating a beginner's diskette for use with Chapter 5, which teaches communication between an MS-DOS microcomputer system and a VAX/VMS computer system. The instructional diskette can be ordered at nominal charge from Digital Press by calling 1-800-366-2665. You may copy and distribute this diskette without charge as often as you wish.[1]

If you choose to use the instructional diskette rather than typing in all the files from the listings in the appendixes, the instructions for using this diskette to upload the files into a TEXTFILES directory on your VAX/VMS system are given in Appendix F. Instructions for creating a beginner's diskette for use with Chapter 5 are also given in Appendix F.

As you use this book, you should keep in mind some important points. Because of the variety of topics and the large quantity of material, it may often seem that just as you are getting familiar with one topic, we move on to another. Here are some things you can do to help reduce confusion: First, read the chapters of this book in an orderly, paced fashion, working through the material at a terminal whenever possible. Rather than hoard confusion, bring your questions to your instructor or user services staff. Second, whether using this book in a course or for self-study, you must *practice* the material on the computer as soon and as often as you can, and *reread* the chapters. It might surprise you how much more sense complicated instructions make on the second reading. You should budget at least two hours per week to practice your work on the computer, so that you

1. Only one chapter is rendered obscure without the instructional diskette: Chapter 5 would be only marginally useful to VAX/VMS beginners unless they are already very familiar with an MS-DOS computer.

don't forget your new skills. Finally, do as many of the exercises as possible. They extend as well as reinforce the text information.

We suggest you read the remainder of this Introduction before moving on to the other chapters; it gives a quick overview of the material you will cover in your study of VAX/VMS. First, you need to know how to get connected to the right computer. Many universities and work sites have an array of different computers. Next, you need to log in using your own account (see Section 1.1). After that, you need to know some fundamental commands of the VMS operating system.

An operating system is a program that performs mundane but vital procedures for the entire computer system. It keeps track of all users who are typing instructions to the main processing unit from terminals in different locations at the same time. Some of its commands can cause files of text to be displayed on the screen of your terminal or to be printed on high-speed line printers. It calls applications programs and utilities such as spreadsheets or text editors into operation. It also makes sure that these programs can find files that they need. When programs create output files, the operating system sees to it that these files are opened, written to, and closed without disturbing other files on the storage disks.

Chapter 2 moves us to the next subject: how to use a text editor. EVE, the text editor covered in this chapter, is not a complete, integrated word processor such as you might find on a microcomputer. EVE allows you to enter text from the keyboard and to save that text on a disk for later use. You may use EVE to revise text, correct errors, and move blocks of text from one place to another within a file or to different files. EVE requires at least a VT100 terminal or its compatible.

After a brief discussion of the DECspell spelling checker program in Chapter 3, we concentrate in Chapter 4 on how to create formatted text using a word processor, WPS-PLUS.

Micro communication with VAX/VMS systems, discussed in Chapter 5, makes use of the KERMIT program for transferring files between MS-DOS microcomputers and VAX/VMS systems. We also look at some fundamentals of the MS-DOS operating system here. The KERMIT program is included on the instructional diskette mentioned previously.

Chapter 6 discusses the area of electronic communications as it relates to VAX/VMS systems. You will learn how to use a method of real-time, on-line communication with the PHONE program. You will also delve into two other methods of electronic communications: MAIL and VAX Notes. Finally, you will see how to communicate with computer systems around the world using the BITNET computer network.

In Chapter 7, we move on to DATATRIEVE, a program that will allow you to create an orderly collection of information known as a database. Once you have created this database, you can extract selective facts that can help you solve problems in business or research. For example, an employer might use DATATRIEVE to produce a list of mid-level executives in the company who are minorities or women.

From DATATRIEVE we turn in Chapter 8 to DECalc, an electronic spreadsheet program. With a spreadsheet program you can represent data in the form of a table, where relations between tabular entries can be defined. You can also make fairly complex calculations quickly and easily. Once you have set up your spreadsheet, you can examine many "what if" scenarios. For example, how would the finances of your organization be affected by a 7 percent cut in revenue?

Finally, Chapter 9 covers some topics that you might use in learning to program in the high-level language BASIC on a VAX computer. VAX BASIC supports several structured commands that are not available in many other BASIC dialects. We clarify some of these constructs by way of several examples.

A special section listing commands and operations related to the program that has been discussed appears toward the end of each chapter. Occasionally, these Quick Reference sections may also include a few items not covered in the chapter, which you will find easy to learn after mastering the chapter material. The Quick References should be helpful when you need a brief reminder about how to do an operation but do not want to review the entire chapter. You may want to keep these summaries handy during your sessions at the terminal.

We strongly suggest that you cover Chapters 1 and 2 (the operating system and the EVE text editor) first.[2] We also suggest that you cover Chapter 3 (DECspell) and Chapter 4 (WPS-PLUS) or Appendix C (SCRIBE) as a unit and in that order. Otherwise, you can work through the topics in any order you prefer, with little loss of continuity.

You are now about to launch yourself into the world of VAX/VMS. You may suffer a few initial frustrations, but as you begin to master the applications presented here, the rewards will become clear.

---

2. If you are using an MS-DOS compatible computer, you should also consult Chapter 5 on the microcomputer–VAX/VMS connection and Appendix G and read the appropriate parts.

*Second Edition*

# A Beginner's Guide to VAX/VMS Utilities and Applications

Chapter 1

# Fundamental VMS Operating System Commands

## 1.1 Logging in to the VAX/VMS System

To begin working on the computer, you need to know how to log in—to gain access—to the system. This chapter assumes that you are already present at a functioning work site and are actually seated before your computer terminal. However, the "real world" is very complicated. Conditions will certainly vary at each work site or university. The number and kinds of computers available will vary, as will the steps necessary to get *to* your VAX or VAXcluster, as a group of interconnected VAX computers are often called. Some of you might not have access to a VAX at the present time but expect to soon. Some sites will provide an initialization file, and others will not. Appendix A gives specific examples to illustrate some of the network obstacles that you might encounter before being able to log in.

For your first interactive terminal session, you will need the user name and password given to you by your instructor or user services staff. You should think up your own password, one that is easier to remember than the long one often assigned to new users. It should not be anything obvious like your first name. You will also need access to a terminal. If you intend to use a personal computer as a remote terminal, review Chapter 5 on the micro–

```
Username: YOUR_USERNAME   ! Type in your user name.
Password:                 ! No echo for the password.
                          ! NOTE: First time users might
                          !       be expected to set a new
                          !       password by issuing the
                          !       command SET PASSWORD
                          !       and following the
                          !       prompts.
        Welcome to VAX/VMS version V5.2 on node MYNODE
     Last interactive login on Wednesday, 24-JUL-1991 08:48

$ .......               ! "$" is the default VMS prompt.
  .
  .                     ! Your terminal session with the VAX.
  .
$ LO                    ! LO is an abbreviation for LOGOUT.


YOUR_USERNAME      logged out at 24-JUL-1991 13:04:53.69
```

**Figure 1.1 Logging in and Logging out**

VAX/VMS connection and Appendix G on modems. For the sake of simplicity, this chapter assumes that your terminal is hardwired into one particular VAX computer.[1]

Press <RETURN> (sometimes referred to as the Carriage Return or the Enter key), or several <RETURN>s, or whatever sequence is required so that the screen of your terminal says `Username:`. Type in your user name and then press <RETURN>. The system will prompt you for a password, and you must type in the password that was given to you and then press <RETURN>. Notice that the password does not *echo to* (appear on) the screen. This is a security measure that prevents onlookers from learning your password. An additional security measure might be in operation on your system: the new password program. If it is, simply follow the prompts for changing your password. Now issue the `LOGOUT` command, often abbreviated `LO`, and then press <RETURN>.

---

1. Appendix A illustrates a more complicated constellation of computer hardware. It is the job of your own user services staff or instructor to acquaint you with the procedures necessary at your own site.

A sample *runstream* of the procedure given so far appears in Figure 1.1. Notice the conventions for runstreams that we follow throughout this book. Anything you type appears in color, while all the computer's responses appear just as they do on your screen. Notes or comments that describe what is going on are preceded by an exclamation point (!). You do not type these notes, nor will they appear on your screen. Note that in these sample runstreams we usually omit the <RETURN> required at the end of each command.

## 1.2 Elementary File Tasks

After a breather, log in again, using the same procedure as before. You will not need to change your password this time. You are now logged in to your directory. This means that you are connected to the disk area reserved for your own files. The amount of data this area can contain is limited. Access to the data is also limited. Here you have control over your own data. Only certain privileged users can access them. No one else may tamper with your files.

Once you get the dollar sign ($) prompt, also called the operating system prompt or the DCL prompt, execute the `DIRECTORY` command by typing `DIR` and pressing <RETURN>. The `DIR` command tells you about the files in your directory. Commands such as `DIR` and `LO` are called DCL (Digital Command Language) commands. DCL commands are instructions to the VAX/VMS operating system to do something. Each applications program, such as a text editor or a spelling checker, has its own set of commands that tell it what to do. Right now, you are issuing commands only to the VAX/VMS operating system. When you issue the `DIR` command, you will probably be told that no files exist. Let's create one.

If your instructor or user services staff has made the initialization file used in this book available on the VAX, carefully type the following line and press <RETURN>:

```
$ COPY - - - - :[ - - - - - - - ]LOGIN1.COM LOGIN.COM
```

The part of the command represented by hyphens is site-specific.

If this initialization `LOGIN.COM` file is not already available on the VAX, create it yourself using one of the two editors described in this book. Turn to Chapter 2 on the EVE screen editor program or (if EVE is not available or you are already familiar with EDT) to Appendix B on the EDT screen editor program. Follow the instructions on creating your own starter `LOGIN.COM` file like the one shown in Section I.1.2 of Appendix I. If you use an editor to create this file, you will have a good head start in using this book. For now, you will need only the starter file. You will be alerted to the necessary changes as they are required. To get through the entire book, you will need a complete `LOGIN.COM` file like the annotated `LOGIN.COM` file given in Section I.1.1 of Appendix I.

Once you have executed the preceding `COPY` command or have used an editor to create the initialization file, there should be at least one file in your directory called `LOGIN.COM;1`. This label is called the *file specification*. The first part, `LOGIN`, is the *file name*. The second part, `.COM`, is the *file type*.[2] The third part, `;1`, is the version number. Issue the command `TY LOGIN.COM` <RETURN>. (`TY` is for `TYPE`.) Notice that the contents of the file "scroll" past on the screen, and shortly the dollar sign prompt reappears. Do not worry about the contents of the `LOGIN.COM` file at this time.

You have now issued a number of commands. You can review these commands by typing the <UP ARROW> key several times. This key has nearly as many locations as there are types of terminals. In nearly all cases the key shows some form of an arrow pointing up. There are also <DOWN ARROW>, <RIGHT ARROW>, and <LEFT ARROW> keys, which you will be using later.

## 1.3 Customizing Your Interactive Session

In the previous section, you copied a special file into your directory, or created it yourself using EVE or EDT. The name of this file is important. The VAX/VMS operating system looks for the file named `LOGIN.COM` in your directory each time you log in. If the file exists, the operating system follows the instructions in the file. The purpose of this file is to customize your interactive session, thereby making things easier for you. Verify that you have altered your interactive session by logging out and logging in again.

---

2. People used to working in other Digital Equipment Corporation environments or microcomputer environments may call the file type the "file extension."

When you log in again, notice that you no longer see the simple dollar sign prompt. The new LOGIN.COM file has changed the prompt symbol for the operating system to a word *and* the $ symbol. The word, called a *node name*, is a simple, unique nickname for the particular VAX computer to which you are logged in. It is not uncommon for one or more VAX nodes to operate together in a cluster (often called a VAXcluster) at a particular computer installation. For purposes of illustration in this book, imagine that your computer is named MYNODE.[3] The operating system prompt, or DCL prompt, will therefore appear in this book as MYNODE$.

Now, if you type the command TY LOGIN.COM and press <RETURN>, you will see the contents of your LOGIN.COM file scroll by on your screen. Do not worry about the contents of this file just now. The important thing to keep in mind is that the VAX/VMS operating system lends itself very easily to customization. However, without substantial tailoring to individual needs, VAX/VMS remains rather cumbersome and unfriendly.

Later, you may wish to prove to yourself that the LOGIN.COM file does tailor the system to your individual needs. You would issue the command RENAME LOGIN.COM NEWLOG.COM <RETURN>. Do not issue this command now. If you did, the next log-in would be just like your second one. The prompt would be the lone dollar sign again instead of the node name and dollar sign.

Now, suppose that you need a hard (printed) copy of your LOGIN.COM file. Execute the PRINT command by typing PR LOGIN.COM and pressing <RETURN>. Within a few minutes, a copy of the file will be printed on one of your site's line printers.

## 1.4 Getting Help on Assorted Commands

VAX/VMS offers on-line help. To see how the help system works, type HELP and press <RETURN>, then follow the screen prompts. To demonstrate HELP, at the DCL prompt, type HELP SHOW and then press <RETURN>. Notice that the screen informs you of what the SHOW command does, and which words you can use with it—for example, USERS. While in HELP, each <RETURN>

3. If you want to find out what your node name really is, type
NODE=F$GETSYI("NODENAME")
and press <RETURN>, then type SHOW SYMBOL NODE and press <RETURN>.

that you press lets you progress one level "higher." For example, if you are at a Subtopic? prompt, <RETURN> will take you to the Topic? prompt, and the next <RETURN> will take you out of HELP and back to the operating system.

After returning to the operating system prompt, type SHO USE (for SHOW USERS) and then press <RETURN>. The screen will display a list of the users currently logged in to your node. Experiment with the SHOW command to discover all the information it discloses. You can use the SHOW command without fear of damaging any of your files because SHOW changes nothing; it only discloses information.

There is also help available for beginners. Browse through this help by typing HELP INSTRUCTIONS <RETURN> or HELP HINTS <RETURN>.

Often you will need to get rid of files that you no longer need. To demonstrate, let's create a trash file so we can delete it. Issue the command COPY LOGIN.COM TRASH.DAT <RETURN>. Now type DIR and then press <RETURN>. Using the TY command, satisfy yourself that the files are, in fact, identical except for their names. Now try to delete the trash file by typing DEL TRASH.DAT and pressing <RETURN>. The system will give you an error message and the DCL prompt will reappear. Using the <UP ARROW> key, cause the last command to reappear. Add a semicolon and a 1 so that the command now reads DEL TRASH.DAT;1. Press <RETURN>. As a safety precaution, the system asks you if you really mean to delete the file. Type Y (for YES) and press <RETURN>. The system will delete the file from your directory. Use the DIR command to check that you have, in fact, deleted the file from your directory.

## 1.5 Control Commands and Command Line Editing

Issue the TY LOGIN.COM command to view the contents of your LOGIN.COM file. If you have the annotated LOGIN.COM file, you noticed that it was longer than one screen of text. Had you wanted to stop and read the top of the file, you would have had to stop it from scrolling off the top of the screen. You can stop the screen movement by holding down the <CONTROL> key and simultaneously typing the letter S. We denote this procedure by <CTRL/s>.[4] <CTRL/q> resumes the movement. Several other <CONTROL> commands are very handy: <CTRL/c> or <CTRL/y> aborts most programs. If you had started a long file typing to the screen and wanted to stop it, <CTRL/c> would abort the scrolling, issue an "interrupt" or "cancel" message, and return you to the DCL prompt.

Several <CONTROL> commands facilitate editing your DCL command line. <CTRL/b> recalls the last command, just like the <UP ARROW> key. The system stores the last twenty DCL commands, which may be recalled in reverse order by repeatedly pressing <UP ARROW> or <CTRL/b>.

On most terminals, pressing the <LEFT ARROW> key allows you to move the cursor backward over characters you have already typed on the DCL command line. For example, if you had typed `DOR` instead of `DIR`, you could press the <LEFT ARROW> key twice to position the cursor at the O. Now type `I` <RETURN>, and the system will execute the `DIR` command.

Pressing <CTRL/a> toggles (switches) back and forth between the insert and replace modes for editing the command line.[5] For example, if you had typed `DR` instead of `DIR`, you could press the <LEFT ARROW> key once, followed by <CTRL/a>. Then type `I` and press <RETURN>. The system will *insert* an I between the D and the R, and then execute the `DIRECTORY` command. You will stay in insert mode until you toggle back to replace mode by pressing <CTRL/a> or until you press <RETURN> to execute the command again.

The <DELETE> or <RUBOUT> key (usually labeled Del or DEL) moves the cursor back one character *and* deletes the character. If you make many mistakes typing, you will find these command line editing options quite useful.

---

4. Throughout this book, when two or more keys appear together within angle brackets, press them simultaneously.

5. "Toggles" reflects what is generally understood by the term: "flip" it once and you have changed modes; "flip" it again and you are back to the original mode. Here, the "flip" is <CTRL/a>.

## Quick Reference: Operating System Commands

These commands are typed at the operating system $ prompt, followed by <RETURN>.

| *Command* | *Description* |
|---|---|
| `TY` *filespec* | Displays (types) the contents of file *filespec* to your terminal. |
| `TY/P` *filespec* | Displays the contents of the file *filespec* to your terminal one page (really one screen) at a time. |
| `DEL` *filespec* | Permanently deletes all versions of the file *filespec* from your directory. |
| `PURGE` *filespec* | Deletes all versions of *filespec* except the highest numbered one. If *filespec* is omitted, the command affects all files in the directory. |
| `PRINT` *filespec* | Places the file *filespec* in the `PRINT` queue. If you delete your file before it has started to print, it will not print. `PRINT` *filespec*`/DELETE` deletes the file *after* printing. |
| `COPY` *old-filespec new-filespec* | Makes a copy of *old-filespec* and names it *new-filespec*. |
| `RENAME` *old-filespec new-filespec* | Renames *old-filespec* as *new-filespec*. |
| `DIR` | Lists the names of *all* the files in your directory. |
| `DIR` *filespec* | Checks to see if you have *filespec* in your directory. |
| `SHOW USERS` | Displays (shows) a list of users currently logged in to your system (node). |
| `SHOW QUEUE` | Shows a list of your files currently printing or waiting to be printed. |

Pressing the following keys issues control commands.

| *Control Command* | *Description* |
|---|---|
| <CTRL/c> or <CTRL/y> | These are "panic buttons" that abort the current program execution and return you to the VMS operating system prompt. |
| <CTRL/o> | Discards output to the terminal. The program continues to execute. |
| <CTRL/s> | Stops scrolling of output on the terminal screen. |

| | |
|---|---|
| <CTRL/q> | Resumes displaying output halted by <CTRL/S>. |
| <CTRL/r> | Retypes the last line entered. |
| <CTRL/u> | Deletes the current line to the left of the cursor. |
| <CTRL/w> | Reconstructs the screen. |

## 1.7 Exercises

If you are new to VAX/VMS computer systems, we suggest that you do at least the first nine exercises that follow, in sequence. As you proceed through the exercises, do not be alarmed if the computer responds with error messages. Error messages can be as instructive as any other system messages. Regardless of the responses you get, you should try to explain why each of them occurred.

The commands that you must type appear in `ALL CAPITALS`, although you need not type them this way. VAX/VMS commands, by and large, are not case-sensitive.

Be *sure* to `LOGOUT` when you complete each session on the computer.

1. Issue the following string of commands:

   ```
   DIR
   TY LOGIN.COM
   TY/P LOGIN.COM
   MORE LOGIN.COM
   MO LOGIN.COM
   ```

   Explain the responses that you get. Reissue the `TY LOGIN.COM` command, using <CTRL/S> and <CTRL/q> to control the scrolling.

2. Issue the following string of commands:

   ```
   PRINT LOGIN.COM
   SHOW QUEUE
   ```

   Reissue the `SHOW QUEUE` command periodically (using the <UP ARROW> command line editing feature) until your print job no longer appears in either the "pending" or "printing" mode.

3. Issue the following string of commands:

```
DIR
COPY LOGIN.COM BYEBYE.COM
DIR
PRINT/DELETE BYEBYE.COM
SHOW QUEUE
```

   As in Exercise 2, reissue the `SHOW QUEUE` command periodically until your print job no longer appears. Then issue the `DIR` command. Explain the results.

4. Issue the following string of commands:

```
COPY LOGIN.COM JUNK.COM
DIR
COPY LOGIN.COM JUNK.COM
DIR
COPY LOGIN.COM JUNK.COM
DIR
COPY LOGIN.COM JUNK.DAT
DIR
DIR *.DAT
DIR *.COM
DIR JUNK.*
PURGE
DIR
```

   Explain the computer's responses. The asterisk (*) is called a wild card. It replaces part of the file specification in order to isolate a file or a group of files. For example, typing `DIR JUNK.*` asks the operating system to list all files with the file name `JUNK` and any file type, whereas `DIR *.DAT` asks the operating system to list all files with file type `.DAT` *regardless of the file name.*

5. Issue the following string of commands:

```
DIR
RENAME JUNK.COM TRASH.COM
DIR
DEL JUNK.COM;*
DEL TRASH.COM
DEL TRASH.COM;*              (respond with a Y)
DIR
```

   Explain the computer's responses.

6. Type HELP at the operating system prompt. When the Topic? prompt appears, type HELP again. Read the results on your screen. Press <RETURN> until you get back to the operating system prompt.

7. Type the following string of commands:

```
DIR *.HLP
HELP/OUTPUT=INFO.HLP INSTRUCTIONS
DIR *.HLP
PRINT/DELETE/NOTIFY INFO.HLP
```

   Explain the computer's responses. (This technique has a parallel on microcomputers. See Chapter 5 for an illustration.)

8. Type the following string of commands:

```
DIR
HELP/OUTPUT=HELP1.HLP HELP
DIR
MO HELP1.HLP
PRINT/NOTIFY/DELETE HELP1.HLP
SHOW QUEUE
```

   Explain the computer's responses.

9. Type the following string of commands:

```
DIR *.HLP
HELP/OUTPUT=HELP2.HLP HELP. . .
DIR *.HLP
PRINT/DELETE/NOTIFY HELP2.HLP
```

   Note that in the second line the ellipses (. . .) are part of the command and are therefore required. There is no space between HELP and the ellipses.

   Compare the printouts of the two files, HELP1.HLP and HELP2.HLP. What can you say about the difference between the two commands HELP/OUTPUT=HELP1.HLP HELP and HELP/OUTPUT=HELP2.HLP HELP?

10. Browse through the on-line help by typing HELP at the operating system prompt. Next, pick a topic. Try APPEND or LOGOUT. Using what you have learned from previous exercises, print out a file containing all the HELP on LOGOUT.

11. Use the on-line help to learn about the `SHOW QUOTA` command. Use the `SHOW QUOTA` command to find out what your disk allocation, or quota, is. On VAX/VMS systems one block is equal to 512 bytes. How many bytes are available to you? What do you think the "overdraft" quota is?

12. Recall the discussion of the `LOGIN.COM` file. At the operating system prompt, type `@LOGIN`. What conclusion can you draw from the result? Use the on-line help to learn about the @ symbol. Does this shed more light on the matter?

13. The kinds of printers available vary greatly from site to site. The following example describes one possible configuration.

    In this example, assume that your site has both a line printer for printing on "narrow" forms (8½ × 11-inch paper) and an LN01 laser printer. In order to print to the narrow forms line printer or the laser printer, type the following commands at the operating system prompt:

    ```
    PRINT/FORMS=NARROW filename      ! For the narrow forms
                                     ! line printer

    PRINT/QUEUE=SYS$LN01 filename    ! For the laser printer
    ```

    Then type the following sequence of commands:

    ```
    NARROW == "PRINT/FORMS=NARROW"
    LASER == "PRINT/QUEUE=SYS$LN01"
    NARROW/NOTIFY LOGIN.COM
    LASER/NOTIFY LOGIN.COM
    ```

    This sequence lets you type `NARROW LOGIN.COM` to print the `LOGIN.COM` file on narrow forms, and `LASER LOGIN.COM` to print the `LOGIN.COM` file on the laser printer. `/NOTIFY` notifies you when the printing is complete (if you are still logged in).

    Now check with your local user services staff to find out the kinds of printers available at your site and the appropriate DCL commands for sending files to them. Print copies of your `LOGIN.COM` file on each of your different printers, using the example given above as a guide.

    The *global symbols* `NARROW` and `LASER` will be in effect for the remainder of the current session. For more information on symbols and DCL, see Bibliography [9]. We discuss the MS-DOS microcomputer equivalent of global symbols in Chapter 5. On the MS-DOS microcomputer, global symbols are called *aliases*.

14. At the operating system prompt, type `HELP SET PASSWORD`. After reading the information, press <RETURN> until you get back to the operating system prompt. Decide on a new password, one that you will *remember*. Then type `SET PASSWORD` and follow the prompts. Log out and then log back in. What conclusions can you draw from this sequence?

15. At the operating system prompt, type `HELP SET PASSWORD/GENERATE`. After reading the information, press <RETURN> until you get back to the operating system prompt. Then type `SET PASSWORD/GENERATE` and follow the prompts, making sure to *remember* the password that you picked. What conclusions can you draw from this sequence?

Chapter 2

# The EVE Screen Editor Program

## 2.1 Getting Started

EVE (Extensible VAX Editor) is the default version of TPU (Text Processing Utility). Both are products of Digital Equipment Corporation. If you come to the VAX with microcomputer experience, you will sense that EVE has a microcomputer feel to it after working with it for a few minutes. It is a screen-oriented text editor that efficiently uses the special keys just to the right of the <RETURN> key on a VT220 terminal. All the functions of which EVE is capable on a VT220 terminal will work on VT100 series terminals as well. All you give up are the neatly labeled special keys. In this chapter, we assume that you are using a VT220. However, we provide key maps for both VT220 and VT100 series terminals for the convenience of all users (see Figures 2.1 and 2.2). EVE can create and revise text as well as move existing text around. It does not perform the complete word processing that can be done with a word processor like WPS-PLUS (see Chapter 4) or a text formatter such as SCRIBE (see Appendix C) or TEX.

Those of you who do not have the `LOGIN.COM` file already available on the VAX and have been directed here from the operating system chapter must use EVE to create your own `LOGIN.COM` file. Follow this chapter through Section 2.4, "Moving the Cursor: Finding and Changing Text." Once you have mastered the material presented in these few pages, you will know enough about using EVE to create the starter `LOGIN.COM` file shown in Section I.1.2 of Appendix I.

## 2.2 *Making and Saving a File*

For a first run at using EVE, begin by logging in. At the DCL prompt (the operating system prompt signified by `MYNODE$` in this book), type `EVE TIPS.TXT` and then press <RETURN> if you already have the annotated `LOGIN.COM` file shown in Section I.1.1 of Appendix I. If you do not have the file, type `EDIT/TPU TIPS.TXT` <RETURN>. Notice that the screen reconstructs and displays a line in reverse video (dark letters against a light background) almost at the bottom of the screen. This line is called the *status line*. Notice the words `Buffer TIPS.TXT` on the status line. This message means that the file you are working on is named `TIPS.TXT`. In VAX terminology, the file name is `TIPS` and the file type is `.TXT`. The version number is 1. You may verify this fact later at the DCL prompt by using the `DIR` command. At the bottom of the screen is information telling you that the file is new.

Note that the words `End of File` are displayed within square brackets near the top of the screen. Nothing is in your file yet. To have some text to work with, type in the first paragraph of this chapter. If you make errors, do not worry about them for now. Do not be concerned about pressing the <RETURN> key to break lines. You may hear an occasional beep as you type toward the right side of the screen, but EVE will make sure that you do not type off into meaningless electronic space. If you are accustomed to typing on a manual typewriter and press the <RETURN> key out of habit, EVE will accept your carriage returns. Whether you continue old habits is your personal choice. EVE's automatic insertion of line breaks is a feature called *automatic word wrap*.

When you have finished typing the paragraph, hold down the <CONTROL> key and type `Z` to save your new file in your directory.

## 2.3 *Getting Help*

When you are ready to do more editing, type `EVE TIPS.TXT` <RETURN> if you have the annotated `LOGIN.COM` file, or `EDIT/TPU TIPS.TXT` <RETURN> if you do not. You may retrieve this command using the <UP ARROW> key if you have not logged out since your last session with EVE. Your screen should reconstruct, displaying the file you just created. Press the key labeled <HELP> (this is the <PF2> key on some terminals). Notice that the screen

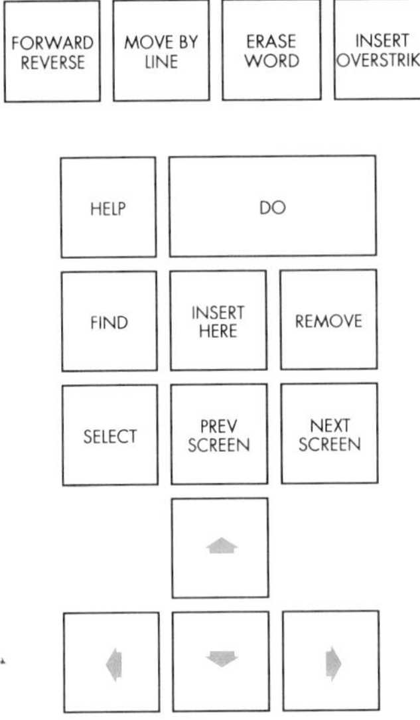


**Figure 2.1 EVE Keys on a VT220 Terminal**

reconstructs again, not with your text, but with information about the special keys. If you are using a VT220 terminal, the display should resemble the schematic diagram in Figure 2.1. If you are using a VT100 series terminal, it should resemble the diagram in Figure 2.2. Follow the instructions EVE provides to learn about the keys labeled <DO> and <FIND> as well as any other key mentioned on the initial HELP screen. Locate the <FORWARD/REVERSE> and <INSERT/OVERSTRIKE> keys. These important keys are not labeled on the VT220.

There is no need to memorize all this information. You can always retrieve it by pressing the <HELP> key. If you are using a VT100 terminal or its equivalent, you will find it worthwhile to keep scratch paper nearby to make a keypad map for your own terminal. You can use it as a quick reference until you become familiar with EVE's keypad. You should take special notice of the <DO> key. It is the gatekeeper to many EVE commands not explicitly assigned to keys. Again, you don't need to memorize lots of key commands because HELP is available for them.

To learn about commands you can execute with the <DO> key, you must first get out of the HELP screen and back to your text by pressing <RETURN>. Once

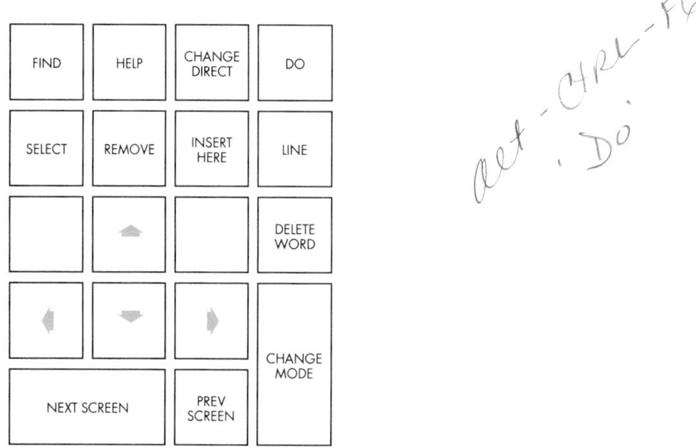


**Figure 2.2 EVE Keys on a VT100 Series Terminal Numeric Keypad**

the text you created reappears on the screen, press the <DO> key. Notice that `Command:` appears at the bottom of the screen.

Type the word `HELP` and then press <RETURN>.[1] Your text is hidden for a moment as the system displays information about commands issued with the <DO> key. Follow the instructions to learn about the `REPLACE` command. When you are finished, use the <RETURN> key to return to your text. If you need a break, press <CTRL/z> to leave the editor, and log out. Since you made no changes during this session, EVE does not create an updated version of your file. However, if you want to tell EVE explicitly to discard changes you have made, press <DO>, type the word `QUIT`, then press <RETURN>.

## 2.4 Moving the Cursor: Finding and Changing Text

Begin editing again by typing `EVE TIPS.TXT` <RETURN> if you have the annotated `LOGIN.COM` file, or `EDIT/TPU TIPS.TXT` <RETURN> if you do not. By simple experimentation with the arrow keys, you will discover that you can easily move the cursor. Then, using combinations of the <WORD/CHAR> key (often called the <BACKSPACE> or <RUBOUT> key) you can correct your errors. The combination <CTRL/h> moves the cursor to the beginning of the current line. <CTRL/e> in like manner moves the cursor to the end of the line.[2]

1. The word `HELP` does not need to be in uppercase letters. We use uppercase letters in this book to distinguish the `HELP` function from other elements.
2. The words "home" and "end" might help you remember these keys.

This is a good time to find the <INSERT/OVERSTRIKE> key, which is a toggle key. Notice that if you press it several times, the words `Insert` and `Overstrike` alternate on the status line. It is a matter of personal preference which of these modes you use to correct unwanted text. Insert mode shifts existing text to the right of the cursor as you insert new text. You must delete old text separately. Overstrike mode merely overwrites old text.

The <RETURN> key also moves the cursor, but in addition it inserts a new line into the text every time you press it. If you accidentally insert a series of blank lines, you can remove them by moving the cursor to the start of the first line in the next paragraph and using the <BACKSPACE> key. If your text were long, using the arrow keys would not be very efficient. The <FIND> key provides a much faster alternative. To demonstrate, press the <FIND> key. In response to the `Forward Find:` prompt that appears at the bottom of the screen, type `SCRIBE` and then press <RETURN>. The cursor moves to the beginning of the word `SCRIBE` in your sample paragraph.[3]

Next, press <FIND> again and, following the prompts, type `DIGITAL` and press <RETURN>. Now EVE acts a little differently. It tells you that it has found the string `DIGITAL` in reverse direction, and asks you if you want to go there. Type `Y` (for `YES`) and press <RETURN>. The cursor will go to the previous occurrence of the string `DIGITAL`.

At the start of any session, EVE begins searching toward the bottom of the file. Remember to look at the status line the next time you begin a session. The word `Forward` will appear at the far right of the status line. Press <DO> and, following the prompts, type `TOP` <RETURN>. Now the cursor is at the very top, or beginning, of the file. If you had typed `BOTTOM`, the cursor would have moved to the bottom, or end, of the file.

Now you know how to locate text using the <FIND> key. In order to change words or sentences, you must use the `REPLACE` command. Press the <DO> key again. In response to the `Command:` prompt, type

```
REPLACE EVE STEVE
```

---

3. Pressing <FIND> twice moves the cursor to the next occurrence of the character string you are looking for, if it exists.

and press <RETURN>. You have just told EVE to replace the existing string EVE with the new string STEVE. The text will emerge as nonsense, but you get the point. Follow the prompts to make the substitutions one at a time. Each time you press <RETURN>, the editor will change the next occurrence of EVE to STEVE and will display the following occurrence of EVE in reverse video. Notice that EVE gives you alternatives to making the substitutions one at a time. You may type NO to skip the current occurrence, ALL to make all substitutions (risky business on long files!), or QUIT to stop the substitution process. The letters A, Q, Y, and N are acceptable abbreviations for ALL, QUIT, YES, and NO.

Quotation marks are important grammatically when replacing more than one word with the REPLACE command. They serve as boundaries when substitution strings contain blanks. After pressing <DO>, type

```
REPLA SCREEN-ORIENTED "SCREEN ORIENTED"
```

and press <RETURN>. This is a laborious way to get rid of one tiny hyphen, but it illustrates the use of quotation marks in the REPLACE command.

There is no point in saving these changes, so whenever you feel like it, press <DO>, and at the Command: prompt type QUIT <RETURN>.

Those of you who have been reading this chapter to learn how to create your own initialization file now know enough about EVE to input the starter LOGIN.COM file given in Section I.1.2 of Appendix I. You should turn to Appendix I now and type in the contents of the starter LOGIN.COM file exactly as they appear there. Once you have done so, you may return to Chapter 1 and continue where you left off in your study of the operating system. When you return to this chapter, you will have a good head start on learning how to use EVE.

## 2.5 The Three Windows of EVE: A Review and More

Much is made of windowing, particularly in microcomputer magazines, and it is often suggested that the complexity of the whole business overshadows its utility. In reality, you have already been using windows. The text you created in Sections 2.2 through 2.4 was held in the *main window*. Whenever you pressed the <DO> key, you typed commands in a different window, the *command window*. As it completed commands, EVE sent you messages in yet another window, the *message window* at the very bottom of the screen. EVE also provides windows that let you edit more than one file at a time.

To demonstrate more advanced windowing, you need another file longer than the first one, one that will cause no damage if altered by mistake. At the DCL prompt, type `COPY LOGIN.COM TRASH.COM` and press <RETURN>. To edit this new file, type `EVE TRASH.COM` <RETURN>. Now you have the opportunity to use keys you have not used so far: the <NEXT SCREEN> and <PREVIOUS SCREEN> keys. Just as you might expect, they cause the text to scroll back and forth.

Next, press <DO> and notice that you are now typing in the command window. Type `TWO WINDOWS` <RETURN> (`TWO WIN` is an acceptable abbreviation) and notice that the screen reconstructs into two windows, one right above the other. Notice also that the same text is found in *both* windows. Press <DO>, then type the command `OTHER WINDOW` <RETURN> (`OTH WIN` is permitted). The cursor jumps to the other window. Press <DO> again and, using the <UP ARROW> key just as you do at the DCL level, retrieve the `OTHER WINDOW` command. As you can see, you can shift the cursor back and forth from window to window using combinations of the <DO>, <UP ARROW>, and <RETURN> keys.

## 2.6 Using Windows to Move Text

Using the <DO> key again, issue the command `GET TIPS.TXT` <RETURN>. Notice that the screens are now different. One contains `TIPS.TXT` and the other contains `TRASH.COM`. Imagine that your goal is to put the smaller file somewhere in the middle of the larger file. First, make sure that the cursor is in the `TRASH.COM` window. Use the <NEXT SCREEN> key to move the cursor away from the top of the file. Now go to the *other window* and make sure that the cursor is at the top of the file. You may need to use the `TOP` command. Press <SELECT>, and notice that EVE tells you, via a message in the message window, that selection has begun. With the <DOWN ARROW> key, go to the last line in the file. Note that each line you select in this manner changes to reverse video with each touch of the arrow key. Once you reach the last line, press the <REMOVE> key. The highlighted text vanishes from the screen—but it is not gone. It is held in a buffer, or storage area, in memory. This area is called the `INSERT HERE` buffer. The text stays in that buffer until you quit

EVE, or <SELECT> and <REMOVE> again. Now go back to the *other window* and press <INSERT HERE>. The text has been moved from one file to another.

You can also use the same combination of <SELECT>, <REMOVE>, and <INSERT HERE> keys to move a block of text or individual characters or words within one file using only one window.

The file you just created has no practical application, so press <DO> and type `QUIT` <RETURN>. Then follow the prompts to quit both files.

## 2.7 Saving and Discarding Your Work: Special Ins and Outs

New users often lose sight of the fact that changes made while editing are not actually made on disk-resident files until you explicitly save a file. When you add, delete, or move characters, you are really only changing buffers in the memory of the computer. For this reason, you should *save your files regularly* if you are confident that your revised work is an improvement over what already exists in the file.

To review, leave the EVE editor by pressing <CTRL/Z>, which saves the file if you have made changes, and quits without saving if you have made no changes. If you have made changes but want to discard them, you must press <DO> and type `QUIT` <RETURN> at the `Command:` prompt.

Begin to edit your old file `TIPS.TXT` again. You may save your changes without leaving the editor. Press <DO> and type `HELP WRITE` <RETURN> in the command window. See if you can follow the instructions to learn how to write (save) a file without leaving your place in the file. If you are successful, a message telling you so will appear in the message window. The `WRITE` command is useful for saving long files if you don't want to lose your place or wait while the editor reloads.

You can also leave the editor without interrupting your work. Press <DO>, then type `SPAWN` <RETURN> to issue the `SPAWN` command. Shortly, the DCL prompt appears. You have created a new interactive job, or *process*. You can now print a file or issue any other DCL command. When you are ready to go back to EVE, issue the `LOGOUT` command to leave the spawned process, and you should return to where you left off in the file. (Microcomputer enthusiasts will recognize the popular concept of keeping programs resident so they may be used again quickly without taking time to reload.)

In EVE, you can issue DCL commands without even leaving the editor. Press <DO> and type `DCL` <RETURN> at the `Command:` prompt. You will be prompted to issue a DCL command. Type `DIR` and press <RETURN>. You will see the screen split and a listing of your directory will appear in the bottom window. You can edit and save the text of the directory using combinations of the `OTHER WINDOW` and `WRITE` commands. You can use this technique to create a commented list of files in your directory. Any time you no longer need two windows, press <DO> and issue the `ONE WINDOW` command.

After returning to the DCL prompt, have a look at the files in your directory by typing the command `DIR` <RETURN>. You will see two versions of your file, `TIPS.TXT;1` and `TIPS.TXT;2`. Version 2 will be the newer. Unless you explicitly specify a version number when you choose a file to edit, the operating system assumes that you want the newer file. If you mean to edit the older version, you need to be specific by typing `EVE TIPS.TXT;1`. The operating system keeps a certain number of the latest versions of your files. This default number is usually set by your system manager, although you can set your own by using the `SET DIRECTORY/VERSION=n` DCL command.[4]

Once you reach the default number of versions, the oldest version (the one with the smallest version number) will vanish each time you leave the editor using the `EXIT` command. If you are certain that the older versions of the file you are editing are no longer of interest, you may issue the `PURGE` command at the DCL prompt. `PURGE` deletes all versions, except the most recent, of all files. You must take care not to delete files you don't mean to delete. To be extra careful, delete files using the `DELETE` command, which requires an explicit version number.

## 2.8 Neater Text, Neater Screens

From time to time you will notice that the screen is a mess and may wonder whether the mess is part of the text or just "noise" on the screen, a common

4. The n designates the number of versions you mean to keep.

problem if you are communicating over a phone line. Press <CTRL/W>. This control command refreshes, or rewrites, the whole screen. Sometimes the problem is not with a noisy line at all. Sometimes your revisions make the file look like a jagged mess. For practice, begin to edit TIPS.TXT again. Introduce single <RETURN>s randomly between words in your file. Be careful not to insert any blank lines. You can cure this unsightly situation by positioning the cursor at the top line of the paragraph, pressing <DO>, and then typing FILL PARAGRAPH (FILL PAR is an acceptable substitute) and pressing <RETURN>. The paragraph will be neat again. EVE recognizes as paragraphs those blocks of text separated by one or more blank lines. *Note*: *Never* do this on a program file, such as LOGIN.COM.

## 2.9 Inserting Often-Used Text: Alternative Approaches

You have already seen how to use the <SELECT>, <REMOVE>, and <INSERT HERE> keys to move blocks of text from one place to ano ther. To quickly review, the first key begins the selection of text to be removed into the INSERT HERE buffer. Since text stays in the INSERT HERE buffer until you leave the editor or press the <REMOVE> key again, you can easily reuse the same text many times within one file by moving the cursor to various locations and pressing the <INSERT HERE> key. Indeed, text can be *copied* (rather than moved) from one INSERT location to another by pressing <INSERT HERE> before moving the cursor from its original location.

You can also use the INCLUDE command to insert a commonly used block of text. Its utility is obvious enough. Say that you wanted to insert your name and mailing address into documents without having to retype them each time. First, create a file containing the information you want to insert. Once that file exists, you can use the INCLUDE command to put it in the right place. To demonstrate, let's INCLUDE the relatively short TIPS.TXT file in the longer TRASH.COM file. Begin editing the TRASH.COM file as you did before. Move the cursor someplace near the middle of the file. Press <DO>. In the command window, type INCLUDE TIPS.TXT <RETURN>. The TIPS.TXT file is now inserted at the current cursor position. As before, you do not need to keep these changes, so issue a QUIT command from the command window.

```
! Here is an example of TPU initialization:
!
! 1. The initialization file must be written in TPU, not
!    EVE. The name should be TPUINI.TPU, and as long as it
!    is in the current directory, it will be executed
!    automatically via the EDIT/TPU command. If TPUINI.TPU is
!    not in the current directory, the following command
!    is required:
!
!    EDIT/TPU/COMMAND=logical_device:[directory]TPUINI
!
! 2. TPU commands must be placed in the file after any
!    procedures. If you have problems concerning the correct
!    execution of commands, you might try to omit the
!    terminating semicolon as it relates to the following
!    quotation from the TPU manual:
!
!            You must separate each executable statement
!            from other statements with a semicolon. (Note
!            that it is a statement separator, not a statement
!            terminator.)
!
! 3. Procedures are executed from within EVE via the TPU
!    command, unless the procedure starts with eve_
!    in which case simply typing the procedure name (following
!    the eve_ prefix) at the "Command:" prompt will execute
!    the procedure. However, before naming a procedure with
!    the eve_ prefix you should check in
!    SYS$LIBRARY:EVESECINI.TPU to see if the name is already
!    in use.
!
************************************************************
!
! Set up an EVE procedure to set the margins in any buffer:
procedure eve_wid
    set (margins,current_buffer,1,70);
endprocedure
!
! Set up a procedure (executed via the TPU command) that
! sets up the current window with a width of 132
procedure w132
   set (width,current_window,132);
endprocedure
!
```

**Figure 2.3 An Example TPUINI.TPU File**

```
! Set up a procedure (executed via the TPU command) that
! sets up the current window with a width of 80
procedure w80
   set (width,current_window,80);
endprocedure
!
! Set the margins of the current buffer between 1 and 70
!
set (margins,current_buffer,1,70);
!
! Define keypad 4 to be the TWO WINDOWS command:
!
define_key ('eve_two_windows',KP4);
!
! Define keypad 6 to be the OTHER WINDOW toggle:
!
define_key ('eve_other_window',KP6);
!
! Define Control-N to be a string containing your name:
!
define_key ('copy_text("YOUR NAME")',ctrl_n_key);
```

**Figure 2.3 (continued) An Example TPUINI.TPU File**

EVE provides a third way to insert text without having to type it in. Section 2.10 gives an example of how to create your own specialized character strings using key combinations.

## 2.10 Programmability: Real Power

Whenever you begin editing, EVE looks for a file called `TPUINI.TPU` in your directory. The file that appears in Figure 2.3 is an example of a `TPUINI.TPU` file that you may adapt to your own needs. The lines beginning with exclamation points are explanatory comments and are not required in order for the commands to work. This file can customize your editor with special margin settings and "hot" keys for commands you use frequently. It can even store your own name (or another character string) on a key so that you can insert it into text without having to type each letter. Notice that this example file has been set up to store the string `"YOUR NAME"` on the key combination <CTRL/n>. Try to edit this file so that you can insert your name into the text during future editing sessions. You should take care with this file. It is a text file and can be changed using EVE. However, it is possible to alter it in such a way that EVE cannot load. If this happens, you must `RENAME` the file until the problem can be resolved.

```
$!        TPU (EVE)-Related Logical Definitions
$!        (REMOVE the ! just to the right of the
$!             dollar sign and to the left
$!               of the DEFINE statement
$!     in order for the DEFINE statement to work)
$!
$! DEFINE MAIL$EDIT CALLABLE_TPU  ! Allows for using TPU in
$!                                ! MAIL
$!
$! DEFINE BASIC$EDIT TPU$EDIT     ! Allows for using TPU in
$!                                ! BASIC
$!
$! DEFINE DTR$EDIT TPU            ! Allows for using TPU in
$!                                ! DATATRIEVE
```

**Figure 2.4 Making EVE Your Default Editor**

Programming in TPU is outside the scope of this book. For now you should simply be aware that EVE is a powerful, programmable text editor.

## 2.11 EVE as Default Editor in Other Programs

In version 5.1 of VMS and earlier versions, EDT (see Appendix B) is the default editor in most applications programs such as MAIL and DATATRIEVE. In order to substitute EVE for EDT in the edit options of MAIL, BASIC, and DATATRIEVE, you will need to remove the ! just to the right of the dollar sign in some of the lines in your annotated `LOGIN.COM` file. If you do not have the annotated `LOGIN.COM` file, you will need to add each line in Figure 2.4 containing a `DEFINE` statement, being careful to omit the exclamation point appearing before the word `DEFINE`.

## 2.12 Quick Reference: EVE Commands and Functions

Remember that EVE is initially in *insert mode*. This means that everything you type from the keyboard is inserted into the text at the current cursor position. Existing text is shifted to the right. In order to change to *overstrike mode*, use the <INSERT/OVERSTRIKE> key.

### Entering and Exiting EVE

| *Command* | *Description* |
|---|---|
| EVE *filespec* | At the operating system MYNODE$ prompt, calls EVE to edit *filespec*. |
| <CTRL/z> or <DO> EXIT | Exits EVE and saves changes. |
| <DO> QUIT | Aborts; exits EVE and discards changes. |

### EVE Keypad Functions

These functions are activated from within EVE by pressing keypad keys.

| *Keypad Function* | *Description* |
|---|---|
| <HELP> | Gives help on functions of labeled keys. |
| <SPACEBAR> | Inserts spaces into current buffer to the left of cursor in insert mode, or erases characters at the cursor position in overstrike mode. |
| <RETURN> | Inserts blank lines in current buffer if cursor is at beginning of a line. Breaks line if cursor is in the middle of line. |
| <DO> | Moves cursor to command window to await typed command. |
| <FIND> *string* | Searches for specified string of characters and moves cursor to beginning of the string. Typing <FIND> twice will search for the string previously entered. |
| <SELECT> | Begins marking text for moving into INSERT HERE buffer. |
| <REMOVE> | Moves marked text into INSERT HERE buffer. |
| <INSERT HERE> | Moves text in INSERT HERE buffer to current cursor position. |
| <NEXT SCREEN> | Displays next screen of text. |
| <PREVIOUS SCREEN> | Displays previous screen of text. |

| | |
|---|---|
| <INSERT/OVERSTRIKE> | Toggles back and forth between overstrike and insert mode. The default when entering EVE is insert mode. This key is the <F14> key on a VT220 terminal. |
| <FORWARD/REVERSE> | Changes direction of cursor movement in search or find operations. |

### EVE Control Commands

These commands are issued from within EVE by pressing the indicated key combinations.

| *Control Command* | *Description* |
|---|---|
| <CTRL/ e> | Moves cursor to end of current line. |
| <CTRL/ h> | Moves cursor to beginning (home) of current line. |
| <CTRL/w> | Reconstructs current window. |
| <CTRL/z> | Exits EVE and saves current buffer if any changes have been made. |

### EVE <DO>-Related Commands

These commands are issued from within EVE by typing the indicated words at the `Command:` prompt, obtained by pressing <DO>.

| *<DO> Command* | *Description* |
|---|---|
| `QUIT` | Discards changes and quits EVE. |
| `EXIT` | Saves file with changes and exits EVE. |
| `HELP` | Displays help on commands that may be issued from the command window. |
| `TOP` | Moves cursor to top, or beginning, of file. |
| `BOTTOM` | Moves cursor to bottom, or end, of file. |
| `REPLACE` *old-string new-string* | Searches for the occurrence of *old-string* and replaces it with *new-string*. You will be prompted at each occurrence as to whether you want to make the replacement (Yes or No), stop the procedure (Quit), or make replacements on all remaining occurrences (All). *Note*: Any string containing a blank must be enclosed in double quotation marks. |
| `TWO WINDOWS` | Breaks screen into two windows. |
| `OTHER WINDOW` | Moves cursor to other window. |

| | |
|---|---|
| ONE WINDOW | Dispenses with one of the windows; goes back to using one window. If two windows are in use, the window containing the cursor fills the screen. |
| GET *filespec* | Begins editing *filespec* in current buffer and displays it in current window. |
| WRITE *filespec* | Saves changes to *filespec* but does not exit EVE. (If *filespec* is not specified, changes will be written to the file you are editing.) |
| SPAWN | Creates another process allowing you to perform DCL commands while the previous process stays in EVE, so that you can return to your editing session without reloading EVE. Re-enter EVE by typing LO (LOGOUT) at the DCL prompt. |
| DCL | Allows DCL commands to be issued from within an EVE window. Text may be edited and saved. |
| INCLUDE *filespec* | Inserts *filespec* into current buffer at current cursor position. |
| FILL PARAGRAPH | Fills paragraph containing cursor within current margins. |

### *EVE Functions Requiring Multiple Keystrokes*

*Moving Text*

- Press <SELECT>
- Move cursor to include all text you want to move
- Press <REMOVE>
- Move cursor to where you want to insert text (possibly a different window or buffer)
- Press <INSERT HERE>

*Finding Strings*

- Press <FIND>
- Type the string for which you want to search
- Press <RETURN>

*Searching/Replacing Strings*

- Press <DO>
- Type REPLACE *old-string new-string*
- Follow the prompts

## 2.13 Exercises

1. Use EVE to personalize the following part of your LOGIN.COM file:

```
$
$WRITE SYS$OUTPUT "    **********************************"
$WRITE SYS$OUTPUT "     *                               *"
$WRITE SYS$OUTPUT "     *    Put Your Own Personalized  *"
$WRITE SYS$OUTPUT "     *           Greeting Here       *"
$WRITE SYS$OUTPUT "     *                               *"
$WRITE SYS$OUTPUT "    **********************************"
$
```

   Also insert the following line just below this part of the file:

```
$SHOW TIME
```

   Once back at the operating system prompt, type @LOGIN, then log out and log in to the system again. What are your conclusions, especially in light of the information that you get when you type HELP at the operating system prompt and then type @ at the Topic? prompt?

2. If you have the annotated LOGIN.COM file, find the following line:

```
$! SET PROCESS/NAME=" - - - - - - "
```

   Remove the exclamation point and replace the dashes with some name by which you would like to be identified. After you log in again, this new name will appear under the Process column generated whenever anyone types the SHOW USERS command at the operating system level.

   If you have the starter LOGIN.COM file, insert the line as described above in your LOGIN.COM file at any place before $ EXIT:.

   Once you have the indicated line in your LOGIN.COM file, type the following commands at the operating system prompt:

```
SHOW USERS
@LOGIN
SHOW USERS
```

   What conclusions concerning your process name can you draw from the results?

3. As you have learned, the operating system reads and executes commands in the `LOGIN.COM` file when you log in. Lines in the `LOGIN.COM` file that begin with `$!` (rather than just `$`) are ignored by the operating system. Using on-line help for `DELETE`, determine which line of the `LOGIN.COM` file must have an exclamation point inserted after the `$` in order to avoid being asked if you want to delete a file each time you issue the `DELETE` command at the operating system prompt.

   If you were not allowed to insert the exclamation point, how would you change the line so that you would get the same result as in the previous paragraph?

4. Use EVE to create the following file named GREETING.COM:

```
$  CONTEXT=""
$  START:
$! Obtain and display PIDs, UICs, and TIME
$!
$  PID=F$PID(CONTEXT)
$  UIC=F$GETJPI(PID, "UIC")
$  PROCESS=F$PROCESS()
$  IF F$EXTRACT(12,2,F$TIME()) .GES. "12" THEN GOTO AFTERNOON
$  MORNING:
$  WRITE SYS$OUTPUT ""
$  WRITE SYS$OUTPUT "Good Morning, ''PROCESS'."
$! WRITE SYS$OUTPUT "Good Morning, ''UIC'."
$  GOTO MORE
$  AFTERNOON:
$  IF F$EXTRACT(12,2,F$TIME()) .GES. "18" THEN GOTO EVENING
$  WRITE SYS$OUTPUT ""
$  WRITE SYS$OUTPUT "Good Afternoon, ''PROCESS'."
$! WRITE SYS$OUTPUT "Good Afternoon, ''UIC'."
$  GOTO MORE
$  EVENING:
$  WRITE SYS$OUTPUT ""
$  WRITE SYS$OUTPUT "Good Evening, ''PROCESS'."
$! WRITE SYS$OUTPUT "Good Evening, ''UIC'."
$  MORE:
$  WRITE SYS$OUTPUT ""
$  WRITF SYS$OUTPUT "Welcome back, on ''F$TIME90'."
$  WRITE SYS$OUTPUT ""
```

   At the operating system level, type `@GREETING`. How would you get this file to be executed upon each log-in? (For more information concerning `.COM` (command) files, see Bibliography [9] and [19].)

5. Copy the file PRAYER.ERR into your directory by issuing the following command at the operating system prompt:

   ```
   COPY TEXTFILES:PRAYER.ERR PRAYER.ERR
   ```

   Section I.2.1 of Appendix I contains a partial listing of this file. You will not be able to copy this file unless the TEXTFILES directory and your LOGIN.COM file have been set up appropriately.

   Use EVE to correct all the errors contained in the PRAYER.ERR file to obtain an error-free copy of Mark Twain's "War Prayer." Be sure to try the REPLACE command and the <FIND> key to help in your task. Remember that after you have used the <FIND> key once to find a string of characters, pressing the <FIND> key again causes EVE to find the next occurrence of the last string found.

6. Apply the instructions given in Exercise 5 to Patrick Henry's "Give me liberty or give me death" speech. To obtain this file, issue the following command at the operating system prompt:

   ```
   COPY TEXTFILES:HENRY.PAT HENRY.PAT
   ```

   Section I.2.2 of Appendix I contains a partial listing of this file.

7. After you have finished the work on Patrick Henry's speech in Exercise 6, get back into EVE to re-edit the HENRY.PAT file. While in EVE, press <DO> to obtain the Command: prompt. At the prompt, type FILL PARAGRAPH <RETURN>. Notice that the paragraph is now substantially less ragged. If you wanted different, perhaps narrower, margins, you could type SET RIGHT MARGIN 60 at the Command: prompt. This command sets the right margin at around column 60. To get help on the SET RIGHT MARGIN command, press <DO> and then <HELP> followed by <RETURN>. Read the information on how the SET RIGHT MARGIN command works. Experiment to determine the shortest legitimate abbreviations for SET RIGHT MARGIN and FILL PARAGRAPH.

8. Assuming that you have the TEXTFILES directory available to you, issue the following two commands at the operating system prompt:

```
COPY TEXTFILES:SET1.TXT SET1.TXT
COPY TEXTFILES:SET2.TXT SET2.TXT
```

If you do not have the TEXTFILES directory, create the two files using EVE. Sections I.2.3 and I.2.4 of Appendix I contain listings of these files.

Assume that these two files represent two test banks of questions and that you are going to compose an exam that contains questions chosen from both of these files. Using what you have learned about moving text around from file to file, create a new file named EXAM.TXT, containing the following header:

```
Computer Literacy Exam I        NAME:________________________

INSTRUCTIONS: Answer the questions in the space
provided. Each numbered question is worth 2 points.
```

*Note*: In the commands given below, we assume that the <RETURN> is included where appropriate.

Below the header, insert questions 1, 2, 3, 5, and 6 from SET1.TXT, numbering them 1 through 5. Below these questions, insert questions 1, 3, and 5 from SET2.TXT, numbering them 6 through 8.

Follow the instructions in Section 2.6, "Using Windows to Move Text," to put the file SET1.TXT into the bottom window. To move the text, you will need to use the following commands or keys: <SELECT>, <REMOVE>, OTHER WINDOW, and <INSERT HERE>.

*Hint*: After selecting all the questions you need from SET1.TXT and moving them to the EXAM.TXT file, you can load the file SET2.TXT into the bottom window by moving the cursor to the bottom window, pressing <DO>, and issuing the command GET SET2.TXT.

9. This exercise shows how to get your own copy of EVE HELP files by accessing a part of a system file that contains all the HELP files for EVE normally accessed by asking for HELP from within the EVE program. The file containing this EVE HELP is named TPUHELP.HLB. Remember that EVE is just a part of the larger program called TPU. To get all the HELP available from within EVE, type the following command at the operating system prompt:

```
LIBRARY/EXTRACT=(EVE)/OUTPUT=EVE.HLP SYS$HELP:TPUHELP.HLB
```

A file called EVE.HLP will now appear in your directory. This file can be typed, edited, or printed like any other text or ASCII file.

10. The kinds of printers available at various computer sites differ greatly. We will give an example of one site and then ask you to construct your own site-specific version.

In this example, assume that your site has both a line printer devoted to printing on "narrow" forms (8½ × 11-inch paper) and an LN01 laser printer. In order to print to the narrow forms line printer or the laser printer, you must type the following at the operating system prompt:

```
PRINT/FORMS=NARROW filename        ! For the narrow forms
                                   ! line printer

PRINT/QUEUE=SYS$LN01/NOFEED/FLAG=ONE -
/NOTRAILER/NOBURST filename        ! For the laser printer
```

Then edit your LOGIN.COM file to include the following lines. The $LAS*ER line, shown on two lines here, must be added to LOGIN.COM as one continuous line.

```
$ NAR*ROW == "PRINT/FORMS=NARROW"
$ LAS*ER == "PRINT/QUEUE=SYS$LN01/NOFEED/FLAG=ONE
/NOTRAILER/NOBURST"
```

If you have the annotated LOGIN.COM file, you need only remove the exclamation points. If you have the starter LOGIN.COM file, you must insert the complete lines exactly as they appear above.

When you have finished editing LOGIN.COM, you can log out and log in again, or type @LOGIN at the operating system prompt. Then type the following commands at the operating system prompt:

```
NARROW/NOTIFY LOGIN.COM
LASER/NOTIFY LOGIN.COM
```

These commands generate a copy of the LOGIN.COM file on narrow forms and from the laser printer.

Now check with your local user services staff to find out what kinds of printers are available at your site, along with the appropriate DCL commands for sending files to these printers. Using the preceding example, edit your LOGIN.COM file appropriately and print out copies of your LOGIN.COM file on the different printers available at your site.

*Note*: The global symbols NARROW and LASER will be in effect at every log-in until the lines you inserted are removed from the LOGIN.COM file, or until the $ is replaced with $! for each of these lines. For more information on symbols and DCL, see Bibliography [9]. See also Chapter 1, Exercise 13.

Chapter 3

# The DECspell Spelling Checker Program

## 3.1 An Interactive Session with DECspell

DECspell is a spelling and capitalization checker available on VAX/VMS systems. Like many Digital-supported programs, it provides on-line help from the DCL command (or operating system) level as well as from within the DECspell program itself.[1] However, DECspell is so straightforward you probably will not need much help—in fact you might just try to operate it now and see how far you can get.

First, copy the file `WACO.RCM` into your directory, using the DCL command `COPY TEXTFILES:WACO.RCM WACO.RCM` if the files have been set up for you. If not, create the file yourself from the listing in Section I.2.5 of Appendix I. Type `SPELL WACO.RCM` <RETURN>. DECspell will tell you that you have no personal dictionary and will ask you if you want to make one. Type `Y` for `YES` as prompted by the program. The file `PERSONAL.LGP` will be created in your directory. The screen will then reconstruct, with the top window of the screen occupied by text from the file `WACO.RCM`. Notice that the string "BBS" is highlighted at the top of the screen. (On some older terminals, misspelled words are put within double angle brackets rather than highlighted.) This highlighting indicates that the string was not found in DECspell's master dictionary. DECspell has found no available corrections for this error and

1. `OVERVIEW` is the beginning `HELP` command from within DECspell.

has made the reasonable assumption that you want to edit it out. Accordingly, the command EDIT is highlighted near the bottom of the screen. However, "BBS" is a conventional abbreviation for the term Bulletin Board System and therefore is not a mistake. ADD it to your personal dictionary so the next time DECspell comes across "BBS" it will not count it as a spelling error.

Using the arrow keys, cause the highlighting to move from the EDIT command to the ADD command, then press <RETURN>. (The same result could have been obtained by typing A for ADD, then pressing <RETURN>.) Notice that DECspell tells you it has added "BBS" to your personal dictionary. Now, at the top of the screen, "BBS" is no longer highlighted, but "Austin" is. Repeat the earlier procedure to add "Austin" to the dictionary.

The next highlighted word is the proper name "James". DECspell has found words that it guesses can be substituted. Use the <DOWN ARROW> key to move to the command line, then the <RIGHT ARROW> to reach IGNORE. Press <RETURN>. Now you see that DECspell has found a "correction" for the proper name "Arthur". The word "earthier" is highlighted, as is the command GLOBAL REPLACE. Press <RETURN>, which indicates that you want to make the replacement throughout the text. (The result yields an incorrect file but demonstrates the GLOBAL REPLACE command.) IGNORE the proper name "Strohm" just as you did "James".

Also IGNORE the word "Waco". Notice what happens: all instances of "Waco" are no longer highlighted. Use GLOBAL REPLACE to change "Blabbie" to "Blabby" following the sequence you used on "Arthur". Now "IH" is highlighted; DECspell wants to do a GLOBAL REPLACE but it would be inappropriate, so type E (for EDIT) <RETURN>. The cursor pops up into the text. Type the words "interstate highway" and notice that DECspell behaves like a text editor in insert mode—that is, it inserts the text and shifts the old text to the right. To get rid of the old text, move the cursor to the right of "IH" and press <BACKSPACE> twice, followed by <RETURN>.

Leave DECspell by typing F (for FINISH) <RETURN>. Follow the prompts to save a corrected version of your text. Notice that DECspell tells you how many errors it corrected. Just as with a text editor, DECspell has preserved WACO.RCM;1 and created WACO.RCM;2. Use the DIR command to verify that two versions exist. Notice that the new file PERSONAL.LGP is now in your directory. TYPE it to the screen and observe that it includes the words you added to it.

## 3.2 Using DECspell Within EVE

Some VAX sites allow DECspell to be called from within EVE. This provides an additional advantage in that it allows the user to select a range of text to check. Using the <SELECT> key and the cursor control keys, mark a block of text just as you do in EVE to remove a block of text. The selected text appears in reverse video. Then press the <DO> key and type SPELL. DECspell then checks the selected text.

When you invoke DECspell at the operating system level, as described earlier, you have to check through the whole file, which can be quite a headache if the doubtful word is in the last line of the file. Another advantage to invoking DECspell from EVE is that you can simply skip over material that you know to be misspelled, such as mail headers and other text with strings that are not real English words.

## 3.3 The Grammar Checker

In addition to DECspell, many sites with VAX/VMS systems provide a grammar checker program. If your site has this program, you can make a good start by first using the on-line help. At the operating system prompt, type HELP GRAMMAR <RETURN>. The on-line help makes it clear that the program cannot discover every kind of grammar or usage error, but the GRAMMAR program can be of immense help to those who use the computer for composing text. Consider the following excerpt from the on-line help:

> Grammar Checker can detect errors resulting from the use of text-editing or word-processing programs. Examples are lack of continuity caused by lack of subject-verb agreement caused by replacing one phrase with another, and redundancies caused by inserting text. These errors are not usually detected in handwritten or typewritten documents.

Those of you are new to computer-based text composition will find the GRAMMAR program useful for this feature alone. The program is called at the operating system level similarly to the way you call DECspell or EVE. Try using it on the now familiar WACO.RCM file. Type

```
GRAMM WACO.RCM
```

followed by <RETURN>. If you look quickly, you will notice the message "loading personal dictionary." This dictionary is the same one you created earlier when you used DECspell to check the same file.

When the screen reconstructs, the words "VAX Grammar Checker" are displayed at the bottom of the screen. You are at an obscure place in the program. No commands are displayed. What do you do? First, select a range of text using the <SELECT> key (begin, perhaps, with the paragraph starting "Now, the Waco Chamber of Commerce. . . ,"). Move the cursor to the end of this paragraph and press <SELECT>. Then move the cursor to the bottom of the file.

The selected text appears in reverse video. Now, press the <DO> key and, as the cursor moves toward the bottom of the screen, type `GRAMMAR` <RETURN>. The following choices will appear at the bottom of the screen:

```
Edit  Replace  Ignore  Add  Pass  Finish  More  Information
```

The GRAMMAR program now begins to have the "look and feel" of DECspell. It finds an "error" and highlights a suggestion for corrective action.

Assuming you are working with a corrected file and have added all the proper names and place names to your dictionary, the first error found is in the sentence beginning with "But". GRAMMAR wants you to Edit the sentence so that it no longer begins with "But". You are not obligated to do what the grammar checker wants. If you wanted to pass over the alleged violation, you would type `P` (for Pass) and then, after the Pass command is highlighted, press <RETURN>. You should experiment with the grammar checker to see if you can improve the style of `WACO.RCM`.

## 3.4 Command Idiosyncracies

The procedure of terminating the Edit command is not the same in DECspell and in GRAMMAR. In DECspell, <RETURN> tells the program that you are finished editing and ready to move on to the next error. In GRAMMAR, pressing <DO> terminates the editing.

Also, GRAMMAR does not automatically save a corrected version of the file when you issue the Finish command. Corrections are saved to a file just as in EVE, by pressing <CTRL/Z>.

Finally, pressing <DO> and typing HELP is of little use in either GRAMMAR or DECspell. The computer acts as though it were giving help for EVE. This is because EVE, DECspell, and GRAMMAR are all specialized applications of TPU, Digital's Text Processing Utility.

## Quick Reference: DECspell Commands

### Entering and Exiting DECspell

| *Command* | *Description* |
|---|---|
| SPELL *filespec* | At the operating system MYNODE$ prompt, runs DECspell on *filespec*. |
| FINISH | Exits DECspell with option of saving corrections. |

The following commands are issued from within DECspell.

| *Command* | *Description* |
|---|---|
| OVERVIEW | Gives beginning on-line help within DECspell. |
| GLOBAL REPLACE | Replaces current error and *all* succeeding occurrences with a correction. |
| REPLACE | Replaces current occurrence of the error with a correction. |
| EDIT | Allows editing the highlighted error in a manner similar to using a text editor in insert mode. |
| IGNORE | Ignores error and *all* succeeding occurrences. |
| ADD | Adds highlighted word to current personal dictionary. |
| PASS | Ignores error. Succeeding occurrences of same word *will* be highlighted as errors. |
| DICTIONARY | Displays names of personal dictionaries being used for verification and allows changing personal dictionary, to which words are added (to the current personal dictionary). |

## 3.6 Exercises

1. Generate a file containing all the on-line help outside of DECspell by typing the following commands at the operating system prompt:

```
HELP/OUTPUT=SPELL1.HLP SPELL...
PRINT/DELETE/NOTIFY SPELL1.HLP
```

2. Demonstrate the on-line help that is available from within DECspell by applying DECspell to a file, moving the cursor to highlight PASS, and pressing <PF2>.

3. Using the LIBRARY command discussed in Chapter 2, Exercise 9, and noting the fact that DECspell's HELP is on the file named SYS$HELP:LNGSPLHLP.HLB, print out a copy of the complete on-line help available from within DECspell.

4. Complete the corrections to the file WACO.RCM using DECspell. However, ADD to the dictionary *all* proper names and slang terms *except* "Waco". Once out of DECspell, read the on-line help on SPELL/FORMAT and SPELL/PACKED, and then type the following commands at the operating system prompt:

```
COPY WACO.RCM JUNK.RCM
SPELL/FORMAT PERSONAL.LGP
SPELL/FORMAT JUNK.RCM
TYPE PERSONAL.LGP
TYPE/P JUNK.RCM
```

   What conclusions can you draw from the results?

5. After doing Exercise 4, apply DECspell to WACO.RCM again. What errors are "flagged"? Using a text editor, edit the file PERSONAL.LGP by inserting the name "Waco". After exiting the text editor, apply DECspell to WACO.RCM again. What conclusions can you draw?

6. Using a text editor, create a file named TEST.LGP, which contains only the name "Waco". After exiting the text editor, type the following command at the operating system prompt:

```
SPELL/PERSONAL_DICTIONARY=TEST.LGP WACO.RCM
```

   What conclusions can you draw from this?

7. Using a text editor, create a file named TEST.TXT, which contains the four words "color", "colour", "honor", "honour." After exiting the editor, read the on-line help on SPELL/MASTER_DICTIONARY. Apply DECspell *three* times to the file TEST.TXT by using *each* of the following commands to start DECspell:

   ```
   SPELL TEST.TXT
   SPELL/MASTER_DICTIONARY=AMERICAN TEST.TXT
   SPELL/MASTER_DICTIONARY=BRITISH TEST.TXT
   ```

   What conclusions can you draw?

8. Apply DECspell to the two *original, uncorrected* files PRAYER.ERR and HENRY.PAT mentioned in the EVE exercises.

9. Does DECspell check for incorrectly used homonyms? To find out, check the word "herd" in WACO.RCM.

Chapter 4

# The WPS-PLUS Word Processor Program

WPS-PLUS is one of several word processors available on VAX computers (see Bibliography [13]). One question that often arises in a discussion of text processing is, "What is the difference between word processors, text editors, and text formatters?" You will probably get as many answers as there are people answering. So as we give our answer, we are not claiming to speak as ultimate authorities.

The distinctions between text editors, word processors, and text formatters are just about as overlapping and ambiguous as those made between micro-, mini-, and mainframe computers. In the case of computers, you will often find distinctions made in terms of size (physical or memory capacity), but these definitions are continually changing. What was once called a minicomputer is now called a microcomputer by some newer definition. This is true simply because computer capability tends to grow while the physical package tends to get smaller.

The same sort of change applies to text editors, word processors, and text formatters. Our measure for distinguishing between these three entities is capability to process text. As a very loose rule of thumb, this capability grows from text editors to word processors to text formatters. They are all used to manipulate text and create documents, be they letters, memos, reports, books, or computer programs. Text editors such as EVE (see Chapter 2) and EDT (see Appendix B) can be used to create documents (we call them files). They work well as long as you want nothing fancy such as boldface or underlining. In most cases, text editors can fill text between specified margins and can move blocks of text around in a given document and between documents. But that's about it.

To be sure, these are useful functions, but if you want more than this, go to a word processor. Word processors, in nearly all cases, can provide boldfacing, underlining, subscripts and superscripts, and many other capabilities that people require when they want to produce a document. Word processors, like text editors, tend to be interactive rather than batch-oriented, that is, you sit at a terminal and see your work being formatted as you progress rather than submitting your job for processing by the computer and then coming back later to see the results. In the acronym-ridden world of modern-day computing, the on-screen presentation of the finished product is often called WYSIWYG (What You See Is What You Get).

There are, however, some things that most word processors cannot do (although this is changing), for example, automatic bibliography production, automatic figure and table numbering, and handling large documents such as books. Many text formatters can easily do these things. SCRIBE is such a text formatter (see Appendix C), as is TEX, a formatter favored by many mathematicians and scientific writers. Text formatters usually run in batch mode, that is, you submit your job to be processed by the text-formatting program, and when it is done, you can look at the results.

In summary, the distinctions between these programs are largely a matter of power and capability, and whether they are used interactively or in batch mode. Let's now begin to learn about one word processor, WPS-PLUS.

## 4.1 Labeling the Keys and Their Functions

If you are reading this section for the first time, you should not expect to understand it fully all at once. Instead, scan the material for an overview and return here for reference as needed throughout the remainder of this chapter. You will probably find Figures 4.2 and 4.3 and the Quick Reference section (4.11) particularly useful for later reference.

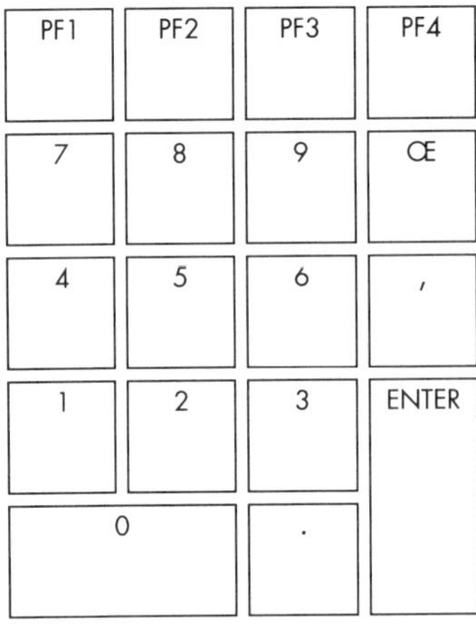


**Figure 4.1 WPS-PLUS Numeric Keypad**

This material is written under the assumption that you are using at least a VT100 series terminal or compatible. However, there are also references to VT200 series terminals, for which it is particularly appropriate. If you are using KERMIT on an MS-DOS microcomputer to emulate a VT102 terminal or higher, you should use KERMIT version 2.30 or higher.

### 4.1.1 *Numeric Keypad*

The numeric keypad of your terminal plays a very important role in processing your text using WPS-PLUS. Your numeric keypad probably looks similar to the one shown in Figure 4.1. The keys on the numeric keypad have special functions when you are working within WPS-PLUS. The WPS-PLUS functions for these keys and their correspondences to the numeric keypad are shown in Figure 4.2.

Let's discuss the use of the <GOLD> key. The <GOLD> key is used in a manner similar to that of the <SHIFT> key on a regular keyboard, that is, in order to get an uppercase letter (assuming that the <CAPITALS LOCK> key is not set), you hold down the <SHIFT> key and type the letter that you want to be capitalized. Hence, pressing a key while holding down the <SHIFT> key gives you a different option than pressing the same key without it. In a similar way, the <GOLD> key gives WPS-PLUS functions to certain keys on the main keyboard when they are pressed after pressing the <GOLD> key, although it is not necessary to hold down <GOLD> while pressing the second key. For example, within a WPS-PLUS menu, if you press the

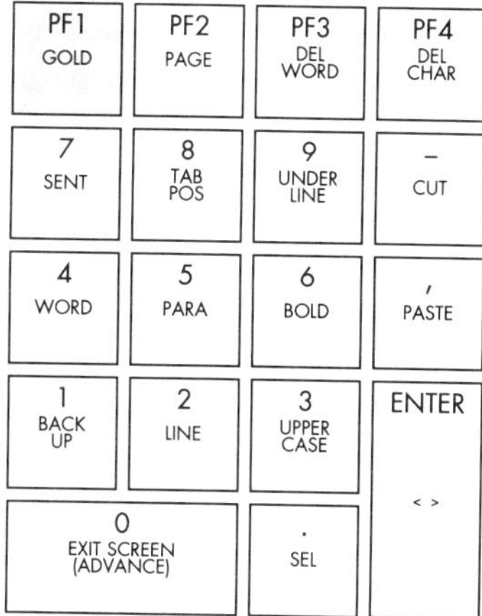


**Figure 4.2 WPS-PLUS Numeric Keypad Functions**

<GOLD> key followed by the <H> key, you will get on-line help. The other WPS-PLUS functions performed by the keys of the numeric keypad, shown in Figure 4.2, will be described as they become relevant to later discussions.

When we refer to a key on the numeric keypad in the context of a WPS-PLUS editor discussion, we usually refer to it by its WPS-PLUS function, followed by a dash and the actual label of the key on your terminal. For example, if we wanted you to use the <keypad COMMA> key, we would say, "Press the <PASTE>–<keypad COMMA> key." We use a similar designation for the keys of the main keyboard when discussing their WPS-PLUS functions (see the next section).

### 4.1.2 *<GOLD> Key Sequences in the WPS-PLUS Editor*

One part of WPS-PLUS is the WPS-PLUS editor. In this editor, many of the keys on the main keyboard provide us with useful functions when pressed after pressing the <GOLD> key. For example, putting the cursor at the end of a line and pressing <GOLD> followed by <C> will center the line within the current margins. In this context, we call <C> the <CNTR> key. Our way of designating the keystrokes involved is to say, "Press <GOLD><CNTR>–<C>," or "Press the <GOLD> key followed by the <CNTR>–<C> key." Notice that every time we refer to one of the keys on the main keyboard by its WPS-PLUS function we follow it with a dash and the actual key name.

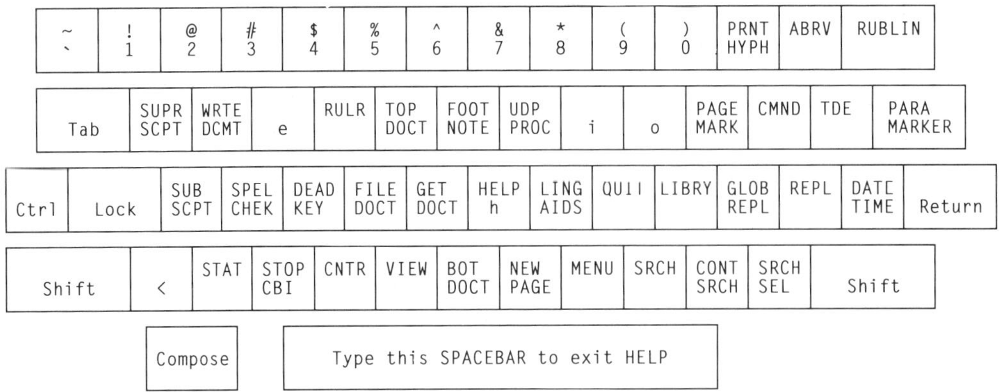


**Figure 4.3 WPS-PLUS Editor Functions for <GOLD> Key Sequences**

The reason for employing both the function names and the actual key names is that in much of the documentation available for WPS-PLUS, either one or the other is given, but not both. We think it is helpful to have both, especially when the function is not mnemonic. Such a non-mnemonic example is seen in getting the linguistic aids function in the WPS-PLUS editor. To do this, you press <GOLD> followed by the <J> key, or <GOLD><LING AIDS>–<J>.

In the WPS-PLUS editor, many such functions are available via <GOLD> key sequences. Figure 4.3 shows the functions available from the main keyboard. The functions are shown in all uppercase letters. The Quick Reference section (4.11) also provides a good summary of the functions associated with <GOLD> key sequences.

There is no need to memorize any of this. You need only keep Figures 4.2 and 4.3 and the Quick Reference section (4.11) handy for reference as you proceed through this chapter.

## 4.2 Setting up to Run WPS-PLUS

There are many ways to implement WPS-PLUS on a VAX/VMS system. If you are using this book as a textbook for a course, your instructor can provide you with the necessary steps to take to use WPS-PLUS on your system; otherwise you should talk to your local user services staff.

The discussion in the remainder of this section is directed to those using WPS-PLUS in a free-standing implementation. If you are using WPS-

```
MYNODE$ @WPSPLUS$SYSTEM:WPLNEWUSR

Creating your WPSPLUS directory...
%CREATE-I-CREATED, MYDISK$:[MYDIR.WPSPLUS] created
Creating WPSPLUS sub-directories...
Creating WPSPLUS default .DAT files....
Creating WPSPLUS user profile...

Now invoking WPSPLUS_LOGIN for you...

WPSPLUS setup completed.

To run WPSPLUS, type WPS.

The following line needs to be added to your LOGIN.COM:

     $@WPSPLUS$SYSTEM:WPSPLUS_LOGIN

MYNODE$
```

**Figure 4.4 Running the Example New User Program**

PLUS from within ALL-IN-ONE, you should skip to the beginning of Section 4.3, keeping in mind that at each point in this chapter where you are told that you will be returned to the operating system, you will have to exit from ALL-IN-ONE by typing EX <RETURN> to get back to the operating system.

### 4.2.1 *A Site-Specific Example*

We demonstrate one implementation of WPS-PLUS to show you the kinds of things that you might expect to do. Your site is likely somewhat different. The first step in our example is to run a "new user" program to set up the necessary file/directory structure that the WPS-PLUS program uses. We do this by typing @WPSPLUS$SYSTEM:WPLNEWUSR at the operating system (DCL) prompt. (In some instances, your instructor might have set up your LOGIN.COM file so that you need only type WPSNEWUSER.) The result of running such a new user program is shown in Figure 4.4.

In this example, the following line is to be added to the LOGIN.COM file after the new user program has been run:

```
$ @WPSPLUS$SYSTEM:WPSPLUS_LOGIN
```

This makes it possible to call WPS-PLUS at any time by typing `WPS` <RETURN> at the operating system prompt. Again, this is only one site-specific example, and your situation will probably differ somewhat from this. For specifics, consult your instructor or local user services staff.

### 4.2.2 WPS-PLUS Directory Structure

Now that you have run the new user program, type `DIR*DIR` <RETURN>. Notice a file called `WPSPLUS.DIR` in your directory. This file indicates the existence of a directory, `WPSPLUS`, containing your WPS-PLUS documents.

WPS-PLUS relies on an elaborate directory structure to take care of the documents that it creates. Understanding this structure is not necessary to do word processing in WPS-PLUS. A more detailed discussion of directories can be found in Appendix D. For now, the main thing you must remember is that the creation and deletion of WPS-PLUS documents should occur from within the WPS-PLUS program. You should not attempt to rename, copy, or delete a WPS-PLUS document from the VMS operating system level.

## 4.3 Entering and Exiting WPS-PLUS

Part of WPS-PLUS is a menu-driven program. This means that your screen fills with a set (menu) of things that you can do (options), and you are to choose one of the options displayed. People sometimes complain that in menu-driven programs they get caught in some menu and cannot escape to previous menus or get out of the program. With this in mind, we discuss how to get out of WPS-PLUS no matter where you find yourself. So if you are stuck in some part of WPS-PLUS, read this section, especially the Summary (4.3.5), to find a way out. We also include a discussion of getting on-line help when available.

Within the WPS-PLUS program, you will find yourself in one of four places:

1. A menu
2. A form
3. The WPS-PLUS editor
4. A CBI (Computer-Based Instruction) module

```
digital                                                Wed 26-Jun-1991
                            WPS-PLUS/VMS 4.0

                 Word and Document Processing Menu

SEL Select     Folder: ____________
               Title:  ____________
               Date:   ____________
C  Create      Number: ____________
E  Edit
D  Delete
P  Print
R  Read                   FC File cabinet
I  Index                  DT Document transfer
RI Recall index           UD User-defined processing

S  Send                   TR Training
EX Exit


_
Enter option and press RETURN,
or press NEXT SCREEN for more options                   (more...)
```

**Figure 4.5 WPS-PLUS Main Menu**

### 4.3.1 *Menus*

If you are in a menu and want to go one step back, for example to a previous menu, press the <EXIT SCREEN> key (also known as the <ADVANCE> key), which is the <keypad 0> key (see Figure 4.2). If you want to exit the WPS-PLUS program and return to the operating system, type EX <RETURN>.

Let's try this by typing the following sequence of commands:

WPS <RETURN>
DT <RETURN>
<EXIT SCREEN>–<keypad 0>
EX <RETURN>

WPS <RETURN> gets you into WPS-PLUS (if this does not work, check with your instructor or local user services staff), and your screen will display the WPS-PLUS Main menu (Figure 4.5). The DT <RETURN> will cause the Document Transfer menu to appear on the screen (Figure 4.6). You will learn later how to use this option. Pressing the <EXIT SCREEN>–<keypad 0> key (also called the <ADVANCE> key) will get you back to the

```
                                                  Fri 28-Jun-1991
                          Document Transfer

 SEL Select             Folder: ____________
                        Title:  ____________
                        Date:   ____________
                        Number: ____________

 RD  Receive a document from DEC workstation
 SD  Send a document to DEC workstation

 RV  Receive a document from VMS
 SV  Send a document to VMS

 RVD  Receive a document from VMS in DDIF format
 SVD  Send a document to VMS in DDIF format

 _
 Enter option and press RETURN,
 or press NEXT SCREEN for more options          (more...)
```

**Figure 4.6 Document Transfer Menu**

WPS-PLUS Main menu, and typing EX <RETURN> will exit you from the WPS-PLUS program, returning you to the operating system.

At any point in this sequence of commands, you can get on-line help by pressing <GOLD><HELP>–<H>. If you have a VT200 series terminal, you can get the same result by pressing the key labeled <HELP> (see Figure 4.35). Try to get on-line help by entering WPS-PLUS again; before typing DT <RETURN>, press <GOLD><HELP>–<H> and follow the prompts, depending on how much information you want. When you are back in the Main menu, type DT, but before pressing <RETURN>, press <GOLD><HELP>–<H>. Notice that this gives you help on the DT command.

To reiterate, when you are in a menu, <EXIT SCREEN>–<keypad 0> will get you to the previous step (if there is one) and EX <RETURN> at the Main menu will get you out of WPS-PLUS to the operating system. If you want on-line help at any point, press <GOLD><HELP>–<H>.

### 4.3.2 Forms

The difference between a menu and a form is that, in the case of forms, instead of choosing from a list of options as in a menu, you fill in blanks (fields) with information. The information you fill in is not taken from a set of options in a menu. When you are in a form, you can get back to the previous screen (menu or form) by pressing the <EXIT SCREEN>–<keypad 0> key. On-line help can be obtained by pressing <GOLD><HELP>–<H>.

In order to exit WPS-PLUS entirely and get back to the operating system, you normally need to be in the Main menu (although there *are* exceptions). From the Main menu, you can get to the operating system by typing `EX` <RETURN>, as described earlier.

Let's try an example. Enter WPS-PLUS by typing `WPS` <RETURN>, and at the Main menu (see Figure 4.5) type `C` <RETURN> to select the Create option. This means that you want to create a new document. The lower half of the screen will fill with the Creating New Document form (Figure 4.7). If the cursor is not in the `Folder:` field, move it there with the <UP ARROW> key and press <GOLD><HELP>–<H>. You will get some on-line help concerning the `Folder:` field. To get back to the Main menu, press <EXIT SCREEN>–<keypad 0>. Exit to the operating system by typing `EX` <RETURN>.

One final note on using forms. As you will see later (for example, in Figure 4.31), some forms have two columns of fields. In this case, moving the cursor with the arrow keys will sometimes not get you to every field. When this happens, try using the <TAB> key.

### 4.3.3 The WPS-PLUS Editor

When you are in the WPS-PLUS editor, there are two ways to exit to the Main menu. One is pressing <GOLD><FILE DOCT>–<F> (see Figure 4.3), which files the document, saving your most current changes, and exits to the Main menu. The other is pressing <GOLD><QUIT>–<K>; you will be asked if you want to exit the editor without saving your work. A response of `Y` <RETURN> gets you back to the Main menu without saving your work, and a response of `N` <RETURN> returns you to the editor.

Let's try an example. Get to the WPS-PLUS Main menu by typing `WPS` <RETURN> at the operating system level. Then type `C` <RETURN> to Create

```
      Creating New Document

Folder:     ____________
Title:      ____________
Keywords:   ____________

Enter information and press RETURN
```

**Figure 4.7 Creating New Document Form**

a new document. The bottom half of your screen will display the Creating New Document form (see Figure 4.7). If the cursor is not in the `Folder:` field, move it there with the <UP ARROW> key and type `DEMO`, using the <SPACEBAR> to blank out any other characters in that field. If you are asked whether you want to create a new folder, respond with `Y` <RETURN>. Next, move the cursor to the `Title:` field and type `LETTER1.DEMO` <RETURN>. Your screen will clear, and at the top of your screen will appear the default ruler for the WPS-PLUS editor (Figure 4.8). You are now in the WPS-PLUS editor, and you could begin to enter text. However, let's postpone that until Section 4.4.

Try getting some on-line help by pressing <GOLD><HELP>—<H>. Your screen will now display a keyboard showing many of the WPS-PLUS keyboard and numeric keypad functions in reverse video (compare with Figures 4.2 and 4.3). When you have finished trying out some of the <GOLD> key sequences as described on your screen, press the <SPACEBAR> (possibly preceded by the <EXIT SCREEN>—<keypad 0> key; check the prompts appearing on your screen carefully), and you will be returned to the editor. Next, press <GOLD><QUIT>—<K> and respond with `N` <RETURN>. This will return you to the editor. A `Y` <RETURN> would have returned you to the Main menu without saving any of your work for that session. In this case, there is no work.

Now press <GOLD><FILE DOCT>—<F>. This will save your document (very little in this case) and return you to the Main menu. At this point, you can exit to the operating system as usual by typing `EX` <RETURN>.

### 4.3.4 A CBI (Computer-Based Instruction) Module

Several Computer-Based Instruction (CBI) modules are available in WPS-PLUS. You can get to them whenever a menu displays the `TR` (TRaining)

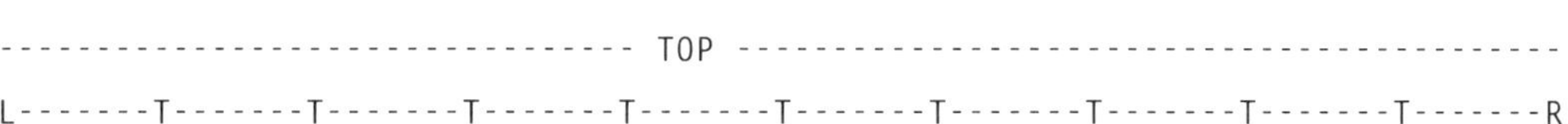


**Figure 4.8 Default Ruler on the Initial WPS-PLUS Editor Screen**

option by typing TR <RETURN>. Usually you will get another menu showing the Training options. Once a Training option is chosen, you can get back to the Training Options menu at any time by pressing <GOLD><STOP CBI>–<X>. From the WPS-PLUS Training menu, you can get to the Main menu by pressing <EXIT SCREEN>–<keypad 0>.

Try this. Get back into WPS-PLUS by typing WPS <RETURN>, and when the Main menu appears, type TR <RETURN>. The WPS-PLUS Training menu will appear. Pick the Getting Started option by typing T1 <RETURN>, then pick the Overview of WPS-PLUS option by typing T3 <RETURN>. Follow the prompts through the entire lesson, unless it seems too simple for you. In that case, type <GOLD><STOP CBI>–<X>. When you return to the WPS-PLUS Training menu, press <EXIT SCREEN>–<keypad 0> twice to get back to the Main menu.

When you are back in the Main menu, EX <RETURN> will return you to the operating system. In fact, you could have exited WPS-PLUS to the operating system while in the WPS-PLUS Training menu by typing EX <RETURN>.

### 4.3.5 Summary

Now let's summarize the actions in the examples we have just discussed. In a menu, press <EXIT SCREEN>–<keypad 0> to get to the previous menu (if there is one). After enough <EXIT SCREEN>–<keypad 0> keystrokes to get you to the Main menu, type EX <RETURN> to exit WPS-PLUS to the operating system. On-line help is available at any point in a menu by pressing <GOLD><HELP>–<H>, or the key labeled <HELP> on VT200 series terminals (see Figure 4.35).

In a form, move between fields with the arrow keys or the <TAB> key. Get to previous forms or menus by using <EXIT SCREEN>–<keypad 0>. Once you are at the Main menu, exit WPS-PLUS by typing EX <RETURN>. On-line help is available at most points via <GOLD><HELP>–<H>, or the key labeled <HELP> on VT200 series terminals. Notice that when you are in a form you may move between fields via the arrow and <TAB> keys correcting your entries, but pressing <RETURN> commits the entries as they appear at that point.

In the WPS-PLUS editor, exit to the Main menu via <GOLD><FILE DOCT>–<F> or <GOLD><QUIT>–<K>. The <FILE DOCT>–<F> option saves your document, including the current changes. With the <QUIT>–<K> option, you are asked if you want to exit without saving your changes; Y <RETURN> gets you back to the Main menu without saving your current changes, and N <RETURN> gets you back into the WPS-PLUS editor. Once you are at the Main menu, EX <RETURN> gets you to the operating system. On-line help can be obtained by pressing <GOLD><HELP>–<H>, or the key labeled <HELP> on VT200 series terminals.

In a CBI (Computer-Based Instruction) module, <GOLD><STOP CBI>–<X> gets you to a Training menu; from there you can get to the Main menu and exit to the operating system, as noted previously.

## 4.4 Getting Started with the WPS-PLUS Editor: Sample Letter

Now that we have finished the preliminaries, let's make a simple document using WPS-PLUS, specifically, a letter. In this hypothetical case, you are a middle-aged university professor who thinks quality undergraduate teaching is being ignored at your university. After reading in the local newspaper about faculty shortages, you decide to write a letter to the editor. We assume that you have legitimate access to a VAX computer and to WPS-PLUS.

### 4.4.1 Using the Default Margins

In the previous section, where you learned how to get in and out of the WPS-PLUS editor, you created a document with the folder name DEMO and title LETTER1.DEMO (see Figure 4.7). You will be editing this document to store your letter.

Before you begin to construct your letter in folder DEMO with title LETTER1.DEMO, notice that for each document you create using WPS-PLUS the conceptual framework is that of an electronic file cabinet containing *folders*; in these folders are specific *documents*, known by their *titles*. However, if you exit WPS-PLUS to the VMS operating system, you will not be able to find a directory named DEMO or a file named LETTER1.DEMO.

```
            Selecting Current Document

Folder:  ____________
Title:   ____________
Number:  ____________

Enter Information and press RETURN
Enter fields and press RETURN to select a document or EXIT
for menu
```

**Figure 4.9 Selecting Current Document Form**

These document designations are known *only* from within WPS-PLUS. The directory structure of WPS-PLUS is explained in Appendix D.

Now begin to compose your letter. Enter WPS-PLUS by typing `WPS` <RETURN> at the operating system prompt; the WPS-PLUS Main menu (see Figure 4.5) will appear. In the upper right-hand corner you will see a highlighted box called the current document block. The current document block contains the fields `Folder:`, `Title:`, `Date:`, and `Number:`. The `Folder:` and `Title:` fields should contain the entries `DEMO` and `LETTER1.DEMO` from your previous work. If they do, simply type `E` <RETURN> to choose the Edit option, and you should see the editor screen reappear.

If your current document block contains other entries, you will need to look around to find your previous work. (We are assuming that you have done the examples in Section 4.3.3. However, if there was a slip-up, then following these instructions should carry you through.) At the Main menu type `SEL` <RETURN>. When the Selecting Current Document form (Figure 4.9) appears, use the arrow keys to move the cursor to the `Folder:` field and type `DEMO` (do *not* press <RETURN>). Next, blank out all other characters in the field using the <SPACEBAR>. With the <DOWN ARROW> key, move the cursor to the `Title:` field and type `LETTER1.DEMO`, blanking out all other characters as before. Now press <RETURN>.

If your document was already in existence, you will be back at the Main menu with the current document block containing `DEMO` in the `Folder:` field and `LETTER1.DEMO` in the `Title:` field. If your document was not in existence, the only difference will be that you will be asked whether you want to create it. This will occur *before* you get back to the Main menu. In this case, answer Y <RETURN>. Now type E <RETURN> to begin editing the document.

Remember, when filling in a WPS-PLUS form, you can move between fields using the arrow or <TAB> keys and change things as much as you like. However, once you press <RETURN>, you have committed all entries in the form. If WPS-PLUS cannot make sense of your entries, you will be informed at this point.

As you begin to edit this document (Folder: DEMO, Title: LETTER1.DEMO), you will see the editor screen reappear. You are now back in the WPS-PLUS editor. Begin by typing the text shown in Figure 4.10. Reproduce all the <RETURN>s as shown. They will not appear on your screen. You will not need to press a <RETURN> at the end of each line. WPS-PLUS will automatically wrap the text to accommodate the margins indicated by the ruler at the top of your document (see Figure 4.8). The default margins are left margin column 1 and right margin column 80. If you make a mistake, use the arrow keys to move the cursor and <BACKSPACE> or <RUBOUT> to delete characters to the left of the cursor.

Also notice that you are in insert mode. This means that whenever you type a character it is inserted into the text, causing everything else on that line to the right of the cursor to move one space to the right. The alternative to insert mode is overstrike mode. To move from insert mode to overstrike mode, press <CTRL/a>, that is, press the <A> key while holding down the <CTRL> key. A message will appear at the bottom of your screen telling you that you are in overstrike mode. To get back into insert mode, press <CTRL/a> again. If you have used the EVE text editor, you will probably remember that this insert/overstrike toggle works the same way in EVE.

Once you have typed your letter, press <GOLD><FILE DOCT>–<F> to File your document in your electronic WPS-PLUS file cabinet. You will now be returned to the Main menu.

Had you wanted to exit the WPS-PLUS editor without saving your work, you could have typed <GOLD><QUIT>–<K>. WPS-PLUS would then have asked you to confirm that you really wanted to quit without saving your

```
<RETURN>
<RETURN>
<RETURN>
<RETURN>
<RETURN>
Local Tribune <RETURN>
P.O. Box ABC <RETURN>
My Town, TX 78XXX <RETURN>
<RETURN>
To the Editor: <RETURN>
<RETURN>
You recently printed an article concerning the possible
upcoming shortage of university faculty. You quoted several
university administrators who expressed their concern over
being unable to fill vacancies. Among those administrators
was one from Third Tier University. <RETURN>
<RETURN>
As one of those "graying" faculty members at TTU, I hope
such a realization on the part of the TTU administration will
signal a need to reduce its abuse of the current faculty.
Specifically, I am referring to the recent inordinate
emphasis on publishing to the detriment of teaching.
Certainly, we continue to hear mouthings about teaching
excellence, but the reality is that most of the rewards now
go to those who publish prolifically and bring in grant
money, while those who continue to emphasize good teaching
are considered "weak sisters." <RETURN>
<RETURN>
Let's hope the faculty shortage will prompt these
administrators to return to their senses and allow faculty
members to develop their individual strengths without being
forced into the publication mill unless they have something
worthwhile to say. Maybe teaching will then be returned to
its rightful place at the university. <RETURN>
<RETURN>
Sincerely yours, <RETURN>
<RETURN>
<RETURN>
<RETURN>
Crank E. Prof <RETURN>
<RETURN>
<RETURN>
CEP/vax
```

**Figure 4.10 Typing LETTER1.DEMO Using the Default Margins**

work. A Y <RETURN> at this point would have returned you to the Main menu.

Let's now print out this draft of your letter.

### 4.4.2 *Printing a Document*

Printing a document in WPS-PLUS is a site-specific task.[1] So as you work through this section, you will probably want to consult your instructor or your local user services staff. However, if you already know what kinds of printers your site has, the examples given here provide a fairly straightforward means of printing your document without knowing anything else about how WPS-PLUS is installed on your system.

Let's assume that a site has three kinds of printers:

1. A line printer, model LP11
2. A laser printer, model LN03
3. A laser printer, model LPS-40 (PostScript)

In reality, your site will probably be different; however, the substitutions you need to make should be clear from this example.

In this section, we use the `P` (Print) command in the Main menu to create a file in your `SYS$LOGIN` directory, in VMS (see Appendix D for a discussion of directories). You can then print this file once you are out of WPS-PLUS and back at the operating system level. So in this case *print* really means "print to a file." You will see a similar use of *print* in Chapter 8 (DECalc).

At the WPS-PLUS Main menu, type `P` <RETURN> (see Figure 4.5). The bottom half of your screen will fill with the Printing Document form (Figure 4.11). In the `Document destination:` field, type `FILE`. Using the <DOWN ARROW>, move to the `Format style:` field and type the appropriate printer designation (in our example, one of the three, LP11, LN03, or LPS), followed by <RETURN>. For definiteness, let's say that you typed `LP11` <RETURN> in the `Format style:` field.

1. The choice of printers and the way WPS-PLUS can be configured to drive those printers is not the same at every VAX/VMS site.

```
                 Printing Document

Document destination: ________
Format style:         ________
Number of copies:     1

Enter information and press RETURN
or NEXT SCREEN to change settings
```

**Figure 4.11 Printing Document Form**

Once you have filled in the Printing Document form, a message will appear at the bottom of your screen: "Formatting document. . .". This means that WPS-PLUS is setting things up for the VMS file that you are going to create, so that when you print it, the results will come out right for the printer you have specified.

In a few moments, another form will appear at the bottom of your screen. It is the Send a Document to VMS form (Figure 4.12). The only field to complete on this form is `VMS File Name:`. Since you indicated `LP11` in the `Format style:` field in this example, you presumably want to print this file on your line printer. Let your file type reflect this by typing `SYS$LOGIN:LETTER1.LPT` <RETURN> in the `VMS File Name:` field. Another message will appear at the bottom of your screen, saying "File copied to VMS", and your screen will then be filled with the Main menu again.

You can then exit WPS-PLUS (`EX` <RETURN>) to the operating system and use the appropriate operating system `PRINT` command to print the file `LETTER1.LPT`, which is in your `SYS$LOGIN` directory. Notice that unless your site has made local changes, forgetting to put `SYS$LOGIN:` in front of the file name and file type will cause your file to be stored in the `WPSPLUS` directory, one level below your `SYS$LOGIN` directory (see Appendix D for a discussion of VMS directories and the WPS-PLUS directory structure).

### 4.4.3 *Deleting a Document*

Soon enough you will have several documents, possibly in different folders. Some will probably have been made by mistake as you learn how to use WPS-PLUS, and others will be old and no longer needed. In any case, you will want to delete some documents from your WPS-PLUS file

```
                    Send a Document to VMS

VMS File Name: ______________________________

Enter the VMS File name, and press RETURN.
```

**Figure 4.12 Send a Document to VMS Form**

cabinet. As you will see, this is a two-step process. First you delete the document, then you empty the WASTEBASKET.

In this example, we make a junk document and then delete it. Following the pattern in Section 4.3.3, use the C (Create) option of the Main menu and follow the steps to create a document with title JUNK in your DEMO folder. After exiting the WPS-PLUS editor with <GOLD><FILE DOCT>–<F>, make sure that your current document block, in the upper right-hand corner of the Main menu, indicates that the current document is indeed entitled JUNK in the DEMO folder. If it is not, use the SELect procedure, discussed in Sections 4.4.1 and 4.4.4, to make it so.

Now type D <RETURN> to choose the Delete option. You might be asked to confirm. If so, type Y <RETURN>. You will be told that this document has been filed in the WPS-PLUS WASTEBASKET. This means that you have not actually removed this file from your VMS directory. It still exists somewhere in the WPS-PLUS directory structure and is taking up space in your disk area. In WPS-PLUS jargon, your document has been placed in the WASTEBASKET folder.

To complete the deletion process in WPS-PLUS, you must empty the WASTEBASKET. Do this by typing FC <RETURN> at the Main menu to choose the File Cabinet option. When the File Cabinet menu appears, type EW <RETURN> to Empty the WASTEBASKET. You will then be asked to confirm your decision, which you do by typing Y <RETURN>. At this point, your document is deleted from WPS-PLUS and from its place in your VMS directory.

You can then return to the Main menu by pressing the <EXIT SCREEN>–<keypad 0> key or exit to the operating system by typing EX <RETURN>.

In summary, the process of deleting a document is as follows:

1. SELect the document for deletion (see Section 4.4.1).

2. In the main menu, Delete the document via

   `D` <RETURN>

   and confirm (if necessary) with

   `Y` <RETURN>

3. In the Main menu, choose the File Cabinet option via

   `FC` <RETURN>

4. In the File Cabinet menu, Empty the `WASTEBASKET` via

   `EW` <RETURN>

   and confirm with

   `Y` <RETURN>

### 4.4.4 Finding the Names of All Folders and All Titles

You will soon want to know what titles are in a given folder or how many folders you have in your WPS-PLUS file cabinet. In this section, we go through a sample procedure to determine these things.

First, let's talk about how to determine all the folders you have. At the Main menu, type `SEL` <RETURN>. When the Selecting Current Document form appears (see Figure 4.9), move the cursor to the `Folder:` field and blank out any characters in that field, using the <SPACEBAR>. Then press <GOLD><LIBRY>–<L>. The upper part of your screen will reconstruct, giving you a list of all your folders. Follow the instructions on your screen and pick a folder.

You should be back to the Selecting Current Document form, with the folder that you just picked in the `Folder:` field. Now move the cursor to the `Title:` field and make the field blank if it is not already. Then press <GOLD><LIBRY>–<L> to get a listing of the titles in the current folder. Following the instructions, pick a title. When your cursor returns to the Selecting Current Document form, press <RETURN>.

Now that you have been returned to the Main menu, the current document block (in the upper right-hand corner) should contain the document you have just SELected.

For a final demonstration, press the <UP ARROW> and <DOWN ARROW> keys. If your current folder contains several titles, these titles will appear in the Title: field as you press the arrow keys. Thus, you now see an easier way to select a particular title in your current folder: just let the <UP ARROW> and <DOWN ARROW> keys do it for you.

To change folders, you still have to use the SELect procedure discussed here or in Section 4.4.1, depending on whether you are SELecting an existing folder or Creating a new one.

### 4.4.5 Changing the WPS-PLUS Ruler

Take a look at the letter you printed earlier. Notice that it has rather narrow margins. Recall that the default margins are left margin column 1 and right margin column 80. In this section, we show how to change these default settings on the WPS-PLUS ruler and how to rewrap, or reflow, your text to fit the new margins.

First, enter WPS-PLUS with the usual `WPS` <RETURN> at the operating system prompt. Then, if the current document block of the Main menu does not have `DEMO` and `LETTER1.DEMO` in the `Folder:` and `Title:` fields, use the SELect procedure (see Sections 4.4.1 and 4.4.4) to SELect these. Next enter the WPS-PLUS editor by typing `E` <RETURN> for the Edit option. Your screen will fill with the letter as shown in Figure 4.10 (without the <RETURN>s).

Make sure that your cursor is at the top of the file; then press <GOLD><RULR>–<R> to change the ruler. The lines shown in Figure 4.13 will be inserted on your screen. The `L` in column 1 indicates that the left margin is set at column 1, and the `R` in column 80 indicates that the right margin is set at column 80. Let's set the left and right margins to 10 and 65, respectively. Using the <LEFT ARROW> and <RIGHT ARROW> keys, move the cursor to column 10 and type `L` and to column 65 and type `R`. Notice that the earlier `L` and `R` disappear.

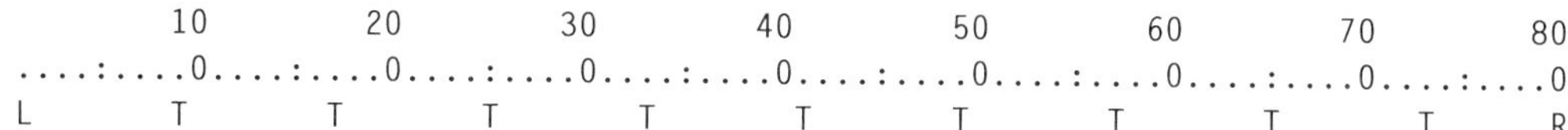

```
        10        20        30        40        50        60        70        80
....:....0....:....0....:....0....:....0....:....0....:....0....:....0....:....0
L       T       T       T       T       T       T       T       T       T      R
```

**Figure 4.13 WPS-PLUS Default Ruler**

Next, delete all the tab stops (indicated by T) by moving the cursor over each T and pressing the <SPACEBAR>. Now set a tab stop at column 45 for the sender's address and date portion of the letter by moving the cursor to column 45 and typing T. Finally, put these settings into effect by pressing <RETURN>. This results in the final commitment of your settings in the same way as the entries in a form are committed only when <RETURN> is pressed. You can now enter your own address, city, and the date on the first three lines by <TAB>ing to column 45 and typing the appropriate information.

Finally, the old text needs to be rewrapped, or reflowed, to conform to the new margins. Notice that the text previously entered is still as it was earlier; the rewrapping was not done automatically. Rewrap the text by moving the cursor to the left margin at the top of the old text and then moving the cursor down the document using the <DOWN ARROW> key or some other distance key (see Section 4.5.1). As you move the cursor down the document, notice that the text is rewrapped according to the new margins of 10 and 65. Exit the editor by pressing <GOLD><FILE DOCT>–<F> to file your work. Unless your site has made local changes, WPS-PLUS does not keep multiple versions of your document, as VMS does in the case of files.

At the Main menu, go through the process of printing a file to VMS (see Section 4.4.2), exit WPS-PLUS, print your VMS file, and compare it to the earlier work.

### 4.4.6 *Some More CBI (Computer-Based Instruction) Modules—Maybe*

At this point, you might want to explore more of the CBI (Computer-Based Instruction) modules. Although these lessons can be a bit confusing if you do not push the right key, they can also be helpful in fixing in your mind some of the things you have already learned. Type TR <RETURN> at

```
                    WPS-PLUS Training

  T1  Getting started
  T2  New features
  T3  Editor training
  T4  File cabinet
  T5  User-defined processes
  T6  View all training

  _

  Enter option and press RETURN, or press EXIT
```

**Figure 4.14 WPS-PLUS Training Menu**

the Main menu and go through some of the modules by picking one of the options on the WPS-PLUS Training menu (Figure 4.14).

Remember, <GOLD><STOP CBI>–<X> will usually get you out of these sessions, and the "panic button", <CTRL/y>, will almost certainly get you back, if rather gracelessly, to the operating system. If you are asked to press the <HYPH PUSH> button, this is <BACKSPACE> on VT100 series terminals and the <F12> or <BS> key on VT200 series terminals. At this point, we strongly recommend using the `T1` (Getting Started) Computer-Based Instruction module.

## 4.5 *More WPS-PLUS Editor Functions*

Now that you know how to create, edit, and print a WPS-PLUS document, we discuss some additional things you can do in the WPS-PLUS editor. So far, you have done nothing more than could have been done more easily with a text editor such as EVE or EDT.

### 4.5.1 *Moving the Cursor Through a Document (the Distance Keystrokes)*

Although you do not yet have a document that is several screens long, when you do, the arrow keys alone will probably be too slow for moving the cursor through your document. When you are editing a document, the cursor movement is associated with certain distance keystrokes. Recalling the discussion of the WPS-PLUS editor functions associated with the numeric keypad and <GOLD> key sequences (see Figures 4.2 and 4.3 and

**Table 4.1 WPS-PLUS Editor Distance Keys**

| Keystrokes | Function |
|---|---|
| <GOLD><TOP DOCT>–<T> | Move to the top of the document. |
| <GOLD><BOT DOCT>–<B> | Move to the bottom of the document. |
| <GOLD><LEFT ARROW> | Move to the beginning of the current line. |
| <GOLD><RIGHT ARROW> | Move to the end of the current line. |
| <GOLD><UP ARROW> | Begin scrolling the document toward the top. Stop the scrolling by pressing <CTRL/c> once. |
| <GOLD><DOWN ARROW> | Begin scrolling the document toward the bottom. Stop the scrolling by pressing <CTRL/c> once. |
| <LINE>–<keypad 2> | Move to the next line. |
| <WORD>–<keypad 4> | Move to the next word. |
| <PARA>–<keypad 5> | Move to the next paragraph. |
| <SENT>–<keypad 7> | Move to the next sentence. |

Section 4.11), read through Table 4.1 to learn some other useful ways to move the cursor through your document.

Now enter the WPS-PLUS editor to edit the `LETTER1.DEMO` document in the `DEMO` folder, and try out some of the functions listed in Table 4.1. As you practice, you will see that when you use the distance keys associated with the numeric keypad, e.g., <PARA>–<keypad 5>, the direction of cursor movement is from top to bottom. In order to reverse this direction, changing cursor movement so that it is from bottom to top, press the <BACK UP>–<keypad 1> key. The direction of movement can be reversed so that it is from top to bottom again by pressing the <ADVANCE>–<keypad 0> key.

On VT200 series terminals, the <PREVIOUS SCREEN> and <NEXT SCREEN> keys (to the right of the main keyboard and to the left of the numeric keypad) also provide a convenient means of scrolling one screen at a time (see Figure 4.35).

### 4.5.2 Bolding, Centering, and Underlining: Creating a Resume

Now let's create a tongue-in-cheek resume that looks like the one in Figure 4.15.

RESUME

Billy Bob Taggart

2501 The Strand
Galveston, TX 78XXX

Born: Comfort, Texas, 1933

Education:

- B.A., Southwest Texas Normal School, 1952
  Major: Physical Education
  Minor: Public Speaking and Elocution
  Honors: Presiding Judge, Luling (Texas) Watermelon Thump, 1950, 1951; Second String Fullback, SWT Bobcats, 1952

- Graduate, La Grange High School, La Grange, Texas, 1948
  Honors: Vice-president, Future Farmers of America; Special Award in Chicken Ranching

- Mirabeau B. Lamar Elementary School, Cotulla, Texas, 1942
  Honors: Captain, English First Hallway Patrol

Experience:

1. 1980-present: Chair, English Department, and Football Coach, Ball High School, Galveston, Texas. Duties: Winning at all costs. Instilling attitudes of conventionality and a positive mental attitude among the student body. Putting the big QT on the subversive notion that varsity players must maintain a particular grade-point average.

2. 1974-1980: Speech Teacher and Debate Coach. Consolidated Middle School, Dime Box, Texas. Duties: Promoting Western capitalist patriotic values among the contestants in the University Interscholastic League; reversing disturbing political trends left over from the sixties. Honors: Fundraising Chair for Burleson County Public Radio.

**Figure 4.15 Sample Resume (RES.DEMO)**

```
3.    1953-1973: United States Air Force. Job at
      retirement: Drill Instructor, Lackland Air Force
      Base, San Antonio, Texas.

Career Interests: Upon completion of my M.Ed. degree, I hope
to advance to the position of principal at the high school
level or perhaps attain the rank of district administrator
for linguistic arts.

Hobbies and Other Interests: I am eligible for early
retirement in three years. My hope is that at that time I can
help my brother with what has become the love of his life
since he embarked on retirement number two: his volunteer
work with the Greater Hidalgo County Recreational Vehicle
Park Owners' Association. I hope to uphold American values of
freedom and family supremacy and to boost attendance at the
Wednesday lodge lunch.
```

**Figure 4.15 (continued) Sample Resume (RES.DEMO)**

At the Main menu, type C <RETURN> to Create a new document, then fill in the Creating New Document form (see Figure 4.7) with RES.DEMO in the Title: field and DEMO in the Folder: field (if necessary). Your screen will reconstruct with only the default ruler at the top of your screen (see Figure 4.8).

Set the left and right margins at 5 and 75 and tab stops at 10 and 15 by pressing <GOLD><RULR>–<R> to initiate the ruler setup. Then move the cursor to column 5 and type L. Next, move the cursor to columns 10, 15, and 75 and type T, T, and R, respectively. Finally, move the cursor to the other tab stops, using the arrow or <WORD>–<keypad 4> keys, and remove the tab stops by pressing the <SPACEBAR> at each location. Signal to WPS-PLUS that you have completed your ruler definition by pressing <RETURN>.

In summary, to change the margins and the tab stops, that is, to change the ruler settings, press <GOLD><RULR>–<R> and move the cursor to the places that you wish to change, pressing the <SPACEBAR> to remove a setting or the appropriate character (L, T, or R) to enter a setting. When you are finished with your settings, press <RETURN> to complete your work. These settings will remain in effect for this document until you reset them.

In Figure 4.15, the first line is "RESUME", centered and boldfaced. To achieve this, first type `RESUME`, then while your cursor is at the end of this line, press <GOLD><CNTR>–<C>. `RESUME` is then centered within the margins you have just set. To make `RESUME` boldfaced, move the cursor to the `R` in `RESUME` and press <SEL>–<keypad PERIOD>. You will see the `R` replaced by a small diamond and `RESUME` will be shifted one line below the diamond. Now move the cursor to the first blank beyond the `E` in `RESUME` and press <BOLD>–<keypad 6>. `RESUME` will then be shifted back up to its original position and will be displayed in boldface.

In summary, to center a line within the current margins, move the cursor to the end of the line and press <GOLD><CNTR>–<C>. To boldface a string of text, move the cursor to the first character of the string and press <SEL>–<keypad PERIOD>, then move the cursor to the end of the string and press <BOLD>–<keypad 6>. Underlining can be done in the same way as boldfacing except that you press <UNDERLINE>–<keypad 9> instead of <BOLD>–<keypad 6>.

We have introduced you to the use of the <SEL>–<keypad PERIOD> key and procedure because they will be useful later in cutting and pasting text and selecting ranges of text for checking spelling. However, there is an easier way to boldface and underline small sections of text.

For boldfacing, simply move the cursor over the first character of the text you want to boldface and press the <BOLD>–<keypad 6>. Repeat as many times as you have characters to boldface. The cursor will move from left to right, boldfacing each character with each keystroke. This procedure also works in the same manner for underlining, except that you use the <UNDERLINE>–<keypad 9> key instead of <BOLD>–<keypad 6>.

Now that `RESUME` is centered and boldfaced, use the arrow keys to move the cursor to the beginning of the next line. If you press <RETURN> while you are at the end of the line containing `RESUME`, you will lose the centering. In case you inadvertently do this, you can restore the centering by pressing the <BACKSPACE> or <RUBOUT> key immediately after the centering is lost. Otherwise, you can redo the centering as described above. Remember *not* to press <RETURN> immediately at the end of any centered line.

Once your cursor is at the beginning of the next line, press <RETURN> to get a blank line and then type `Billy Bob Taggart`. Center this line, insert another blank line, and type the next two lines, containing the address, as shown in Figure 4.15.

Insert another blank line and type `Born:`. Now underline the `Born:` by moving the cursor to the first character and pressing <SEL>–<keypad PERIOD>. As happened in the case of boldfacing, the line will be shifted below the select diamond. Now move the cursor to the first space after the colon and press <UNDERLINE>–<keypad 9>. Your line will then be shifted to its original position, with `Born:` underlined.

Insert another blank line, type `Education:`, and underline it, using the procedure we have just discussed (or by successively pressing the <UNDERLINE>–<keypad 9> key, as discussed earlier. After inserting another blank line, use the two tab stops to create the three Education sections as shown in Figure 4.15. Next, after inserting another blank line, type `Experience:` and underline it.

Now you will see another feature of the ruler in WPS-PLUS. Once you have inserted a blank line after `Experience:`, start the process of setting a new ruler by pressing <GOLD><RULR>–<R>. Then set the left margin at 10 by moving the cursor to column 10 and typing `L`. Next, move the cursor to column 15 and type `W` (for tab-Wrap). Set the new ruler definition by pressing <RETURN>.

The `W` that you typed in column 15 while setting the new ruler will allow you to produce the output in Figure 4.15. What happens is that when you press <TAB> the cursor moves to column 15. You can then type as much text as you like; your work will be automatically wrapped at the right margin (75), and at each wrap the cursor will return to column 15 instead of to the left margin, column 10. When you press <RETURN>, the cursor returns to the left margin, column 10. You can now see why this is called the tab-wrap feature.

To get the results as shown in Figure 4.15, type `1.` and press <TAB>. Type the rest of the paragraph without pressing <RETURN> until you have finished the paragraph. Your text will automatically be wrapped between columns 15 and 75. When you finish the first paragraph, press <RETURN> twice and proceed in a similar manner for numbers 2 and 3.

Complete the resume by resetting the ruler as it was at the beginning (left and right margins at 5 and 75) and typing the remaining paragraphs shown in Figure 4.15, including the underlining.

### 4.5.3 Searching for and Replacing Strings of Text

One of the standard functions of any text editor is searching for a particular string of text. Another is searching for a particular string of text and replacing it with another string of text. If you have worked through either the EVE chapter or the EDT appendix, you already know about these functions. The key functions discussed in this section are pictured in Figures 4.2 and 4.3.

First, let's use the WPS-PLUS editor to search for a string without replacing it with another. Enter the editor and prepare to edit the `LETTER1.DEMO` document in the `DEMO` folder. In this example, you will search for the string "you". If the cursor is not already at the top of the document, move it there by pressing <GOLD><TOP DOCT>–<T>. Next, press <GOLD><SRCH>–<COMMA>. At the bottom of your screen you will see "Enter search string:" with the cursor below. Type `you` <RETURN>. The first occurrence of "you" will be found, and the cursor will move there. Notice that it is actually "You" at the beginning of a sentence.

On VT200 series terminals, the <FIND> key can be used for the same purpose of initiating a search (see Figure 4.35).

In order to search for another occurrence of the same string, "you", press <GOLD><CONT SRCH>–<PERIOD>. The cursor will move to the next occurrence of the string "you". Again the string is at the beginning of a sentence. A second press of <GOLD><CONT SRCH>–<PERIOD> will put the cursor at the beginning of "yours" in the closing of the letter. A third press of <GOLD><CONT SRCH>–<PERIOD> will result in the message "SEARCH phrase was not found" at the bottom of your screen. In this example, the search disregarded uppercase and lowercase; both "you" and "You" were considered to be proper matches. This convention is the same as in the EVE text editor. If the initial search string is all lowercase, the case of the string is ignored; however, if the initial search string contains any uppercase letters, an exact match is sought. Test this out by searching for "You".

If you are familiar with the EVE editor, you know that on a VT200 series terminal the <FIND> key can be pressed twice to initiate a search for the next occurrence of a string. This is not true in WPS-PLUS, despite the fact that an initial search can be started using the <FIND> key. To continue the search you must press <GOLD><CONT SRCH>–<PERIOD>, as discussed.

In summary, <GOLD><SRCH>–<COMMA> starts the search for a given string of text and <GOLD><CONT SRCH>–<PERIOD> continues it.

Now you will learn how to search for a particular string and replace it with another. To use this function in WPS-PLUS, you first need to understand that there are several buffers (temporary storage areas) in use while you are working in the WPS-PLUS editor. One of these buffers, which we discuss in detail in the next section, is the `PASTE` buffer. This buffer is used to hold text that can be inserted (pasted) at any location in your document. The search-and-replace function in the WPS-PLUS editor requires that you first put the text that will replace a particular string into the `PASTE` buffer. Then, after you initiate the search-and-replace sequence, the contents of the `PASTE` buffer are used to replace the string for which you are searching.

Let's do an example. Move to the top of the `LETTER1.DEMO` document by pressing <GOLD><TOP DOCT>–<T>. You are going to replace the first occurrence of "shortage" with "dearth" and leave the second occurrence of "shortage" as it is. First select the replacement string, "dearth", which is to be put into the `PASTE` buffer, by pressing <SEL>–<keypad PERIOD>. The select diamond will appear with the cursor directly below it. Type `dearth` <CUT>–<keypad MINUS>. This puts `dearth` into the `PASTE` buffer.

Now set up for the search by pressing <GOLD><SRCH>–<COMMA>. At the `Enter search string:` prompt, type `shortage` <GOLD><SRCH SEL>–<SLASH>. The cursor will advance to the first occurrence of the string "shortage", and the select diamond will appear, with the text, starting with `shortage`, shifted down one line. Press <GOLD><REPL>–<APOSTROPHE>. You will see `shortage` replaced by `dearth`, and the cursor will move to the end of the string that has just been replaced. To continue the process, press <GOLD><SRCH SEL>–<SLASH>. Now, instead of pressing <GOLD><REPL>–

**Table 4.2 WPS-PLUS Editor Search/Replace Keys**

| Keystrokes | Function |
|---|---|
| *Search Only* | |
| <GOLD><SRCH>–<COMMA><br><FIND> (VT200 series terminal) | Initiate search for search string |
| <GOLD><CONT SRCH>–<PERIOD> | Search for next instance of search string |
| *Search and Replace* | |
| <SEL>–<keypad PERIOD><br><SELECT> (VT200 series terminal) | Select replacement string to be put in `PASTE` buffer |
| <CUT>–<keypad MINUS><br><REMOVE> (VT200 series terminal) | Place replacement string in `PASTE` buffer |
| <GOLD><SRCH SEL>–<SLASH> | Select each instance of search string |
| <GOLD><REPL>–<APOSTROPHE> | Replace current instance of search string with replacement string from `PASTE` buffer |

<APOSTROPHE> to replace `shortage` with `dearth`, press <GOLD><SRCH SEL>–<SLASH>. The text will not be replaced by the contents of the `PASTE` buffer, and the search-and-replace process continues. Since there are no other occurrences of the string "shortage" in the document, you are informed of this and the cursor does not move.

If you want to keep the change you have just made (`shortage` to `dearth`), exit the WPS-PLUS editor with <GOLD><FILE DOCT>–<F>; otherwise use <GOLD><QUIT>–<K> to exit without keeping any changes.

To help you remember the key sequences that we have been discussing, we list them in Table 4.2.

In summary, the search-and-replace sequence for strings of text is as follows:

1. Move to a place in the document above the area of text that you wish to search and replace.

2. Put your replacement string into the `PASTE` buffer by pressing <SEL>–<keypad PERIOD> and typing *replacement string* <CUT>–<keypad MINUS>.

3. Start the search by pressing <GOLD><SRCH>–<COMMA> and typing *search string* <GOLD><SRCH SEL>–<SLASH>.

4. Replace each occurrence with <GOLD><REPL>–<APOSTROPHE>, or move to the next occurrence without replacing the string by pressing <GOLD><SRCH SEL>–<SLASH>.

If you are using a VT200 series terminal, you can use the <SELECT> and <REMOVE> keys (see Figure 4.35) to put the replacement string into the `PASTE` buffer. In the previous example, you would move the cursor to the top of the document, then press the <SELECT> key and type `dearth`. Finally, put `dearth` into the `PASTE` buffer by pressing the <REMOVE> key. You can begin the search sequence by pressing the <FIND> key, but after that, the search-and-replace sequence continues with the appropriate sequences of <GOLD><SRCH SEL>–<SLASH> and <GOLD><REPL>–<APOSTROPHE>, as discussed in this section.

### 4.5.4 Moving Text Within a Document or Between Documents

You will now see the `PASTE` buffer in action again. This time it will be holding text that is to be moved to another place in the same document or to some other document. First let's move a paragraph within a single document. Get into the WPS-PLUS editor, editing the `RES.DEMO` document in the `DEMO` folder. This example involves moving the next-to-last paragraph (the one starting with `Career Interests:`) to the end of the document.

Move the cursor to `Career Interests:`, placing the cursor over the `C`. Now press <SEL>–<keypad PERIOD> and notice, as before, that the select diamond appears where your cursor was located and the text is shifted down one line. Now move the cursor to the blank line between the paragraphs and press <CUT>–<keypad MINUS>. The paragraph will disappear. It has been placed into the `PASTE` buffer.

Now move the cursor to the end of the document and insert a blank line between the last paragraph and the current cursor position by pressing <RETURN>. Then press <PASTE>–<keypad COMMA> and notice that the paragraph reappears.

Exit the WPS-PLUS editor with <GOLD><QUIT>–<K> unless you wish to save this work. If you do, exit with <GOLD><FILE DOCT>–<F>.

In summary, to move a piece of text within a document, proceed as follows:

1. Place the text to be moved into the PASTE buffer by moving the cursor to the beginning of this text and pressing <SEL>–<keypad PERIOD>.

2. Move the cursor to the end of the text to be moved and press <CUT>–<keypad MINUS>.

3. Move the cursor to the place where you want the text to appear and press <PASTE>–<keypad COMMA>.

Notice that until you have carried out another <SEL> . . . <CUT> sequence, the PASTE buffer contains the text previously cut; pressing <PASTE> at any time will cause the same text to be inserted at the current cursor position. In fact, the PASTE buffer retains the same text when you move between documents. But there's a bit more to this, and if storage space (usually disk space) is sometimes a problem for you, pay special attention: The contents of the PASTE buffer are saved *between* WPS-PLUS sessions. So if you came back days later, entered the WPS-PLUS editor, and pressed <PASTE>–<keypad COMMA>, the results of your last <SEL> . . . <CUT> sequence would still be inserted at the current cursor position. This means that if your PASTE buffer contains a substantial amount of text, you could be using a lot of storage quota and not even be aware of it. Thus, *it's a good idea to let your last <SEL> . . . <CUT> operation be one that puts only a small amount of text into the PASTE buffer.*

The fact that the PASTE buffer holds onto text until you <SEL> . . . <CUT> is convenient when you want to transfer text between documents.

1. Use <SEL> . . . <CUT>, as discussed, to fill the PASTE buffer with the text that you want to transfer.

2. Exit the editing of your current document.

3. Either SELect or Create (at the Main menu) the document that is to contain the text currently in the PASTE buffer.

4. Once in the second document and at the position where you want the text in the PASTE buffer to be located, press <PASTE>–<keypad COMMA>.

5. You will be asked whether you want the current contents of the PASTE buffer to be transferred. Respond with Y <RETURN>, and the text will be transferred.

As we explained in Section 4.5.3, if you are using a VT200 series terminal, you can fill the PASTE buffer by using the keys labeled <SELECT> and <REMOVE> (see Figure 4.35). You can also insert the contents of the PASTE buffer with the key labeled <INSERT HERE>, just as you did with the <PASTE>–<keypad COMMA> key earlier.

As long as we are discussing buffers, we should mention that WPS-PLUS, much like the EDT screen editor, has two other buffers, a WORD buffer and a CHARACTER buffer. And just as you can insert the contents of the PASTE buffer wherever you like and as many times as you like, you can insert words or characters with these other two buffers. To put a word or character into the WORD or CHARACTER buffer, press <DEL WORD>–<keypad PF3> or <DEL CHAR>–<keypad PF4>. The word or character at the current cursor position will be deleted and placed into the appropriate buffer. You can retrieve the contents of these buffers by pressing <GOLD><DEL WORD>–<keypad PF3> or <GOLD><DEL CHAR>–<keypad PF4>. Only the most recent word or character deletion is contained in these buffers.

### 4.5.5 Inserting Entire Documents

So far, we have transferred text between documents via the PASTE buffer. The text transferred could be an entire document if we choose. Proceed as follows:

1. Move the cursor to the place where you want a particular document inserted.

2. Press <GOLD><GET DOCT>–<G>, and notice that the GOLD GET menu appears (Figure 4.16).

3. Pick the DOC option (to get a document from your file cabinet) by typing DOC <RETURN>, then fill in the Selecting Document to Insert form (see Figure 4.17) that appears at the bottom of your screen. Fill in the Folder: and Title: fields for the document you want transferred. Press <RETURN> when you have finished filling in the form.

One thing to keep in mind: The last ruler in force within the inserted document will also be in force in the remainder of your current document

```
                    GOLD GET Menu

DOC   Get a document from your file cabinet
VMS   Get a VMS file
UDP   Get a UDP
DEC   Get a document from your DEC Workstation

_
Enter option and press RETURN
```

**Figure 4.16 GOLD GET Menu**

```
                 Selecting Document to Insert

Folder:  _______________
Title:   _______________
Number:  _______________

Enter Information and press RETURN
Enter fields and press RETURN to select a document or EXIT
for menu
```

**Figure 4.17 Selecting Document to Insert Form**

below the place where the document was inserted. If the inserted ruler is different from the one for your current document, you should restore the original ruler for the current document at the end of the inserted text, using <GOLD><RULR>—<R>, as discussed earlier.

## 4.6 Transferring Documents to and from VMS

If you have been looking for the WPS-PLUS documents at the VMS operating system level, you have probably not had much success finding them. Your documents are saved in files in a WPSPLUS directory (see Appendix D). However, these files do not have the same names as the documents you specified while in WPS-PLUS, nor can they be read outside of WPS-PLUS. In this section, you will learn how to transfer these WPS-PLUS documents to recognizable VMS files.

Also, you will learn how to transfer VMS files, created outside of WPS-PLUS, into your WPS-PLUS file cabinet. These VMS files might have

```
                                              Fri 28-Jun-1991
                       Document Transfer

SEL Select                              Folder: DEMO________
                                        Title:  ____________
                                        Date:   ____________
                                        Number: ____________

RD  Receive a document from DEC workstation
SD  Send a document to DEC workstation

RV  Receive a document from VMS
SV  Send a document to VMS

RVD  Receive a document from VMS in DDIF format
SVD  Send a document to VMS in DDIF format
_
Enter option and press RETURN
```

**Figure 4.18 Document Transfer Menu with DEMO Folder**

been created by text editors such as EVE or EDT, or by some other program such as the spreadsheet program DECalc.

First, you will transfer a file from your root directory into WPS-PLUS. This example will involve getting the file we used to demonstrate the spelling checker (DECspell) in Chapter 3, the WACO.RCM file. Get the file to your root directory by issuing the following command at the operating system level (if you have access to the TEXTFILES directory):

```
COPY TEXTFILES:WACO.RCM SYS$LOGIN:WACO.RCM
```

If you do not have access to the TEXTFILES directory and did not create the file for the DECspell chapter, use one of the text editors, EVE or EDT, to create it, or use another text file in your root directory. A listing of the WACO.RCM file can be found in Section I.2.5 of Appendix I.

Now, enter WPS-PLUS, make certain that you are in the DEMO folder (if you are not, type SEL <RETURN>, as discussed earlier), and at the Main menu type DT <RETURN> to call the Document Transfer menu (Figure 4.18). Recall that we obtained this menu earlier when we were demonstrating the use of the <EXIT SCREEN>—<keypad 0> key. Next, pick the Receive a Document from VMS option by typing RV <RETURN>.

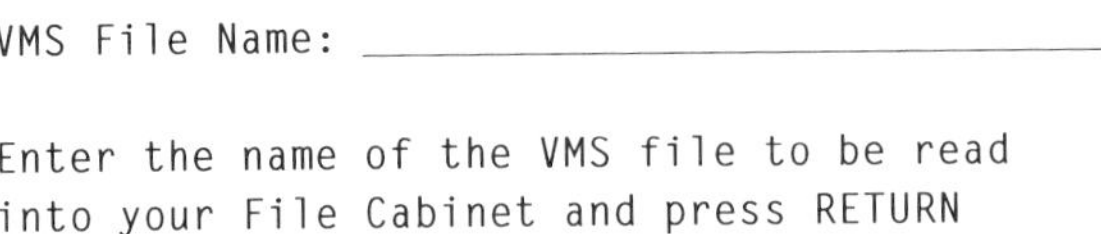
```
                 Receive a Document from VMS

VMS File Name: ______________________________

Enter the name of the VMS file to be read
into your File Cabinet and press RETURN
```

**Figure 4.19 Receive a Document from VMS Form**

```
                 Creating from VMS File

Folder:    DEMO________
Title:     ____________
Keywords:  ____________

Enter information and press RETURN
Enter information for the document you want to create and
press RETURN
```

**Figure 4.20 Creating from VMS File Form**

When the Receive a Document from VMS form appears (Figure 4.19), type `SYS$LOGIN:WACO.RCM` <RETURN> in the single field, `VMS File Name:`. (If you are transferring another file, substitute the appropriate file name after the colon.) If you forget to type the `SYS$LOGIN:` part of the file specification, WPS-PLUS will probably give you an error message saying that it cannot find the file. This is because WPS-PLUS is looking for the file in the `WPSPLUS` directory rather than in `SYS$LOGIN` or in the directory where you were when you entered WPS-PLUS. We think this is a defect in WPS-PLUS and hope that it will be remedied so that WPS-PLUS looks first in the directory that you are in when entering WPS-PLUS rather than always looking in the `WPSPLUS` directory first. Some sites might have had their user services staff alter this. So, if you're lucky, this will not be a problem for you, and you can ignore the need to put the prefix `SYS$LOGIN:` everywhere.

Finally, you will see the Creating from VMS File form (Figure 4.20). Move the cursor to the `Title:` field if the cursor is not already there, and type `WACO.RCM` <RETURN> (or the appropriate file name). You will then see a message at the bottom of your screen, "Creating document . . .". You will be back in the Document Transfer menu (see Figure 4.18). The document is now in your WPS-PLUS file cabinet. Hence, if you wanted to edit the document at this time, you would simply press the <EXIT SCREEN>–<keypad 0> key to return to the Main menu and then type E <RETURN> to edit the WACO.RCM document in your DEMO folder.

The first time you want to rewrap, or reflow, a paragraph in a document imported into your WPS-PLUS file cabinet from your VMS directory, you must use a different procedure than the one described in Section 4.4.5, where you reflowed text within new margins by moving the cursor down through the text.

Your first-time reflowing of any paragraph will start by pressing the <SEL>–<keypad PERIOD> key to select the paragraph (or more text, if desired). The text will shift down under the select diamond. At the end of the text to be reflowed, press <GOLD><PARA>–<keypad 5>.

The reason for using the <SEL> sequence the first time you reflow text in an imported file is to remove the <RETURN>s that are at the end of each line of the imported document.

Subsequent reflowing of such a paragraph may proceed as discussed in Section 4.4.5.

Now, let's reverse the process and send a WPS-PLUS document to VMS. Notice that when you send a file to VMS, as described in this section, you lose most of your formatting except for margins, tab stops, and centering. For example, the boldfacing and underlining will be lost.

You will get what is often referred to as an ASCII file or a text file, which contains no special control characters for printers. One effect of this is that you can use the operating system command TYPE (or TY) *filespec* without fear that your terminal will lock up. However, if you have spent a lot of time putting in special formatting, this will be lost. (There is one exception, which is discussed later in this section.)

In this example, you will export your RES.DEMO document from WPS-PLUS to VMS. First, at the Main menu, SELect the RES.DEMO document in the DEMO folder, then type DT <RETURN> to call the Document Transfer menu (see Figure 4.18). Choose the Send a Document to VMS option by typing SV <RETURN>. The lower part of your screen will fill with the Send

```
your_spelling
corrections [More...]

Replace  Edit  Ignore  Add  Pass  Dictionary  Finish
```

**Figure 4.21 Menu for Checking the Spelling of a Single Word**

a Document to VMS form (see Figure 4.12). Type SYS$LOGIN:RES.DEMO <RETURN> in the single field, VMS File Name:. (If you omit the SYS$LOGIN: part of the file specification, the file will go into the WPSPLUS directory.) You will shortly see the message, "File copied to VMS" appear at the bottom of your screen. As in the previous discussion of transferring VMS files to WPS-PLUS, when the transfer is complete, you are in the Document Transfer menu (see Figure 4.18). Return to the Main menu as before by pressing the <EXIT SCREEN>–<keypad 0> key, or exit from WPS-PLUS to VMS by typing EX <RETURN>.

To keep all your formatting when transferring a document from WPS-PLUS to VMS, specify the VMS file type as .WPL. You will not be able to do much with the file in VMS, however. For example, if you TYPE the file to your screen your terminal will likely lock up. So why do this? You might want to store this file on tape or some other storage medium and delete it from your VMS directory and WPS-PLUS file cabinet. This could give you more storage space to use for other applications. You could then retrieve this work, including all your special formatting, by importing it back into WPS-PLUS.

## 4.7 Linguistic Aids

Several aids are available in WPS-PLUS to help you with your writing. One is a spelling checker. This aid can be applied to a single word, to a selected part of your document, or to all of your document. Two other linguistic aids that can be applied to a particular word are the thesaurus and what is called usage alert. Finally, some installations of WPS-PLUS will include a grammar checker.

### 4.7.1 Applying the Spelling Checker to a Single Word

When you are in the WPS-PLUS editor and are uncertain about the spelling of a word, simply place the cursor somewhere in the word and press <GOLD><SPEL CHEK>–<S>. At the bottom of your screen will be a mess-

```
Thesaurus  Usage  Spell  Grammar  Language
```

**Figure 4.22 Linguistic Aids Menu**

age that WPS-PLUS is "Invoking the spell checker . . .". If your word is spelled correctly, a fleeting message will flash at the bottom of your screen to the effect that it is spelled correctly. If your word is misspelled, the Spelling Checker menu (Figure 4.21) will appear at the bottom of your screen. Then proceed as discussed in the DECspell chapter (Chapter 3).

Try applying this procedure to the string "Arthur" in the WACO.RCM document in the DEMO folder, which you just imported into your WPS-PLUS file cabinet from VMS.

### 4.7.2 *Applying the Spelling Checker to a Selected Region*

You might want to apply the spelling checker to part of your document, say, only to newly entered text. To do this, first select the region to be checked. The method is similar to selecting part of your text to move into the PASTE buffer. First, move the cursor to the beginning of the region where you want the spelling checked, and press <SEL>–<keypad PERIOD>. The select diamond will appear, with the text shifted down under it. Using one or more of the distance keys, move to the end of the text that you want checked for spelling.

Now the procedure becomes different from putting text into the PASTE buffer. Ask for the Linguistic Aids menu by pressing <GOLD> <LING AIDS>–<J>. This menu (Figure 4.22) will appear at the bottom of your screen. Move the cursor to the Spell option with the appropriate arrow key and press <RETURN>, or simply type S <RETURN>. Then proceed as discussed in the DECspell chapter.

If you type <GOLD><LING AIDS>–<J> before selecting a region, WPS-PLUS will remind you that you must select a region. This reminder comes *after* you choose the Spell option.

Try out this procedure on the first paragraph of the WACO.RCM document.

```
digital                                          Wed 26-Jun-1991
                          WPS-PLUS/VMS 4.0

                Word and Document Processing Menu

SEL  Select          Folder:  __________
                     Title:   __________
                     Date:    __________
                     Number:  __________

         Word and Document Processing - continued (1)

SC  Spell check             LP List processing
DIC Dictionaries            DP DECpage document formatting
                            PN Paragraph numbering
GC  Grammar checker
GCD Grammar checker defaults

_
Enter option and press RETURN
```

**Figure 4.23 Second Part of WPS-PLUS Main Menu**

### 4.7.3 Applying the Spelling Checker to an Entire Document

To apply the spelling checker to an entire document, you make your choice at the Main menu. However, you will see that the first part of the Main menu (see Figure 4.5) has no option related to the spelling checker. The reason is that there is actually *more* to the Main menu. Notice the `(more. . .)` at the lower right-hand corner of the Main menu. This means that there was not enough room to put all the options on one screen and that there is at least one more screen of options. To see the next screen, type `M` <RETURN>. Your screen will reconstruct with more options (Figure 4.23). Indeed, any time that a menu displays the `(more. . .)` line near the bottom right-hand corner of your screen, typing `M` <RETURN> should call another screenful of options.

On the second screen of the Main menu, you will see the `SC` (Spell Check) option. Pick this option by typing `SC` <RETURN>. Your screen will fill with the contents of the document listed in the current document block (displayed in the upper right-hand corner of both screens of the Main menu). Then follow the steps from the DECspell chapter.

```
effect
                                                No More
Noun: Something brought about by a cause.
Noun: The condition of being in full force or operation.
Noun: The power or capacity to produce a desired result.
Verb: To be the cause of.
Verb: To carry to a successful conclusion.
Verb: To compel observance of.
                                                No More

effect, result, issue, event, consequence, fruit, sequence,
outcome, harvest, corollary, aftermath, upshot, precipitate,
sequel
```

**Figure 4.25 Thesaurus Example**

```
effect

effect;(consequence; to bring about)
affect;(to influence or alter; to simulate)
```

**Figure 4.24 Usage Alert Example**

Try applying the spelling checker to the entire `WACO.RCM` document in your `DEMO` folder.

## 4.7.4 *Applying the Thesaurus and Usage Alert to Specific Words*

The Thesaurus and Usage options can be applied to any particular word as you go through your document.[2] To demonstrate this option, select any document, get into the WPS-PLUS editor, move to the bottom of the document, insert a couple of blank lines, and type `effect`. Now press <GOLD><LING AIDS>–<J>. The Linguistic Aids menu (see Figure 4.22) will appear.

---

2. At the present time, there is one known bug in WPS-PLUS version 4.0 that relates to this section. If you try to do the work in this section without having already used one of the Spelling Checker options, your terminal will lock up. Therefore, use one of the Spelling Checker options (e.g., <GOLD><SPEL CHECK>–<S> applied to a single word) before proceeding with this section. This bug will no doubt be fixed in subsequent releases of the WPS-PLUS program.

```
                    Sending Document by VMS MAIL

To:

______________________________________________________________
Subject:
RES.DEMO
______________________________________________________________

Enter information and press RETURN
```

**Figure 4.26 Sending Document by VMS MAIL Form**

Pick the Thesaurus option by moving the cursor there or by typing `T` <RETURN>. Your screen will reconstruct in a manner similar to that shown in Figure 4.24. The first definition is highlighted, and synonyms for this definition are shown at the bottom of the screen. Synonyms for other definitions will appear when another definition is highlighted by pressing the <DOWN ARROW> or <UP ARROW> key. Once the appropriate definition is chosen, the word you wish to use in place of `effect` can be chosen by highlighting your choice with the <RIGHT ARROW> or <LEFT ARROW> key. Once your appropriate choice is highlighted, a single <RETURN> will cause the replacement. If you wish to keep things as they are, highlight the original word, `effect`, and press <RETURN>, or alternatively, press <EXIT SCREEN>–<keypad 0>. To continue this example, do the latter.

Once you have completed the thesaurus example, and with the cursor still at the end of `effect`, press <GOLD><LING AIDS>–<J> again. Now choose the Usage option by moving the cursor there or by typing `U` <RETURN>. You should then see the information displayed in Figure 4.25. As you can see, this tells you how this word and words sounding like it (homonyms) are used. You can move to the appropriate option by pressing the arrow keys and choose it by pressing <RETURN>.

Try applying the thesaurus and usage alert to several words in the `RES.DEMO` document.

### 4.7.5 *The Grammar Checker*

The grammar checker functions in essentially the same manner as the spelling checker when it is applied to a selected block of text or to an entire document. The only additional thing you need to keep in mind is that when you pick the Edit option, press <keypad ENTER> to return to the

```
                    Print Settings Menu

CO  Change control settings
PG  Change pagination settings
PL  Change page layout
FS  Change footnote settings

RB  Remove blank lines at top of page (Y/N): N
SS  Save print settings                      # 0
RS  Restore print settings                   # 0

P  Print with current settings

_

Enter option and press RETURN
```

**Figure 4.27 Print Settings Menu**

Grammar Checker menu at the bottom of your screen. Recall that when you used the grammar checker at the operating system level (see Section 3.4 in Chapter 3) you returned to the Grammar Checker menu after terminating the Edit option by pressing <DO>.

## 4.8 Mailing WPS-PLUS Documents

You can send any of your WPS-PLUS documents via VMS MAIL (see Chapter 6 for details on MAIL) by using the S (Send) option at the Main menu. The document is sent in the same form as when you export a WPS-PLUS document to VMS. The file sent via MAIL is stripped of all its formatting except for margin settings, tab stops, and centering. Underlining and boldfacing are lost.

Try this option by sending yourself a copy of the RES.DEMO document in the DEMO folder. First, SELect this document. When you are back at the Main menu, type S <RETURN>. The bottom part of your screen will reconstruct with the Sending Document by VMS MAIL form (Figure 4.26). In the To: field, enter your own user name. If you want to change the subject, RES.DEMO, press <DOWN ARROW> to get into the Subject: field and type your new subject, followed by <RETURN>. If you wish to keep the subject as given, just press <RETURN> after typing your user name. As with any form, the <UP ARROW> and <DOWN ARROW> keys, and possibly the <TAB> key, move between fields, and pressing <RETURN> commits the current

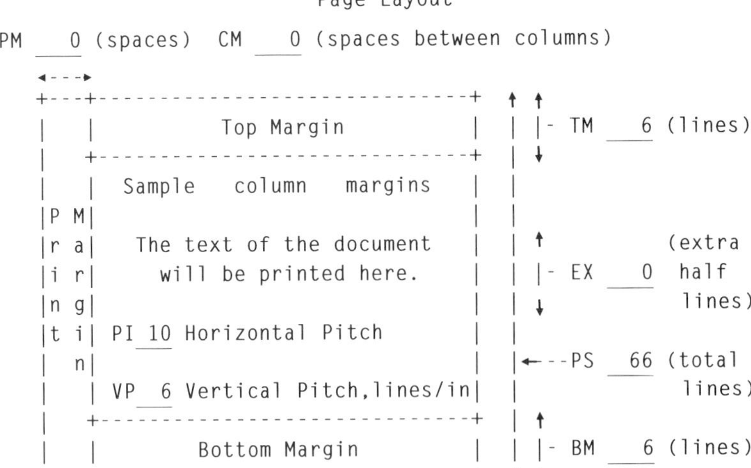

```
                      Page Layout
PM    0 (spaces)  CM    0 (spaces between columns)
   <-->
   +---+----------------------------+   ^ ^
   |   |         Top Margin         |   | |- TM    6 (lines)
   |   +----------------------------+   | v
   |   | Sample   column   margins  |   |
   |P M|                            |   |
   |r a|  The text of the document  |   | ^         (extra
   |i r|    will be printed here.   |   | |- EX    0  half
   |n g|                            |   | v           lines)
   |t i| PI 10 Horizontal Pitch     |   |
   |  n|                            |   |<--PS   66 (total
   |   | VP  6 Vertical Pitch,lines/in|  |             lines)
   |   +----------------------------+   | ^
   |   |        Bottom Margin       |   | |- BM    6 (lines)
   +---+----------------------------+   v v

Enter new settings and press RETURN
```

**Figure 4.28 Page Layout Form with Default Settings**

field entries. You will shortly be informed that your "Document has been posted via VMS MAIL". When you enter VMS MAIL, you will find that you have new mail from yourself.

In summary, to send a WPS-PLUS document via VMS MAIL, proceed as follows:

1. SELect the document you wish to send.
2. At the Main menu, type S <RETURN> to choose the Send option.
3. Fill in the Sending Document by VMS MAIL form with the appropriate information, terminating with <RETURN>.

## 4.9 Things You Might Want to Know

We have really only covered the fundamentals of WPS-PLUS. However, there are still a few more things that you will probably want to know, even as a new user of WPS-PLUS.

### 4.9.1 Changing Page Layout for the Printer

You might find, after you print out one of your documents, that you do not like the layout. For example, perhaps there are too many or too few lines per page. Perhaps you would like to change the number of blank lines at the top or bottom of your printed pages. To do these things, you need to go back to the Print option in the Main menu and take a somewhat different path than before. In this example, you will change the total number of lines on a page from the default 66 lines to 54.

To do this, get to the Main menu and pick the Print option by typing P <RETURN>. When the Printing Document form appears (see Figure 4.11), fill the Document destination: and Format style: fields with FILE and LP11 (or whatever printer type is appropriate to your site). Then press <GOLD><A> to call the Print Settings menu (Figure 4.27) to the screen. (Note that pressing <GOLD><A> within the Printing Document form has a different effect than pressing <GOLD><SUBSCPT>–<A> within the WPS-PLUS editor to indicate that a subscript is desired.)

On the Print Settings menu, choose the Change Page Layout option by typing PL <RETURN>.[3] When the screen reconstructs, you will see the Page Layout form (Figure 4.28). In this example, you are changing the PS field (total lines) from the default 66 to 54, so press <DOWN ARROW> until the cursor appears in the PS field, then replace 66 with 54. When this has been done, press <RETURN> to commit the current settings. The Print Settings menu (see Figure 4.27) will reappear; type P <RETURN> to select the Print with Current Settings option. You will see the "Formatting document. . ." message and then the familiar Send a Document to VMS form (see Figure 4.12). Fill in the single field with SYS$LOGIN:*filespec*, where *filespec* is a VMS file specification of your own choosing. Remember, omitting SYS$LOGIN: will probably cause the file to be placed in your WPSPLUS directory.

Any of the fields shown in Figure 4.28 can be changed to suit your page layout preference by using the <UP ARROW> and <DOWN ARROW> keys to move to the appropriate field and changing it. These settings remain in effect only for this one document (the document listed in your current document block when you made the changes) until you change them again

---

3. The material in this section related to the PL (Page Layout) option applies to versions of WPS-PLUS below version 4.0. For version 4.0, choose PG (Change Pagination Setting) at the Print Settings menu. The resulting Pagination Settings menu will contain the fields discussed in reference to the Page Layout form.

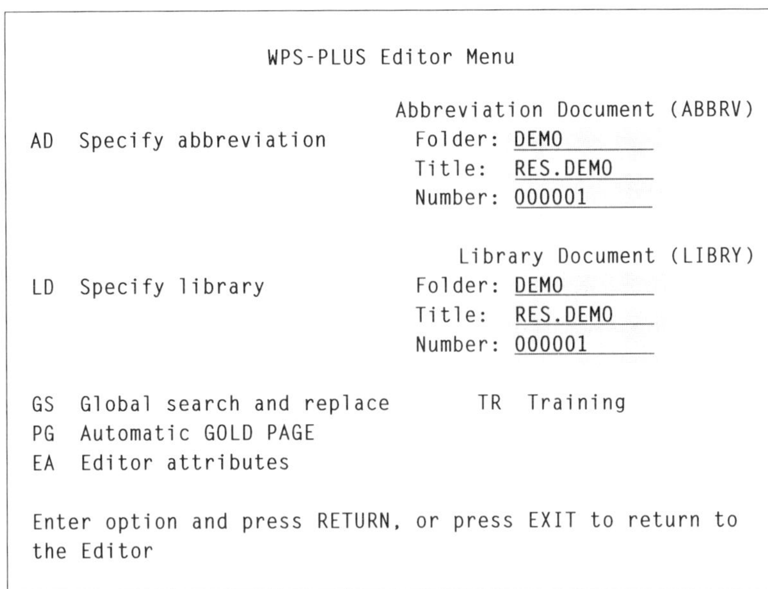

```
                    WPS-PLUS Editor Menu

                                   Abbreviation Document (ABBRV)
AD  Specify abbreviation             Folder: DEMO
                                     Title:  RES.DEMO
                                     Number: 000001

                                       Library Document (LIBRY)
LD  Specify library                  Folder: DEMO
                                     Title:  RES.DEMO
                                     Number: 000001

GS  Global search and replace        TR  Training
PG  Automatic GOLD PAGE
EA  Editor attributes

Enter option and press RETURN, or press EXIT to return to
the Editor
```

**Figure 4.29 WPS-PLUS Editor Menu with RES.DEMO Document**

by this same process. The page layout settings for other documents retain the defaults unless you change them by the process just discussed.

In summary, to change the page layout of your document, proceed as follows:

1. At the Main menu, type `P` <RETURN> to choose the Print option.
2. At the Printing Document form, make sure that the fields are set with `FILE` and the appropriate printer specification; then press <GOLD><A> to obtain the Print Settings menu.
3. Type `PL` <RETURN> at the Print Settings menu to choose the Change Page Layout option.
4. Make appropriate changes in the Page Layout form. Press <RETURN> to commit the new settings.
5. Back in the Print Settings menu, type `P` <RETURN> to Print with current settings.
6. Enter the appropriate file specification in the Send a Document to VMS form.

```
                         Editor Attributes

Set wide screen (Y/N): N
Set math option (Y/N): Y

Redline enabled (Y/N):  N
Redline characteristic: DOUBLE UNDERLINE

Set current text lines/page:  54 (current default)
Set standard text lines/page: 54 (default for all documents)

GET DOCMT screen on (Y/N): N
Status line enabled (Y/N): N
Word choice - with trailing symbols (Y/N): Y

Widow/orphan control lines: 0
Hyphenation checking (Y/N): Y

Enter information and press RETURN
```

**Figure 4.30 Editor Attributes Form with Example Settings**

Our discussion so far might be all you will ever need to know about page layout. However, if you use WPS-PLUS for fairly large documents, you will probably find that page breaks occur in undesirable places. One way to fix this is to use the <GOLD><NEW PAGE>–<N> function to force new pages. This can, of course, cause problems at some later time if you add new text above that point in your document. So how can you find out before printing where the page breaks are going to occur? We explain this in the rest of this section. The process is a little complicated, so if you are not working with large documents at this time, skip to Section 4.9.3 and come back when you need this information.

Enter the WPS-PLUS editor, editing one of your documents. Press <GOLD><MENU>–<M>. The Editor menu will appear. (Figure 4.29 shows the result of editing the RES.DEMO document in the DEMO folder.) If you have made *no* changes in the page layout of this document for the printer (recall, in an earlier example, we changed PS—total lines—from 66 to 54), then type PG <RETURN> for the Automatic GOLD PAGE option. When WPS-PLUS stops giving you the message that it is "Performing auto pagination. Please wait. . .", you will be at the bottom of your document. Move to the top by pressing <GOLD><TOP DOCT>–<T>, then move successively to each of the page markers by pressing the <PAGE>–<keypad PF2>. The cursor will stop either at a line with `---NEW PAGE---` (a result of your having pressed <GOLD><NEW PAGE>–<N> at an earlier time) or at a line with `---PAGE MARKER---` (a result of the auto pagination that you have just caused to occur). You can then examine the pagination before printing your document and decide if you need to make any further adjustments.

### 4.9.2 Making Editor Attributes Conform to Page Layout Settings

Recall that we said to type `PG` <RETURN> in the Editor menu if you had not changed the page layout settings for your printer. If you did previously change the page layout settings for your printer with respect to a particular document, then in order for the automatic pagination (Automatic GOLD PAGE), used within the WPS-PLUS editor, to reflect your printer page layout settings, you need to change some of the editor attributes of the WPS-PLUS editor to parallel the printer page layout settings. If you do not make these changes, the automatic pagination that you see within the WPS-PLUS editor will *not* be reflected in your printed document. It might seem appropriate for these editor attributes to change automatically any time you change the printer page layout settings for a particular document, but this is not the case. So we need to make some changes in the editor attributes.

Let's continue our example for a situation where have we changed the total number of lines from 66 to 54. The automatic pagination determines the placement of PAGE MARKERS based on a parameter called "current text lines/page" (`CT`), and changing the page layout for the printer as described earlier does *not* change this setting. The "current text lines/page" parameter is equal to (total lines per page) – (lines in top margin) – (lines in bottom margin). So with the changes we made in our previous example, `CT` was 66 – 6 – 6 = 54. We now need to change this to 54 – 6 – 6 = 42 to accommodate the changes made in the previous example. Here's how.

After pressing <GOLD><MENU>–<M> in the WPS-PLUS editor, yielding the Editor menu (see Figure 4.29), pick the Editor Attributes option by typing `EA` <RETURN>. This will call the Editor Attributes form (Figure 4.30) to the screen. Move to the field `Set current text lines/page:` and change 54 to 42. When you have made the change, commit the new settings by pressing <RETURN>. If you want all the documents you edit to have this number of lines per page, you can change the field `Set standard`

```
                    WPS-PLUS Pagination Settings

Number on the first page:      1      Auto paginate (Y/N):            Y
First page printed:            1      Lines in the top margin:        6
Last page printed:             0      Lines in the bottom margin:     6
Total lines per page:         54      Spaces between columns:         0
Print quality:             DRAFT      Spaces in left print margin:    0
Vertical lines per inch:       ?      Replacement character 1:        _
Characters per inch (pitch):  10      Replacement character 2:        _
Extra half-lines                      Print darkness:            NORMAL
   between lines:              0      Shadow print (Y/N):             N
Sheet feeder tray:          REAR      Widow/orphan control lines:     0

Enter new settings and press RETURN
```

**Figure 4.31 Printer Pagination Settings Form**

text lines/page: from 54 to 42 before pressing <RETURN>. Pressing <RETURN> will get you back to the Editor menu (see Figure 4.29), and pressing <EXIT SCREEN>–<keypad 0> will return you to the WPS-PLUS editor.

Notice that if you change the Set standard text lines/page: field, you will need to make certain that the printer page layout is changed for each document to reflect this (see Section 4.9.1). By now you can probably see that you simply need to keep the page layout settings for your printer in sync with the editor attributes of the WPS-PLUS editor, *and vice versa*.

Now you can proceed as before to get the automatic pagination, by pressing <GOLD><MENU>–<M> in the WPS-PLUS editor and then typing PG <RETURN> in the Editor menu (see Figure 4.29). The PAGE BREAKS will now occur so that they correspond to the page layout settings that you set earlier for your printer.

So far, you have seen how to preview the PAGE MARKERS before you print your document and how to make sure that they correspond to any printer page layout changes you have made. But what if you have checked the results of automatic pagination and want to delete one of the PAGE MARKERS or insert your own? You can insert your own ---PAGE MARKER--- line by moving the cursor to the place where you want it and pressing <GOLD><PAGE MARK>–<P>. If you want to delete a PAGE MARKER, move the cursor to one of the ---PAGE MARKER--- lines and press <DEL CHAR>–<keypad PF4>.

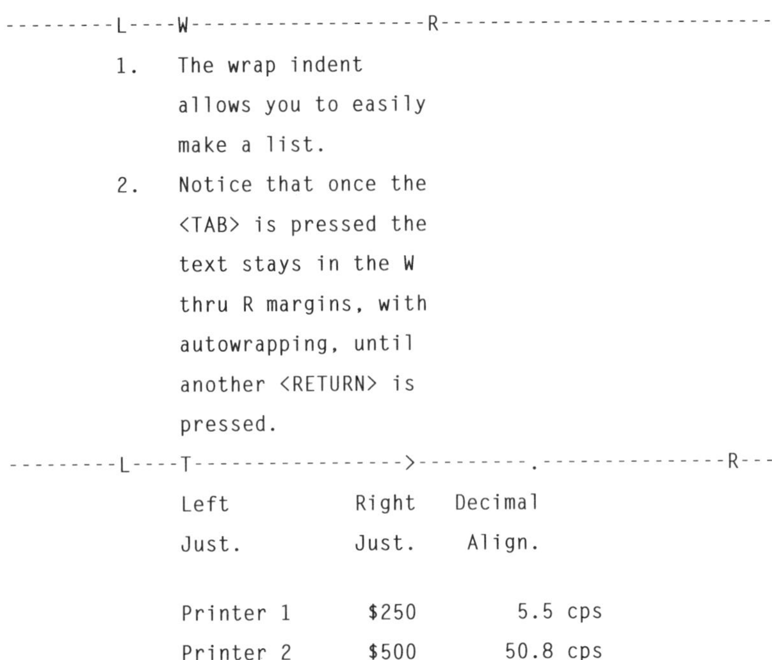

```
---------L----W------------------R-------------------------
          1.   The wrap indent
               allows you to easily
               make a list.
          2.   Notice that once the
               <TAB> is pressed the
               text stays in the W
               thru R margins, with
               autowrapping, until
               another <RETURN> is
               pressed.
---------L----T---------------->---------.--------------R---
               Left           Right   Decimal
               Just.          Just.    Align.

               Printer 1       $250          5.5 cps
               Printer 2       $500         50.8 cps
```

**Figure 4.32 Examples of Tab/Indent Settings**

However, if you do nothing more, your extra PAGE MARKERS will be ignored when your document is printed. You must make one more change: turning off the automatic pagination related to the Print option at the Main menu level. So get to the Main menu by saving your document with <GOLD><FILE DOCT>–<F> and type `P` <RETURN> for the Print option. When the Print Document form (see Figure 4.11) appears, verify the settings and then press <GOLD><A> for the Print Settings menu (see Figure 4.27). Choose the Change Pagination Settings option by typing `PG` <RETURN>. The Printer Pagination Settings form (Figure 4.31) will appear. Change the `Auto paginate (Y/N):` field to `N` (you will need to use <TAB> rather than the arrow keys to get to this field). Press <RETURN> to get back to the Print Settings menu. Then type `P` <RETURN> to Print with current settings. When prompted for a VMS file, give an appropriate file specification.

It is very important to remember that if you ever want to go back to the page layout settings, discussed in Section 4.9.1, you will need to change

**Table 4.3 Tab/Indent Settings**

| Tab/Indent Setting | Description |
|---|---|
| T | Left-justified tab setting (the usual) |
| > | Right-justified tab (typing in text at these tab stops inserts text from right to left) |
| . | Decimal-aligned tab (text aligned on decimal point) |
| W | Word-wrap indent (for making lists) |

**Table 4.4 Margin Settings**

| Margin Setting | Description |
|---|---|
| *Left Margin* | |
| L | Single spacing |
| N | Line-and-a-half spacing |
| D | Double spacing |
| H | Half-line spacing |
| *Right Margin* | |
| R | Ragged right margin |
| J | Right-justified text |

the `Auto paginate (Y/N):` field back to `Y`. This is done by replicating the procedure just discussed except for putting `Y` in the field instead of `N`.

### 4.9.3 More on Tabs and Margins

You have already seen the simplest examples of margin and tab setting. Recall that you pressed <GOLD><RULR>–<R> to bring the current ruler onto the screen (see Figure 4.13 for the default ruler) and used the distance keys to reach the appropriate columns and set tabs with `T` and left and right margins with `L` and `R`. The <SPACEBAR> deletes any tab setting at the current cursor position. Pressing <RETURN> commits the settings as currently displayed.

There are, however, several other tab settings available. Table 4.3 lists them and Figure 4.32 gives examples using these settings. There are also several other margin setting options (see Table 4.4).

```
[------------------------------ START FOOTNOTE ------------------------------]
L-------T-------T-------T-------T-------T-------T-------T-------T-------T-------R
```

**Figure 4.33 Footnote Editor**

### 4.9.4 *Printing Page Numbers (Headers and Footers)*

Printing page numbers in your document is a special case in the category of headers and footers, that is, text printed at the top or bottom of each page of your document. The example we use will place centered page numbers at the bottom of each page. First, move the cursor to the top of your document and press <GOLD><CMND>—<LEFT BRACKET>. You will see the first line of what is called a control block, designated by `---START CONTROL---` centered on your screen. It is in this control block that you designate the text to go into your footer. The cursor is on the line following `---START CONTROL---`, which is labeled `---END CONTROL---`. Type `BOTTOM` (`TOP` for a header), followed by two <RETURN>s.

Next, type `\p`, that is, backslash (not slash) followed by a lowercase `p`. Center this as usual with <GOLD><CNTR>—<C>. Then proceed with any other editing chores you might have.

Notice that you must place this control block at the beginning of a page. We have taken care of this by going to the top of the document. However, if you want to begin headers or footers some pages into your document, you will have to find the beginning of a page in your document. Certainly, you could look for a `---NEW PAGE---` that you placed there yourself using <GOLD><NEW PAGE>—<N>. However, if you want to know where all the other PAGE MARKERS are hidden, follow the procedure discussed in Sections 4.9.1 and 4.9.2.

### 4.9.5 *Footnotes and End Notes*

Footnotes and end notes are an easy matter now that you have come this far in learning how to use WPS-PLUS. First, move the cursor to the place where you want to insert the footnote or end note (from now on, we use just the term *footnote,* although *end note* is also appropriate). Next, type <GOLD><FOOT NOTE>—<Y>. Three lines will appear at the bottom of your screen (Figure 4.33). One of the lines is a ruler, which you can adjust by using <GOLD><RULR>—<R>, as discussed earlier.

```
                    WPS-PLUS Footnote Settings

Footnotes or endnotes (F/E):                                  F

Minimum lines per page:                                       1
Lines in the top margin:                                      2
Lines in the bottom margin:                                   6
Total lines per page:                                         56

Separator character (press SPACE for default setting):        _
Separator length:                                             10
Separator position:                                           LEFT

Blank lines between last text line and separator line:        1
Blank lines between separator line and first footnote:        0
Blank lines between footnotes:                                1

Enter information and press RETURN,
or press NEXT SCREEN for more
```

**Figure 4.34 Footnote Settings Form**

As you type your footnote, your typing is inserted after the ruler and before the `---END FOOTNOTE---` line. When you have finished your footnote, if you want to keep it, press <GOLD><FILE DOCT>–<F>. You will be returned to the place you left in editing your document. A capital F, in reverse video, will appear at the place where the footnote will go in the formatted output document for the printer. As you might expect, pressing <GOLD><QUIT>–<K> while in the footnote editor will allow you to exit the footnote editor without saving your footnote text, but you will have to use the <SEL> . . . <CUT> sequence to remove the footnote marker (F) from the document text.

In order to designate a footnote or an end note, there is one more thing that must be done. Having already changed the page layout format (see Section 4.9.1), you will find this a fairly simple matter. Simply proceed as you would for printing a document: type `P` <RETURN> at the Main menu, and at the Print Document form, press <GOLD><A>. When the Print Settings menu (see Figure 4.27) appears, type `FS` <RETURN> to choose the Change Footnote Settings option. When the Footnote Settings form (Figure 4.34) appears, type either `E` <RETURN> or `F` <RETURN> in the `Footnotes or endnotes (F/E):` field. Next press <EXIT SCREEN>–<keypad 0> to get back to the Print Settings menu. Then type P <RETURN> to Print with current settings, and proceed as discussed earlier.

For on-line help on footnotes and end notes, enter the WPS-PLUS editor and press <GOLD><HELP>–<H> to get the keyboard help screen, press <GOLD><FOOT NOTE>–<Y>, and follow the prompts.

### 4.9.6 Some WPS-PLUS Capability in the EVE Editor Program

If you have already learned the EVE text editor (Chapter 2), you might be interested to know that some of the WPS-PLUS capabilities can be used while in EVE. To do this, you need to create a file named EVE$INIT.EVE (if you don't already have one) and put the following line into it:

```
SET KEYPAD WPS
```

Although you cannot get bolding and underlining, you can get other options such as centering, ruler changes, and the Get Document option. Several of the numeric keypad functions work as discussed earlier in this chapter. One thing you might find especially useful is that while in EVE you can type <GOLD><SPEL CHEK>–<S> and the spelling checker will be invoked to check the spelling in your entire file. If you want to apply the spelling checker to certain parts of your file, proceed as discussed earlier, by placing the cursor at the beginning of the text that you want to check for spelling. Press <SEL>–<keypad PERIOD> and move the cursor to the end of that text. Finally, press <GOLD><SPEL CHEK>–<S> and then use the spelling checker as described in the DECspell chapter.

### 4.9.7 Miscellaneous

If you have set the parameter for "current text lines/page" (CT) to correspond to your printer page layout (see Sections 4.9.1 and 4.9.2), or if you have simply taken the WPS-PLUS defaults, you can find out where your cursor is located within your document with respect to these editor attribute settings by pressing <GOLD><STAT>–<Z>. At the top of your screen will appear the page, row, and column numbers for the current cursor location.

If you want the status information displayed continuously, press <GOLD><MENU>–<M> while in the WPS-PLUS editor. This will give you the Editor menu (see Figure 4.29). Choose the Editor Attributes option by typing EA <RETURN>. When the Editor Attributes form appears (see Figure

4.30), change the `Status line enabled (Y/N):` field to `Y`. You can get back to the Editor menu by pressing <RETURN> and back to editing your document by typing <EXIT SCREEN>–<keypad 0>.

You might also want to see the hidden formatting characters that were entered as you used the WPS-PLUS editor, for example, the character that tells WPS-PLUS to center a line. To view these hidden characters, move to some part of one of your documents and press <GOLD><VIEW>–<V>. Repeat this for every screen of interest to you. To get your screen back the way it was before, press <GOLD><VIEW>–<V> again. The <GOLD><VIEW>–<V> function acts as a toggle.

## 4.10 Other Options to Investigate

In this chapter, we have given you a useful set of basic tools available in WPS-PLUS. For much more information, consult Bibliography [22, 29].

Some things you might be interested in learning about are the Two-Dimensional Editor and the Mathematics Editor. The Two-Dimensional Editor allows the easy creation of boxed diagrams. The Mathematics Editor allows you to put columns of numbers into your document and obtain totals while in the editor. You can also create simple spreadsheets. Mail/merge operations can be done easily with the `LP` (List Processing) option of WPS-PLUS.

Pressing the <GOLD>—<PF1> key before other keys on the main keyboard or the numeric keypad endows those keys with special functions. As was true in the chapter, this summary shows both the function and the actual key label of each key, connected by a dash.

Pressing <GOLD><HELP>—<H>, or the <HELP> key on VT200 series terminals (see Figure 4.35), calls on-line help from virtually any place in WPS-PLUS. Pressing <EXIT SCREEN>—<keypad 0> usually exits on-line help.

### Entering and Exiting

We assume that the appropriate site-specific preliminary work has been done (see Section 4.2.1).

| *Command or Key Sequence* | *Description* |
|---|---|
| `WPS` <RETURN> | At the `MYNODE$` operating system prompt, enters WPS-PLUS Main menu. |
| `EX` <RETURN> | Exits to the VMS operating system from the Main menu. |
| <EXIT SCREEN>—<keypad 0> | Exits to previous form or menu from menus or forms other than the Main menu. |
| <GOLD><FILE DOCT>—<F> | Exits to Main menu from WPS-PLUS editor, saving the changes of the current session. |
| <GOLD><QUIT>—<K> | Exits to Main menu from WPS-PLUS editor, discarding the changes of the current session. |
| <GOLD><STOP CBI>—<X> | Exits a CBI (Computer-Based Instruction) module, usually to a Training menu. |

### Main Menu Options

For on-line help on individual options, type the option and then press <GOLD><HELP>—<H>, or <HELP> on VT200 series terminals.

The Main menu is shown in Figures 4.5 and 4.23. Type each option followed by <RETURN>.

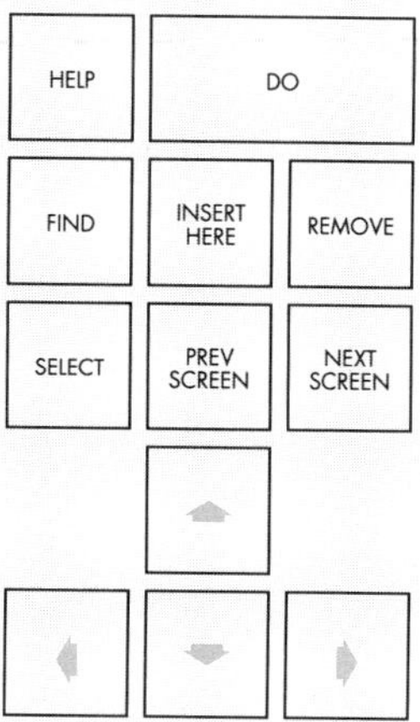


**Figure 4.35 VT200 Series Terminal Non-Numeric (Cursor) Keypad**

| *Option* | *Description* |
|---|---|
| C | Creates a new document. |
| D | Deletes the document listed in the current document block of the Main menu. To completely delete the document from the files attached to your account, you must also Empty the WASTEBASKET by typing EW <RETURN>. |
| DT | Begins the process of Document Transfer, i.e., importing and exporting files and documents to and from WPS-PLUS and VMS. |
| E | Edits the document listed in the current document block of the Main menu. |
| EX | Exits the Main menu and WPS-PLUS to the VMS operating system. |
| FC | Provides options for managing your File Cabinet. |
| GC | Applies the grammar checker (if available on your system) to the document listed in the current document block of the Main menu. |
| LP | Begins the List Processing option of WPS-PLUS. |
| P | Prints (to a file or to some specified printer) the document listed in the current document block of the Main menu. Pressing <GOLD><A> at the Printing Document form (Figure 4.11) calls the Print Settings menu (Figure 4.28) for changing settings related to the printer. |

R
Reads the document listed in the current document block of the Main menu. The document is displayed one screen at a time. <RETURN> displays the next screen, and <EXIT SCREEN>—<keypad 0> discontinues the process.

S
Sends the document listed in the current document block of the Main menu to some user via VMS MAIL.

SC
Applies the spelling checker to the document listed in the current document block of the Main menu.

SEL
Begins the process of SELecting a document for listing in the current document block of the Main menu. Subsequently pressing <GOLD><LIBRY>—<L> will give a listing of folders or titles, depending on the *blank* field where the cursor is located when <GOLD><LIBRY>—<L> is pressed.

TR
Begins one of the TRaining CBI (Computer-Based Instruction) modules.

---

### Forms

For on-line help on what a particular field should contain, try blanking out the field (with the <SPACEBAR> or <RUBOUT> key) and pressing <GOLD><HELP>—<H>, or <HELP> on VT200 series terminals.

Move between fields using the arrow keys or <TAB>. Once the fields are specified to your satisfaction, press <RETURN> to commit your entries.

---

### WPS-PLUS Editor

For on-line help on <GOLD> key sequences or keypad functions, press <GOLD><HELP>—<H>, or <HELP> on VT200 series terminals, followed by the sequence or function.

<CTRL/a>, or <F14> on VT200 series terminals, toggles between insert and overstrike mode in the WPS-PLUS editor.

The editor functions for <GOLD> key sequences are shown in Figure 4.3.

| *Main Keyboard Key Sequence* | *Description* |
|---|---|
| <GOLD><BOT DOCT>—<B> | Moves the cursor to the bottom of the document. |
| <GOLD><CNTR>—<C> | Centers the text line according to the current ruler. *Note*: You must place the cursor at the end of the line that you want to center. |

<GOLD><FILE DOCT>–<F>

Exits the WPS-PLUS editor by filing the document. This saves all changes made during the current session.

<GOLD><GET DOCT>–<G>

Begins the procedure for inserting an entire document (or VMS file) starting at the current cursor location.

<GOLD><LING AIDS>–<J>

Begins the process of applying one of the following linguistic aids: (1) spelling checker applied to a section of text selected by pressing <SEL>–<keypad PERIOD>; (2) thesaurus applied to the word at the current cursor location; (3) usage alert (homonyms) applied to the word at the current cursor location; (4) grammar checker, if available, applied to a section of text selected by pressing <SEL>–<keypad PERIOD>.

<GOLD><QUIT>–<K> Exits the WPS-PLUS editor without saving the changes of the current session. You will be prompted for a confirmation before leaving the WPS-PLUS editor. Typing Y <RETURN> in response to the prompt allows you to continue exiting.

<GOLD><MENU>–<M> Begins sequences allowing for the settings related to the display of your document (e.g., page length) within the WPS-PLUS editor. *Note*: There can sometimes be conflicts between these settings and those for printers, set via the Main menu: P <RETURN>, <GOLD><A>, and so on (see Sections 4.9.1, 4.9.2).

<GOLD><NEW PAGE>–<N>

Places a `---NEW PAGE---` marker in your document so that when it is printed, the material below the marker will start a new page. This is always in force, whether automatic pagination is in effect or not (see Sections 4.9.1, 4.9.2).

<GOLD><PAGE MARK>–<P>

Allows for forcing new pages if automatic pagination is off; it is ignored if automatic pagination is on (see Sections 4.9.1, 4.9.2).

<GOLD><RULR>–<R> Begins the process of changing the current ruler (margin and tab settings). Pressing the <SPACEBAR> removes a tab setting (if it exists) at the current cursor location. When settings are finished, <RETURN> commits the new ruler. See Section 4.9.3 for details on setting margins and tabs.

<GOLD><SPEL CHEK>–<S>

Applies the spelling checker to the word at the current cursor location.

<GOLD><TOP DOCT>—<T>

Moves the cursor to the top of the document.

<GOLD><VIEW>—<V> Allows you to see the hidden formatting symbols embedded in the document. Pressing this key a second time brings back the original view of the document without the formatting symbols.

<GOLD><WRTE DCMT>—<W>

Allows you to create (Write) a new document (containing a SELected region of your current document) in your WPS-PLUS file cabinet or to create a new VMS file. The WPS-PLUS document option preserves the formatting, whereas the VMS file option loses some of the formatting.

<GOLD><FOOT NOTE>—<Y>

Begins the footnote editor for inserting footnote text into the document at the current cursor location. <GOLD><FILE DOCT>—<F> or <GOLD><QUIT>—<K> exits the footnote editor. The first exit saves the contents of the footnote editor; the second does not.

<GOLD><STAT>—<Z> Shows the status of the cursor location—page, row, column. Pressing this key a second time turns off the status display. This status information can be displayed every time you edit a document (see Section 4.9.7).

<GOLD><CMND>—<LEFT BRACKET>

Opens a control block (see Section 4.9.4).

<GOLD><SRCH>—<COMMA>

Begins a search for a string that you specify. Not for search-and-replace function.

<GOLD><CONT SRCH>—<PERIOD>

Continues a search for a string that you have specified with <GOLD><SRCH>—<COMMA>. Not for search-and-replace function.

<GOLD><SRCH SEL>—<SLASH>

In a search-and-replace sequence, allows for specification of the search string.

<GOLD><REPL>—<APOSTROPHE>

In a search-and-replace sequence, causes replacement of the current search string with the contents of the PASTE buffer (the replacement string).

The numeric keypad and its functions are shown in Figures 4.1 and 4.2. Notice that certain sets of keys work in a similar fashion: distance keys, formatting keys, and keys used in conjunction with the `PASTE`, `WORD`, and `CHARACTER` buffers.

*Numeric Keypad Key Functions* — *Description*

<ADVANCE>—<keypad 0>

Moves the cursor forward one character. Pressed before one of the distance keys—<LINE>—<keypad 2>, <WORD>—<keypad 4>, <PARA>—<keypad 5>, or <SENT>—<keypad 7>—it causes subsequent cursor movement to be toward the bottom of the document. The direction of movement can be reversed again (toward the top) by pressing <BACK UP>—<keypad 1>.

<BACK UP>—<keypad 1>

Moves the cursor back one character. Pressed before one of the distance keys—<LINE>—<keypad 2>, <WORD>—<keypad 4>, <PARA>—<keypad 5>, or <SENT>—<keypad 2>—it causes subsequent cursor movement to be toward the top of the document. The direction of movement can be reversed again (toward the bottom) by pressing <ADVANCE>—<keypad 0>.

<LINE>—<keypad 2>

The distance that, by default, moves the cursor to the beginning of the *next* line. Pressing <BACK UP>—<keypad 1> causes subsequent <LINE> presses to move the cursor to the beginning of the *preceding* line (toward the top of the document). Pressing <ADVANCE>—<keypad 0> restores the direction of cursor movement to the *next* line (toward the bottom of the document).

<WORD>—<keypad 4>

The distance key that, by default, moves the cursor to the beginning of the *next* word. A blank space designates the end of a word. Pressing <BACK UP>—<keypad 1> causes subsequent <WORD> presses to move the cursor to the beginning of the *preceding* word (toward the top of the document). Pressing <ADVANCE>—<keypad 0> restores the direction of cursor movement to the *next* word (toward the bottom of the document).

<PARA>—<keypad 5>

The distance key that, by default, moves the cursor to thc beginning of the *next* paragraph. A blank line designates the end of a paragraph. Pressing <BACK UP>—<keypad 1> causes subsequent <PARA> presses to move the cursor to the beginning of the *preceding* paragraph (toward the top of the document). Pressing <ADVANCE>—<keypad 0> restores the direction of cursor movement to the *next* paragraph (toward the bottom of the document).

<SENT>–<keypad 7> The distance key that, by default, moves the cursor to the beginning of the *next* sentence. A period designates the end of a sentence. Pressing <BACK UP>–<keypad 1> causes subsequent <SENT> presses to move the cursor to the beginning of the *preceding* sentence (toward the top of the document). Pressing <ADVANCE>–<keypad 0> restores the direction of cursor movement to the *next* sentence (toward the bottom of the document).

<GOLD><ARROW> The distance functions of <GOLD> with <LEFT ARROW>, <RIGHT ARROW>, <UP ARROW>, and <DOWN ARROW> are listed in Table 4.1.

<UPPER CASE>–<keypad 3>

A formatting key that makes the character at the current cursor location uppercase. Pressed after a <SEL>–<keypad PERIOD> sequence is started, it makes all the characters in the selected region uppercase.

<BOLD>–<keypad 6> A formatting key that makes the character at the current cursor position boldfaced. Pressed after a <SEL>–<keypad PERIOD> sequence is started, it makes all the characters in the selected region boldfaced.

<UNDERLINE>–<keypad 9>

A formatting key that underlines the character at the current cursor location. Pressed after a <SEL>–<keypad PERIOD> sequence is started, it underlines all the characters in the selected region.

<SEL>–<keypad PERIOD>

Begins the procedure for selecting text to put into the PASTE buffer. After moving from the beginning to the end of the text that you want in the PASTE buffer, press <CUT>–<keypad MINUS>; the text will be removed and replaced into the PASTE buffer.

<CUT>–<keypad MINUS>

Pressed after a <SEL>–<keypad PERIOD> sequence is started, this key moves everything in the selected region into the PASTE buffer.

<PASTE>–<keypad COMMA>

Causes the contents of the PASTE buffer (if any) to be inserted *before* the character at the current cursor location.

<PAGE>–<keypad PF2> Moves the cursor to the next page marker in the current search direction.

<DEL WORD>–<keypad PF3>

Deletes characters from the current cursor location to the end of the current word and places them in the WORD buffer.

<GOLD><DEL WORD>–<keypad PF3>

Inserts the contents of the WORD buffer *to the right of* the current cursor location.

<DEL CHAR>–<keypad PF4>

Deletes the charater at the current cursor location and places it in the CHARACTER buffer.

<GOLD><DEL CHAR>–<keypad PF4>

Inserts the contents of the CHARACTER buffer at the current cursor location, moving the character that was at the cursor to the right.

<TAB POS>–<keypad 8>

Moves the cursor to the next tab stop or to the beginning of the next line. This differs from using the main keyboard <TAB> key in that if you are in the middle of some text and type the main keyboard <TAB> key, blank space will be inserted from the cursor position to the next tab stop, whereas with <TAB POS>–<keypad 8> the cursor moves to the next tab stop without inserting any blank space.

<GOLD><SWAP>–<keypad ENTER>

Causes the character at the current cursor location to be swapped with the character immediately to the right of the cursor (great for "teh" and "ti").

<GOLD><PARA>–<keypad 5>

Pressed after a <SEL>–<keypad PERIOD> sequence is started, this key reflows a paragraph or longer section of text. Use it to reflow text the first time after importing a file from VMS to WPS-PLUS.

---

Some of the functions described earlier can also be performed with keys that are on VT200 series terminals but not on VT100 series terminals. This is especially true with respect to the non-numeric (cursor) keypad that lies between the numeric keypad and the main keyboard (see Figure 4.35).

| *VT200 Series Cursor Keypad Key Functions* | *Description* |
|---|---|
| <FIND> | Performs the same function as <GOLD><SRCH>–<COMMA>. *Note*: <FIND><FIND> does not perform the same function as does <GOLD><CONT SRCH>–<PERIOD>. |

| | |
|---|---|
| <INSERT HERE> | Performs the same function as <PASTE>–<keypad COMMA>. |
| <REMOVE> | Performs the same function as <CUT>–<keypad MINUS>. |
| <SELECT> | Performs the same function as <SEL>–<keypad PERIOD>. |
| <PREV SCREEN> | Moves the editor window toward the top of the document by one screenful, if possible. |
| <NEXT SCREEN> | Moves the editor window toward the bottom of the document by one screenful, if possible. |

***Training: CBI (Computer-Based Instruction) Modules***

Training modules can be accessed by typing TR <RETURN> at the Main menu and choosing from the menus that follow. Usually you can exit a training module to the main Training menu by pressing <GOLD> <STOP CBI>–<X>.

## 4.11 Exercises

1. Suppose you are graduating from your college or university with a major in your chosen field. You are now seeking employment. Part of this process will involve composing your resume and a cover letter, introducing yourself to your prospective employer. Use WPS-PLUS to create these two documents. In your documents, be sure to meet the following requirements.

   Using Section 4.4 as a starting point, construct your cover letter as follows:

- Set left and right margins at 10 and 65, respectively.
- Include your return address (can be made up) and date in the appropriate place.
- Introduce yourself, say why you want a job with this employer, and say why you think you are qualified (refer to items in your resume).
- The text of your letter should be at least half a page long, single-spaced. Follow any standard business letter format.

   Using Section 4.5 and Figure 4.15 as a guide, construct your resume as follows:

- Include the bolding, underlining, margins, and categories as shown.

- Fill in with your qualifications.

2. Apply the spelling checker and grammar checker (if available) to the text of the cover letter created in Exercise 1.

3. Using the `WACO.RCM` document imported in Section 4.6, change the margins to left margin 5 and right margin 50. Next, press <GOLD><VIEW>–<V> to see the hidden characters. Then use the <SEL> sequence discussed in the same section to reflow the paragraphs. Which hidden characters have been removed?

4. Construct a hypothetical course schedule having the following four columns: Course, Section, Day–Time, Instructor. Change the margin settings, tab stops, and so on, as necessary. Underline the headings and put in at least five course entries.

5. Mail yourself a copy of the document created in Exercise 4.

6. Write a short research paper (no more than five pages double-spaced). Include at least five references and use the footnote/end note option to cite your references. Print your paper using the footnote option and then the end note option.

Chapter 5

# Micro Communication with VAX/VMS Systems

5.1

## Why You Should Know How to Transfer Files

In this application of MS-DOS[1] microcomputers, your goal will be to learn how to save work produced on the VAX in such a form that you can refer to it later on an MS-DOS microcomputer, another VAX, or some other host computer. We will deal primarily with text files, but the concept applies to nearly all kinds of files on your computer system.

You may be wondering why you would want to be able to transfer your files among different systems. Here is an illustration of how you might actually put the contents of this chapter to practical use. Let's say that you are a student and you get sick toward the end of the spring semester. You miss almost two weeks of classes. The professor in one of your upper-division courses posts your course grade as "incomplete" with the Registrar and expects an almost-finished term paper by the sixth week of the fall semester. The company that has hired you for the summer has a fleet of MS-DOS microcomputers, which employees may use for personal work after normal business hours. If you had studied the contents of this chapter, you could take

1. MS-DOS stands for Microsoft Disk Operating System. Computers that use this operating system are often called IBM PC clones because the International Business Machines Personal Computer was the first popular home and business computer to use MS-DOS, which Microsoft Corporation developed specially for IBM.

the source file of your research paper in its draft form, perfect it during the summer on your employer's microcomputers, and turn it in to your professor *before* the deadline, all without falling behind in your classes. In fact, anyone who needs to switch from one type of equipment to another will find the information in this chapter useful.

## 5.2 What You Need for This Chapter

The first step is to browse through this chapter once so that you become relatively familiar with its goals and focus. Then determine whether you will be using a microcomputer "hardwired" to a VAX (an assumption followed throughout this chapter), or whether you will connect to the VAX by telephone. In the event of the latter, you should review the notes in Appendix G on the proper use of a modem.[2]

You will need a couple of blank diskettes on which to make backup copies of your beginner's program diskette. You will also need several adhesive diskette labels.[3] Keep scratch paper handy when you are working on the microcomputer so that you can make notes on matters that need clarification.

## 5.3 Getting Started on the Microcomputer

Before you can start the MS-DOS computer "talking" to the VAX, you have to learn some fundamental MS-DOS commands to start an interactive session. Insert the prepared distribution copy of the beginner's diskette in drive-A of the microcomputer. Close the drive door and turn the computer

2. Modem stands for modulator/demodulator. This equipment translates terminal activity into signals that computers can understand. A modem, along with the programs that operate them, must be at each end of the line for the computers to communicate via telephone.

3. We assume that someone at your site has already prepared a local version of the distribution copy of the beginner's diskette, and that the distribution diskette has been formatted with the system files appropriate for your particular kind of MS-DOS microcomputer. If this is not the case, you will have to secure a copy of the instructional diskette from Digital Press (see Introduction) and then prepare your own beginner's diskette. Instructions for this procedure are in Appendix F. If time does not permit you to secure the instructional diskette, this chapter will not be very meaningful. However, you may approximate its contents by securing your own copies of KERMIT.EXE, CED.COM, and ROFF4.EXE, programs that are in the public domain and available from most MS-DOS microcomputer users' groups. It is greatly to your advantage to select a text editor for use on the microcomputer, but we leave that choice to you. EDLIN.COM, which comes with MS-DOS, is an unspectacular but easily learned editor. Consult Appendix H for instructions on how to customize MS-KERMIT to enable the use of EVE.

on. If the computer is already on, do not turn it off. Instead, press the <CONTROL>, <ALT>, and <DEL> keys simultaneously. From here on, we denote this key combination as <CTRL/ALT/DEL>.[4] This will end the previous interactive session and begin yours. Within two minutes, the computer should "come to life." The screen displays certain information as the system boots. The booting process, which involves loading the operating system into memory and performing other initialization procedures, ends when you see a message reminding you to make your own copy of the boot diskette. The screen stops scrolling and you see the prompt `A>`. This is called the *DOS prompt*. Notice that you do not log in or use a password the way you did on the VAX. But you *do* have a directory similar to your VAX directory. For now, your directory is the space reserved for the set of files contained on the diskette in drive-A.

Many DOS commands are remarkably similar to VMS operating system commands. For instance, typing `DIR` <RETURN> results in a list of files with information similar to that shown in Figure 5.1. The first of these files, `COMMAND.COM`, contains many of the commands of MS-DOS.[5] You have already used one of these commands: `DIR`. `TYPE` is another familiar one.[6] Try typing a file. Issue the command `TYPE FILES.DIR` <RETURN>. The result is similar to what you get when you issue the `DIR` command, but notice that some comments appear on the side. These comments explain the contents of each file. It is a good idea to keep a current commented directory on each diskette you use; later you will do an exercise that shows you how.

## 5.4 Backing up Your Work

Once the DOS prompt has returned to your screen, remove the diskette from drive-A to check that the write-protect notch has been covered with tape. Insert the diskette again. You are now going to prepare an unused diskette to make a working copy of your beginner's diskette. Prepare a diskette label that reads "Boot Disk, Working Copy." *Do not write on diskette labels after they have been applied to the diskette.* Verify that the new diskette does *not*

4. On many MS-DOS compatible computers you also have the choice of pressing the <RESET> button. Check local sources to find out if such a button exists on your microcomputer.

5. Commands contained in this file, which are issued at the DOS prompt, are called *internal commands* in MS-DOS documentation.

6. The beginner's diskette also contains the command `LIST`. It is like `TYPE`, but it allows you to scroll backwards and forwards.

```
Volume in drive A has no label
 Directory of A:\

COMMAND  COM     17664   3-08-83  12:00p
AUTOEXEC BAT        16   1-04-87  12:00p
MYDISK   BAT       259   1-04-87  12:23p
NEWEXEC  BAT        80   1-04-87  12:02a
CED      CFG       306   1-04-87  12:02p
CED      COM      7040   7-23-85  10:07p
CHKDSK   COM      9819   8-19-86   1:00p
FORMAT   COM     11122   8-19-86   1:00p
LIST     COM      3072  11-01-85
SCRNSAVE COM       310  12-10-83   8:32p
FILES    DIR      1217   8-27-91   6:14p
DATE     DOC       939   1-05-87  12:15p
LIST     DOC      5376   1-25-86   3:52p
OWNER    DOC      3587   1-18-87   3:58p
TIP      DOC      1909   1-18-87   4:15P
WARN     DOC       782   1-18-87   5:29p
ROFF4    EXE     35696   8-10-85   5:20p
MSKERMIT INI      3026   8-28-91   2:36p
ROF1     TUT      1186   1-18-87   2:46p
ROF2     TUT       686   1-18-87   3:02p
KERMIT   EXE    145907   3-27-91   9:59a
        21 File(s)     168960 bytes free
```

**Figure 5.1 Directory Listing of Drive-A**

have tape on its write-protect notch, and insert it into drive-B. Shut the drive door. To verify that the diskette is new, type `DIR B` <RETURN>. Drive-B will spin for a while, and then you will see on your screen a notification similar to this:

```
Not ready error reading Drive B
Abort, Retry, Ignore?
```

Type `A` (for abort), and the DOS prompt will return. You have verified that the diskette contains no data that the computer can read. Now type `FORMAT B:/S` <RETURN> and follow the instructions on the screen.[7] After a couple of minutes, you will be asked if you want to format another diskette. Type `N`

7. This command prepares a new diskette to receive programs and data. The `/S` in the command causes a copy of the operating system files to be written onto the diskette. As the message on the screen indicates, the `FORMAT` command will destroy data on the diskette being formatted. You verified moments ago, however, that the diskette contains no readable data. Always check to make sure that a diskette has no valuable data before you format it.

(for NO). Now issue the command COPY *.* B: <RETURN>. All the files from the diskette in drive-A will be copied to the diskette in drive-B. Now take both diskettes out and take a breather. Return the distribution copy of the beginner's diskette to the person responsible for it.

For reinforcement of the concepts covered so far, read "A Quicky Guide to DOS," reproduced in Appendix E and cited as Bibliography [15]. This article gives a good introduction to MS-DOS commands.

## 5.5 A Fancier Session Using Familiar Commands

Your second MS-DOS session begins by booting the system with your working copy of the boot diskette. Once you get the MS-DOS prompt, review the contents of your diskette by typing DIR <RETURN>. Notice the file AUTOEXEC.BAT. This file is analogous to the LOGIN.COM file on the VAX. Also notice the file NEWEXEC.BAT. Now issue the following commands (with <RETURN>s) at the MS-DOS prompt:

```
REN AUTOEXEC.BAT OLD.BAT
REN NEWEXEC.BAT AUTOEXEC.BAT
DIR *.BAT
```

You now have on your screen a listing of all files with the extension .BAT: OLD.BAT, MYDISK.BAT, and AUTOEXEC.BAT.[8] Using the TYPE command, display the contents of these files to the screen. The new AUTOEXEC.BAT file is longer and more complicated than the older one. Your sessions will now be more customized. For the moment, do not worry about the contents of the new file. Just demonstrate that it works by forcing the system to boot by pressing <CTRL/ALT/DEL>.

When the microcomputer boots again, you will notice that the amount of text displayed to the screen is greater. The prompt has also changed, so that the date and time are displayed. Notice too that they may be wrong! Many MS-DOS microcomputers cannot remember the date and time of day as the system reboots unless an optional clock-calendar has been added. It is important to learn to set the time and date so that your files reflect the proper

8. On the VAX/VMS system, file extensions are called *file types*. VAX/VMS allows multiple versions of the same file. For example, LOGIN.COM;1 is expected to be an older version of LOGIN.COM;2. MS-DOS does not allow version numbers to follow the file extension. Accordingly, some text editors will leave a backup file with a slightly altered file extension. Before you do any serious editing on the microcomputer, you should determine if and how your editor saves previous versions of your files.

file creation date. Type DATE <RETURN>. Follow the prompts to enter the correct date, then press <RETURN>. Notice that the prompt has changed to the right date. Now type TIME <RETURN> and follow the prompts to enter the correct time. Keep in mind that the difference between a colon and a period is critical when entering the time. When you press <RETURN>, the MS-DOS prompt should give the correct time as well as the right date. (If you want some general information about your diskette, as well as a partial summary of commands, type the special, customized command TIPS <RETURN>. Use the <ESC> (for <ESCAPE>) key to return to the MS-DOS prompt.)

## 5.6 *Logging a Session with the VAX: The Microcomputer as a Smart Terminal*

Now that your microcomputer knows the right time and date, call KERMIT by typing MSKERMIT[9] and pressing <RETURN>. Some information comes to the screen but goes away before you can read it. A highlighted bar appears at the bottom of the screen. It is full of information, which you can disregard for now.

Press <RETURN> a couple of times until the microcomputer begins to act like a VAX terminal. Log in to your account, using your own user name and password. (If you get a string of meaningless characters, don't panic. Press <CONTROL> and <BREAK> at the same time twice, and then <RETURN>. If the microcomputer acts "dead," ask your local user services staff to see if your computer has been properly wired to communicate with the VAX. Modem users will have to add the additional step of setting the baud rate and dialing as described in Appendix G.)

Now that you are logged in to the VAX, take a minute to consider how many computer programs are running here, all at the same time. On the VAX, the VMS operating system is running. Applications programs could also be

---

9. The version of KERMIT that operates on the microcomputer might be called micro-KERMIT, MS-KERMIT, or local KERMIT, depending on the background and bias of the instructor or system manager. This chapter was written using version 3.10. To save keystrokes, you might later choose to RENAME KERMIT.EXE to something shorter, such as MSK.EXE. See the exercises at the end of this chapter for another method to accomplish this goal.

running. On the micro, the operating system MS-DOS is running, along with some background programs.

If you pause to read this book for more than three minutes, the screen will have blacked out. Typing any key will cause it to light up again. (The <ALT> or <SHIFT> keys are good ones to use to revive the screen because they do not actually enter any characters into the mainframe or the microcomputer.) This screen blackout is a consequence of the `SCRNSAVE.COM` program, called by your `AUTOEXEC.BAT` file, which the operating system read when the microcomputer booted. This screen-save program serves the purpose of keeping often-used sections of the screen from burning out prematurely.

Everything you type now will be sent directly to the VAX. For all practical purposes, the entire microcomputer is operating in the background. MS-KERMIT is causing the microcomputer to emulate a VT200 series terminal.[10]

One of the most useful applications of a microcomputer in combination with a host computer is to make a log file of an interactive session. The first step is to tell MS-KERMIT that you want to make such a file by typing what is known as an escape sequence. While holding down the <CONTROL> key, type a right square bracket ]. Then type `C`. The prompt changes to `MS--KERMIT>`. Type the command `LOG SESSION` and press <RETURN>. Then type `CONNECT` and another <RETURN>. You are now talking to the VAX again. Type something that you know will cause text to be sent to the screen. (`TYPE LOGIN.COM` would display the contents of the `LOGIN.COM` file to the screen. You will learn from experience that some of the more powerful screen-oriented programs such as PHONE do not log very well. However, line-oriented commands such as `TYPE` cause no problems.) Notice that, as text scrolls across the screen, the light on drive-A indicates accesses are occurring as the diskette spins. When the screen is finally still, type the escape sequence, <CTRL/ ]> followed by `C`, again so that you can issue a command in response to the `MS-KERMIT>` prompt. Type `CLOSE` <RETURN>. The diskette in drive-A gives a last spin, indicating that the file `KERMIT.LOG` has been closed. Type `CONNECT` <RETURN> and log off the VAX.

10. Version 3.10 requires that you type `SET TERM/DEVICE=VT200/NOEIGHT` at the operating system `MYNODE$` prompt.

Once again, type the escape sequence, <CTRL/ ]> followed by C. When you see the MS-KERMIT> prompt, type EXIT <RETURN>. This sequence gets you out of the KERMIT program on the micro. Now use the DIR command to display a directory of your local files (those on your microcomputer diskette). Notice that you created a new file called KERMIT.LOG. Display it to the screen using the TYPE command. You may keep this file or delete it. If you keep it, future LOG commands from KERMIT would *append* new text to the *bottom* of the file KERMIT.LOG.

## 5.7 *File Transfers*

Follow the steps in earlier sections to begin a session on the microcomputer, call MS-KERMIT, and log in to your VAX account. Working with another version of KERMIT on the VAX, you can perform verified, or protocol, file transfers.[11] To illustrate the point, *download* your LOGIN.COM file from your VAX directory to the microcomputer and *upload* the AUTOEXEC.BAT file from the MS-DOS microcomputer to your VAX directory.

To call VAX-KERMIT, type KERMIT <RETURN>. The VAX will respond by changing from the node prompt to KERMIT-32>.[12] In answer to this prompt, type SERVER <RETURN>. Next you see a message that KERMIT is running in server mode and that you need to type your escape sequence to return to your microcomputer. Type the now familiar <CTRL/ ]> followed by C.

In plain English, you are being asked to give some commands to KERMIT on your micro so that the VAX-KERMIT server will have something to do. Respond to the MS-KERMIT> prompt by typing GET LOGIN.COM <RETURN>. Presently the screen reconfigures and you are told the name of the file coming to your micro. Notice that the diskette in drive-A spins occasionally as the

---

11. This version of KERMIT might be called VAX-KERMIT, KERMIT-32, or mainframe KERMIT, according to the preference of the instructor or system manager. Verified file transfers involve complicated error-checking procedures that ensure, within a range of certainty, that data sent match data received. (For detailed information, see the explanation set forth by the author of KERMIT, Bibliography [5].)

12. You should check with your system manager or local user services staff to see how the line

```
$! KER*MIT == "$SYS$SYSTEM:KERMIT.EXE"
```

in your annotated LOGIN.COM file should be modified. The form of the string on the right-hand side of the == is site-specific, and the ! will have to be removed. Of course, if you have the starter LOGIN.COM file, the line will have to be inserted (without the !).

file is being transferred. Your LOGIN.COM file is being downloaded to the microcomputer. When the operation is over, the MS-KERMIT> prompt returns, and you hear a beep.

This time, type SEND *.BAT <RETURN>. Now all the files on your micro with extension .BAT are being uploaded to the VAX, one right after the other. These files are AUTOEXEC.BAT, MYDISK.BAT, and OLD.BAT. When the MS-KERMIT> prompt returns, type SEND *.INI <RETURN>. When the transfer is over, type FINISH <RETURN>. Then type CONNECT <RETURN>. Another <RETURN> should cause the VAX operating system prompt, MYNODE$, to reappear. If the KERMIT-32> prompt appears instead, type EXIT <RETURN> and you should be back to the operating system prompt, MYNODE$. Type DIR *.BAT <RETURN>.

Your screen should inform you that your VAX directory holds three such files—the same three files you just sent from the micro via KERMIT. After bringing them to the screen with TYPE, PRINT a copy of them for review. Also, PRINT a copy of MSKERMIT.INI. Now log out from the VAX. Once you read the VAX log-out message, type the same escape sequence, <CTRL/ ]> followed by C, that you used earlier so that your keystrokes are sent to your local KERMIT rather than out to the VAX. When the MS-KERMIT> prompt appears, type EXIT <RETURN>. Issue the command TYPE LOGIN.COM <RETURN>. Your own personalized LOGIN.COM file from the VAX should scroll on the screen. After the scrolling is finished, remove your diskette and take a break.

## 5.8 A Review of What Went on Behind the Scenes

If you insert your own copy of the beginner's diskette into drive-A and boot the system as you did before, you might notice the commands as they scroll across the screen. When you get the MS-DOS prompt, the system has booted and your interactive session has been customized by the AUTO EXEC.BAT file. In turn, this file has called some programs that operate in the background. For example, SCRNSAVE.COM causes the screen to go blank after three minutes of no keyboard input, thereby reducing screen burn-out problems. CED.COM, in combination with CED.CFG, allows you to use aliases, synonyms, or abbreviated commands, as well as to retrieve and edit the entire MS-DOS command line (just as you did command line editing on the VAX).

On the micro, the interactive job has been customized by the AUTOEXEC.BAT file. In like manner, the operation of MS-KERMIT has been customized by the MSKERMIT.INI file. (We will discuss customizing KERMIT later.) For now, just keep in mind the fact that your sessions on an MS-DOS machine and on the VAX are customized when the operating system on each computer reads instructions from initialization files. Often applications programs on both machines have initialization files as well. For example, the VAX file TPUINI.TPU and the MS-DOS file MSKERMIT.INI customize the operations of the EVE editor on the VAX and of KERMIT on the MS-DOS microcomputer, respectively.

The exact details of how KERMIT works are beyond the scope of this book. Generally speaking, here is what happened: You called micro-KERMIT into operation by typing MSKERMIT <RETURN>. The file MSKERMIT.INI was read by MS-KERMIT on the microcomputer. This file reset some defaults to facilitate your use of KERMIT from your work site or your home computer. (Home computer users might find it useful to review the notes to modem users found in Appendix G.) Once you were logged in to the VAX, you called VAX-KERMIT by issuing the command KERMIT <RETURN>. Your first command to VAX-KERMIT was SERVER <RETURN>. From then on, VAX-KERMIT waited for commands and data, not from your keyboard, but from micro-KERMIT. Some of those commands were started by the GET and SEND commands, which you really did enter. Other commands were issued automatically as the file transfers were completed. Those transfers involved a complex error-checking procedure to increase the probability that your information was received in the form in which it was sent.

When, at the MS-KERMIT> prompt, you typed FINISH <RETURN>, CONNECT <RETURN>, and finally a couple of <RETURN>s, KERMIT terminated on the VAX. The microcomputer running MS-KERMIT resumed acting like a computer terminal. Then you logged off the VAX and, using the escape sequence of <CTRL/]> followed by C, you returned to the MS-KERMIT> prompt. At this point, your keystrokes were no longer sent to the VAX; they were sent only to the local KERMIT. You typed EXIT <RETURN>, which terminated the local KERMIT. Thereafter, your keystrokes were sent to the operating system on the microcomputer.

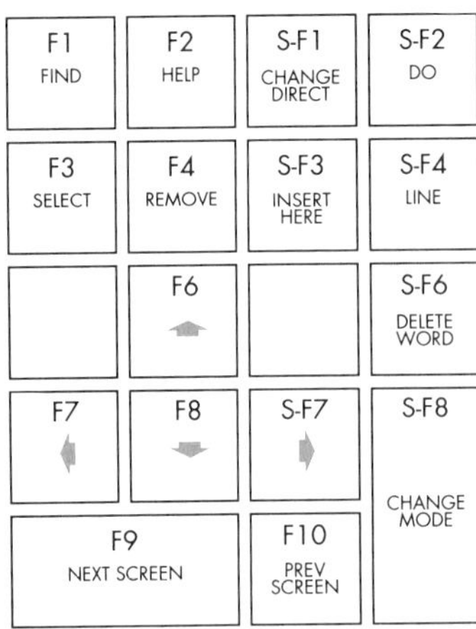


**Figure 5.2 Sample EVE Keypad Map for Keyboards with Vertical Function Keys**

## 5.9 *Using EVE from the Microcomputer*

In Chapter 2, you used EVE to create and edit files. Now you can use this editor from the microcomputer because MS-KERMIT emulates a VT102 (or higher) terminal. The only peculiarity is that different microcomputers have different keyboards.

To use EVE with MS-KERMIT, refer to Figure 5.2 for the appropriate mapping of the EVE keys for keyboards with vertical function keys (S-F1 means <SHIFT/F1>). The IBM PC and many compatibles have such keyboards. The EVE keys are programmed (mapped) by the `MSKERMIT.INI` file on your beginner's diskette. For more information on using this file with EVE, see Appendix H.

## 5.10 *Transferring Binary MS-DOS Files Using KERMIT*

So far, all the files you have transferred between the VAX and the MS-DOS microcomputer have been ASCII files. That is, they are made up of printable characters you can display to the screen by issuing the `TYPE` command. Not all MS-DOS files are printable. Program files may not be displayed to the screen with the `TYPE` command. There might come a time that you will want to transfer MS-DOS binary files—those files with `.COM` or `.EXE` extensions. Such a situation could arise when one of your fellow VAX users has a nice public domain program (the `.EXE` version) that you want. (Note that we emphasize this procedure should be followed only with programs in the public domain.) You need not actually make contact and copy diskettes in order to get a copy of the program. Once the program has been uploaded to the VAX, and the protection properly lowered, you can download the file using KERMIT.

In order to ensure error-free file transfers as you follow the transfer procedures we have discussed, you should be sure to do the following:

- At the VAX-KERMIT prompt, `KERMIT-32>`, type `SET FILE TYPE BINARY` <RETURN> *before* typing `SERVER` <RETURN>.
- At the `MS-KERMIT>` prompt, type `SET EOF NOCTRL-Z` before beginning the file transfer.

## 5.11 Quick Reference: MS-DOS, VAX-KERMIT, and Micro-KERMIT Commands

### MS-DOS Commands

(Assume you are logged in to drive-A.)

| *Command* | *Description* |
|---|---|
| DIR | Displays to the screen a list of all files on drive to which you are logged in. |
| DIR **.ext* | Displays only files that have an extension of *.ext*. |
| TYPE *file.ext* | Types contents of file *file.ext* to the screen. |
| REN *oldfile.ext newfile.ext* | Changes name of file from *oldfile.ext* to *newfile.ext*. |
| COPY *old.ext new.ext* | Makes a copy of file *old.ext* on file *new.ext*. |
| COPY **.ext* B: | Copies all files with extension *.ext* to drive-B. |
| DEL *file.ext* | Deletes file *file.ext* from directory. |
| FORMAT B: | Prepares diskette in drive-B for reading and writing by MS-DOS. This destroys all data already on the diskette. |
| FORMAT B:/S | Same as FORMAT B: except that DOS system files are added to the diskette. This allows use of the diskette for booting but leaves less room to store files. |
| MSKERMIT | Calls MS-KERMIT. |

### VAX-KERMIT Commands

| *Command* | *Description* |
|---|---|
| SERVER | Causes VAX-KERMIT to await commands from MS-KERMIT to transport files between the two computers. |
| HELP | Gives VAX-KERMIT on-line help. |

### Micro-KERMIT Commands

| *Command* | *Description* |
|---|---|
| <CTRL/]> C | The sequence for escaping to MS-KERMIT. Hold down the <CONTROL> key and type a right square bracket ], then type a lowercase or uppercase C. |

Terminal stops sending keystrokes to the VAX computer and starts sending instructions to MS-KERMIT> prompt. The following commands are typed at that prompt:

`FINISH` — Sends a message to VAX-KERMIT server that all file transfers have been completed.

`CONNECT` — Connects to host computer via serial port.

`LOG SESSION` — Saves text displayed on screen to file named `KERMIT.LOG` on microcomputer. New text is appended at the bottom of an existing file. This command does not work with full-screen applications such as DECalc or PHONE.

`LOG SESSION` *filespec*

Same as `LOG SESSION` except that log file has been given an explicit name, represented here by *filespec*.

`CLOSE` — Stops saving text to log file.

`HELP` — Displays list of MS-KERMIT commands along with short explanation.

`EXIT` — Exits the MS-KERMIT program.

### Other Micro-KERMIT Control Commands

| *Command* | *Description* |
|---|---|
| <CTRL / ]> P | Escapes to DOS, i.e., keeps MS-KERMIT in background, does not disturb connection to the VAX, while returning to MS-DOS prompt. Return to MS-KERMIT by typing EXIT <RETURN> and pressing the <SPACEBAR>. |
| <CTRL / ]> ? | Gives the HELP menu for micro-KERMIT. |

## 5.12 Exercises

1. Follow the instructions to send the file CED.CFG from your beginner's diskette to the VAX. TYPE the file to the screen. PRINT a copy for further study. Notice the line that reads SYN TY TYPE. This line defines TY as an acceptable synonym, or alias, for TYPE. Now, using a VAX text editor, add the line that would make MSK an acceptable synonym for MSKERMIT. When you have finished editing, follow the procedure to download the new CED.CFG to your own copy of the beginner's diskette. After you have logged off the VAX and left MS-KERMIT, issue a DIR command. Notice the odd name given to your new version of CED.CFG. Review the instructions to RENAME files. First rename CED.CFG to OLD.CFG. Then RENAME the new version of CED.CFG, which you downloaded from the VAX, to CED.CFG, so that it will be properly recognized the next time the system boots. If you have followed the instructions correctly, you should then be able to call MS-KERMIT with MSK.

2. TYPE the file AUTOEXEC.BAT to the screen of your microcomputer. Notice the line that reads CED -FCED.CFG. Consider the fact that AUTOEXEC.BAT and CED.CFG are initialization files for COMMAND.COM and ED.COM, respectively. Together these files help customize your interactive session on the MS-DOS microcomputer. You can alter these files to customize your session some different way. What is the name of the file that customizes your work on the VAX?

3. You have already downloaded a copy of TPUINI.TPU to your diskette. Without changing it at all, follow the instructions in this chapter to upload it to the VAX. After you have left KERMIT with the FINISH and the CONNECT commands, use the DIR command to see if you can figure out how the VAX/VMS operating system renamed the earlier version of TPUINI.TPU. Discard that now useless version by using the PURGE command.

4. It is possible to use the VAX as a storage place for binary MS-DOS files, as detailed in Section 5.10. These files, if they are programs, cannot execute on the VAX, but you can share them with other users provided you follow the proper procedures for transferring binary files. To prove the point, make a copy of LIST.COM using the MS-DOS COPY command. At the MS-DOS prompt, type COPY LIST.COM LIST1.COM <RETURN>. LIST is the program that types a file to the

microcomputer screen. LIST also allows backward as well as forward scrolling of text. LIST AUTOEXEC.BAT will display the contents of the file named AUTOEXEC.BAT to the screen. Satisfy yourself that LIST1 works the same way. Follow the instructions to upload LIST1.COM to the VAX. Then, while still in KERMIT, download the same file using the GET command. After you have logged out from the VAX and are back at the MS-DOS prompt, use the DIR command to discover that you have a new file, which has been renamed in a manner similar to the CED.CFG file in Exercise 1. After you have tested the programs to see that they both work like LIST.COM, delete both of these new test files.

5. From the MS-DOS prompt, issue the command TYPE FILES.DIR <RETURN>. What you see on the screen is very similar to what you see with the DIR command, except that there are explanations of the contents of each file. Now you can make your own annotated directory. Issue the command DIR>NEWFIL.DIR <RETURN>. The characters normally displayed to the screen are instead put into the file called NEWFIL.DIR. The MS-DOS manual calls this process "redirection of output." Using the editor of your choice, you can add comments about the contents of each file. Maintaining a commented directory is a good idea so that you can remember what each file contains without having to call it up to the screen or print it.

6. Generate a file containing all the on-line help outside of VAX-KERMIT by typing, at the operating system prompt, the commands

```
HELP/OUTPUT=KERMIT1.HLP KERMIT...
PRINT/DELETE/NOTIFY KERMIT1.HLP
```

7. Using the LIBRARY command discussed in Chapter 2, Exercise 9, and keeping in mind the fact that the HELP within KERMIT is on the file named SYS$HELP:KERMIT.HLB, print out a copy of the complete on-line help available from within the VAX-KERMIT program.

Chapter 6

# Electronic Communications Programs on VAX/VMS Systems

One of the quickest ways to get over feeling bewildered by computers is to learn how to communicate with other computer users. Many programs available for VAX/VMS systems enable you to set up communications. One such program, PHONE, simulates a telephone conversation printed on the screen with two users talking back and forth, and even talking at the same time. Another program, MAIL, allows users to write each other "letters," which may be read immediately if the recipient is logged in at the time they are sent, or later at the recipient's convenience. The VAX Notes program, which falls in the category of BBS (Bulletin Board System) programs, is a computer simulation of a public bulletin board. As a user, you can post notices of interest to many other users. Just like some conventional bulletin boards on the walls of classrooms or dormitories, VAX Notes can be divided into interest areas. However, as you will see, it provides much more relevance and immediacy than most conventional bulletin boards. Finally, BITNET, a network of computer systems, allows communication among computer users around the world.

## 6.1 The PHONE Program

### 6.1.1 An Interactive Session with PHONE

To operate PHONE, you need at least a VT100 terminal. As with any other program supported by Digital Equipment Corporation, it is a good idea to make your first step a look at what HELP the system has to offer. At the operating system (DCL) prompt (your node name followed by $ if you have either of the LOGIN.COM files), type HELP PHONE <RETURN>. Follow the prompts on the screen to learn PHONE's fundamental commands. Like many other programs on VAX/VMS systems, PHONE has on-line help also. Type PHONE <RETURN>. When you locate the blinking cursor next to the percent sign (%), which is PHONE's default "switch hook" symbol, type HELP <RETURN>. The on-line help will prompt you about how to get additional information. Make notes for future reference on the DIAL, DIR, ANSWER, and HANGUP commands. When you feel you know enough to use PHONE, you are ready for your interactive session.

The interactive session described here shows you how to search for someone you know who might be logged into the system. In order to guarantee success on this score, you might consider accompanying a friend, who also has an account on your VAX/VMS system, to some location that has at least two terminals.

Some systems are set up so that the PHONE DIR (discussed below) is disabled for security reasons. In such situations, you might try the SHOW USERS command, which is issued at the operating system prompt. However, this will show only the users logged in to your node. If you encounter problems, check with your local user services staff.

Recall the instructions you followed to set your process name to something besides your non-mnemonic user name (Chapter 2, Exercise 2). Before trying to PHONE your friend, get the user name as well as the process name. When you think your friend is logged in, and while you are at the DCL prompt, type PHONE DIR <RETURN>. Notice that the screen reconstructs as you enter the PHONE program. Several columns of categories appear: User Name, Process Name, Terminal Type, and Availability. Search for your friend's user name. If you don't find it, clear the screen by typing any key. Now notice that the screen has been divided into two windows. One is labeled with your own user name; the other is not labeled. Opposite the percent sign, type EX (for EXIT), followed by <RETURN>.

You are back at the operating system prompt, which we generically call MYNODE$. If you are logged into MYNODE, for example, you have just seen a list of users who are also currently logged into MYNODE. If you did not find your friend in that list, and your VAXcluster or network contains another

VAX/VMS node called NODE2, you need to use your <UP ARROW> key to get the command `PHONE DIR` back onto the command line. Then type `NODE2::`, so that the whole command says `PHONE DIR NODE2::`, and press <RETURN>. The screen will now reconstruct as it did moments before. Suppose your friend is described on the PHONE screen as

```
DEC-wizard        CS33595007        VTA1488        available
```

`DEC-wizard` is the process name or, if you will, the name given to the interactive job every time your friend logs in. Making your process name distinctive is a way to help other users know when you are using the system. The next string of numbers you see is the user name for a unique computer account and directory on your computer system. When you PHONE someone, you *must* include the user name. The next string, `VTA1488`, designates which terminal your friend is using. Finally, `available` means that your friend has not blocked out incoming messages from other users. (Shortly, you will see how to do that.) Write down your friend's user name. Clear the screen by typing any key. The cursor should now be just to the right of the percent sign. Now type

```
DIAL NODE2::CS33595007
```

and press <RETURN>. PHONE advises you each time it "redials" or "rings" the other user. At the same moment, your friend DEC-wizard gets a message that you are trying to PHONE. If DEC-wizard wants to answer, he must first exit the program he is currently using and return to the operating system prompt. At this prompt, answering is just a simple matter of DEC-wizard's typing `PHONE ANSWER` <RETURN>. At that moment, both screens display two separate windows with node and user name labels. You and your friend can type at the same time—just as both parties can talk simultaneously in a real telephone call. Often, typing two blank lines indicates that the current speaker is finished and will now listen to the other person, in much the same way as the word "over" is used on CB radios. As a window fills with text, the old text scrolls off the top. Because PHONE is an informal means of communication, most users do not spend a lot of time correcting typographical errors.

When the "conversation" is over, one user will type <CTRL/Z>, which sends a message to the other user saying he has hung up. A touch of any key will then return the cursor to the percent sign, PHONE's prompt. That user may `DIAL` someone else or return to the operating system prompt by typing `EXIT` <RETURN>, or simply <CTRL/Z> if he wishes to make no more calls.

Any time you are in the PHONE program, but the cursor is *not* at the % "switch hook" prompt, you can obtain the prompt by typing <%> and whatever PHONE command you want to execute. This technique works even while you are having a conversation with someone.

It is important to remember that, although PHONE can be very useful, its use should not be abused. You should call only those people who you think are willing to receive a call from you. Furthermore, if you do not want to receive PHONE calls, you may issue the DCL command

```
SET BROADCAST=(NOPHONE)
```

which will preclude calls during that *one* interactive session.

If you want to preclude PHONE interruptions upon *each* log in, then the `SET BROADCAST` command can be included in the `LOGIN.COM` file you are using. This command is already included in the annotated `LOGIN.COM` file; just remove the ! from the line to make the command functional. If you are operating with the starter `LOGIN.COM` file, insert the entire line

```
$ SET BROADCAST=(NOPHONE)
```

just before the `$ EXIT:` line.

## 6.1.2 Quick Reference: PHONE Commands

**Entering and Exiting PHONE**

| *Command* | *Description* |
|---|---|
| PHONE | Issued at the operating system MYNODE$ prompt, this command executes PHONE while at the operating system level. |
| EXIT | Issued at the % prompt, this command exits PHONE. |

These commands are issued from within PHONE at the % prompt.

| *Command* | *Description* |
|---|---|
| HELP | Enters PHONE's on-line help system. |
| DIR or DIR *nodename*:: | Obtains directory of those people with whom you could talk on your system (node) or any other system (node) in the network. |
| DIAL *username* | Places call to another person. Requires the person's user name and node name, if the node is different from your own. |
| ANSWER | Answers when someone calls you. |
| REJECT | Tells a caller that you do not want to answer. |
| HANGUP or <CTRL/Z> | Disconnects when you have finished a PHONE call. |

### 6.1.3 Exercises for PHONE

1. Generate a file containing all the on-line help outside of PHONE by typing the following commands at the operating system prompt:

```
HELP/OUTPUT=PHONE1.HLP PHONE...
PRINT/DELETE/NOTIFY PHONE1.HLP
```

2. Using the `LIBRARY` command discussed in Chapter 2, Exercise 9, and keeping in mind the fact that the `HELP` within PHONE is on the file named `SYS$HELP:PHONEHELP.HLB`, print out a copy of the complete on-line help available from within PHONE.

3. Find a willing colleague and perform the terminal exercises outlined in Section 6.1.1. If you can find no one on your system whom you know, try to PHONE yourself. What happens?

4. Check with your local user services staff to see how your VAX/VMS nodes are networked. If your VAX is in a VAXcluster, try the `PHONE DIR` *nodename*`::` command on each node to see if you can find out who is currently logged in to each of the nodes in the VAXcluster. *Note*: Not all systems allow this much access, so do not be surprised if it does not work on all the nodes you try.

5. Use PHONE's on-line help to read about the `FACSIMILE` command. Test your understanding of what you read: create a small greeting file, PHONE yourself (if nobody else is available), and try out this command. What uses can you see for such a facility?

6. PHONE yourself or someone else. While you are conversing, return to PHONE's % prompt and ask for `HELP`. For details on this maneuver, see Section 6.1.1, look through the on-line help from within PHONE, or look through the files you obtained from Exercises 1 and 2. Note especially any `HELP` related to the "switch hook."

## 6.2 The MAIL Program

Electronic mail, or e-mail,[1] has become a popular mode of communication in many large organizations. The VMS version, called MAIL, is different from PHONE in that it does not require the receiving user to be logged in when the message is sent. However, a logged-in recipient will usually see a message indicating the presence of a new mail message. As with PHONE, MAIL has HELP available at the DCL level when you type HELP MAIL <RETURN>. In like manner, you can get HELP by typing HELP <RETURN> from within the MAIL program.

### 6.2.1 An Interactive Session with MAIL

To send electronic mail when at the operating system level, type MAIL <RETURN>. Notice that the screen does not clear as it did with PHONE, but the prompt changes. It now says MAIL>. In response to this prompt, type SEND <RETURN>. The program prompts you through everything you need to do to complete a message. As with PHONE, you send your message to your colleague's user name. On your first try, it might be a good idea to send mail to your *own* user name. When prompted for subject, you may enter a subject, or simply press <RETURN>. Then MAIL will prompt you to enter the text of your message. End your message by typing <CTRL/Z>. Notice that if you have been sending mail to yourself, MAIL informs you that you have received mail. To read mail sent to you while you are in the MAIL program, you should use the EXIT command to leave the MAIL program, then enter it again.[2] When you get the MAIL> prompt again, you will be notified that you have new mail. Type READ <RETURN>. After your message has been displayed to the screen, you must decide what to do with it; you can either store it for future reference or delete it. At the MAIL> prompt, type DEL <RETURN>. Your test message will now be discarded when you leave the MAIL program.

---

1. For those interested in the history of e-mail, see Bibliography [23], which also contains several interesting articles concerning telecommunications, including one on buying a modem.

2. There is a more elegant way to do this. MAIL, in fact, automatically creates folders to keep track of mail that has not been read as well as mail that has been marked for deletion. These folders are MAIL, NEWMAIL, and WASTEBASKET. Let's say you are reading old mail and you get notification that you have new mail. Typing SELECT NEWMAIL will connect you to the folder of unread messages. Once you have read a message, it is moved from the NEWMAIL to the MAIL folder. In like manner, deleting a message does not erase it. Instead the message is merely transferred to the WASTEBASKET folder. WASTEBASKET's contents are not actually discarded until you exit the MAIL program.

You might want to store some of your mail, such as an important assignment, as a file in your directory so that you can PRINT it from the operating system level or edit it for some other purpose. In such cases, you should type EXTRACT, followed by the name of the file into which you want the message saved. Then press <RETURN>. After this save process is complete, you should delete the message by typing DEL <RETURN>.

Now try sending a test message to another user. Remembering the user name of a colleague willing to receive test mail from you, at the MAIL> prompt type SEND <RETURN>. When MAIL asks you to whom you want to send the letter, enter your colleague's user name, then the subject and text of your message. When you are done, type <CTRL/Z>. Within your message, ask your colleague to use the command ANSWER, or REPLY, just after your message has been displayed to her screen. The two of you will discover that the ANSWER command forces the recipient to make an immediate acknowledgment of the message. Whenever you ANSWER a message, MAIL does not prompt for addressee or subject matter (if a subject has already been given); it just instructs you to insert text and dispatch the letter with <CTRL/Z>.

As you learn more about MAIL, you will discover that a good way to produce neater and better correspondence is to send files you have tidied up using DECspell and a text-editing or text-formatting program. To find out the proper commands for sending a file that exists in your directory, type HELP SEND <RETURN> from within the MAIL program. Pay special attention to the examples there.

Once you have received mail, you will notice that a new file, named MAIL.MAI, appears in your directory. You should *not* delete this file, nor should you attempt to EDIT or TYPE it. The MAIL.MAI file contains your messages in a form that can be read while in the MAIL program but not easily read otherwise. If you delete the file, you may be notified that you have mail *but* you will not be able to READ it. If you TYPE or EDIT the MAIL.MAI file, you may sometimes cause your terminal to "lock up."

### 6.2.2 Editing Messages to SEND, REPLY, and FORWARD

You may be wondering whether you can edit your messages the same way you edited a file with a text editor. The answer is yes.

If you are using EVE, remove the ! from the lines

```
$! MA*IL == "MAIL/EDIT=(SEND,FORWARD,REPLY)"
$! DEFINE MAIL$EDIT CALLABLE_TPU
```

in your annotated LOGIN.COM file. For the starter LOGIN.COM file, simply insert the lines (without the !) immediately preceding the $ EXIT: line.

If you are using EDT (see Appendix B), remove the ! from the line

```
$! MA*IL == "MAIL/EDIT=(SEND,FORWARD,REPLY)"
```

in your annotated LOGIN.COM file. For the starter LOGIN.COM file, simply insert the line (without the !) immediately preceding the $ EXIT: line.

It does not matter whether you SEND, REPLY, or FORWARD your messages. When you are ready to type your message, you will see your screen clear and you may begin typing your message much as you would in the text editor. When you are finished, exit as you would exit the text editor saving your work, and your message will be sent. If you exit as you would exit the text editor not saving your work, your message will not be sent.

## 6.2.3 Quick Reference: MAIL Commands

**Entering and Exiting MAIL**

| *Command* | *Description* |
|---|---|
| MAIL | Issued at the operating system MYNODE$ prompt, this command starts execution of MAIL. |
| EXIT | Issued at the MAIL> prompt, this command exits MAIL to the operating system. |

These commands are issued from within MAIL at the MAIL> prompt.

| *Command* | *Description* |
|---|---|
| HELP | Executes MAIL's on-line help system. |
| READ | Reads next MAIL message. |
| SELECT NEWMAIL | Accesses folder of unread messages. |
| SEND | Sends mail to specified user. |
| SEND *filespec* | Sends file *filespec* to specified user. |
| DELETE | Deletes the message just read. |
| DIR | Lists directory of current MAIL messages. |
| ANSWER or REPLY | Replies to MAIL message currently being read. |
| <CTRL/z> | Indicates completion of MAIL message being typed. |
| EXTRACT *filespec* | Sends MAIL message currently being read to file *filespec*. |
| FORWARD | Forwards current message to specified user. |

### 6.2.4 Exercises for MAIL

1. Generate a file containing all the on-line help available outside of MAIL by typing the following commands at the operating system prompt:

```
HELP/OUTPUT=MAIL1.HLP MAIL...
PRINT/DELETE/NOTIFY MAIL1.HLP
```

2. Using the LIBRARY command discussed in Chapter 2, Exercise 9, and keeping in mind the fact that the HELP within MAIL is on the file named SYS$HELP:MAILHELP.HLB, print out a copy of the complete on-line help available from within MAIL.

3. After reading through the on-line help available to you on READ, FORWARD, REPLY, and EXTRACT, send yourself a test message. Apply each of these commands to show that you understand how they work.

4. Make the changes discussed in Section 6.2.2 for using a text editor with MAIL. For EVE, make sure that the following two lines are in your LOGIN.COM file:

```
$ MA*IL == "MAIL/EDIT=(SEND,FORWARD,REPLY)"
$ DEFINE MAIL$EDIT CALLABLE_TPU
```

   For EDT (see Appendix B), make sure that the *first* preceding line is in your LOGIN.COM file. Repeat your work from Exercise 3. How do things differ? What do you think the result would be if the first line were changed to

```
$ MA*IL == "MAIL/EDIT=(READ,SEND,FORWARD,REPLY)"
```

   Test your hypothesis and explain the results.

5. After doing Exercise 4, SEND a message. While you are editing your message, press the <HELP> key for the text editor. Now press the other keypad keys, one at a time. Are all the functions the same as in the text editor?

6. Use the PRINT command from within MAIL. How could this supplant some uses for the EXTRACT command?

7. Read the on-line help from within MAIL regarding COMPRESS. Try the command. Is there a new file in your directory? What could be the value of this command?

8. Look through the on-line help, both from within and from outside the MAIL program, and figure out how to send an already prepared file via MAIL. Send a test file to yourself or to a colleague on your system.

9. Browse through the on-line help concerning `MAIL`, both from within and outside the MAIL program. Pay special attention to discussions of distribution lists. Get an agreement from two other users on your system to try out this concept. Send them *and yourself* a test message, using a distribution list *and* a message file that have been prepared before entering the MAIL program. What value can you see in distribution lists, beyond sending a lot of junk mail?

## 6.3 The VAX Notes Conferencing Program

So far, we have looked at electronic communications between just a couple of users. However, on many occasions, you might want to send messages to a great many users. You might want to canvass your campus for a ride during your college's spring break, or you might want to confer with colleagues about a report on which you are working together. You could use MAIL, but it would be less cumbersome if all the interested parties could post their ideas in a single place, where all could read and respond to them. This is a bulletin board system, or BBS. The acronym BBS is well known among many microcomputer users. Some microcomputer hobbyists dedicate an entire system for use as a community bulletin board.

One program that can serve as a BBS is VAX Notes. VAX Notes is described by Digital as a "computerized conferencing system."[3]

### 6.3.1 Getting Started

First, let's enter and exit the VAX Notes program. At the operating system prompt, type `NOTES` <RETURN>. Your screen will reconstruct with the first display screen of VAX Notes (Figure 6.1). The cursor is located after `Notes>` on the first line of the display screen. To leave VAX Notes and return to the operating system prompt, type `EXIT` <RETURN>. Once back in the operating system, you will see that you have a new file, `NOTES$NOTEBOOK.NOTE`, in your directory. This file is used by VAX Notes to keep information that is specific

3. Bibliography [10]. See this source for more details on VAX Notes.

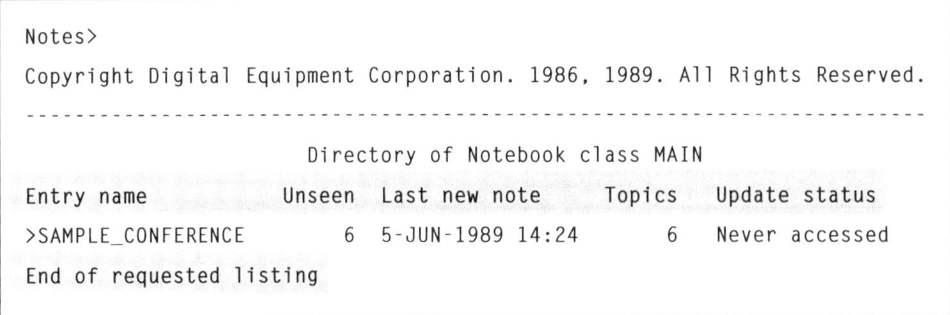

```
Notes>
Copyright Digital Equipment Corporation. 1986, 1989. All Rights Reserved.
--------------------------------------------------------------------------

                 Directory of Notebook class MAIN
Entry name            Unseen  Last new note      Topics   Update status
>SAMPLE_CONFERENCE         6  5-JUN-1989 14:24        6   Never accessed
End of requested listing
```

**Figure 6.1 First Display Screen of VAX Notes**

for your use of the program. You have already seen such a file, the MAIL.MAI file that accompanies the MAIL program. Just as with MAIL.MAI, you should not delete the NOTES$NOTEBOOK.NOTE file unless you are no longer going to use VAX Notes.

The first display screen of VAX Notes contains the four parts that characterize most VAX Notes display screens:

- Command line
- Message line
- Heading
- Viewing area

The *command line,* the first line on the screen, contains the Notes> prompt. Any time you type a command for VAX Notes, it will appear on this line. You can use command line editing the same way you do at the operating system level, that is, <CTRL/a> toggles you in and out of insert and overstrike mode, and the <UP ARROW> and <DOWN ARROW> keys allow you to recall previously typed commands.

The *message line,* the second line, initially contains a copyright notice, but once you have typed a complete command (including <RETURN>), it becomes blank unless there is a message for you before your first <RETURN> press. Any VAX Notes error messages are displayed here, as are other system messages, such as one telling you that a print job has finished printing or that you have new MAIL.[4]

4. Type EVE BUFFER MESSAGE to see these messages displayed in an EVE buffer.

```
Command_Summary

 If you are new to VAX Notes, type New_User for examples of how to use
 Getting Started commands, type Terms_and_Concepts for an explanation of
 your Notebook and other VAX Notes terms and concepts, or type a question
 mark (?) for a list of all VAX Notes commands.

 Getting Started Commands:

  ADD ENTRY               CLOSE                   DIRECTORY
  EXIT                    EXTRACT                 HELP
  NOTES (DCL command)     OPEN                    PRINT
  READ                    REPLY (or ANSWER)       WRITE

 The following topics have information on more advanced VAX Notes commands:

  Choosing_an_Editor      Information_Commands    Keypad
  Keyword_Commands        Logical_Names           Moderator_Commands
  Notebook_Commands       Other_Utilities         Reading_Notes
  Software_Licenses       Specifying_Notes        Subprocess_Commands

Help buffer  Press CTRL/z to leave prompts.

Press RETURN to continue...
```

**Figure 6.2 First Command Help Screen**

The *heading,* displayed in reverse video, simply designates what type of information is displayed in the columns below, in the viewing area. We explain these headings later.

What is contained in the *viewing area,* directly below the heading, depends on where you are in VAX Notes. In Figure 6.1, it contains a notification about a conference in your notebook. We explain "notebook" and "conference" in subsequent sections.

Now, let's summarize the on-line help available in VAX Notes. First, enter VAX Notes by typing NOTES <RETURN>. At the Notes> prompt, type HELP <RETURN>. Your screen will reconstruct with a help screen similar to that shown in Figure 6.2. Follow the prompts, and read the on-line help concerning the DIRECTORY/CONFERENCES command. When you have read all you want to, press <CTRL/Z>, and you will be returned to the first display screen.

There is another way to get on-line help within VAX Notes. This body of on-line help is related to the numeric keypad functions that are available in

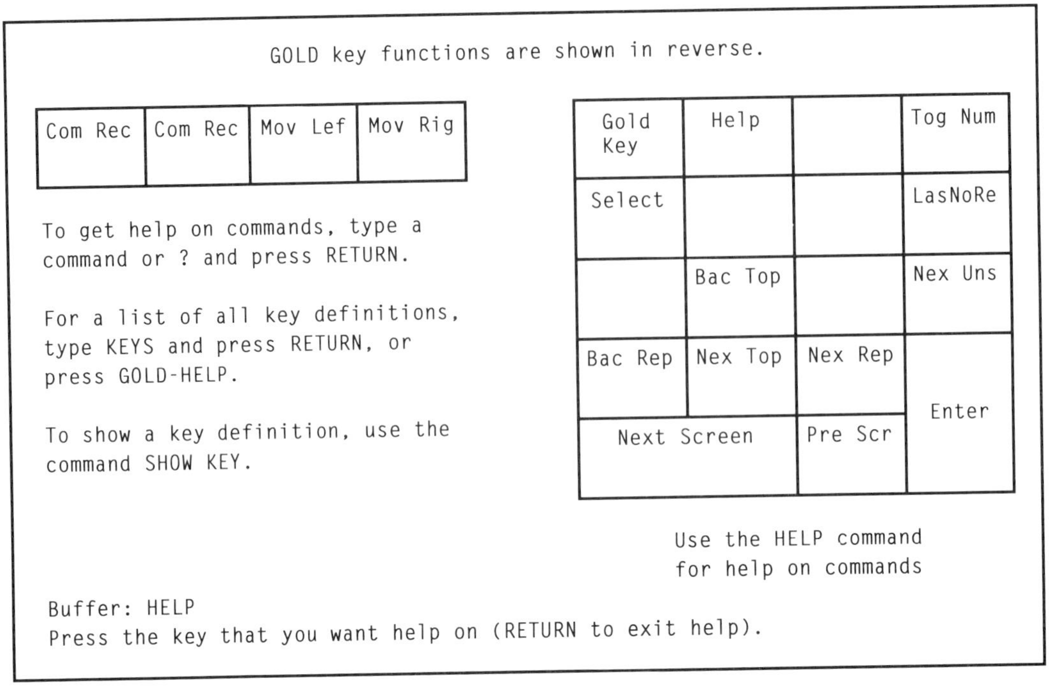

GOLD key functions are shown in reverse.

| Com Rec | Com Rec | Mov Lef | Mov Rig |
|---|---|---|---|

To get help on commands, type a command or ? and press RETURN.

For a list of all key definitions, type KEYS and press RETURN, or press GOLD-HELP.

To show a key definition, use the command SHOW KEY.

| Gold Key | Help | | Tog Num |
|---|---|---|---|
| Select | | | LasNoRe |
| | Bac Top | | Nex Uns |
| Bac Rep | Nex Top | Nex Rep | Enter |
| Next Screen | | Pre Scr | |

Use the HELP command for help on commands

Buffer: HELP
Press the key that you want help on (RETURN to exit help).

**Figure 6.3 Keypad Help Screen**

VAX Notes. To see this help, press the <PF2> key if you are using a VT100 series terminal or the <HELP> key if you are using a VT200 series terminal. Your screen will reconstruct in a manner similar to that shown in Figure 6.3 if you are using a VT100 series terminal. We are illustrating this here so that you will be aware of the existence of this on-line help, but we suggest that you do not use these keys until you have mastered the rest of the material in Section 6.3. Press <RETURN> to exit this part of VAX Notes on-line help. Leave VAX Notes by typing `EXIT` <RETURN> at the `Notes>` prompt, and read through the material on terminology, presented at the beginning of Section 6.3.2.

### 6.3.2 *Reading Notes in the SAMPLE_CONFERENCE*

Before you find out what is available on your system's implementation of VAX Notes, we need to discuss a small amount of VAX Notes terminology.

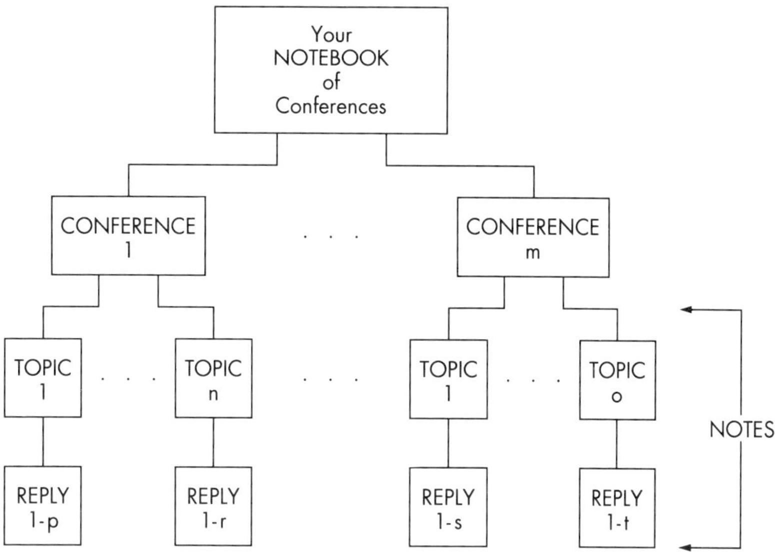


**Figure 6.4 Some VAX Notes Relations**

For a conceptual framework, suppose you teach chemistry in a public high school, and you and your colleagues in the other sciences are going to have a conference to produce a budget request for equipment. The subject of the conference would be "equipment purchases." If things were organized reasonably well, your conference would begin with a list of agenda items, for example, "equipment for biology," "equipment for chemistry," "equipment for physics." Each of these items would be discussed in turn. Someone would begin the discussion of a particular item and others would, in a sense, reply to the preceding remarks. As the conference proceeded, you or your colleagues might add new items (topics) to the agenda.

With this example in mind, let's generalize for VAX Notes. In VAX Notes, a *conference* is a set of discussions related to a particular subject, for instance, "equipment purchases." A *topic* is a particular agenda item, for example, "equipment for biology," "equipment for chemistry." Further discussion on a particular topic is called a *reply*. Both topics and replies are called *notes*. Figure 6.4 might be useful for keeping these relations in mind.

Now, enter the VAX Notes program by typing NOTES <RETURN>, and type UPDATE <RETURN> at the Notes> prompt. If the number of unseen notes (those you have not seen yet) has changed since you were last in VAX Notes, the UPDATE command brings this count up to date.

You will again see a screen similar to the first display screen (Figure 6.1). Your first display screen might differ a little from Figure 6.1, but this example should be similar enough for you to interpret your particular implementation of VAX Notes. Notice the viewing area. This lists the contents of your *notebook,* that is, the conferences that you are currently able to read. In our example, we are able to read only the notes in SAMPLE_CONFERENCE. Most installations of VAX Notes will have a SAMPLE_CONFERENCE. If yours does not, read the next two paragraphs and then skip to the beginning of Section 6.3.3, where the ADD ENTRY command is discussed.

Looking at the heading directly above the viewing area in Figure 6.1, we see that the conference name is designated as Entry Name. The number of Unseen notes is six and Last new note was added on June 5, 1989. There are also six Topics in this conference (this means that there are no replies to any of the topics). Update status indicates that you have not looked at any of these topics.

The viewing area of the first display screen contains the conferences that you are currently able to read. In VAX Notes terminology, the viewing area contains the conferences that are in your notebook, that is, it displays the contents of your notebook. Before reading a note, find out how many conferences are available on your system by typing DIRECTORY/CONFERENCES <RETURN> at the Notes> prompt. Figure 6.5 shows an example set of conferences. Yours will probably be different. If you see More. . . at the bottom of your viewing area, this means there are additional conferences available. Press <RETURN> to see the next screen. If you are using a VT200 series terminal, the <NEXT SCREEN> and <PREV SCREEN> keys can be used to good effect. If you are using a VT100 series terminal, the numeric keypad <0> key performs the NEXT SCREEN function and the numeric keypad <PERIOD> key performs the PREV SCREEN function. Take note of the different conferences available to you, and decide on one that you would like to read. But first, let's read a note in SAMPLE_CONFERENCE.

```
Notes>
--------------------------------------------------------------------------------
                    Directory of conferences on NOTES$LIBRARY:
 Conference file
>GENERAL
  Title:  General Discussion
  Moderator:  SWT::SYSTEM
  Created:  2-JUN-1989 13:35  46 topics, 52 notes  Updated:  15-JUL-1989 01:37

 INFO-AMIGA
  Title:  INFO-AMIGA
  Moderator:  SWT::SYSTEM
  Created:  10-MAR-1989 16:21  1080 topics, 274 notes  Updated:  15-JUL-1989 02:00

 INFO-CPM
  Title:  INFO-CPM
  Moderator:  SWT::SYSTEM
  Created:  13-MAR-1989 18:01 93 topics, 13 notes  Updated:  14-JUL-1989 01:46

 INFO-FUTURES
  Title:  INFO-FUTURES
More...
```

**Figure 6.5 Example Partial Directory of Conferences**

```
Notes>
--------------------------------------------------------------------------------
Note 1.0                         Usage guidelines                        No replies
SWT::SYSTEM                                              15 lines  5-JUN-1989 12:12
--------------------------------------------------------------------------------
   VAX Notes is a computer conferencing system that lets you conduct
   convenient online conferences among system users.

   Notes containing the following are specifically disallowed:

   - vulgar, obscene, racially oriented or sexually oriented language

   - libelous statements

   - the advocation of the deliberate violation of a federal or state law
     or a published university policy

   Users are responsible for any notes written from their account. Notes
   that are not in keeping with the above usage guidelines will be removed
   and the offending user will lose access to VAX Notes.
End of note
```

**Figure 6.6 Example Note 1.0 of SAMPLE_CONFERENCE**

```
Notes>
------------------------------------------------------------------------------
                            Introduction to VAX Notes
Created:  5-MAY-1989 11:39      6 topics        Updated: 5-JUN-1989 14:24

  Topic      Author          Date          Repl     Title
>     1      SWT::SYSTEM     5-JUN-1989       0     Usage guidelines
      2      SWT::SYSTEM     5-JUN-1989       0     VAX Notes terminology
      3      SWT::SYSTEM     5-JUN-1989       0     The DIRECTORY command
      4      SWT::SYSTEM     5-JUN-1989       0     Using your favorite editor
      5      SWT::SYSTEM     5-JUN-1989       0     Improving readability
      6      SWT::SYSTEM     5-JUN-1989       0     Suggestions and etiquette
End of requested listing
```

**Figure 6.7 Example Directory of SAMPLE_CONFERENCE**

Type OPEN SAMPLE_CONFERENCE <RETURN> at the Notes> prompt. Your screen will reconstruct with the first note in the conference named SAMPLE_CONFERENCE. Figure 6.6 shows note 1.0 of our example implementation of VAX Notes. The first note of your SAMPLE_CONFERENCE might differ, although most VAX Notes installations have a SAMPLE_CONFERENCE available.

Notice above the viewing area, in the heading, the designation Note 1.0. At this point, it is appropriate to discuss how notes are designated. The first note, the one to open the discussion (begin a new topic), is designated with a zero to the right of the period. The number to the left of the period is the topic number. If there were any replies to the note (topic), they would be designated by an appropriate number to the right of the period. For example, if there were three replies to this note (topic) 1.0 (it turns out there are not), then they would be numbered 1.1, 1.2, and 1.3.

Let's see exactly how many notes (topics and replies) there are in this SAMPLE_CONFERENCE. Type DIR *.* <RETURN> at the Notes> prompt. Figure 6.7 shows what occurs in our example implementation of VAX Notes: there are six topics with no replies to any of the topics. In the next section, we discuss an example where there are replies to topics.

If you want to read the note that begins topic 2, type READ 2 <RETURN>, or simply 2 <RETURN>. Figure 6.8 shows Note 2.0 of our example VAX Notes implementation.

```
Notes>
--------------------------------------------------------------------------------
Note 2.0                    VAX Notes terminology                     No replies
SWT::SYSTEM                                          30 lines  5-JUN-1989 14:21
--------------------------------------------------------------------------------
   VAX Notes is a computer-mediated conferencing system that lets you
   conduct online conferences or meetings.

   This sample conference has been provided to help you quickly get
   started using VAX Notes. It contains definitions of terms, ways to
   read notes, and helpful hints for running and participating in an
   online conference.

   A CONFERENCE has an agenda to focus discussion on a SUBJECT. Agenda
   items in a VAX Notes conference are called TOPICS, and participants'
   comments on these topics are called REPLIES. Topics and replies are
   referred to collectively as NOTES.

   A single topic with its associated replies is called a DISCUSSION.
   Topic notes are identified as n.0, where n is a number assigned
   sequentially by the system. Replies to a topic note are also numbered
13 more lines...
```

**Figure 6.8 Example Note 2.0 of SAMPLE_CONFERENCE**

Next, let's get back to the first display screen of VAX Notes (see Figure 6.1). You can leave SAMPLE_CONFERENCE, which you entered earlier with the OPEN SAMPLE_CONFERENCE command, in one of three ways: type CLOSE <RETURN>, or EXIT <RETURN>, or press the <CTRL/z> key.

Once the first display screen reappears, you may exit to the operating system either by typing EXIT <RETURN>, as mentioned earlier, or by pressing <CTRL/z>. If you want a break, leave VAX Notes and come back to Section 6.3.3 later; otherwise proceed to the discussion of how to read notes in other conferences.

### 6.3.3 Reading Notes in Other Conferences

We now discuss how to get access to other conferences. First make sure that you are in the first display screen of VAX Notes. This is the screen that appears when you type NOTES <RETURN> at the operating system prompt (see, for instance, Figure 6.1). Our example conference is taken from a particular implementation of VAX Notes, so your site's version of VAX Notes will undoubtedly have different conferences. However, the principles

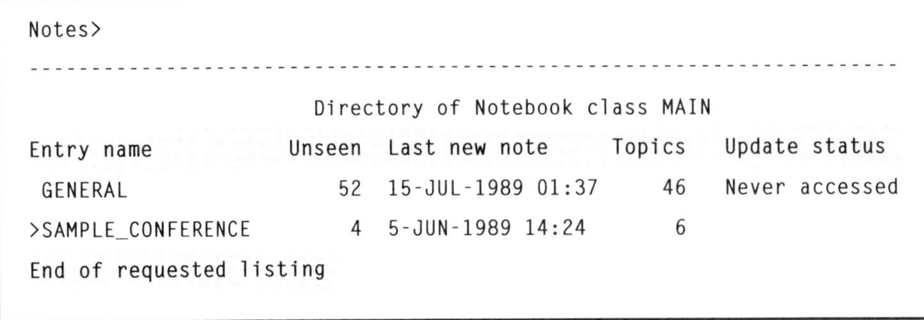
```
Notes>
--------------------------------------------------------------------------
                     Directory of Notebook class MAIN
Entry name          Unseen  Last new note      Topics   Update status
 GENERAL                52  15-JUL-1989 01:37      46   Never accessed
>SAMPLE_CONFERENCE       4  5-JUN-1989 14:24        6
End of requested listing
```

**Figure 6.9 First Display Screen after a Conference Has Been Added to the Notebook**

involved are simple, and you should be able to make the easy substitutions that are necessary.

Recall that previously, when you checked to see what conferences were available (by typing `DIRECTORY/CONFERENCES` <RETURN>), you saw the screen shown in Figure 6.5. Let's now see what is in the `GENERAL` conference. (*Note*: At this point, you should pick a conference from the list that appears on your own screen and substitute the name of that conference wherever we ask you to type `GENERAL`.) In order to be able to read the notes in a conference, you must have the conference in your notebook. To effect this, use the `ADD ENTRY` command. The format of the command is `ADD ENTRY` *conference-name,* so type `ADD ENTRY GENERAL` <RETURN> at the `Notes>` prompt. You will be informed that the conference you specified has been added to your notebook.

In order to verify this, type `UPDATE` <RETURN>. This will cause your first display screen to change and show the notes in each conference that are still unseen by you. In our example, the screen reconstructs as shown in Figure 6.9 (compare with Figure 6.1).

To look at the notes contained in the new conference that you added to your notebook, type `OPEN GENERAL` <RETURN>, substituting for `GENERAL` the name of the conference that you added. If you have not used the `ADD ENTRY` command as mentioned before, you will get a message such as "No Notebook entry". If you have added the conference to your notebook, your screen will reconstruct and show the first unseen note in the conference you opened.

```
Notes>

--------------------------------------------------------------------------------
Note 1.0           Introduction to the GENERAL conference            No replies
SWT::SYSTEM                                         15 lines   5-JUN-1989 11:57
--------------------------------------------------------------------------------
   This conference is for items of general interest for which a more
   specific conference has not been established.

   Notes containing the following are specifically disallowed:

   - vulgar, obscene, racially oriented or sexually oriented language

   - libelous statements

   - the advocation of the deliberate violation of a federal or state law
     or a published university policy

   Users are responsible for any notes written from their account. Notes
   that are not in keeping with the above usage guidelines will be removed
   and the offending user will lose access to VAX Notes.
End of note
```

**Figure 6.10 Example Note of a Newly Opened Conference**

Figure 6.10 shows that the first note in our example GENERAL conference regales folks with the guidelines for posting notes in this conference.

Notice that the heading now contains information about the conference where you are currently located, along with the topic and other related notes (if there are any).

Now, let's see what notes (topics and replies) are contained within this conference. Recall that the numbering convention for notes is that the number to the left of the period is the topic number and the number to the right of the period is the reply number (if any). To get a listing of all notes within a particular conference, type `DIR *.*` <RETURN>. If there is more than one screenful of notes, pressing <RETURN> will bring the next screen into view. On a VT200 series terminal, use the <PREV SCREEN> and <NEXT SCREEN> keys to move the information in the viewing area back and forth; on a VT100 series terminal, the numeric keypad <0> key serves the NEXT SCREEN function and the numeric keypad <PERIOD> key the PREV SCREEN function.

```
Notes>
--------------------------------------------------------------------------------
                                General Discussion
Created:  2-JUN-1989 13:35          46 topics          Updated: 15-JUL-1989 01:37
  Topic     Author             Date          Repl     Title
            SWT::CC_SIMMONS    11-JUL-1989   41.1     ut to swt connection
            SWT::MME4FF16      11-JUL-1989   41.2     In Case of Lack of UTto SWTSU
     42     SWT::MME4FF16      11-JUL-1989    10      SWTSU Computer Rumors, v2no7, M
            SWT::JB127DBC      11-JUL-1989   42.1     rumormongering
            SWT::MWOB5A        12-JUL-1989   42.2     Hate-Hate relationship
            SWT::RS01          12-JUL-1989   42.3     Amen!
>           SWT::JB12DBC       12-JUL-1989   42.4     Who turned out th' lights?
            SWT::DH71FE        12-JUL-1989   42.5     for want of a few 'D cells'..
            SWT::MWOB5A        12-JUL-1989   42.6     ASD:KLFUASDFNADSF
            SWT::CC_SIMMONS    13-JUL-1989   42.7     asdasdasd
            SWT::MWOB5A        13-JUL-1989   42.8     "a title for your reply"
            SWT::CC_SIMMONS    13-JUL-1989   42.9     LAKSDLSLDKFSAD
            SWT::MWOB5A        14-JUL-1989   42.10    The Greatest Show on Earth
     43     SWT::CC_BRYSON     12-JUL-1989    0       EVE and NOTES
     44     SWT::PHBA129E      12-JUL-1989    2       Program for Jowers
            SWT::DE71FE        12-JUL-1989   44.1     Action> Use Thermonuclear Devil
More...
```

**Figure 6.11 Example Listing from Applying the DIR *.* Command**

Figure 6.11 shows one of the screens that appears for our example GENERAL conference after DIR *.* <RETURN> has been typed. Notice that topic 42 has ten replies.

In order to read a note, type READ, followed by the note number and <RETURN>. In this example, we want to read reply 2 of topic 42, that is, note 42.2, so we type READ 42.2 <RETURN>. You may also type just the note number, followed by <RETURN> (for instance, 42.2 <RETURN>) to get the same result. Figure 6.12 shows the text of note 42.2 in our GENERAL conference example.

If you want to save the note you are currently reading to a file in your log-in directory, simply decide on a file specification and type EXTRACT *filespec* <RETURN>. Try this by typing EXTRACT EXAMPLE.TXT <RETURN>. After leaving VAX Notes, you can print out your file at the operating system level as discussed in Chapter 1.

```
Notes>

--------------------------------------------------------------------------------
Note 42.2          SWTSU Computer Rumors, v2no7, Monday, June 10          2 of 10
SWT::MWOB5A                                         18 lines    12-JUL-1989 08:08
                          -< Hate-Hate relationship >-

--------------------------------------------------------------------------------
    There was a system crash yesterday. Rumor has it out here on west
    campus that the power in MCS went down. I am really getting tired of
    this. I WANT A PUBLIC ERROR LOG SOMEPLACE THAT EXPLAINS WHAT IS
    HAPPENING WITH THE *&%^ COMPUTER! When something goes wrong, we should
    have a right to know what it was, why, and who was at fault. There
    are weird things happening to the system every day. Like someone
    de-activating SPSS while I am using it and not telling anyone, thus
    preventing any productive work in my office until it mysteriously
    appears again. Un-updated. And like the mysterious UP-DOWN
    relationship with userdir. My login script DEPENDS on some of those
    files. And whats the problem with ACLs and access to files I created
    two minutes ago? Half the time I log on TEGAN, I find out I can't get
    access to my own LOGIN.COM file! But hardly any problem on NYSSA or LEELA,
    however.

    I WANT AN ERROR LOG. Write your congress(wo)man today.

2 more lines...
```

**Figure 6.12 Example of Reading a Note**

Another option for obtaining a printed copy of a note is to send the current note directly to the printer from within VAX Notes without saving it to a file. You can do this by typing PRINT <RETURN> at any time after you have begun reading a particular note. The EXTRACT and PRINT commands in VAX Notes work similarly to those in the MAIL program.

Now, let's exit the notes and return to the operating system. As with SAMPLE_CONFERENCE or on-line help, you essentially "back out of" the program. Type CLOSE <RETURN> or EXIT <RETURN>, or press <CTRL/z>, and you will leave the notes you have been reading in the conference you opened. You will return to the first display screen (see Figure 6.9). Then, to reach the operating system, either type EXIT <RETURN> or press <CTRL/z>.

In summary, to read notes in a particular conference, proceed as follows:

1. If the conference is new to you (if not, skip to the next step), add it to your notebook by typing

   ADD ENTRY *conference-name* <RETURN>

   Then update your notebook by typing

   UPDATE <RETURN>

2. Access the conference by typing

   OPEN *conference-name* <RETURN>

3. Check out all the notes by typing

   DIR *.* <RETURN>

   (We discuss a less cumbersome method later.)

4. Read the notes you choose by typing

   READ *note-number* <RETURN> or *note-number* <RETURN>

5. When you are finished with the conference, move to the screen containing your notebook (the first display screen) by typing

   CLOSE <RETURN> or EXIT <RETURN>

   or by pressing <CTRL/z>

### 6.3.4 Writing, Replying to, and Deleting Notes

Now that you know how to add a conference to your notebook, open a conference, and read notes, let's discuss how to post your own notes. Some conferences might be set up so that only certain users can post notes, but if you are allowed to post notes, here is how you do it.

Open the conference in which you wish to post a note. If you want to start a new topic, type WRITE <RETURN>. Your screen will reconfigure to look like the screen in Figure 6.13. Type in your note, and when you are finished and want to post it, press <CTRL/z>. You will then be prompted for a title. Type one in, followed by <RETURN>, or simply press <RETURN> if you want the title field to be blank. You will be asked if everything is as you want it. Reply appropriately, and your note will either be posted or not, depending on your reply.

```
   New Note goes here...
[End of buffer]
```

**Figure 6.13 Default Editor Screen for Posting a Topic**

The default editor for posting notes in VAX Notes is EVE (see Chapter 2). In Section 6.3.5, we explain how to specify other editors.

If you are reading a note and want to reply to it, type `REPLY` <RETURN>. Your screen will reconstruct to show two windows, as in the EVE editor. The top window will contain the note to which you are replying, and the bottom window is for your reply. Figure 6.14 shows an example of a reply screen. When you have finished, press <CTRL/Z> and proceed as discussed for writing a new topic.

To delete a note that you have posted, open the appropriate conference and type `DELETE NOTE` *note-number* <RETURN>. As you might expect, this normally works only if *note-number* identifies one of your own notes.

### 6.3.5 Additional Commands in VAX Notes

Now that you know the fundamentals of how to use VAX Notes, there are several extras that might be very useful if you expect to be a regular user of the program. First, let's summarize how you check on notes in a conference that is in your notebook and that you read regularly:

1. Enter VAX Notes by typing

   `NOTES` <RETURN>

   at the operating system prompt.

2. Once in VAX Notes, reset the counters so that the number of unseen notes is brought up to date by typing

   `UPDATE` <RETURN>

```
    <<< Note 47.0 by SWT::MME4FF16 “Mr. Mike (Michael A. Moore)” >>>
         -< SWTSU Computer Rumors, v2no08, Sunday, July 16 >-
+-----------------------------------------------------------------+
| SWTSU Computer Rumors                         Volume 2 Number 08 |
|                        Sunday, July 16, 1989                     |
| “Efforts to improve a program’s user friendliness invariably lead |
|    to work in improving users’ computer literacy.” -Don Stokes    |
Buffer: NOTES$SCRATCH               | Read-only | Insert | Forward
    Reply goes here...

End of buffer

Buffer: NOTE$EDIT                   | Read-only | Insert | Forward
Press F10 or CTRL/Z to add your note.
```

**Figure 6.14 Example Reply Screen**

3. Choose a conference and prepare to read the first unseen note by typing

   `OPEN` *conference-name* <RETURN>

4. The first unseen note will be displayed as the conference is opened. Press <RETURN> until you get the message “No more replies”; then type

   `NEXT UNSEEN` <RETURN>

   This will take you to the next unseen note, if it exists. If there are no more, you will get the “No more new notes” message. If there is another unseen note, proceed as mentioned at the beginning of this step.

5. Exit the conference via

   `CLOSE` <RETURN>, `EXIT` <RETURN>, or <CTRL/z>

6. Exit VAX Notes by typing

   `EXIT` <RETURN> or <CTRL/z>

   if you are finished using VAX Notes, or go to step 3 if you want to read notes in another conference.

Now for some miscellaneous tips. At any time you are in a conference that you have opened, you can get a listing of all unseen notes by typing

DIR *.*/UNSEEN <RETURN>

If you do not want to read any more unseen notes but want to mark them as already having been seen, type

SET SEEN <RETURN>

while you have that particular conference open.

If VAX Notes gives you an error message, you can get an explanation of the error message by typing

SHOW ERROR <RETURN>

If you want to use the text editor EDT instead of EVE when you reply to notes or begin a new topic using the WRITE command, you should be aware of the SET PROFILE command. To make the change from EVE (the default) to EDT, type

SET PROFILE/EDITOR=EDT <RETURN>

From then on, you will get EDT edit functions. Similarly, if you want to use functions that are available in the WPS-PLUS editor, type

SET PROFILE/EDITOR=WPS <RETURN>

The SET PROFILE command is also useful for displaying more information alongside your user name in the heading portion of any note that you post. You can effect this by typing

SET PROFILE/PERSONAL_NAME="*string*" <RETURN>

Replace *string* with the desired information (up to 63 characters) between the double quotes. For example, you might want to display your name or telephone number next to your user name. After you type this command, whatever you chose for *string* will be displayed in the heading area every time you post a note.

When you have opened a conference, you can use the DIRECTORY command to get partial listings of the notes it contains. For example, DIR 1-5 <RETURN> will list the titles of topics 1 through 5, and DIR 1.*-5.* <RETURN> will list the titles of all the topics *and* replies for topics 1 through 5. A little experimentation should set this in mind.

**Table 6.1 Comparison of Commands in VAX Notes and BULLETIN**

| VAX Notes Command | BULLETIN Command | Description |
|---|---|---|
| DIR/CONFERENCE | DIR/FOLDER | Get a listing of folders |
| OPEN *conf-name* | SELECT *folder-name* | Access messages in a folder |
| WRITE | ADD | Add a message |
| REPLY | REPLY | Reply to a message |
| DELETE | DELETE/IMMEDIATE | Delete a message of yours |
| PRINT | PRINT | Print a message |
| EXTRACT | FILE or EXTRACT | Put a message in a file |

If you are in the VAX Notes program and want to get to the operating system but would like to return to where you left off in VAX Notes once you have finished with your other job, you can use the SPAWN command. For example, suppose you are reading the notes in a particular conference and someone begins to call you with the PHONE program. In this case, you could simply type SPAWN <RETURN>, followed by PHONE ANSWER <RETURN>. Once you have finished your phone conversation, return to where you were in VAX Notes by typing LO <RETURN> (for LOGOUT). The reason for using the LOGOUT command is that the SPAWN command causes another "process" to be started. This is similar to having logged in a second time. Indeed, when you log in, your "job" is called a process. So it makes sense that to stop your second process you should LOGOUT.

If you use VAX Notes regularly, you might remember that you saw a particular note covering some topic, but you cannot remember exactly what one it was. In these circumstances, the SEARCH command can be quite helpful. If you can remember any distinctive string, such as "terminal gossip", you need only type SEARCH "*terminal gossip*" <RETURN> and if the string is contained in the notes of the conference that you currently have opened, VAX Notes will find it and display the part of the note containing the first occurrence of that string. The general form of the command is

SEARCH "*string*"

where you provide the string.

Finally, if you would like to review the concepts that have been discussed in this section, enter the VAX Notes program, type HELP NEW_USER <RETURN>, and follow the prompts. Much of this material will be familiar to you, but you might pick up a few extra pointers.

### 6.3.6 *Comparing VAX Notes with the BULLETIN Program*

For those familiar with the BULLETIN program, Table 6.1 compares some VAX Notes commands and their analogues in BULLETIN.[5]

---

5. This comparison first appeared in VAX Notes on the Southwest Texas State University VAXcluster and is adapted here with the consent of its author, Michael A. Moore.

### *Entering and Exiting VAX Notes*

| *Command* | *Description* |
|---|---|
| NOTES | Issued at the operating system MYNODE$ prompt, this command enters VAX Notes. |
| EXIT | Issued at the NOTES> prompt, this command exits from the notebook screen to the operating system. |

These commands are issued from within VAX Notes at the NOTES> prompt.

| *Command* | *Description* |
|---|---|
| HELP | Enters the on-line help system of VAX Notes. Exit HELP by pressing <CTRL/Z>. |
| HELP *command* | Calls on-line help for the specified command. |
| HELP NEW_USER | Gives a brief introduction to VAX Notes. This is a good review tool. |
| <PF2> (VT100 series terminal) or <HELP> (VT200 series terminal) | Pressing this key calls on-line help for numeric keypad functions. Exit HELP by pressing <RETURN>. |
| ADD ENTRY *conference-name* | Adds *conference-name* to the list of conferences in your notebook. |
| CLOSE | Leaves the conference that you currently have open and returns you to your notebook. EXIT <RETURN> and <CTRL/Z> have the same effect. |
| DELETE ENTRY *conference-name* | Deletes *conference-name* from the list of conferences in your notebook. |
| DIRECTORY | If you have opened a conference, lists all the topics in that conference. If you are in your notebook, lists all the conferences in your notebook. |
| DIRECTORY *.* | If you have opened a conference, lists all the notes (topics and replies) in that conference. |
| DIRECTORY *.*/UNSEEN | If you have opened a conference, lists all the notes (topics and replies) in that conference that you have not yet seen. |
| DIRECTORY/CONFERENCES | Lists all conferences available in your VAX Notes implementation. |

`DIRECTORY/NOTEBOOK` Lists the entries in your notebook.

`EXIT` If you have opened a conference, this command has the same effect as `CLOSE`. If you have the contents of your notebook displayed, it returns you to the operating system. <CTRL/Z> has the same effect.

`EXTRACT` *filespec* Creates a file named *filespec* in your log-in directory containing the contents of note you are currently reading.

`EXTRACT/APPEND` *filespec*
Appends the contents of the note you are currently reading to the file named *filespec*.

`OPEN` *conference-name* Allows you to begin reading notes in *conference-name* if you have *conference-name* in your notebook. Otherwise, you must `ADD ENTRY` *conference-name* first.

`PRINT` Prints the contents of the note you are currently reading to the default printer, `SYS$PRINT`.

`READ` *topic-number.reply-number*
Displays the first screen of the specified note. Omitting `READ` and typing the note number alone has the same effect.

`REPLY` Initiates the process of replying to a note. It puts you into the reply editor, which has two windows. The top window contains the note to which you are replying, and the bottom window is for your reply.

`REPLY` *filespec* Has the same effect as `REPLY` except that you edit *filespec* in your reply window.

`SEARCH` "*string*" Allows you to search the conference that you currently have open for the first occurrence of *string*.

`SET SEEN` Sets all the unseen messages in the currently opened conference to the status of having been seen.

`SET PROFILE/EDITOR=EDT`
Allows the reply and write editor to be EDT rather than the default editor, EVE.

`SET PROFILE/PERSONAL_NAME=`"*string*"
Allows customization of your user name by displaying *string* alongside your user name in the heading of any note that you post.

`SHOW ERROR` Explains error messages produced by VAX Notes.

| | |
|---|---|
| SPAWN | Allows you leave VAX Notes, work at the operating system level, and return to where you left off in VAX Notes (by typing LO for LOGOUT). |
| UPDATE | Brings the unseen message count up to date. Also updates the list of conferences in your notebook if you have added any conferences since the last UPDATE. |
| WRITE | Enters the write editor and initiates the process of beginning a new topic. |
| WRITE *filespec* | Has the same effect as WRITE except that you edit *filespec* in the write editor. |
| <CTRL/z> | Performs the function of CLOSE when you are reading notes in a conference. In your notebook, performs the function of EXIT. In an editor, performs the usual <CTRL/z> function for that editor. |

### 6.3.8 Exercises for VAX Notes

1. At the operating system prompt, type NOTES <RETURN>. When you are in VAX Notes, type HELP <RETURN>. Follow the instructions, reading as many help screens as you like. At the Notes> prompt, type DIRECTORY/CONFERENCES <RETURN>. Pick the name of a conference that seems interesting. At the Notes> prompt, type HELP ADD <RETURN>. Using the information you get from help, add the name of a conference to your notebook.

2. Leave the VAX Notes program by pressing <CTRL/z> until you are back at the operating system. Enter the VAX Notes program again, as you did in Exercise 1. Following the same procedure as in Exercise 1, add another conference to your notebook. Exit VAX Notes.

3. Enter VAX Notes. Use the OPEN command to begin reading some of the notes in one of the conferences that you just added to your notebook. At the Notes> prompt, type HELP EXTRACT <RETURN>. After reading through the help, attempt to extract all the notes in topic 1 to a file named ONE.TXT. Leave the VAX Notes program and verify that you have in fact saved such a file to your log-in directory.

4. WRITE and REPLY are commands that allow you to add new notes to a conference. If your instructor has prepared a classroom exercise conference, open that conference and use the WRITE and REPLY commands

to add new notes to that conference. (Do not add notes to any other conference.) What can you say about the differences between the WRITE and REPLY commands?

5. Both WRITE and REPLY will insert text from a file in your directory into a note. For example, typing WRITE NOTE1.TXT would put the contents of NOTE1.TXT into a new note. If you have a classroom exercise conference, use this command to put the contents of your LOGIN.COM file into a new note.

6. At the Notes> prompt, type HELP DELETE NOTE <RETURN>. Then, as a favor to your classmates, delete the note you have just posted.

7. Type HELP DELETE ENTRY <RETURN>, and using the information you get from help, delete from your notebook a conference you are no longer interested in reading.

8. Typing EVE BUFFER MESSAGES <RETURN> will cause all error messages as well as any messages that came to your screen from other programs (such as MAIL) to appear in an EVE window while you are still in VAX Notes. Use this command, and the <DO> key in combination with the EVE WRITE command, to write these messages to a file named MESS1.TXT. Press <CTRL/Z> twice to return first to VAX Notes and then to the operating system. Verify that a new file named MESS1.TXT exists in your directory.

## 6.4 BITNET

You already know how to communicate with users on your own and other appropriately networked VAXclusters by way of MAIL, PHONE, and VAX Notes. You can even log in to other VAXclusters via the SET HOST *nodename* command (see Section 9.3), assuming you have a valid account on that particular node. Examples of such computer networks of VAX-clusters are networks within a state, educational system, or corporation.

We now discuss another type of computer network that provides a means of communication between "users."[6] This kind of computer network consists of many different brands of computers; they are not restricted to the VAX or other Digital Equipment Corporation computers. The key to networking

6. The term "user" is used advisedly here; we might actually be communicating with computer programs such as file servers (see Section 6.4.2).

such diverse machines lies in the individual computer systems' possessing software that allows them to interact appropriately with other network partners. There are several kinds of software for the VAX alone. In this discussion, we assume that your VAX/VMS system is using a software package named Jnet.[7] We refer to this configuration as a VAX/VMS/Jnet system.

We need to point out that, even with a VAX/VMS/Jnet system, these kinds of computer networks lead you into one of the least standardized and most rapidly changing areas for application of a VAX/VMS system. In this book, we have tried to be as clear and up-to-date as possible, but it might be that your system has been customized for some special purpose or that changes in the way the network operates occurred after this book was published. If things do not work precisely as we describe them, check with your local user services staff for the local or current "incantation" that will accomplish the task being described. This sounds like a nuisance, and it is. However, once you get past the initial hurdles, the rewards will outweigh the trouble.

There are many computer networks, often called Wide Area Networks (WANs), that connect diverse types of computers. BITNET is just one such network. A network of more than 2,500 computers, BITNET is composed of over 500 institutional members internationally, primarily institutions of higher learning and research centers. Many of the other WANs can be accessed using one of BITNET's *gateways*, which we discuss later in this section. At this point, it is sufficient to note that through BITNET gateways you can communicate with more than 3,600 computers throughout the world.

The chartered purpose of BITNET is to "facilitate the noncommercial exchange of information consistent with the academic purposes of its members." But what can *you* do with BITNET? Here are a few possibilities:

- Obtain files on many subjects from various computer systems by way of *file servers*.
- Be included on mailing lists of discussion groups on various subjects by way of *list servers*.
- Use other kinds of *servers*.

---

7. Jnet is a product of Joiner Associates Inc., 3800 Regent Street, P.O.B. 5445, Madison, Wisconsin 53705-0445; telephone: (608) 238-8637.

- Communicate by way of MAIL with other BITNET users.
- Communicate with users and server programs on other networks by way of BITNET gateways.

Before you proceed further, it is probably advisable to check with your local user services staff to see if your site places any particular restrictions on using BITNET, and whether there are some locally available files about BITNET. You might find that your system has a BITNET directory containing files on some of the latest BITNET newsletters, an up-to-date list of BITNET sites, and files on several other topics of interest. If such files exist, you should print out copies of them and at least scan them. You probably will not understand everything in the files, but as you progress through our discussion you should find that more and more of the information they offer becomes clear.

If your system uses the VAX Notes program, there might be a `NETWORK` conference as well as several conferences containing the mailings of particular mailing lists (discussed later in this section) that are available by way of BITNET.

### 6.4.1 BITNET Addresses and Sending BITNET Mail

Before we go into the details of how to take advantage of the many opportunities available through BITNET, we need to discuss a couple of terms. BITNET's terminology has no easy standardization. Although we are consistent in our use of terms throughout this discussion, you might find variations of these terms as you begin to use BITNET. For example, we use the term *node name* to mean a computer or set of computers in a "logical" group. You will sometimes see node names referred to as "domains" containing "nodes." The second bit of terminology that we use, *user name*, is the way the local computer system normally identifies a particular user.

BITNET *addresses* have the format

*username@nodename*

For example, the BITNET address of this book's authors is

`RS01@SWTEXAS`

`RS01` is the user name, and `SWTEXAS` is the node name of our VAXcluster. By now you can probably make a good guess as to what your own BITNET address is. Check with your local user services staff, however, just to make sure. BITNET node names can be different from local VAXcluster names.

As you become acquainted with BITNET, you will see that some node names contain periods. This is part of the domain-node arrangement. Just accept the addresses as they are given to you, and you will find, most of the time, that everything works out.

If you have an account on a VAX/VMS/Jnet system, sending mail to someone who has an account on a computer system attached to BITNET is an easy matter. For instance, to send mail to the authors at the preceding BITNET address, enter the MAIL program, as described in Section 6.2, and proceed as you normally would to send a MAIL message. Then fill in the `To:` field by typing

`JNET%"RS01@SWTEXAS"` <RETURN>

The quotation marks are *required*. The `JNET%` part of the address might have to be `BITNET%` or something else, depending on the specific installation at your site. If neither of these works, check with your local user services staff. Continue as you would to send any MAIL message.

### 6.4.2 Accessing the LISTSERV Program by MAIL

In this section, we discuss how to use a computer program called a server. This particular server, called "revised LISTSERV," was developed at École Centrale de Paris; we refer to it simply as LISTSERV.

In the current context, a *server* is a program that runs on a particular computer (just like any other job or process) and that can interpret a limited set of commands transmitted to it. A server can perform one or more functions, depending on its design. We will examine two functions that LISTSERV can perform: those of a *file server* and a *list server*.

#### 6.4.2.1 LISTSERV's File Server Function

A *file server* is a server whose basic function is to transmit files to users who request them. Users can request files by transmitting the appropriate command to the file server (over BITNET). One means of sending commands to a server is via MAIL. This is the only method that we discuss here.

The LISTSERV program resides on many computer systems connected to BITNET. We will send commands to the LISTSERV server at a node named BITNIC, an acronym for BITNET Network Information Center. We will

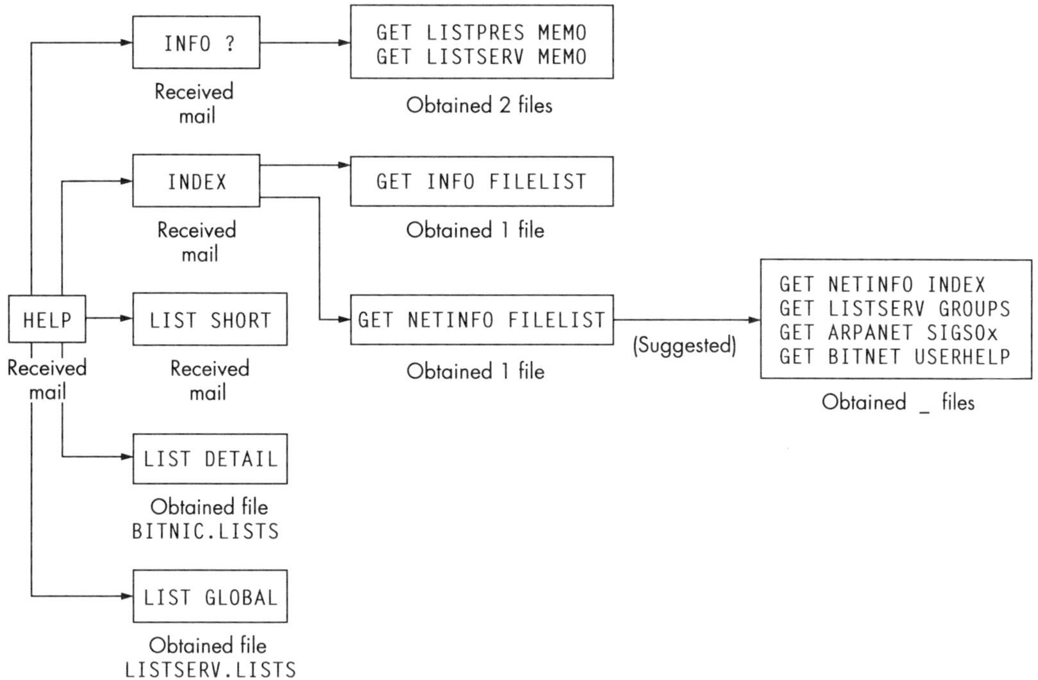


**Figure 6.15 Summary of Some LISTSERV Commands Discussed in Section 6.4**

mail our commands to the file server's user name, LISTSERV. Hence, the BITNET address is `LISTSERV@BITNIC`.

The first command we will send is one that is usually sent to any server when you know relatively little about its capabilities and functions, namely, `HELP`. So enter the MAIL program by typing `MAIL` <RETURN> at the operating system prompt, and at the `MAIL>` prompt type `SEND` <RETURN>. Respond to the prompts as you would in sending any MAIL message except that when you are prompted to fill in the `To:` field, type

`JNET%"LISTSERV@BITNIC"` <RETURN>

Again, the quotation marks are *required,* and the `JNET%` part might need to be something else, such as `BITNET%`. If neither `JNET%` nor `BITNET%` works, check with your local user services staff. When you get to the part of MAIL that prompts you to enter your message, type `HELP` and press <CTRL/Z> to indicate completion of the message. Thus, the command (message) that we have sent to `LISTSERV@BITNIC` is `HELP`, as indicated earlier.

This section describes commands that we will send to LISTSERV@BITNIC and the responses we get. Figure 6.15 summarizes the commands that we discuss. The commands are shown in boxes, and additional information appears below the boxes.

One thing to keep in mind is that when you have completed the process of sending your mail, the network might inform you of the network nodes through which your mail is passing as it travels to the file server LISTSERV@BITNIC. These system messages crossing your screen may be a bit disconcerting, so be prepared. If you decide that you don't want to see these messages every time you send BITNET mail, inserting the following line in your LOGIN.COM file should suppress them:

```
$ SET BROADCAST=(NOUSER1)
```

After a time, you will receive notification of new mail from LISTSERV@BIT-NIC. The amount of time that passes depends on many factors, for example, the load on the network, or a system between you and LISTSERV@BITNIC being off-line. Hence, you could get a mail reply in a matter of minutes or, in rare cases, a few days. Normally you can expect a reply within a few hours. When your reply does come, it will look something like the response shown in Figure 6.16.

Notice that the mail contains a list of most commonly used commands. Since we are just getting started, the INFO command seems a reasonable one to try. So get back into the MAIL program and, following the procedure just discussed, send the command

```
INFO ?
```

to LISTSERV@BITNIC. Figure 6.17 shows an example reply that you might expect to receive.

Figure 6.17 indicates that there are several information guides available. The items in parentheses are file specifications. The first string is the file name and the second is the file type. Notice that the file name and file type are separated by at least one blank space rather than by a period. This is the convention followed for file specifications when communicating with the LISTSERV program; it is required by the various computers running the program. These are not necessarily VAX computers, so it should not be surprising that the file name conventions are a bit different.

```
From:   BITNET%"LISTSERV@BITNIC"    "Revised List Processor" 22-JUL-1989 13:02:18.70
To:     RS01@SWTEXAS
CC:
Subj:   Output of your job "RS01"

Received:  From BITNIC(MAILER) by SWTNYSSA with Jnet id 6547
           for RS01@SWTEXAS; Sat, 22 Jul 89 13:02 CDT
Received:  by BITNIC (Mailer R2.03B) id 6546; Sat, 22 Jul 89 13:58:55 EST
Date:      Sat, 22 Jul 89 13:58:54 EST
From:      Revised List Processor (1.6a) <LISTSERV@BITNIC>
Subject:   Output of your job "RS01"
To:        RS01@SWTEXAS

>HELP

Revised LISTSERV version 1.6a -- most commonly used commands

Info          <topic|?>                 Get detailed information files
List          <Detail|Short|Global>     Get a description of all lists
SUBscribe     listname <full_name>      Subscribe to a list
SIGNOFF       listname                  Sign off from a list
SIGNOFF       * (NETWIDE                - from all lists on all servers
REView        listname <options>        Review a list
STats         listname <options>        Review list statistics
Query         listname                  Query personal distribution options
SET           listname options          Set personal distribution options
INDex         <filelist_name>           Obtain a list of LISTSERV files
GET           filename filetype         Obtain a file from LISTSERV
REGister      full_name|OFF             Tell LISTSERV about your name

There are more commands (AFD, FUI, PW, etc). Send an INFO REFCARD
for a complete reference card, or INFO ? for a list of available
documentation files.

Postmasters are:
 BITNIC Staff <BABEL@BITNIC>
 Michael Hrybyk <HRYBYK@BITNIC>
 Amanda Spiegel <SPIEGEL@BITNIC>
 NICMAINT@BITNIC
 POSTMAST@BITNIC
 Jim Conklin <CONKLIN@BITNIC>
 ROBINSON@BITNIC


Summary of resource utilization
-------------------------------

CPU time:        3.39 sec         Device I/O:   61
Overhead CPU:    0.27 sec         Paging I/O:    0
CPU model:       4361             DASD model: 3370
```

**Figure 6.16 Example of LISTSERV's Response to the HELP Command**

```
From:   BITNET%"LISTSERV@BITNIC"  "Revised List Processor" 22-JUL-1989 15:36:31.92
To:     RS01@SWTEXAS
CC:
Subj:   Output of your job "RS01"

Received:  From BITNIC(MAILER) by SWTNYSSA with Jnet id 7193
           for RS01@SWTEXAS; Sat, 22 Jul 89 15:36 CDT
Received: by BITNIC (Mailer R2.03B) id 7192; Sat, 22 Jul 89 16:33:21 EST
Date:        Sat, 22 Jul 89 16:33:18 EST
From:        Revised List Processor (1.6a) <LISTSERV@BITNIC>
Subject:     Output of your job "RS01"
To:          RS01@SWTEXAS

> INFO ?

List of information guides available from LISTSERV@BITNIC:

PResent      (LISTPRES MEMO    )     Presentation of LISTSERV for new users
GENintro     (LISTSERV MEMO    )     General information about Revised LISTSERV
REFcard      (LISTSERV REFCARD)      Command reference card
KEYwords     (LISTKEYW MEMO    )     Description of list header keywords
AFD          (LISTAFD  MEMO    )     Description of Automatic File Distribution
FILEs        (LISTFILE MEMO    )     Description of the file-server functions
LPunch       (LISTLPUN MEMO    )     Description of the LISTSERV-Punch file format
JOB          (LISTJOB  MEMO    )     Description of the Command Jobs feature
DISTribute   (LISTDIST MEMO    )     Description of Relayed File Distribution
COORDinate   (LISTCOOR MEMO    )     Information about LISTSERV Coordination
FILEOwner    (LISTFOWN MEMO    )     Information guide for file owners
DATABASE     (LISTDB   MEMO    )     Description of the database functions

The following files are restricted to list owners:

LINKing      (LISTLINK MEMO    )     Guidelines for linking list servers together
OWNers       (LISTOWNR MEMO    )     Description of list-owners commands
PUT          (LSVPUT   EXEC    )     An exec to facilitate sending PUT commands

You should order the PResentation or GENintro manual
if you are new to LISTSERV.

Summary of resource utilization
-------------------------------

CPU time:           0.80 sec         Device I/O:    4
Overhead CPU:       0.03 sec         Paging I/O:    1
CPU model:          4361             DASD model: 3370
```

**Figure 6.17 Example of LISTSERV's Response to the INFO? Command**

The first two lines are related to available information guides:

```
PResent  (LISTPRES MEMO ) Presentation of LISTSERV for new users
GENintro (LISTSERV MEMO ) General information about Revised LISTSERV
```

Let's request the two files (using VMS naming conventions) LISTPRES.MEMO and LISTSERV.MEMO from LISTSERV@BITNIC. Use MAIL to send the following requests to LISTSERV@BITNIC:

```
GET LISTPRES MEMO
GET LISTSERV MEMO
```

You have just used the GET command. It is mentioned in the mail that you received when you sent the HELP command to LISTSERV@BITNIC (see Figure 6.16). The format is GET *filespec*, and as you might guess, it just tells the file server to send (GET) you the specified file. Notice that the LISTSERV program can interpret more than one command at a time, so you only had to send one MAIL message to receive two files. Some file servers require that you send only one command at a time. As you branch out and begin to communicate with file servers other than LISTSERV, be aware of this possibility.

Eventually you will be notified by MAIL that LISTSERV@BITNIC is sending along the files that you requested. If you are not notified while you are still logged in, you will probably get a message like this the next time you log in:

```
Last interactive login on Sunday, 23-JUL-1989 08:59
Last non-interactive login on Sunday, 23-JUL-1989 09:00
  You have 1 new Mail messages.
  Type RECEIVE to process 2 new network files.
```

You certainly will have no problem reading your mail. The text of your mail from LISTSERV@BITNIC will look something like the following:

```
> GET LISTPRES MEMO
File "LISTPRES MEMO" has been sent to you in Punch format.

> GET LISTSERV MEMO
File "LISTSERV MEMO" has been sent to you in Punch format.
```

But what is the meaning of "Type RECEIVE to process 2 new network files"? You will have to use another utility program available on the VAX/VMS/Jnet system, which allows you to get the network files that LISTSERV@BITNIC has placed in a system storage area. This utility program's namc is RECEIVE.[8]

---

8. RECEIVE has a very useful companion command, which is also provided by Joiner Associates. This command is SEND. It allows you to send unreadable files such as those with .EXE or .OBJ extensions. These files can be sent to users on the same node or users on remote computers via BITNET. Assuming your node has subscribed to the Jnet package from Joiner Associates, you can learn about SEND and its syntax by typing HELP SEND <RETURN>.

The two files that you requested, LISTPRES.MEMO and LISTSERV.MEMO, are not sent directly to you as MAIL messages are. Instead, they are placed in a temporary storage or holding area on your system. You must decide whether you really want these files. If you do, use the RECEIVE program to transfer the files from the system storage area to your own directory.

How long these files stay in the temporary storage area depends on the decisions of your system manager. The files might stay there no more than a few days or much longer. In any case, it is not a good idea to leave these files in storage indefinitely.

To get into the RECEIVE program, type RECEIVE <RETURN> at the operating system prompt. You will be notified of the files that have arrived for you, and the prompt will change to RECEIVE>. Here's a sample of what you can expect to see:

```
Files received for RS01
Source file      Class  Node User        Date         Time  Records
LISTSERV.MEMO;2  PUN N  BITNIC LISTSERV 23-Jul-1989 03:06       777
LISTPRES.MEMO;1  PUN N  BITNIC LISTSERV 23-Jul-1989 03:05       398
RECEIVE>
```

At the RECEIVE> prompt, type HELP <RETURN>. Notice that several commands are available. Scan the help available on the commands DIRECTORY, TYPE, RECEIVE, COPY, and DELETE. Try the DIRECTORY command by typing DIRECTORY <RETURN>. As you see, it just lists the network files that have arrived for you. Next type TYPE LISTPRES.MEMO <RETURN>. This causes the file LISTPRES.MEMO to be displayed on your screen. The file is long, so if you get tired of watching it scroll across your screen, press <CTRL/O> to turn off this output.

The commands RECEIVE and COPY may both be used to transfer a copy of a network file from the temporary storage area to your own directory. In concept, COPY works like the VMS COPY command, and RECEIVE works like the VMS RENAME command. Let's demonstrate both of these commands. First, type COPY LISTPRES.MEMO <RETURN> and then RECEIVE LISTSERV.MEMO <RETURN>. You will be notified that both files have been placed in your VMS directory. Now, at the RECEIVE> prompt, type DIR <RETURN>. You will see that LISTPRES.MEMO is still available in the storage area, but LISTSERV.MEMO is not.

Thus, you see the difference between the COPY and the RECEIVE commands. The COPY command keeps the original file in your system's storage area for network files, and the RECEIVE command does not. Save some system space for network files by typing DELETE *.* <RETURN>.[9] If you type DIR <RETURN> now, you will see that there are no network files for you to obtain using the RECEIVE program. Leave the RECEIVE program by typing EXIT <RETURN>.

Once back at the operating system, check your current directory. You will have two new files: LISTPRES.MEMO and LISTSERV.MEMO. Print and scan these two files. Much of their contents will be pretty obscure to you at this time. However, as we progress through this BITNET section, you should review the files from time to time. You will find them increasingly enlightening. We especially recommend the "Terminology and General Information. . ." and "GENCOM" parts of LISTSERV.MEMO. In the "GENCOM" part, you will find a description of commands discussed in this section.

You now know how to ask LISTSERV@BITNIC to send you files via the GET *filespec* command, and you can transfer the files to your own directory, once they arrive at your site, by using the RECEIVE program. But you still need to know which files are available; a whole wealth of files are available from a LISTSERV file server. The MAIL message that you received in response to the HELP command (see Figure 6.16) contains an appropriate command: INDEX. The line related to this command is

```
INDex      <filelist_name>   Obtain a list of LISTSERV files
```

The format of the command is INDEX *filelist-name*. Since you do not know the name of any file list, enter the MAIL program and send just the following command to LISTSERV@BITNIC:

```
INDEX
```

LISTSERV@BITNIC will respond with a MAIL message telling you that a file named LISTSERV.FILELIST is being sent. After a while, you will be notified that a network file is available to you. Use the RECEIVE program, as discussed, to transfer this file into your directory and print it out.

---

9. This command must be issued at the RECEIVE> prompt, not at the operating system MYNODE$ prompt.

The file named LISTSERV.FILELIST is a little hard to read because it was initially written using more than 80 columns. Since files sent over BITNET are restricted to a width of 80 columns, the extra columns of text have been wrapped to the next line. With a little effort, though, you can see that several files describing particular file lists are available. A *file list* is a set of files on a particular subject. For example, the two lines

```
104/2/ INFO FILELIST ALL LMC V 102 103 89/06/22 09:46:23 List
of information files about LISTSERV
```

indicate that a file named INFO.FILELIST describes the files contained in the INFO file list. Similarly, the lines

```
101/2/ NETINFO FILELIST ALL DOC V 114 631 89/07/21 16:15:32
Directory of BITNET Info & Other Help
```

indicate that a file named NETINFO.FILELIST contains a listing of files in the NETINFO file list, that is, a "Directory of BITNET Info & Other Help."

Obtain copies of these two files by entering the MAIL program and sending the following message (commands) to LISTSERV@BITNIC:

```
GET INFO FILELIST
GET NETINFO FILELIST
```

The file that we have been reading, LISTSERV.FILELIST, indicates that there are several other file lists available from LISTSERV@BITNIC. How would you get more information on the files contained in these file lists? Also, a file obtained from a LISTSERV program and residing on another computer system might have a substantially different set of file lists. You might want to check this out by issuing the commands we have already discussed to another LISTSERV program, for example, LISTSERV@RUTVM1. If you are losing track of the files that you have been requesting, refer to Figure 6.15.

Eventually LISTSERV@BITNIC will send you a mail message indicating that the files INFO.FILELIST and NETINFO.FILELIST are being sent. When you are notified of their arrival at your site, use the RECEIVE program to transfer them to your own directory. Print them out and scan their contents. As you look through the file INFO.FILELIST, notice that you have already obtained two of the listed files: LISTPRES.MEMO and LISTSERV.MEMO.

In looking through the file NETINFO.FILELIST, notice the following lines near the beginning of the file:

```
101/2/ NETINFO INDEX ALL DOC V 73 685 89/06/28 13:00:46 This
file in an easier to read format
```

Since NETINFO.FILELIST has a lot of useful information in it, you might want to get a copy of the NETINFO.INDEX file, which has "an easier to read format." We continue to refer to NETINFO.FILELIST for people who do not want to gather too many files, but our remarks should apply equally well to the more easily read NETINFO.INDEX. One file in the NETINFO file list that has some useful introductory material concerning BITNET is noted in NETINFO.FILELIST. Its name is BITNET.USERHELP. If you want to build on what you are learning in this section, get a copy of this file also.

This concludes our introduction to LISTSERV@BITNIC as a file server. As we have already observed, the LISTSERV program resides on many computers, not just at BITNIC. These other installations can contain their own sets of interesting file lists. To get some idea of where other implementations of LISTSERV are, obtain a copy of the file LISTSERV.GROUPS (also noted in NETINFO.FILELIST). We will use the file LISTSERV.GROUPS in our discussion of LISTSERV's list server function, so have a copy of it handy as you begin to read the next section.

### 6.4.2.2 *LISTSERV's List Server Function*

There are many kinds of BITNET-related lists (we sometimes refer to these as mailing lists) to which you can have your name attached. (By "name" we mean your BITNET address and possibly your actual name.) One kind of list helps users communicate with members of a discussion group on some topic; another ensures that you will receive all sorts of electronics magazines, digests, and the like.

How do you sign up on a particular list, and which lists are available? One way to sign up is via a list server. A *list server* is a server that keeps updated mailing lists of subscribers (participants) and that is used for sending mail on a particular topic to those subscribing to the list.

We discuss here how to use the list server function of the LISTSERV server. LISTSERV is not the only server available on BITNET, but it is one of the most prevalent. As you branch out in your use of BITNET, you might have to deal with other servers that have a somewhat different way of operating.

First, let's discuss how to find out which lists are available. Recall the `LIST` command, given in the first command summary that you received from sending the `HELP` command to `LISTSERV@BITNIC` (see Figure 6.16). Three options are available with this command: `SHORT`, `DETAIL`, and `GLOBAL`. Send these three commands to `LISTSERV@BITNIC` by entering MAIL and sending the following message (commands):

```
LIST SHORT
LIST DETAIL
LIST GLOBAL
```

The first two commands (`LIST SHORT` and `LIST DETAIL`) give information concerning mailing lists that are available from the LISTSERV program residing on the BITNIC node. `LIST SHORT` results in mail that gives a "short" list of mailing lists to which you can subscribe from `LISTSERV@BITNIC`. Figure 6.18 shows the relevant part of this mail.

The `LIST DETAIL` command causes a file named `BITNIC.LISTS` to be sent. You will need to use the RECEIVE utility to transfer this file to your directory from your system's network file storage area. `BITNIC.LISTS` is just an amplification of the mailing lists to which you can subscribe using `LISTSERV@BITNIC`.

To demonstrate that different lists are available from LISTSERV programs residing on nodes other than BITNIC, send the same two commands, `LIST SHORT` and `LIST DETAIL`, to `LISTSERV@RUTVM1`.

Since many more mailing lists are available from LISTSERV servers residing on other computer systems (nodes), we need a way of easily getting more information. This is where the third command, `LIST GLOBAL`, is helpful. This command causes a file named `LISTSERV.LISTS` to be sent to you. The first part of the file `LISTSERV.LISTS` states that it is a "List of all LISTSERV lists known to `LISTSERV@BITNIC` on . . .". Figure 6.19 shows a fragment of the `LISTSERV.LISTS` file.

Notice that only the list titles are given in the third column, so if you are not sure of the topics covered in a particular list, there is no amplification. One way you can usually get such amplification is to look at the file

```
> LIST SHORT
APPLICAT  Applications under BITNET
BITNEWS   BITNET Network News List
BITTECH   Meeting attendees
CCNEWS    Campus Computing Newsletter Editors
CYBER-L   CYBER List
DOMAIN-L  Domains Discussion Group
EARNTECH  EARN Technical Group
FINTF     Name of list:  FinTF
FUTURE-L  BITNET Futures List
GGUIDE    BITNET User's Guide List
HEDSDIRS  HEDSDIRS Mailing List
IBM-NETS  BITNIC IBM-NETS List
INFONETS  Info-Nets List
JNET-L    JNET Discussion Group
LIAISON   Network Site Liaisons
LICENSE   Software Licensing List
LINKFAIL  Link failure announcements
MAIL-L    Mail Transfer/User Agents
MON-L     BITNET Monitoring List
NETMON-L  Discussion of NETMON
NODMGT-L  Node Management Discussion
POLICY-L  Discussion about BITNET policies
RSCSV2-L  The RSCS version 2 List
SIMULA    The SIMULA Language List
SPIRES-L  SPIRES Conference List
STD-L     BITNET Standards List
TECH-L    TECH-L List
TECHNEWS  BITNET Technical News List
TRAFIC-L  Traffic Monitoring List
TRANS-L   File Transfer List
UG-L      Usage Guidelines List
USRDIR-L  User Directory List
XMAILER   The Columbia Mailer List
X400-L    BITNET X.400 Discussion
```

**Figure 6.18 Part of the Mail from LISTSERV@BITNIC in Response to the LIST SHORT Command**

LISTSERV.GROUPS. Recall that you were asked to get a copy of this file at the end of Section 6.4.2.1. Figure 6.20 contains a fragment of LISTSERV.GROUPS, giving an amplification of the AIDSNEWS mailing list.

So, working with the LISTSERV.LISTS and LISTSERV.GROUPS files, you can decide to which mailing lists you want to subscribe. To subscribe to a mailing

```
......
Network-wide ID    Full address         List title
---------------    ------------         ----------
......
AGRIC-L            AGRIC-L@UGA          Agriculture Discussion
AIDS               AIDS@EBOUB011        (Peered) Sci.Med.AIDS Newsgroup
                   AIDS@RUTVM1          (Peered) Sci.Med.AIDS Newsgroup
                   AIDS@USCVM           (Peered) Sci.Med.AIDS Newsgroup
AIDS_INTL          ICECA@RUTVM1         Intl Committee for Elec Comm on AIDS
AIDSNEWS           AIDSNEWS@EBOUB011    (Peered) AIDS/HIV News
                   AIDSNEWS@RUTVM1      (Peered) AIDS/HIV News
                   AIDSNEWS@USCVM       (Peered) AIDS/HIV News
AILIST             AILIST@DBOTU111      (Peered) Artificial Intelligence List
                   AILIST@FINHUTC       (Peered) Artificial Intelligence List
                   AILIST@NDSUVM1       (Peered) AILIST Artificial Intelligence List
                   AI-L@TAUNIVM         (Peered) Artificial Intelligence List
......
```

**Figure 6.19 Part of the LISTSERV.LISTS File Obtained via the LIST GLOBAL Command**

```
......
List: AIDSNEWS@RUTVM1
Coordinator: Michael Smith (MNSMITH@UMAECS)
  AIDS Treatment News reports on experimental and alternative treatments
  available now. It collects information from medical journals, from
  interviews with scientists, physicians and other health practitioners
  and persons with AIDS or ARC. This list does not recommend particular
  therapies, but seeks to increase the options available. Ethical and
  public-policy issues of AIDS treatment research will also be examined.
  This list is also used for discussion of AIDS and related issues.
  ARPAnet sites may subscribe by sending mail to the coordinator.
......
```

**Figure 6.20 Part of the LISTSERV.GROUPS File**

list with a LISTSERV server, look in the `Full address` column of `LISTSERV.LISTS` (see Figure 6.19) and pick the node name from this address. Recall that the node name is the part following the @ symbol. Next, note the name in the `Network-wide ID` column. Then send the following command via MAIL to `LISTSERV@`*nodename* (the node name you just located):

`SUB Network-wide_ID` *your-name*

For example, if you wanted to subscribe to the `AIDSNEWS` mailing list, you would send the following command via MAIL to `LISTSERV@RUTVM1`:

`SUB AIDSNEWS` *your-name*

In most instances, you will eventually receive mail telling you that you have been added to the mailing list. If you later decide you want to be taken off a particular mailing list, follow the same procedure as when you subscribed except that the message you send to LISTSERV@*nodename* is

```
SIGNOFF Network-wide_ID
```

In our example of AIDSNEWS, you would send the following message to LISTSERV@RUTVM1:

```
SIGNOFF AIDSNEWS
```

For the AIDSNEWS list, there are actually two other nodes (EB0UB011 and USCVM) to which we could have sent our SUB command (see Figure 6.19). You should send your subscription request to just one node.

If you want to contribute to the mailings distributed by a particular mailing list, simply send mail to the address given in the Full address column of LISTSERV.LISTS. In our AIDSNEWS example, you could send your contribution to one of the three addresses given, e.g., AIDSNEWS@RUTVM1.

Notice in Figure 6.19 that some mailing lists are labeled "Peered". This usually means that a "moderator" reads the messages before they are circulated. If the "Peered" designation is missing, the mail is usually forwarded to everyone on the mailing list as it arrives at the list server.

One word of caution: Remember that when you subscribe to or sign off from a particular mailing list, you send your mail to LISTSERV@*nodename*, where *nodename* is given in the Full address column of LISTSERV.LISTS. However, to send a message to everyone on a particular mailing list, you send to the "full address" given in the second column of LISTSERV.LISTS. If you get mixed up and send your subscription or resignation message to the "full address" in the second column, it could happen that everyone on the mailing list will get your message but the LISTSERV program, to which you must direct this information, will not.

The correspondence between LISTSERV.GROUPS and LISTSERV.LISTS is not one-to-one. In reading LISTSERV.GROUPS, you might find some variations from the instructions given here for subscribing. So read carefully when you find a mailing list that interests you.

### 6.4.3 *Other Servers on BITNET*

As mentioned earlier, there are other servers on BITNET besides the LISTSERV server. To learn about their capabilities, start at the same place you did with `LISTSERV@BITNIC`. Use MAIL to send the command `HELP` to the server and proceed from there, based on the response you get. Some other servers to explore are

- `INFO@NSF`
- `UMNEWS@MAINE`
- `VMSSERV@UBVMSD`

As you expand your knowledge of what is available from BITNET, you should consider getting the following files, which are associated with the `NETINFO` file list (`NETINFO.FILELIST`):

- `USING.SERVERS`
- `BITNET.SERVERS`
- `NETSERV.HELPFILE`
- `DATABASE.HELPFILE`
- `BITNET.LINKS`
- `NODES.INFO1` and `NODES.INFO2`
- `NSFNET.NETWORK`

### 6.4.4 *Gateways to Other Networks*

Several other national and international wide area networks (WANs) exist in addition to BITNET. Some of the other WANs are

- ARPANET
- CSNET
- UNIDATA
- USAN

The file `NSFNET.NETWORK` (available from `LISTSERV@BITNIC`) gives a brief description of these WANs.

Thus, if you find that a colleague to whom you wish to send mail is not on BITNET, you still have at least one more possibility for communication, that is, to get in touch with another network through a BITNET *gateway*. Usually this requires special preparation of your mail message in the form of "headers." These headers give special required information to the programs that handle your mail as it makes its way to its destination. One of the easiest ways to prepare your message is to use a special gateway mail utility. At this point, check with your local user services staff to find out if your system has such a gateway mail utility and which networks besides BITNET you can access via gateways.

An example of a gateway mail utility is a program called GMAIL. GMAIL functions like VMS MAIL with respect to its commands. If GMAIL is available on your system, you should have little trouble sending mail to other networks that are available to you, provided you have the recipient's correct address. The file `GMAIL.INFO` from `LISTSERV@BITNIC` should give you more information on GMAIL. At present, distribution information on GMAIL can be obtained from Ed Miller, `GMAIL@SLACTWGN`, or `ESMP09@SLACTWGN`.

File servers and list servers are also available on these other networks. One set of files describing servers available on BITNET as well as on other networks is the set of files `ARPANET.SIGS01` through `ARPANET.SIGS07` (see the file `NETINFO.FILELIST`, where they are noted). These files are available from `LISTSERV@BITNIC`.

At present, you can also get yet another "list of lists" if you have access to a program called FTP. Check with your local user services staff for the FTP status of your site. If you do have access to FTP, you can get a set of files named `INTEREST-GROUPS-1.TXT` through `INTEREST-GROUPS-9.TXT`. Figure 6.21 shows an example FTP session for obtaining `INTEREST-GROUPS.TXT`. When you are prompted for a password, any string will do, but some people think that your BITNET address is the preferred response. Your responses are shown in color in Figure 6.21.

It is not our intention to discuss in detail how to use the FTP program. However, at this writing, the `INTEREST-GROUPS.TXT` files noted here contain a wealth of up-to-date information that is unavailable (as far as we know) from any BITNET file server.

### 6.4.5 Additional Tips on Using BITNET

As your use of BITNET increases, you will likely find that typing some of the lengthy addresses can be inconvenient as well as error-prone. There is a

```
VMS User FTP version 1.08 13-Nov-1986
[Establishing connection to DECnet/TCP gateway]
FTP> OPEN SRI-NIC.ARPA
220 SRI-NIC.ARPA FTP Server Process 5Z(47)-6 at Fri 28-Jul-89 15:31-PDT
[Now login using the USER command]
FTP> USER ANONYMOUS
Password:
230 User ANONYMOUS logged in at Fri 28-Jul-89 15:32-PDT, job 20.
FTP> CD NETINFO:
250 Connected to TS:<NETINFO>.
FTP> DIR IN*.*
200 Port 9.102 at host 128.83.1.26 accepted.
150 List started.
TS:<NETINFO>
INTEREST-GROUPS.TXT.30,31
INTEREST-GROUPS-1.TXT.16
INTEREST-GROUPS-2.TXT.16
INTEREST-GROUPS-3.TXT.16
INTEREST-GROUPS-4.TXT.16
INTEREST-GROUPS-5.TXT.16
INTEREST-GROUPS-6.TXT.16,17
INTEREST-GROUPS-7.TXT.16,17
INTEREST-GROUPS-8.TXT.12,13
INTEREST-GROUPS-9.TXT.3
INTERNET.GATEWAYS.10001
INTERNET.PINGING.13
INTERNET-NUMBER-TEMPLATE.TXT.19,20
2 buffers, 365 bytes, 0 index
365 bytes in 4.0 seconds = 726 bits/second
226 Transfer completed.
FTP>
200 Port 9.103 at host 128.83.1.26 accepted.
150 ASCII retrieve of <NETINFO>INTEREST-GROUPS-1.TXT.16 (6 pages) started.
17 buffers, 13677 bytes, 0 index.
13677 bytes in 13.9 seconds = 7894 bits/second
226 Transfer completed. 13677 (8) bytes transferred.
FTP> EXIT
221 QUIT command received. Goodbye.
```

**Figure 6.21 Example FTP Session for Obtaining the File INTEREST-GROUPS.TXT**

way to use abbreviations by putting appropriate lines in your LOGIN.COM file. Consider, for example, the following two lines:

```
$ DEFINE MSMITH "JNET%" "MNSMITH@UMAECS""
$ DEFINE ATNSERV "JNET%" "LISTSERV@RUTVM1""
```

The first line allows you to type MSMITH instead of JNET%"MNSMITH@UMAECS" in the To: field if you want to send MAIL to the coordinator of the AIDSNEWS list. Similarly, the second line allows you to type ATNSERV instead of JNET%"LISTSERV@RUTVM1" to send MAIL to LISTSERV@RUTVM1. In general, the form of the DEFINE command is

$ DEFINE *abbrev* "JNET$" "*username@nodename*""

where you supply the information for the categories shown in italics.

This abbreviation method works in MAIL as well as in GMAIL (if GMAIL is installed at your site). It is an example of defining logical symbols. For more information on this and other DCL topics, see Bibliography [1].

### LISTSERV Commands

These commands are issued as messages via MAIL. The `To:` field contains a BITNET address of the form `JNET%"LISTSERV@`*nodename*`"`, where the double quotes are required and *nodename* is a computer system on BITNET that runs the LISTSERV program. (The `JNET%` part may vary; for instance, `BITNET%` could be required. Check with your local user services staff if neither name works.)

Figure 6.15 summarizes the LISTSERV commands and files discussed in the BITNET section. For additional information on LISTSERV commands, see Figure 6.16 and the files `LISTPRES.MEMO`, `LISTSERV.MEMO`, and `BITNET.USERHELP`.

| *Command* | *Description* |
|---|---|
| `HELP` | Gets introductory information concerning LISTSERV. |
| `INFO ?` | Gets a summary of the available files giving information about BITNET and LISTSERV. |
| `INDEX` | Gets summary information on the file lists available. |
| `GET` *filename filetype* | Requests that a copy of *filename.filetype* be sent to you. |
| `LIST` *option* | Gives information concerning mailing lists. Three options are available: `SHORT`, `DETAIL`, and `GLOBAL`. |
| `LIST SHORT` | Gives a brief list of the mailing lists available from LISTSERV at the particular node to which you sent this command. |
| `LIST DETAIL` | Gives an amplification on the list sent in response to the `SHORT` option. |
| `LIST GLOBAL` | Gives a list of *all* LISTSERV lists known to the particular LISTSERV receiving your command. |
| `SUB` *list-name your-name* | Initiates your subscription to a mailing list. (See Section 6.4.2.2 for details on how to address this command using MAIL.) |
| `SIGNOFF` *list-name* | Signs you off a mailing list. (See Section 6.4.2.2 for details on how to address this command using MAIL.) |

### RECEIVE Commands

Called by typing RECEIVE <RETURN> at the operating system MYNODE$ prompt, the RECEIVE program allows you to transfer network files (requested earlier) from a system temporary storage area to your own directory.

The following commands are issued at the RECEIVE> prompt.

| *Command* | *Description* |
|---|---|
| HELP | Gets on-line help. |
| DIRECTORY | Lists the network files sent to you and available in the system storage area. |
| TYPE *filespec* | Displays the contents of *filespec* to your screen. |
| RECEIVE *filespec* | Transfers *filespec* from the system storage area to your directory. The file is no longer contained in the storage area. |
| COPY *filespec* | Copies *filespec* from the system storage area to your directory. The file is also retained in the system storage area. |
| DELETE *filespec* | Deletes *filespec* from the system storage area. |
| EXIT | Leaves the RECEIVE program and returns to the operating system. |

### 6.4.7 *Exercises for BITNET*

1. Generate a file containing all the on-line help on RECEIVE by typing the following commands at the operating system prompt:

```
HELP/OUTPUT=RECEIVE.HLP RECEIVE...
PRINT/DELETE/NOTIFY RECEIVE.HLP
```

2. Go through all the examples mentioned in this chapter. If some of the list servers or file servers are no longer functioning or are currently out of service, go through the current lists and try some that might be of interest to you.

3. Some sites have their own local list server programs whereby you can receive all mail generated by different interest groups without actually requesting to be placed on the originating list. This means that only one piece of mail need be sent to your site, and can then be routed to all users there. Why might this be a good idea? Check with your local user services staff to see if you have such a facility. If so, what lists can you sign up for without trying to make contact with the originating file server? At some sites, selected file servers are posted in specified folders in the bulletin board system. Is this done at your site? If so, how can you get access to these postings?

4. If you plan to study Chapter 7 on the DATATRIEVE database management program, issue the following command at the operating system prompt:

   ```
   SEND DATABASE@BITNIC HELP
   ```

   Begin studying how to use this database server, and be ready to contrast it with DATATRIEVE.

5. One useful thing to know if you are a programmer and have object or executable files is that the files can be sent from one VAX/VMS system to another via the following command at the operating system prompt:

   SEND/FILE/VMSDUMP *filespec*

   These VMSDUMP files can be received with the usual RECEIVE command. Try this by sending and receiving one of your own executable files.

# Chapter 7

# The DATATRIEVE Database Management Program

As we have mentioned before in the course of our discussions, a database program allows you to create an orderly collection of data, from which you can extract selected facts. For example, if you are the benefits and salary administrator for a large firm, you might want to develop a database of employee information so you can easily find out facts like how many full-time employees earn over $29,000. DATATRIEVE, one of several database management programs available for VAX/VMS systems, could help you obtain this and a wealth of other information quickly and easily without the struggle of sorting through traditional paper files.

## 7.1 DATATRIEVE Terminology and the NEWUSER Installation Program

When you execute the DATATRIEVE program, you are utilizing three fundamental units:

1. The record (or data) definition

2. The raw data

3. The domain definition

To understand how these units relate, consider an example. Suppose you have a simple personal phone book that contains the names and phone numbers of your friends and acquaintances. For each person, you have a place for first and last name and phone number (including area code). This set of information on each person is called a *record*, and each part of the record is called a *field*.

You decide to make a computerized database of your phone book. You construct it so that each record has two fields, NAME and PHONE. The NAME field would have two parts, or *subfields*: LAST_NAME and FIRST_ NAME. The PHONE field would have only one part: the entire phone number, including area code. In DATATRIEVE's terminology, the NAME field is a *group field*, since it has subfields. The PHONE field is an *elementary field* because it has no subfields. In constructing this phone book database, you also have to decide the maximum number of characters each field can have. For example, you might allot space for ten characters each to the FIRST_NAME and LAST_NAME fields, and twelve characters to the PHONE field. A complete specification of the structure of each record—field name, sizes, and so on—is called the *record definition* or *data definition*.

For your simple phone book, you will, of course, also need the actual names and numbers of your friends and acquaintances. DATATRIEVE requires these data to be in a *raw data file*. This means that the data (names and numbers) can be compressed into a file in such a way that they are stored efficiently. The price for this efficiency and compression is that the data can be read and understood easily only when we know how the records are defined.

The last of the three fundamental units of DATATRIEVE is the *domain definition*. The domain definition simply points to where the record definition and the raw data file reside on the computer system. So, when we execute DATATRIEVE, we have to specify which domain, or domain definition, we want. DATATRIEVE can then retrieve the raw data file and the record definition, which it combines in a way that we can easily understand.

Back to the phone book example. Once you are in DATATRIEVE, you will need to specify the phone book domain. Then you will be able to make queries of the database—such as how many Smiths you know, what Jerry Doe's phone number is, or which phone numbers with the area code 212 appear in the database.

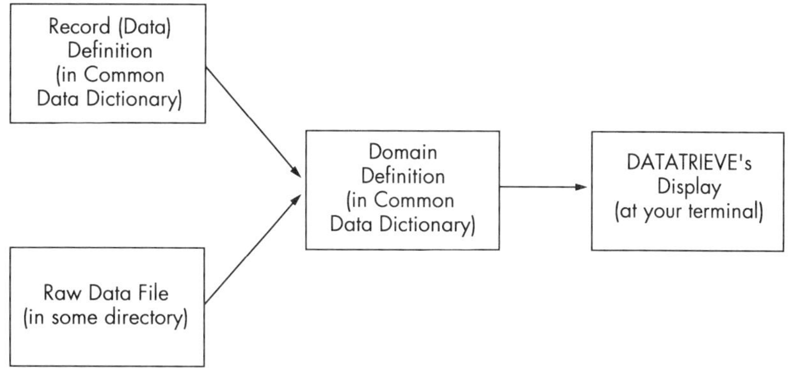


**Figure 7.1 DATATRIEVE's Domain Structure**

Figure 7.1 shows a diagram of the basic structure of the DATATRIEVE domains. From our perspective, we see only the raw data files in our directory. The record definitions and the domain definitions reside elsewhere on the system in a place called the Common Data Dictionary (CDD).[1]

Now let's get started. DATATRIEVE offers a NEWUSER program, which sets up several example domains, record definitions, and raw data files for us. Because we will use these domains in the examples that follow, our first step is to run this NEWUSER program.

After logging in and while at the operating system prompt, type `NEWUSER` <RETURN> if you are using the annotated `LOGIN.COM` file, or type `@DTR$LIBRARY:NEWUSER` <RETURN> if you are using the starter `LOGIN.COM` file. As NEWUSER executes, you might be asked whether you want to delete some `*.TMP` files. If so, simply respond by typing `Y` <RETURN>. Figure 7.2 shows what to expect on your screen.[2] You will see two remarks near the end of this procedure; they indicate that you need to add two lines to your `LOGIN.COM` file. If the two lines shown on your screen do not agree with those in Figure 7.2, be sure to write down the two lines shown on your screen.

1. For more information on CDD, see Bibliography [11, 25, 26, 27].

2. For brevity's sake, we omit the <RETURN>s that follow the DCL and DATATRIEVE commands in figures in this chapter. For example, in Figure 7.2, <RETURN> should follow `NEWUSER`. In all figures, <RETURN> is understood to follow the commands that you type, shown in color.

```
MYNODE$ NEWUSER

NEWUSER helps new users to get started with DATATRIEVE. It
gives you the necessary files to perform the introductory
examples in the VAX DATATRIEVE "Handbook" and the examples in
the VAX DATATRIEVE "User's Guide" and "Reference Manual."

    NEWUSER is working . . . It will take a few minutes.

    All data copied successfully.

    The following commands have been defined for you but you
    will need to add them to your LOGIN.COM file for the next
    time you log in:

$ DTR32 == "$sys$system:DTR32.EXE"
$ assign/process "CDD$TOP.DTR$USERS.MY_Username" cdd$default
If you need help, see the person responsible for DATATRIEVE
    on your system.

    To invoke DATATRIEVE just type    DTR32

MYNODE$
```

**Figure 7.2 Executing the NEWUSER Program**

If you are using the starter `LOGIN.COM` file, insert the two lines (those shown on your screen) just before the `$ EXIT:` line in your `LOGIN.COM` file. Be sure to insert your own user name in the `ASSIGN/PROCESS` line.

If you are using the annotated `LOGIN.COM` file, lines similar to those on your screen are already in the file. After taking careful note of the two lines that appeared on your screen while running NEWUSER, edit your `LOGIN.COM` file. Locate the string `DTR32` and make the characters to the right of the == identical to those that appeared during the running of NEWUSER. Make the same kind of corrections to the `ASSIGN/PROCESS` line. Finally, remove the ! from both lines. It is *critical* that you make these changes; otherwise, the next time you log in, you will *not* be able to function as we outline in this chapter.[3]

Before proceeding, check your directory. You should see that you have seven new files: ACCOUNTS.DAT;1, FAMILY.DAT;1, OWNER.DAT;1, PERSON.DAT;1, PET.DAT;1, PROJECT.DAT;1, and YACHT.DAT;1. These are the raw data files for your sample domains. *Do not delete* these files until we are finished with our DATATRIEVE work. (The actual number of files in your directory will depend on the version of DATATRIEVE available on your system. For example, the ACCOUNTS.DAT file might not be available on earlier versions.)

We are now ready to explore the sample DATATRIEVE domains.

## 7.2 Interactive Session 1: Showing Some NEWUSER Domain and Record Definitions

First, execute the DATATRIEVE program. At the operating system prompt, type DTR32 <RETURN>. You can see in Figure 7.3 that the prompt changes to DTR>. As with most of the software packages you have studied, on-line help is available. Within the DATATRIEVE program, it is available by typing HELP <RETURN>. Try this and see what happens. If you need some comic relief, ask for help on WOMBAT, then on the ADVANCED subtopic.

DATATRIEVE distinguishes between commands and statements. *Commands* refer to data definitions stored in the CDD (Common Data Dictionary), such as record and domain definitions. *Statements* refer to the storing, modifying, erasing, reporting, and querying functions of DATATRIEVE. You can learn about these distinctions from the on-line help within DATATRIEVE, but you don't have to know them in order to do the work in this chapter.

---

3. It is possible that your system has been set up in such a way that you will have to edit the $! ASSIGN/PROCESS line more extensively. You should change it to agree with the two lines that appeared on your screen when you ran the NEWUSER program. Also note that the /NOLOG option shown in the annotated LOGIN.COM file is not mentioned when you run the NEWUSER program. The /NOLOG option can be omitted, but having it can keep you from getting an occasional warning that serves no real purpose for the beginner.

```
MYNODE$ DTR32

Vax Datatrieve V4.0
DEC Query and Report System
Type HELP for help
DTR> SHOW ALL

Domains:
    ACCOUNT_BALANCES;1              FAMILIES;1       OWNERS;1
    PERSONNEL;1      PETS;1         PROJECTS;1       YACHTS;1
Records:
    ACCOUNT_BALANCE_REC;1           FAMILY_REC;1     OWNER_RECORD;1
    PERSONNEL_REC;1 PET_REC;1       PROJECT_REC;1    YACHT;1
The default directory is _CDD$TOP.DTR$USERS.MY_Username
No established collections.
No ready sources.
No loaded tables.

DTR> SHOW DOMAINS

Domains:
    ACCOUNT_BALANCES;1              FAMILIES;1       OWNERS;1
    PERSONNEL;1      PETS;1         PROJECTS;1       YACHTS;1

DTR> SHOW RECORDS

Records:
    ACCOUNT_BALANCE_REC;1           FAMILY_REC;1     OWNER_RECORD;1
    PERSONNEL_REC;1 PET_REC;1       PROJECT_REC;1    YACHT;1

DTR> READY PERSONNEL
DTR> READY YACHTS, OWNERS
DTR> SHOW READY

Ready sources:
   OWNERS:  Domain, RMS indexed, protected read
          <_CDD$TOP.DTR$USERS.MY_Username.OWNERS;1>
   YACHTS:  Domain, RMS indexed, protected read
          <_CDD$TOP.DTR$USERS.MY_Username.YACHTS;1>
   PERSONNEL:  Domain, RMS indexed, protected read
          <_CDD$TOP.DTR$USERS.MY_Username.PERSONNEL;1>
No loaded tables.

DTR> EXIT

MYNODE$
```

**Figure 7.3 DATATRIEVE's SHOW and READY Commands**

```
DTR> SHOW PERSONNEL_REC

RECORD PERSONNEL_REC USING
01 PERSON.
   05 ID                        PIC IS 9(5)
   05 EMPLOYEE_STATUS           PIC IS X(11)
                                QUERY_NAME IS STATUS
                                QUERY_HEADER IS "STATUS"
                                VALID IF STATUS EQ "TRAINEE", "EXPERIENCED"
   05 EMPLOYEE_NAME             QUERY_NAME IS NAME
     10 FIRST_NAME              PIC IS X(10)
                                QUERY_NAME IS F_NAME
     10 LAST_NAME               PIC IS X(10)
                                QUERY_NAME IS L_NAME
   05 DEPT                      PIC IS XXX
   05 START_DATE                USAGE IS DATE
                                DEFAULT VALUE IS "TODAY"
   05 SALARY                    PIC IS 9(5)
                                EDIT_STRING IS $$$,$$$
   05 SUP_ID                    PIC IS 9(5)
                                MISSING VALUE IS 0
;

DTR>
```

**Figure 7.4 Displaying the PERSONNEL Record Definition Using SHOW**

As illustrated in Figure 7.3, type `SHOW ALL` <RETURN>. DATATRIEVE shows you that you have seven domains and seven record definitions in your "dictionary." For example, the `PERSONNEL` domain has `PERSONNEL_REC` as its record definition. Other options of the `SHOW` command are also displayed in Figure 7.3. The next two, `SHOW DOMAINS` and `SHOW RECORDS`, are self-explanatory. Try them and see the results.

You can see what the record definition for the `PERSONNEL` domain looks like by typing `SHOW PERSONNEL_REC` <RETURN>. Figure 7.4 displays the result. We can see that the `PERSONNEL` domain contains fields named `PERSON`, `ID`, `EMPLOYEE_STATUS`, `EMPLOYEE_NAME`, `DEPT`, `START_DATE`, `SALARY`, and `SUP_ID`. Notice that under `EMPLOYEE_NAME` there is an indentation, after which the fields `FIRST_NAME` and `LAST_NAME` appear. This indentation means that `EMPLOYEE_NAME` is a group field containing the two elementary fields `FIRST_NAME` and `LAST_NAME`. Except for `PERSON`, the rest of the fields are elementary fields. The `PERSON` field is the name given to the entire record; it is considered a group field containing all other fields in the record. These distinctions between different kinds of fields can be quite important, so make sure you understand them.

One of the items you saw displayed by typing the SHOW ALL command (see Figure 7.3) was the message No ready sources. In order for you to be able to make queries of a domain (source), DATATRIEVE requires that you READY that domain. The READY command gives you access to the domain you specify. Type the READY PERSONNEL and READY YACHTS, OWNERS commands, and then type SHOW READY. You can now make queries of any of the three readied domains (sources), OWNERS, YACHTS, and PERSONNEL.

Before learning how to make queries of the database, return to the operating system level by typing EXIT <RETURN> (see Figure 7.3).

## 7.3 Interactive Session 2: Queries That Do Not Change the Database (Printing Record Streams)

Re-enter DATATRIEVE by typing DTR32 <RETURN>, and READY the PERSONNEL domain by typing READY PERSONNEL <RETURN>. First, display *everything* in this domain by typing PRINT PERSONNEL <RETURN>. Once having readied any domain, you can see its entire contents by typing PRINT, followed by the domain name and <RETURN>. Figure 7.5 shows the result of following these instructions. You now see that there are twenty-three records in this domain and eight fields (ID, STATUS, FIRST_NAME, LAST_NAME, DEPT, START_DATE, SALARY, and SUP_ID). Another way to get the same result would be to type PRINT ALL PERSONNEL <RETURN>. Try it and see.

Let's take a look at some of the options available for making inquiries, or queries, of the database. For example, follow the sequence of statements in Figure 7.6. Type PRINT FIRST 3 PERSONNEL <RETURN>. You will see that the first three records in the PERSONNEL domain, which you saw in its entirety in Figure 7.5, are printed to your screen. In DATATRIEVE's terminology, you have used a *record selection expression*, or *RSE*, to create a record stream, which is displayed to your terminal. An RSE is simply a phrase defining a specific condition or conditions that records must meet. In this case, the condition is FIRST 3. The record stream is a temporary set of related

```
MYNODE$ DTR32

VAX DATATRIEVE V4.0
DEC Query and Report System
Type HELP for help
DTR> READY PERSONNEL
DTR> PRINT PERSONNEL

                        FIRST      LAST                   START               SUP
ID    STATUS            NAME       NAME         DEPT      DATE        SALARY  ID

00012 EXPERIENCED CHARLOTTE SPIVA         TOP 12-Sep-1972 $75,892 00012
00891 EXPERIENCED FRED      HOWL          F11  9-Apr-1976 $59,594 00012
02943 EXPERIENCED CASS      TERRY         D98  2-Jan-1980 $29,908 39485
12643 TRAINEE     JEFF      TASHKENT      C82  4-Apr-1981 $32,918 87465
32432 TRAINEE     THOMAS    SCHWEIK       F11  7-Nov-1981 $26,723 00891
34456 TRAINEE     HANK      MORRISON      T32  1-Mar-1982 $30,000 87289
38462 EXPERIENCED BILL      SWAY          T32  5-May-1980 $54,000 00012
38465 EXPERIENCED JOANNE    FREIBURG      E46 20-Feb-1980 $23,908 48475
39485 EXPERIENCED DEE       TERRICK       D98  2-May-1977 $55,829 00012
48475 EXPERIENCED GAIL      CASSIDY       E46  2-May-1978 $55,407 00012
48573 TRAINEE     SY        KELLER        T32  2-Aug-1981 $31,546 87289
49001 EXPERIENCED DAN       ROBERTS       C82  7-Jul-1979 $41,395 87465
49843 TRAINEE     BART      HAMMER        D98  4-Aug-1981 $26,392 39485
78923 EXPERIENCED LYDIA     HARRISON      F11 19-Jun-1979 $40,747 00891
83764 EXPERIENCED JIM       MEADER        T32  4-Apr-1980 $41,029 87289
84375 EXPERIENCED MARY      NALEVO        D98  3-Jan-1976 $56,847 39485
87289 EXPERIENCED LOUISE    DEPALMA       G20 28-Feb-1979 $57,598 00012
87465 EXPERIENCED ANTHONY   IACOBONE      C82  2-Jan-1973 $58,462 00012
87701 TRAINEE     NATHANIEL CHONTZ        F11 28-Jan-1982 $24,502 00891
88001 EXPERIENCED DAVID     LITELLA       G20 11-Nov-1980 $34,933 87289
90342 EXPERIENCED BRUNO     DONCHIKOV     C82  9-Aug-1978 $35,952 87465
91023 TRAINEE     STAN      WITTGEN       G20 23-Dec-1981 $25,023 87289
99029 EXPERIENCED RANDY     PODERESIAN    C82 24-May-1979 $33,738 87465

DTR>
```

**Figure 7.5 Displaying the Entire PERSONNEL Domain**

records that an RSE has defined. In this case, the record stream displayed to the screen is

```
00012 EXPERIENCED CHARLOTTE SPIVA TOP 12-Sep-1972 $75,892 00012
00891 EXPERIENCED FRED      HOWL  F11  9-Apr-1976 $59,594 00012
02943 EXPERIENCED CASS      TERRY D98  2-Jan-1980 $29,908 39485
```

```
DTR> PRINT FIRST 3 PERSONNEL

                        FIRST      LAST                  START               SUP
ID     STATUS           NAME       NAME       DEPT       DATE       SALARY   ID

00012 EXPERIENCED  CHARLOTTE  SPIVA      TOP  12-Sep-1972  $75,892  00012
00891 EXPERIENCED  FRED       HOWL       F11   9-Apr-1976  $59,594  00012
02943 EXPERIENCED  CASS       TERRY      D98   2-Jan-1980  $29,908  39485

DTR> PRINT PERSONNEL WITH SUP_ID = 87289

                        FIRST      LAST                  START               SUP
ID     STATUS           NAME       NAME       DEPT       DATE       SALARY   ID

34456 TRAINEE      HANK       MORRISON   T32   1-Mar-1982  $30,000  87289
48573 TRAINEE      SY         KELLER     T32   2-Aug-1981  $31,546  87289
83764 EXPERIENCED  JIM        MEADER     T32   4-Apr-1980  $41,029  87289
88001 EXPERIENCED  DAVID      LITELLA    G20  11-Nov-1980  $34,933  87289
91023 TRAINEE      STAN       WITTGEN    G20  23-Dec-1981  $25,023  87289
```

**Figure 7.6 Some Simple Record Selection Expressions (RSEs) and Record Streams**

Recall that there are eight elementary fields in each record of the PERSONNEL domain. Let's look at a few more examples of RSEs. Referring to Figure 7.6, type PRINT PERSONNEL WITH SUP_ID = 87289 <RETURN>. In this case (as in most), the part following the word WITH is the RSE. The result: the record stream created by the RSE is printed to your terminal, and looks like what is shown in Figure 7.6. In response to your query, DATATRIEVE displayed all employees in the database whose supervisor identification number is 87289.

Try these other queries of a similar nature:

```
PRINT PERSONNEL WITH START_DATE = "2-Aug-1981"
PRINT PERSONNEL WITH LAST_NAME = "WITTGEN"
PRINT FIRST 7 PERSONNEL WITH DEPT = "G20"
PRINT FIRST 5 PERSONNEL WITH STATUS = "EXPERIENCED"
```

Notice that if a field contains *characters* rather than being strictly *numeric*, it is placed in double quotes in the RSE. Further observe that field names do *not* contain blank characters; you must type the underline character instead of a blank, for example, LAST_NAME. (A hyphen is an acceptable substitute for the underline character in queries.) In order to demonstrate

```
DTR> PRINT PERSONNEL WITH DEPT = "T32" SORTED BY L_NAME

                  FIRST      LAST                START                SUP
ID     STATUS     NAME       NAME       DEPT     DATE        SALARY   ID

48573 TRAINEE     SY         KELLER     T32   2-Aug-1981   $31,546  87289
83764 EXPERIENCED JIM        MEADER     T32   4-Apr-1980   $41,029  87289
34456 TRAINEE     HANK       MORRISON   T32   1-Mar-1982   $30,000  87289
38462 EXPERIENCED BILL       SWAY       T32   5-May-1980   $54,000  00012
```

**Figure 7.7 An RSE with a Sort Option**

DATATRIEVE's statement-editing function, try making an error on purpose: Leave out the underscore in the field name LAST_NAME. You will immediately get an error message. Then, type EDIT <RETURN>. The screen clears and your bad line is displayed. You are in the statement editor, which simulates your text editor.[4] Insert the underscore where it belongs, delete the offending space, and exit as you normally do from your text editor when saving a file. This sequence causes your corrected command to be executed.

Now suppose you need your PERSONNEL records sorted alphabetically in your record stream. Following Figure 7.7, type PRINT PERSONNEL WITH DEPT = "T32" SORTED BY L_NAME <RETURN>. This command not only prints all employee records in the PERSONNEL domain in department T32 but also sorts the results alphabetically by LAST_NAME (or, as abbreviated here, L_NAME).

Try your hand at some of the following PRINT statements with a sort option:

```
PRINT PERSONNEL WITH DEPT = "G20" SORTED BY SALARY, LAST_NAME
PRINT PERSONNEL WITH DEPT = "G20" SORTED BY LAST_NAME, SALARY
PRINT PERSONNEL WITH DEPT = "G20" SORTED BY DESC SALARY
PRINT PERSONNEL WITH DEPT = "G20" SORTED BY ASCENDING SALARY
PRINT PERSONNEL SORTED BY LAST_NAME, DEPT
PRINT PERSONNEL SORTED BY ASCENDING DEPT, DESCENDING SALARY
```

Notice that the sorting process can extend over more than one field, can occur in ascending or descending order, or can extend over the entire domain.

---

4. If you are using EVE and the annotated LOGIN.COM file, just remove the ! from the following line in your LOGIN.COM file:

```
$! DEFINE DTR$EDIT TPU
```

If you are using EVE and the starter LOGIN.COM file, you will need to insert the above line (without the !) in your LOGIN.COM file immediately preceding $ EXIT:.

```
DTR> PRINT PERSONNEL WITH START_DATE AFTER "1-JAN-1982"

                      FIRST      LAST                START          SUP
ID    STATUS          NAME       NAME        DEPT    DATE     SALARY ID

34456 TRAINEE         HANK       MORRISON    T32   1-Mar-1982 $30,000 87289
87701 TRAINEE         NATHANIEL  CHONTZ      F11  28-Jan-1982 $24,502 00891

DTR> PRINT PERSONNEL WITH SALARY BETWEEN 20000 AND 25000

                      FIRST      LAST                START          SUP
ID    STATUS          NAME       NAME        DEPT    DATE     SALARY ID

38465 EXPERIENCED JOANNE         FREIBURG    E46  20-Feb-1980 $23,908 48475
87701 TRAINEE         NATHANIEL  CHONTZ      F11  28-Jan-1982 $24,502 00891
```

**Figure 7.8 RSEs with Different Relational Operators**

So far, our RSEs have only contained the equal sign, so that DATATRIEVE sends us *exact* matches. However, there is more flexibility available in writing RSEs. As in Figure 7.8, type PRINT PERSONNEL WITH START_DATE AFTER "1-JAN-1982" <RETURN>, followed by PRINT PERSONNEL WITH SALARY BETWEEN 20000 AND 25000 <RETURN>. In the first instance, you are checking for dates greater than 1-JAN-1982; in the second instance, you are checking for salaries greater than $20,000 but less than $25,000.

Terms like "equal to," "greater than," and "less than" are called *relational operators*. Table 7.1 summarizes the relational operators available in DATATRIEVE for making more detailed RSEs.[5]

Try the following commands to demonstrate how some of the other relational operators work:

```
PRINT PERSONNEL WITH SALARY > 20000
PRINT PERSONNEL WITH SALARY > 20000 AND STATUS = "EXPERIENCED"
PRINT PERSONNEL WITH DEPT = "G20" AND SALARY BT 20000 AND 40000
PRINT PERSONNEL WITH STATUS NE "TRAINEE"
PRINT PERSONNEL WITH DEPT CONT "T" BUT DEPT NE "TOP"
PRINT FIRST 5 PERSONNEL WITH SALARY > 26000 SORTED BY SALARY
PRINT PERSONNEL WITH SUP_ID = 39485, 48475
PRINT PERSONNEL WITH DEPT CONTAINING "F", "T"
```

5. See Bibliography [11] for more information.

**Table 7.1 Simple Relational Operators in DATATRIEVE**

| Operator | Meaning | Example |
|---|---|---|
| EQUAL<br>EQ<br>= | Equal to<br>(case-sensitive) | DEPT = "G20" |
| NOT-EQUAL<br>NE | Not equal to | STATUS NE "TRAINEE" |
| AFTER<br>GREATER-THAN<br>GT<br>> | Greater than | SALARY > 26000<br>DATE AFTER "1-AUG-1981" |
| GREATER-EQUAL<br>GE | Greater than<br>or equal to | ID GE 27009 |
| BEFORE<br>LESS-THAN<br>LT<br>< | Less than | DATE BEFORE "3-AUG-1983"<br>SALARY LT 27000 |
| LESS-EQUAL<br>LE | Less than<br>or equal to | SUP_ID LE 30000 |
| BETWEEN x AND y<br>BETWEEN x y<br>BT x AND y<br>BT x y | Between and<br>including the<br>two values<br>specified | SALARY BT 25000 35000 |
| CONTAINING<br>CONT | Containing the<br>specified value<br>(case-sensitive) | DEPT CONTAINING "T"<br>STATUS CONT "F" |

So far, we have used RSEs to find and print records we are seeking—in other words, to create a record stream. However, in all these cases, we have printed *every* field when the record stream was created. DATATRIEVE also allows us to print only *specified* fields of records sought. For example, follow Figure 7.9 by typing `PRINT NAME, SALARY OF FIRST 5 PERSONNEL WITH SALARY > 25000 SORTED BY SALARY` <RETURN>. Notice that only the two fields `NAME` and `SALARY` are printed. The reason three columns appear is that `NAME`, or `EMPLOYEE_NAME`, is a group field containing two elementary fields, `FIRST_NAME` and `LAST_NAME` (see Figure 7.4). Try typing the same command, except specify other fields to be displayed, such as `START_DATE` and `SUP_ID`.

```
DTR> PRINT NAME, SALARY OF FIRST 5 PERSONNEL-
CON> WITH SALARY > 25000 SORTED BY SALARY

FIRST     LAST
NAME      NAME          SALARY

STAN      WITTGEN       $25,023
BART      HAMMER        $26,392
THOMAS    SCHWEIK       $26,723
CASS      TERRY         $29,908
HANK      MORRISON      $30,000
```

**Figure 7.9 PRINTing Only Specified Fields of Record Streams**

In this section, we have discussed several ways to create and print record streams using the PRINT statement. In the next section, you will learn how to create collections of records and use them to produce simple reports, which can be sent to files and printed as hard copy.

## 7.4 Interactive Session 3: Collections and Report Writing

The goal of this section is to teach you to generate simple reports to files in your directory. You can then print these files on paper and distribute them to colleagues or clients.

Once logged in, execute DATATRIEVE, and READY the PERSONNEL domain, as shown in Figure 7.10. Again, notice that if you did not put a line similar to the following

```
$ ASSIGN/PROCESS/NOLOG "CDD$TOP.DTR$USERS.-----" CDD$DEFAULT
```

into your LOGIN.COM file, as indicated earlier, you might not even be able to READY the PERSONNEL domain. The exact form of this line is displayed when you run the NEWUSER program.

The first new statement we discuss is the FIND statement. FIND is much like the PRINT statement except that instead of printing a record stream to the terminal, it creates a *collection* that can be referenced later. Type FIND PERSONNEL WITH SUP_ID = 00012 <RETURN> and notice that the line [7 records found] appears (see Figure 7.10). You then know that DATATRIEVE has created a collection with the default name CURRENT (not shown

```
MYNODE$ DTR32

VAX DATATRIEVE V4.0
DEC Query and Report System
Type HELP for help
DTR> READY PERSONNEL
DTR> FIND PERSONNEL WITH SUP_ID = 00012

[7 records found]
DTR> PRINT ALL

                         FIRST      LAST                 START                 SUP
ID     STATUS            NAME       NAME         DEPT    DATE         SALARY   ID

00012 EXPERIENCED  CHARLOTTE  SPIVA       TOP   12-Sep-1972  $75,892  00012
00891 EXPERIENCED  FRED       HOWL        F11    9-Apr-1976  $59,594  00012
38462 EXPERIENCED  BILL       SWAY        T32    5-May-1980  $54,000  00012
39485 EXPERIENCED  DEE        TERRICK     D98    2-May-1977  $55,829  00012
48475 EXPERIENCED  GAIL       CASSIDY     E46    2-May-1978  $55,407  00012
87289 EXPERIENCED  LOUISE     DEPALMA     G20   28-Feb-1979  $57,598  00012
87465 EXPERIENCED  ANTHONY    IACOBONE    C82    2-Jan-1973  $58,462  00012
```

**Figure 7.10 Creating a Collection Using FIND**

on screen). We can view the collection by typing PRINT CURRENT <RETURN> or simply PRINT ALL <RETURN>.

Although you can create several collections with different names, it will suffice now simply to deal with the default, the CURRENT, collection. Try creating new collections by typing each of the following commands, making sure you follow each of the FIND commands with PRINT ALL <RETURN> or PRINT CURRENT <RETURN>:

```
FIND PERSONNEL WITH SUP_ID = 39485
FIND PERSONNEL WITH DEPT = F11
FIND PERSONNEL WITH SALARY > 26500
```

Notice that the previous CURRENT collection is *destroyed*, or *overwritten*, when a new FIND statement is executed.

Now that you understand the idea of creating collections with the FIND statement, type FIND PERSONNEL WITH SUP_ID = 00012 <RETURN>. Again you see the message [7 records found]. Next follow the pattern set in

```
DTR> FIND PERSONNEL WITH SUP_ID = 00012

[7 records found]
DTR> REPORT CURRENT
RW> PRINT PERSON
RW> END_REPORT

                                                        22-July-1987
                                                        Page 1

                     FIRST      LAST                START                SUP
ID     STATUS        NAME       NAME       DEPT     DATE        SALARY   ID

00012 EXPERIENCED  CHARLOTTE  SPIVA      TOP  12-Sep-1972  $75,892  00012
00891 EXPERIENCED  FRED       HOWL       F11   9-Apr-1976  $59,594  00012
38462 EXPERIENCED  BILL       SWAY       T32   5-May-1980  $54,000  00012
39485 EXPERIENCED  DEE        TERRICK    D98   2-May-1977  $55,829  00012
48475 EXPERIENCED  GAIL       CASSIDY    E46   2-May-1978  $55,407  00012
87289 EXPERIENCED  LOUISE     DEPALMA    G20  28-Feb-1979  $57,598  00012
87465 EXPERIENCED  ANTHONY    IACOBONE   C82   2-Jan-1973  $58,462  00012
```

**Figure 7.11 Using DATATRIEVE's Report Writer**

Figure 7.11 and type REPORT CURRENT <RETURN>. We see that the DTR> prompt changes to RW>, indicating that you are now running DATATRIEVE's Report Writer.

Now type PRINT PERSON <RETURN>, which types every field of each record in your collection. It types *every* field because, as you will recall from the discussion of the record definition PERSONNEL_REC (see Figure 7.4), the entire record is viewed as a group field with the name PERSON. Next exit the Report Writer by typing END_REPORT <RETURN>.[6] DATATRIEVE's Report Writer then prints a simple report to the screen. The report looks almost the same as when you executed the PRINT ALL command in Figure 7.10 except that the columns are a little differently spaced and there is a page number and date in the upper right-hand corner.

It is a simple matter to save this report to a file in your directory rather than display it to the screen. Before typing any other commands, type EDIT <RETURN>. The last several commands (those since initiating the Report

6. The underscore between END and REPORT is required.

```
DTR> FIND PERSONNEL WITH STATUS = "TRAINEE"

[7 records found]
DTR> REPORT CURRENT SORTED BY DEPT, SALARY ON TEST2.TXT
RW>  SET REPORT_NAME = "TRAINEE EMPLOYEES "/"BY"/" DEPARTMENT -
CON> AND SALARY"
RW>  SET COLUMNS_PAGE = 50
RW>  PRINT ID, NAME, DEPT, SALARY
RW>  END_REPORT
DTR> EXIT

MYNODE$ TY TEST2.TXT

               TRAINEE EMPLOYEES    22-JUL-1987
                      BY           PAGE 1
              DEPARTMENT AND SALARY

       FIRST        LAST
ID     NAME         NAME        DEPT    SALARY

12643  JEFF         TASHKENT    C82     $32,918
49843  BART         HAMMER      D98     $26,392
87701  NATHANIEL    CHONTZ      F11     $24,502
32432  THOMAS       SCHWEIK     F11     $26,723
91023  STAN         WITTGEN     G20     $25,023
34456  HANK         MORRISON    T32     $30,000
48573  SY           KELLER      T32     $31,546
```

**Figure 7.12 Another Example Using DATATRIEVE's Report Writer**

Writer) will be displayed to the screen. Change the command REPORT CURRENT (see Figure 7.11) so it reads REPORT CURRENT ON TEST1.TXT. When you are satisfied with your correction, exit as though you were leaving your text editor and saving a file. The sequence of commands is now executed. The report is *not* displayed to the screen. It has been saved in a file called TEST1.TXT.

Now let's create a report with a little more meat to it, using the commands contained in Figure 7.12. First, create a collection containing seven records that have the STATUS of TRAINEE. Call the Report Writer and request that the collection, CURRENT, be sorted by DEPT and then by SALARY. Once in the Report Writer, give the report a title containing three lines; each line of the title is contained in quotation marks and separated by slashes. The report title is long enough to require a continuation, which is indicated with a hyphen. Notice the CON>, which is the continuation prompt.

Continuing with the Report Writer, specify that the report be only fifty columns wide, and that only the ID, NAME, DEPT, and SALARY fields are to be printed. End the Report Writer commands with END_REPORT <RETURN>; the report is saved to file TEST2.TXT, which is shown in Figure 7.12. Using the DIR command, satisfy yourself that you have indeed created two new files of type .TXT. PRINT them so you can verify that you have issued your commands correctly.

## 7.5 Changing Your Data Records with STORE and MODIFY

So far, you have learned several ways to query, sort, retrieve, and report data that were already in the domain. But you also need to know how to add data to the domain. We start our session as usual, with one exception: the READY command reads READY PERSONNEL WRITE (see Figure 7.13). The sequence in Figure 7.13 shows how to add a new employee to the PERSONNEL domain. Notice that DATATRIEVE prompts you for everything it needs. It rejects the wrong kind of data; for instance, it rejects an all-character string for the numeric field ID. If, at any point, you type <CTRL/Z>, you terminate the storing of the new record (the record is not added to the database). Recall that <RETURN> is assumed at the end of each line you type.

Remember that the record definition part of the domain has specified the kind of data allowed in each field. If you enter incorrect data, the program will prompt you for the correct kind. Sometimes you will not know all the information pertaining to a new record. Whenever you come to a field that asks for a fact you do not have, press the <SPACEBAR> or <TAB> and then <RETURN>. You can fill in those fields later using the MODIFY statement. For now, leave DATATRIEVE, and take a break.

Now start up DATATRIEVE in the conventional way, but this time, at the DTR> prompt, type READY PERSONNEL MODIFY <RETURN>, yielding an example like the one in Figure 7.14. Say you want to change employee Barbie Newcomer's salary to reflect her recent promotion. The first step is to get at the record you need with a combination of FIND and SELECT statements. The PRINT statement verifies that you have found and selected

```
DTR> READY PERSONNEL WRITE
DTR> STORE PERSONNEL
Enter ID: KEN

Non-digit in string "KEN", ignoring character(s).
Re-enter ID: 53112
Enter EMPLOYEE_STATUS: EXPERIENCED
Enter FIRST_NAME: KEN
Enter LAST_NAME: NEWCOMER
Enter DEPT: <CTRL/z>

Execution terminated by operator.
DTR> STORE PERSONNEL
Enter ID: 53112
Enter EMPLOYEE_STATUS: EXPERIENCED
Enter FIRST_NAME: KEN
Enter LAST_NAME: NEWCOMER
Enter DEPT: T44
Enter START_DATE: 23-AUG-1986
Enter SALARY: 54500
Enter SUP_ID: 39485
DTR> REPEAT 2 STORE PERSONNEL
Enter ID: 53113
Enter EMPLOYEE_STATUS: TRAINEE
Enter FIRST_NAME: BARBIE
Enter LAST_NAME: NEWCOMER
Enter DEPT: T32
Enter START_DATE: 27-AUG-1986
Enter SALARY: <TAB>
Enter SUP_ID: 87289
Enter ID: 53114
Enter EMPLOYEE_STATUS: EXPERIENCED
Enter FIRST_NAME: HEIDI
Enter LAST_NAME: ABRAMOWITZ
Enter DEPT: T32
Enter START_DATE: 28-AUG-1986
Enter SALARY: 69000
Enter SUP_ID: 87289
DTR> EXIT
```

**Figure 7.13 Adding New Data Records Using STORE**

the right record for modification. It also displays existing data. The MODIFY statement begins a process similar to the STORE command you used earlier. For each field you want to leave unchanged, simply press <TAB> and then <RETURN>. Pressing the <SPACEBAR> and then <RETURN> will cause a field to be empty (even if it previously contained data).

```
DTR> READY PERSONNEL MODIFY
DTR> FIND PERSONNEL WITH L-NAME = "NEWCOMER"

[2 records found]
DTR> SELECT; PRINT

                     FIRST       LAST                  START                SUP
ID     STATUS        NAME        NAME        DEPT      DATE       SALARY    ID

53112 TRAINEE        KEN         NEWCOMER    T44   23-Aug-1986   $54,500   39485

DTR> SELECT NEXT; PRINT

                     FIRST       LAST                  START                SUP
ID     STATUS        NAME        NAME        DEPT      DATE       SALARY    ID

53113 TRAINEE        BARBIE      NEWCOMER    T32   27-Aug-1986             87289

DTR> MODIFY
Enter ID: <TAB>
Enter EMPLOYEE_STATUS: <TAB>
Enter FIRST_NAME: <TAB>
Enter LAST_NAME: <TAB>
Enter DEPT: <TAB>
Enter START_DATE: <TAB>
Enter SALARY: 24500
Enter SUP_ID: <TAB>
DTR> PRINT

                     FIRST       LAST                  START                SUP
ID     STATUS        NAME        NAME        DEPT      DATE       SALARY    ID

53113 TRAINEE        BARBIE      NEWCOMER    T32   27-Aug-1986   $24,500   87289

DTR> EXIT
```

**Figure 7.14 Changing Data Records Using MODIFY**

As illustrated in Figure 7.13 during the STORE PERSONNEL discussion, <CTRL/ Z>will terminate the process and leave the data unchanged. After you have successfully modified the record, a PRINT command will display the new data.

## 7.6 *Handling Your Own Data Using ADT*

A database management program would be a mere curiosity if you could not organize your data according to your own needs. The Application Design Tool (ADT) lets you do this. Specifically, ADT is an automated way to define your domains by setting up the corresponding record definitions and initializing the raw data files. ADT thus saves you the trouble of learning the intricacies of DATATRIEVE's high-level programming language. To use ADT at its simplest level, you need to decide on only a very few items: domain name, raw data file name, and record definition. Recall that the record definition is essentially the set of field names and their data types.

Returning to an example we used earlier in this chapter, consider making the simplest phone directory with a domain name `FRIENDS` and a raw data file called `FRND`.[7] Let one field, called `NAME`, contain ten alphabetic characters. Call the other field `TEL_NO`, with space for seven numbers to the left of the decimal point. You now have enough information to use ADT and DATATRIEVE to keep a primitive phone directory composed of first names and seven-digit telephone numbers. Call ADT from within DATATRIEVE simply by typing `ADT` <RETURN>. ADT's full-screen prompts are simple and straightforward, especially if you respond with a `Y` (for `YES`) when you are initially queried, `Do you want detailed prompts?`. The only thing that might be a bit confusing comes near the end of your session with ADT, when you are asked, `Do you want your data file to be indexed?`. For simplicity, respond with an `N` <RETURN> (for `NO`). When ADT finally queries you with `Do you want to add the domain and record definition to your current default directory?`, respond with a `Y` <RETURN> if you are satisfied. If you sense that you are making, or have already made, some error in the creation of your new database, you can abort the process by pressing <CTRL/z>, just as you did with `STORE` or `MODIFY` data in earlier sessions. Furthermore, if you are in the middle of your ADT session and you want to go back one step in the process, simply type the left angle bracket (<). Multiple typings of < will take you back an equivalent number of steps in the current ADT session.

---

7. DATATRIEVE will automatically supply the file type `.DAT`.

Once your domain is set up with ADT, READY the domain with the WRITE option and STORE a few sample records, following the example given in Figure 7.13.

If you want to write a report using your new FRIENDS domain, notice that the group field containing all the other fields has been given the name FRIENDS_REC, as has the record definition. You can see this group field by typing SHOW FRIENDS_REC <RETURN> at the DTR> prompt. This means that when you are in DATATRIEVE's Report Writer program and you want to display every field in this domain, you should use the command PRINT FRIENDS_REC at the appropriate place in the Report Writer.

For a little more practice, you might try to create a more complicated phone book domain with the domain name FRIENDS2 and a raw data file named FRND2. The fields could look like these:

| Field Name | Data Type | Field Size |
|---|---|---|
| NAME | | |
| LAST_NAME | Character | 10 |
| FIRST_NAME | Character | 10 |
| PHONE_NUMBER | | |
| AREA_CODE | Number | 3 |
| LOCAL_NUMBER | Character | 8 |

You will need to designate the NAME and PHONE_NUMBER fields as GROUP fields. You will be prompted for abbreviations of the field names when they are relatively long.

Finally, be sure to notice the symbols displayed at the top of your screen while you are in ADT. You might find them helpful from time to time during your ADT session. They are as follows:

| Symbol | Function |
|---|---|
| ? | Gives HELP on the last ADT command typed. |
| ! | Prints all the record definitions up to this point. |
| < | Backs up to the previous step in the ADT session. |
| <PF2> | Gives the "overview" screen HELP. |

### Entering and Exiting DATATRIEVE

| *Command* | *Description* |
|---|---|
| DTR32 | Issued at the operating system MYNODE$ prompt, this command starts execution of DATATRIEVE program. |
| EXIT | Issued at the DTR> prompt, this command exits DATATRIEVE. |

The following commands or statements are issued at the DTR> prompt while in the DATATRIEVE program.

| *Command or Statement* | *Description* |
|---|---|
| HELP | Enters DATATRIEVE's on-line help system. |
| SHOW... | Displays. |
| SHOW DOMAINS | Shows domains available with current dictionary. |
| SHOW RECORDS | Shows record definitions available with current dictionary. |
| SHOW READY | Shows domains ready to be queried. |
| SHOW ALL | Shows all the above along with collections and tables. |
| PURGE; | Deletes all but the highest version of each "dictionary object" (e.g., domain definitions and record definitions) from each domain. The semicolon is required. |
| READY *domain-name* | Gives access to *domain-name*. Required before queries can be made of this domain. |
| READY *domain-name* WRITE | Prepares a domain for the addition of records. |
| STORE *domain-name* | Begins addition of a new record to a domain's data file. |
| READY *domain-name* MODIFY | Prepares a domain for the modification of records. |
| MODIFY | Begins modification of a selected record in a domain. |

`PRINT...` Displays.

`PRINT` *domain-name* Prints the entire contents of this domain. `PRINT ALL` *domain-name has the same effect.*

`PRINT FIRST` *n domain-name*

Prints first *n* records in this domain.

`PRINT` *domain-name* `WITH` *rse*

Prints all elements (record stream) in this domain that satisfy the RSE.

`PRINT FIRST` *n domain-name* `WITH` *rse*

Prints first *n* elements in this domain that satisfy the RSE.

`PRINT` *domain-name* `SORTED BY` *field-name*

Prints entire contents of this domain sorted by the specified field.

`PRINT` *domain-name* `WITH` *rse* `SORTED BY` *field-name*

Prints all elements in this domain that satisfy the RSE, sorted by the specified field.

`PRINT` *domain-name* `WITH` *rse* `SORTED BY ASCENDING` *field-name*

The same as previous statement except sorted by the specified field in ascending order. `DESCENDING`, or `DESC`, order is also an option.

`PRINT` *field-name(s)* `OF` *domain-name* `WITH` *rse*

Prints the specified field(s) of domains that satisfy the RSE.

`PRINT` *collection-name* Prints the collection created by a `FIND` statement.

---

`FIND` Creates a collection.

`FIND` *rse* Creates a collection satisfying the RSE, and names it `CURRENT`.

---

`REPORT` Executes DATATRIEVE's Report Writer.

`REPORT` *collection-name*

Executes the Report Writer using the specified collection.

`REPORT` *collection-name* `SORTED BY` *field-name(s)*

Executes the Report Writer using the specified collection and sorted by the specified field(s).

`END_REPORT` Exits the Report Writer.

---

`ADT` Calls the Application Design Tool to customize your own database. (Set up your domain with its record definition and initial raw data file.)

---

## 7.8 Exercises

1. Generate a file containing all on-line help outside of DATATRIEVE by typing the following commands at the operating system prompt.

```
HELP/OUTPUT=DTR1.HLP DATATRIEVE...
PRINT/DELETE/NOTIFY DTR1.HLP
```

2. Using the `LIBRARY` command discussed in Chapter 2, Exercise 9, and keeping in mind the fact that the `HELP` within DATATRIEVE is on the file named `SYS$HELP:DTRHELP.HLB`, print a copy of the complete on-line help available from within DATATRIEVE.

3. Test the following statements:

```
PRINT PERSONNEL WITH START_DATE = "2-Aug-1981"
PRINT PERSONNEL WITH LAST_NAME = "WITTGEN"
PRINT FIRST 7 PERSONNEL WITH DEPT = "G20"
PRINT FIRST 5 PERSONNEL WITH STATUS = "EXPERIENCED"
```

   Explain your results in each application. Try using the `EDIT` command if you type a line incorrectly and get an error message. Also try <UP ARROW> to edit a previous command. (Compare this to the command line editing at the DCL level.)

4. Test the following statements:

```
PRINT PERSONNEL WITH DEPT = "G20" SORTED BY SALARY, -
LAST_NAME
PRINT PERSONNEL WITH DEPT = "G20" SORTED BY LAST_NAME, -
SALARY
PRINT PERSONNEL WITH DEPT = "G20" SORTED BY DESC SALARY
PRINT PERSONNEL WITH DEPT = "G20" SORTED BY ASCENDING -
SALARY
PRINT PERSONNEL SORTED BY LAST_NAME, DEPT
PRINT PERSONNEL SORTED BY ASCENDING DEPT, DESCENDING SALARY
```

   Explain your results in each application. Is the default sort (i.e., the sort where you do not specify ascending or descending) ascending or descending?

5. Test out the following statements:

```
PRINT PERSONNEL WITH SALARY > 20000
PRINT PERSONNEL WITH SALARY > 20000 -
AND STATUS = "EXPERIENCED"
PRINT PERSONNEL WITH DEPT = "G20" -
AND SALARY BT 20000 AND 40000
```

```
PRINT PERSONNEL WITH STATUS NE "TRAINEE"
PRINT PERSONNEL WITH DEPT CONT "T" BUT DEPT NE "TOP"
PRINT FIRST 5 PERSONNEL WITH SALARY = 26000 SORTED BY SALARY
PRINT PERSONNEL WITH SUP_ID = 39485, 48475
PRINT PERSONNEL WITH DEPT CONTAINING "F", "T"
```

Explain your results in each application. Try the following variation on one of the above statements:

```
PRINT PERSONNEL WITH STATUS NE "Trainee"
```

Is DATATRIEVE case-sensitive? Does this indicate that you should take any particular precautions when issuing RSEs?

6. Try all the examples in Table 7.1. Explain all your results.

7. Returning to Exercises 3 through 6, do several involving the PERSONNEL domain, except PRINT (to your terminal) only the NAME and SALARY fields. Then do the same thing, except PRINT (to your terminal) only the NAME, START_DATE, and SUP_ID fields.

8. Create and PRINT (to your terminal) the collections suggested by the following statements:

```
FIND PERSONNEL WITH SUP_ID = 39485
FIND PERSONNEL WITH DEPT = F11
FIND PERSONNEL WITH SALARY = 26500
```

9. Returning to Exercises 3 through 7, do several, applying the FIND statement in conjunction with DATATRIEVE's Report Writer to create reports on separate files in your directory. Make sure that the reports have appropriately descriptive titles.

10. Your boss wants a report on all experienced employees. Use DATATRIEVE on the PERSONNEL domain to create a report on all personnel with the status EXPERIENCED. In your report, print only the ID, NAME, DEPT, and SALARY fields. Sort the results *only* by the SALARY field. Entitle the report "Experienced Employees"/ "by"/ "Salary".

11. Follow the instructions in Exercise 10, except report on trainees and entitle your report appropriately. Then use WPS-PLUS (if you have studied Chapter 4) to prepare a memo concerning the report (from DATATRIEVE), including the tabular part of that report. Take the memo format to be

DATE
MEMO TO:
FROM:
CONCERNING:
Body of the memo

12. Use DATATRIEVE on the FAMILIES domain contained in your directory to create a report on a file so that you are reporting all families with more than two children. Entitle the report "Non-Zero Population Growth" / "Families", and have your report include *all* fields. *Hint*: While inside the Report Writer, you will need to type PRINT FAMILY, instead of PRINT FAMILIES. (You should know why.)

13. Following the suggested outline in Section 7.6, use ADT to create the simple FRIENDS phone book domain. When the domain has been set up, use the READY FRIENDS WRITE command, followed by REPEAT 5 STORE FRIENDS. Next, add five records to the domain.

14. Use DATATRIEVE to create a phone book database that contains at least fifteen records with at least three different zip codes, at least three different area codes, and at least three different cities. The records should have the following form:

| Field Name | Data Type | Field Size |
|---|---|---|
| NAME | | |
| LAST_NAME | Character | 10 |
| FIRST_NAME | Character | 10 |
| ADDRESS | | |
| STREET_NUMBER | Number | 5 |
| STREET_NAME | Character | 10 |
| CITY | Character | 10 |
| STATE | Character | 10 |
| ZIP | Number | 5 |
| PHONE_NUMBER | | |
| AREA_CODE | Number | 3 |
| LOCAL_NUMBER | Character | 8 |

Now generate three different reports:

a. All records and all fields, sorted by ZIP code

b. All records and all fields, sorted by LAST_NAME and AREA_CODE

c. All records and *only* the NAME and PHONE_NUMBER fields, and CITY fields sorted by city

15. Examine the record definition (ACCOUNT_BALANCE_REC) of the ACCOUNT_BALANCES domain contained in your directory. How many group fields does it have? Name two of the group fields and give the number of elementary fields that comprise each of the two group fields.

16. Use DATATRIEVE and Report Writer with the ACCOUNT_BALANCES domain to create a report file that contains the first ten (if there are that many) REVENUE_FIELDS with RENTAL_INCOME greater than $10,000.

Chapter 8

# The DECalc Spreadsheet Program

A spreadsheet is just an electronic worksheet, like any worksheet you have used to create a home or business budget. Spreadsheets have many kinds of applications, most readily apparent in the areas of business and institutional administration.[1] For example, suppose you are the president of a small company with three departments and a projected annual income of $300,000. A well-designed spreadsheet can model the finances of your company so that you can specify how you allocate your resources to each department and, in turn, how each department spends its budget.

When you complete this spreadsheet model of your company, you can realize its usefulness by asking a few "what if?" questions. For example, what if my income projections are too optimistic? Which departments will be hit first or hardest? What if I allocate a greater percentage of this decreased income to one of these departments? How would this reallocation affect the other departments?

If you have done your work on the spreadsheet design properly, these kinds of questions are easily examined because the financial interrelations between departments are built in. You can examine many different scenarios, both optimistic and pessimistic, and make contingency plans accordingly.

1. For more details, see texts such as Bibliography [16, 20].

You can see that this kind of planning tool could easily be applied to governmental administration as well as to the management of your own personal finances. In the next sections, we look at how to use DECalc, a spreadsheet program available on VAX computers, to construct a very simple gradebook and checkbook. Although the complexity of our examples is not great, you should be able to see how larger spreadsheet applications can be set up.

## 8.1 Interactive Session 1: A Simple Gradebook

In this section, we ask you to take the role of a teacher who wants to use DECalc to keep track of student grades. As an example you will create a simple gradebook containing two students, their two exam grades, homework averages, and calculated final averages.

In this interactive session, you will learn

- How to enter and exit DECalc
- How to observe the files automatically created by DECalc
- How to get HELP in DECalc
- The screen configuration of DECalc, with accompanying terminology
- How to move the box cursor
- How to enter label and value data into a DECalc spreadsheet
- How to enter formulas and functions
- How to reproduce the contents of a box over a given target range
- Simple column formatting
- How to save and retrieve your spreadsheets

Now, invoke the DECalc spreadsheet program by typing CALCULATE (or CALC) <RETURN> at the operating system level. In a few moments your screen will reconstruct and resemble Figure 8.1. In Figure 8.1, you can see the major part of the screen. However, the items you see in the figure that are printed on the light color area will appear on your screen in reverse video. Reverse video means that the letters are dark against a light background, the opposite of the screen's normal appearance. The basic structure of the spreadsheet is that of a grid, or matrix, made up of vertical columns and horizontal rows. Each row and column intersection is called a *box*, or *cell*.

When DECalc appears on your screen, it tells you that HELP is available by pressing the <PF2> key. Try this and see what happens. You will notice that the bottom half of the screen fills with text concerning OVERVIEW. Alternately

```
A1                  DECalc                   Version 3.0A...
     Press the PF2 key for HELP...
     Press the PF2 key for HELP...
       A     |    B    |    C    |    D    |    E    |...
 1
 2
 3
 4
 5
 6
 7
 8
 9
10
11
12
13
15
16   COPYRIGHT (C) DIGITAL EQUIPMENT CORPORATION 1987
 .
 .
```

**Figure 8.1 Part of the Initial DECalc Screen**

pressing the <UP ARROW> and <DOWN ARROW> keys will cause this HELP window to scroll up and down provided that you are not at the top or bottom of the HELP text. Moving the <LEFT ARROW> and <RIGHT ARROW> keys will move you through several options on HELP. Move to some other topic with the <RIGHT ARROW> and press <RETURN> to see what happens. You should have been able to get HELP on some other topic. Press the <SPACEBAR> when you think that you understand how to use DECalc's on-line help system. Pressing the <SPACEBAR> will return you to the spreadsheet, with its display of columns A through G and rows 1 through 20.

You will soon see that DECalc has two parts (not counting the HELP screens). The bottom part is called the *window* because it allows you to see a portion of the spreadsheet that is seven columns wide and twenty rows long. When you first run DECalc, you get columns A through G and rows 1 through 20.

The top part of the DECalc display is composed of three lines, which are part of the *Information Area* of the display (some spreadsheets call this area the control panel):

1. The BOX/CONTENTS line

2. The DIRECTIONS line

3. The ENTRY line

The BOX/CONTENTS line will contain the contents of the current box as well as its coordinates. At this point, you are located at box A1 (column A, row 1). There are no data in the box, so all you see on the first line is A1.

Once you begin to enter commands, the second line, the DIRECTIONS line, will begin to provide limited directions concerning what DECalc expects for input. Any time you are confused, you can press <PF2> to get additional HELP on the command being issued.

Finally, the ENTRY line will contain anything you type from the keyboard. As you type your commands, you will see them appear here. If you type entries for a box, they will also appear on the ENTRY line.

Before doing anything more in DECalc, exit and make a few observations. To exit, simply type /E. Notice what happens on the DIRECTIONS and ENTRY lines before you are returned to the DCL prompt.

If you issue a DIR command, you will find a new file in your directory. Its name is DECALC_GRIDS.DIR.[2] What DECalc has done is create a subdirectory of your current directory; this subdirectory's name is DECALC_GRIDS. As you begin to work in DECalc, some of the spreadsheet files you save will reside in this subdirectory.

2. Version 4.0 of DECalc, available in a field test version, does *not* create this directory. Grids that are saved will now be placed by default in the directory you are in when you enter DECalc.

Whenever you want to see what is in this directory, simply

1. Type `DIRC` in order to get to the subdirectory.[3]
2. Type `DIR` for a directory of the files in this subdirectory.
3. In order to get back to your other files (your "root" directory), type `ROOT`, then type `DIR`.[4]

Now that the preliminaries are out of the way, re-enter DECalc and start on the gradebook. (See Figure 8.2 for the finished grid.) Type `CALC` <RETURN>. The screen will again reconstruct, and you will see the familiar grid of boxes and the three lines of the Information Area.

Begin by moving the box cursor around a little. (When the context is obvious we refer to the box cursor simply as the cursor.) Press the arrow keys and notice the result. See if you can get to the G4 box. Moving the cursor using the arrow keys is a good way to move to nearby locations within your spreadsheet, say, from box A1 to box A4. However, if you want to move the cursor to some distant location—say from A1 to K75—with one command, the | (vertical bar) command is much more efficient. For example, move back to box A1 by typing `|A1` <RETURN>. Notice this puts the cursor at the A1 location; the `BOX/CONTENTS` line notes this by registering `A1`.

In our applications of DECalc, the boxes can contain either *labels*, such as Budget or Expenses, or *values*, such as 300 or 2. Now enter some labels. Once you are located at box A1, type `Name` <RETURN>. You see that, as you type, `"Name` appears on the `ENTRY` line; once you press <RETURN>, `"Name` appears on the `BOX/CONTENTS` line. Most important, the contents of A1 become the label, `Name`, which is left-justified. When DECalc recognizes that you are typing a label, it automatically puts the label in quotes on the `ENTRY` line but not within the spreadsheet itself.

Now move the cursor to the B1 box and type `Exam 1` but instead of pressing <RETURN>, press the <RIGHT ARROW> key. By doing so, you see that pressing

---

3. If you are using the starter `LOGIN.COM` file, you will need to add the line
`$ DIRC == "SET DEFAULT [.DECALC_GRIDS]"`
to your `LOGIN.COM` file directly preceding the `$ EXIT:` line

4. If you are using the starter `LOGIN.COM` file, you will need to add the line
`$ ROOT == "SET DEFAULT SYS$LOGIN"`
to your `LOGIN.COM` file directly preceding the `$ EXIT:` line.

<RETURN> or moving the cursor will cause whatever is on the ENTRY line to be placed in the box where the cursor is located. Continue this process by putting Exam 2, Homework, Final, Average, and Average in cells C1, D1, E1, D2, and E2, respectively.

Next move to box A3 and try to put in ten hyphens (-) to create a horizontal line that will separate your headers from the students' names and grades below them (see Figure 8.2). However, when you type the second hyphen, you are greeted with a beep and the indication of an error. The problem is that the hyphen symbol indicates to DECalc the arithmetic operation of subtraction, so DECalc interprets what you have typed as two minus signs. In order to get DECalc to accept the hyphen as a label rather than as a value, you *must* preface the ten hyphens with a double quote ("). Do this, press <RETURN>, and observe that you get the desired result. You want this same result to occur in the other boxes in row 3 in columns B, C, D, and E. You could get this result by repeating the operation just done in box A3 another four times, which could become tedious. Instead, use the first of many DECalc *slash commands*, so called because they are preceded by a slash /.

To execute the REPRODUCE command, type /R and notice that the DIRECTIONS line begins to prompt you with information. If you want some on-line help, simply press <PF2>. Read some of the HELP screen, then return to your work by pressing the <SPACEBAR>.

In this session, you will probably make some mistakes and then not know what to do next. In such cases, the on-line help relating to the command with which you are working at that moment can be quite useful. You should become familiar with DECalc's on-line help system. It could save you substantial grief later on.

Now back to the REPRODUCE command. After /R press <RETURN>. You have just told DECalc that you want to reproduce the default *source range* A3:A3, read "A3 through A3." You are next prompted to give the *target range*, the range into which you want the contents of A3:A3 to be reproduced. Now type B3:E3 <RETURN>. Notice that you get the desired result: the ten hyphens in box A3 are reproduced in boxes B3 through E3.

Your gradebook will contain only two students, J. Doe and G. Smith. Enter their names in the A4 and A5 boxes, respectively.

To this point, you have entered only labels in the boxes. Now begin to enter some values. You will soon see that values are not only numbers, they can also be mathematical formulas and functions. If you are curious about values, you might check DECalc's on-line help for `ENTERING DATA`. For now, simply enter a few grades for the two scholars. Enter the grades `75`, `90`, and `88` in boxes B4, C4, and D4, respectively, for J. Doe. Then enter `66`, `73`, and `90` in boxes B5, C5, and D5, respectively, for G. Smith.

Spreadsheet programs like DECalc do a wonderful thing: they take the place of a calculator or scratch pad by performing calculations on data you enter. First, though, you must tell the program how the calculations are to be performed (added or subtracted, for example) by entering formulas in the appropriate boxes. Before you begin entering formulas and doing calculations, there is a command that you should enter *unless* you want your calculations to be done in a strictly left-to-right order (to within grouping symbols). If you intend the arithmetic to be done the way you learned it in algebra class, type `/GMMA`. This command will guarantee that you have "Globally set the Mode of Mathematical calculations to be done Algebraically." We suggest that you get into the habit of typing `/GMMA` before beginning to set up your calculations.

To compare these two methods of calculation, consider the expression 40 + 10/2. If the operations are done left to right, first 40 and 10 are added, giving 50. Then 50 is divided by 2, giving 25. This is DECalc's default. On the other hand, performing the operations algebraically, multiplication and division are done before addition and subtraction unless there are grouping symbols. In the algebraic calculation, 10 is divided by 2, giving 5. Next, 40 and 5 are added, giving 45.

Now enter a formula to tell DECalc how to compute the simple average of the three grades for J. Doe. Move the cursor to box E4 and type `(B4+C4+D4)/3` <RETURN>. Notice that you must enclose the items to be added in parentheses; a / symbolizes division. Also notice that, when you press <RETURN>, the average of the three grades is calculated and entered in the box as `84.3333333`. Next, move the cursor to box E5. Instead of a formula similar to the one above, we will use one of the many functions that DECalc provides. Type AVE(B5:D5) <RETURN>. This command tells DECalc to compute the average of the values in boxes B5 through D5. Again, you see that the average, 76.3333333, appears in the box and that the BOX/CONTENTS line of the Information Area tells you that the function AVE was used in calculating the contents of box E5.

At this point, we can ask a few "what if?" questions. For example, what if J. Doe received a grade of 90 on Exam 1, or a 42? How would her average change? To find out, move the cursor to J. Doe's Exam 1 box, B4, and enter these numbers, first one, then the other. Notice that, in each case, the Final Average column changes appropriately. Now return the value to 75.

Before saving your work, tidy up the Names column with a couple of applications of the FORMAT command. Move the cursor to box A1, and type /FC <RETURN>. This command tells DECalc to Format a Column; because the cursor is at box A1, it will format column A. The New Width option appears on the DIRECTIONS line of the Information Area. Choose this option by typing either N or, simply, <RETURN>. Pressing <RETURN> picks up the highlighted option, which in this case is N. Next, type 15 <RETURN> to set a new column width of 15. You can now see the result: column A has a width of fifteen characters instead of the default value of ten characters.

The sequence you just completed shows that DECalc works in a manner similar to that of DECspell. When the DIRECTIONS line gives several options, you can move the cursor along the DIRECTIONS line to the option you want and press <RETURN>. The option highlighted will be entered. Or you can type the first letter of one of the options followed by <RETURN> with the same result.

You still have a little work to do on the gradebook. Box A3 now does not have enough hyphens; it needs five more. Edit the contents of this box. Move the cursor to box A3 and press <PF3>. The ENTRY line now contains the contents of A3, and the DIRECTIONS line indicates that we are in EDIT mode. Move the cursor on the ENTRY line to the end of the hyphens and type five more, followed by <RETURN>. Now you know how to edit a box to change its contents without completely retyping those contents.

Continuing the tidying-up process, center the contents of some boxes using the FORMAT command. Type /FBA1:A6 followed by <RETURN>. This

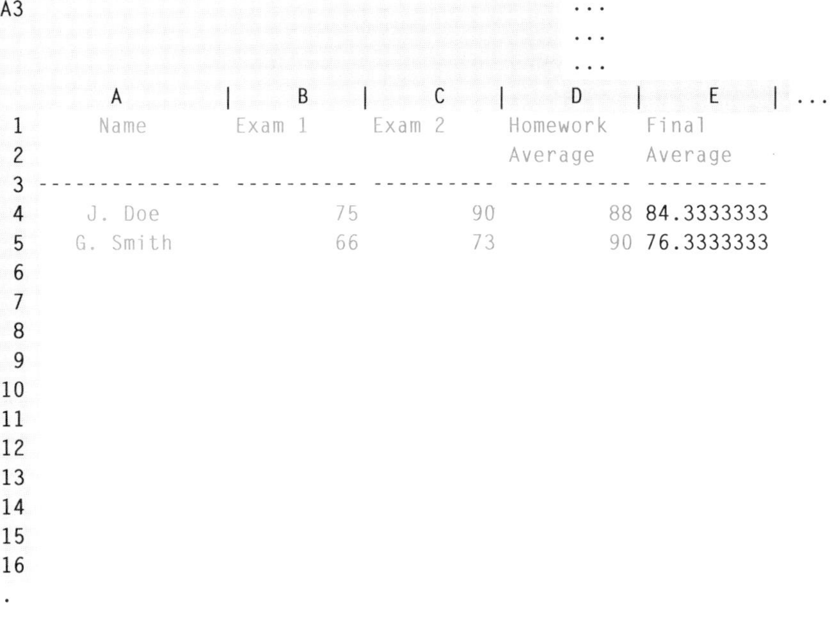

A3
A | B | C | D | E | ...
1 Name Exam 1 Exam 2 Homework Final
2 Average Average
3
4 J. Doe 75 90 88 84.3333333
5 G. Smith 66 73 90 76.3333333
6
7
8
9
10
11
12
13
14
15
16


**Figure 8.2 The Simple Gradebook Grid**

sequence indicates to DECalc that you want to Format Boxes in the range A1 through A6. Press <RETURN> again to specify a New format, as indicated by the `DIRECTIONS` line. Next type `C` (for Center) and <RETURN>. You can now see that the labels in column A have been centered. Your grid should look like the one in Figure 8.2.

Finish this session by saving your work. Execute the `STORAGE` command by typing `/SS` for Storage, Save. Then type `GRADES` <RETURN>. If asked about a password, specify `NONE` by pressing <RETURN>. Then exit by typing `/E`.

If you are using a version of DECalc earlier than 4.0, check your DECalc subdirectory by typing `DIRC` <RETURN> and the usual `DIR` command. You will see one new file with the name `GRADES.CALC$GRD;1`.[5] This file contains

5. If you are using version 4.0 (or higher) of DECalc, typing `DIR` <RETURN> will reveal a new file, `GRADES.CALC$DTF`. (The file type for version 4.0 or higher is `.CALC$DTF` rather than `.CALC$GRD` as in earlier versions.)

the encrypted version of your grid; that means that you can read the file *only* when you are in DECalc, which deciphers the code for you. You will not be able to make much of this file by typing it. Now return to your root directory by typing ROOT <RETURN>.

Execute DECalc again. When you are in the DECalc program, type /SR (for Storage, Retrieve), followed by GRADES <RETURN>. In a few moments, the grid will be restored, just as you left it. We will start here in the next session.

## 8.2 Interactive Session 2: More DECalc Commands

In this section, you will learn how to use several of the commands that come up on the DIRECTIONS line when you type /. If you logged out from session 1, you will need to log in and execute DECalc again. First, let's restore our gradebook. From what you learned in the previous section, you know that you can simply type /SRGRADES <RETURN> to regain your original gradebook grid.

In the remainder of this chapter, you will often be told to type a string of characters. You should pay special attention that you type these commands exactly as they are given. Type spaces with the <SPACEBAR> only when there is a space in the string given. Do *not* type a space when none is indicated. The ENTRY line might put in a space for readability, but your typing should be as indicated in the text. We emphasize this point because, for DECalc commands, pressing the <SPACEBAR> will often have the same effect as pressing <RETURN>.

Now suppose that you have forgotten the name of the grid you saved earlier. In this case, type /SL (for Storage, List) and <RETURN>. The bottom of the screen fills with a list of the grids you have saved. In this case you will see GRADES, the grid you saved.

In versions of DECalc earlier than 4.0, there is one problem with the /SL command: you will get a list of only those files in the DECALC_GRIDS subdirectory that have the file type .CALC$GRD. This means that if you saved your grid using the /SS command and gave your file a new file type rather than using the default supplied by DECalc, the file will not be listed even though it exists.[6]

In most business situations, it will be important to obtain a hard copy, or printout, of your spreadsheets. You can do so by using the PRINT command. Type /PSA1:E5 GRADES, which tells DECalc that you want to Print the Selected display of the range A1 through E5 (the diagonal corners of the grid) to a file named GRADES.LIS. Then press <RETURN> twice. The second <RETURN> commits you to a 132-column printout. As long as you are printing your work on a line printer, the 132-column option will be acceptable.

If you now exit DECalc with /E, you will find a file named GRADES.LIS in your root directory. If you TYPE the file, you will see the following result:

```
MYNODE$ TY GRADES.LIS
     Name      Exam 1       Exam 2       Homework   Final
                                         Average    Average
-----------------------------------------------------------
     J. Doe    75           90           88         84.3333333
     G. Smith  66           73           90         76.3333333
```

It is important to notice that .LIS files *cannot* be retrieved while you are in DECalc. They are useful *only* for displaying a part of the grid *outside* of the DECalc program. This is not true, however, for the command we discuss next. It is another of the PRINT command options. Get back into DECalc. Retrieve GRADES by typing /SRGRADES <RETURN>, and issue the command /PDA1:E5 GRADES <RETURN>. This command tells DECalc to Print, using the Dump select option, the grid range A1 through E5 (the diagonal corners of the grid) to the file named GRADES.CALC$COM. Now, exit DECalc with /E, and TYPE the file GRADES.CALC$COM. You should see something similar to the following:

```
MYNODE$ TY GRADES.CALC$COM
!DECalc Version 3.0A
! Setting globals for PRIMARY WINDOW
\GC10
\GFLL
\GFVGR
```

6. In DECalc version 4.0 (or higher), the /SL command searches only for files with the file type .CALC$DTR in the directory you were in when you entered DECalc.

```
\GFR
\GFU
\GMMA
\GMTC
\GMRA
! Restoring individual column widths for PRIMARY WINDOW
\FCA N15
! Restoring PRIMARY WINDOW box formats and contents
|A1 "Name
! "Name
\FB N C
|B1 "Exam 1
! "Exam 1
|C1 "Exam 2
! "Exam 2
|D1 "Homework
! "Homework
|E1 "Final
! "Final
|A2
\FB N C
|D2 "Average
! "Average
|E2 "Average
! "Average
|A3 "--------------
! "--------------
\FB N C
|B3 "----------
! "----------
|C3 "----------
! "----------
|D3 "----------
! "----------
|E3 "----------
! "----------
|A4 "J. Doe
! "J. Doe
\FB N C
|B4 75
! 7.50000000000000E+01
|C4 90
! 9.00000000000000E+01
|D4 88
! 8.80000000000000E+01
|E4 (B4+C4+D4)/3
! 8.43333333333333E+01
|A5 "G. Smith
! "G. Smith
\FB N C
```

```
|B5 66
! 6.60000000000000E+01
|C5 73
! 7.30000000000000E+01
|D5 90
! 9.00000000000000E+01
|E5 AVE(B5:D5)
! 7.63333333333333E+01
! Restoring marker to original position
|A3
! End of DECalc Dump file
```

This PRINT command is another way of storing your grid that allows you to see what is stored in each box. Recall that if you save the grid with the /SS (Storage, Save) command, you are unable to learn anything about the grid *unless* you are in the DECalc program. Now go back into DECalc and retrieve the grid GRADES.CALC$COM, which you saved in the Dump file. Once in DECalc, type /SCGRADES, followed by <SPACEBAR> or <RETURN>, for the STORAGE option of retrieving a Command file named GRADES.CALC$COM. The familiar gradebook grid will reappear after a few moments. There are other methods of saving and retrieving your grids. If you are interested in pursuing them, have a look at Bibliography [6].

Now let's examine several other DECalc commands you should find useful. Before discussing each command throughout the rest of this section, we assume that you have restored the grid to its initial condition via the /SR or the /SC commands. Do so whenever you see the phrase "restore the gradebook grid" in this book.

Sometimes you will want to get rid of the contents of one or more boxes. You can clear boxes with the BLANK command. Type /BSA1:B5 B Y, and notice that you have Blanked the Section of boxes A1 through B5 for Both values and formats. (In this instance, you must confirm with a Y that you really mean to do this. As irritating as such confirmation requirements might be, it can sometimes save you from making expensive mistakes.)

Restore the gradebook grid, move the cursor to box A3, and type /BGBY. This command Blanks the Grid of Both values and formats, after you give a confirming Y.

Restore the gradebook grid, move the cursor to box A3, and type `/DR3 4 Y`. This command Deletes Rows 3 through 4 after your confirming `Y`. Notice that this is different from blanking in the sense that the contents of the boxes are not simply erased. The rows themselves are deleted, and any rows below are moved up to take their place. Similar results can be obtained for columns by using the `/DC` option. For example, `/DCA A Y` will Delete Columns A through A after your confirming `Y`. This process can be more complicated when boxes are referenced in formulas contained in other boxes, as is the case with the grades and their averages. You should get more experience with DECalc before using the `DELETE ROW` or `DELETE COLUMN` options where formulas are involved.

Restore the gradebook grid, move the cursor to box A3, and type `/ICB 2` <RETURN>. This command Inserts two Columns *before* column B. Move the cursor to column G4 and note that the relation necessary for calculating the correct Final Average is maintained, that is, the formula has been altered to use boxes D4, E4, and F4 instead of B4, C4, and D4, as before. The same principle is followed for box G5.

Restore the gradebook grid, move the cursor to box A3, and type `/MR3 5 10` <RETURN>. This command Moves Rows 3 through 5 to a position *before* row 10. Move to boxes E8 and E9 and notice that, again, the appropriate boxes are referenced for calculating the correct Final Averages.

This concludes your second interactive DECalc session. Although there is still much about DECalc you do not know, you are now in a position to make use of many of its powerful features. We discuss one more topic, functions, in our next two interactive sessions. We will construct a fairly simple checkbook grid that can keep track of how much you spend in a single, coded category.

## 8.3 Interactive Session 3: A Simple Checkbook Grid

In our last two sessions, we discuss an extension of the `REPRODUCE` and `FORMAT` commands, along with some new functions. (If you want to learn about all the functions available in DECalc, enter the DECalc program and press <PF2>, then type `E` <RETURN> `F` <RETURN> (for Entering Data, Functions). Next, pick a Functions option—for example, Special—that you want to read about.

```
F5   \F D5-E5

    A  |           B           |    C    |    D    |    E    |    F
 1 My   Checkbook:
 2
 3 No.        Description          Code     Deposit     Check     Balance
 4 ----- ------------------------- --------- --------- --------- ---------
 5                                          $2,500.00            $2,500.00
 6                                                        $25.00 $2,475.00
 7                                                               $2,475.00
 8                                                               $2,475.00
 9                                                               $2,475.00
10                                                               $2,475.00
11                                                               $2,475.00
12                                                               $2,475.00
13                                                               $2,475.00
14                                                               $2,475.00
15                                                               $2,475.00
16                                                               $2,475.00
17                                                               $2,475.00
18                                                               $2,475.00
19 ----- ------------------------- --------- --------- --------- ---------
20                                          $2,500.00     $25.00 $2,475.00
 .
 .
```

**Figure 8.3 First Checkbook Grid**

Now let's begin creating a simple checkbook. Figure 8.3 shows how the finished checkbook grid should look. Enter DECalc. Because column A will contain the check number, make it only five characters wide with the command `/FCA N 5` <RETURN>. This command tells DECalc to Format Column A with a New width of five characters. Next, widen column B to twenty-five characters in order to accommodate the number of characters in our second column, Description. This can be done by typing `/FCB N 25` <RETURN> (or <SPACEBAR>). This command tells DECalc to Format Column B with a New width of twenty-five characters.

Now enter the column labels by typing `My`, `Checkbook:`, `No.`, `Description`, `Code`, `Deposit`, `Check`, and `Balance` in columns A1, B1, A3, B3, C3, D3,

E3, and F3, respectively. Next, center the labels in row 3 with the command /FBA3:F3 N C <RETURN>, which tells DECalc to Format Boxes A3 through F3 with a New format of Centering.

Next, put hyphens in boxes A4 through F4 by moving the cursor to the appropriate box, typing the double quote (") and the appropriate number of hyphens, or through some combination of this and the REPRODUCE command, as discussed in Section 8.1. Do the same for boxes A19 through F19. (For example, if you had already entered hyphens in row 4, you could simply issue the command /RA4:F4 A19 <RETURN>, which would Reproduce the work in the range A4 through F4 in the corresponding range beginning in box A19.) We set aside row 20 for entering formulas that calculate the totals of the deposits, checks, and the final balance.

Let's do a few formatting operations before defining the necessary arithmetic for correct calculation of the checkbook balances. First, type /FZC5:F18 <RETURN>. This command Formats the boxes that will contain the amounts of the codes, deposits, checks, and balances (boxes C5 through F18) in such a way that, if you do not enter any data in them, their values are assumed to be zero for the purposes of calculating and testing. Do the same operation for the totals (boxes D20 through F20) by typing /FZD20:F20 <RETURN>. If you do not, DECalc will give you errors when the balances being calculated involve boxes where you have *not* entered a value.

There is one other formatting chore: you need to make sure that the columns involving dollars will display the data appropriately. To make sure, type /FBD5:F18 N $ <RETURN>, which tells DECalc to Format Boxes D5 through F18 with a New format that includes a dollar sign. You need to do the same for the totals in row 20. Type /FBD20:F20 N $ <RETURN>.

Before saving your grid, type /GMMA. As mentioned earlier, this command guarantees that your calculations are done as you expect.

So far, we have little visible to show for this rather tedious session. You will find this aspect of spreadsheet setup to be the most time-consuming, but it *will* pay off in the end! Save your work with the familiar STORAGE command by typing /SSCHECK <RETURN> <RETURN> (for Storage, Save). Now we can demonstrate a few things and then return you to this point to continue your work on constructing a checkbook. Your grid is now saved in a file called CHECK.CALC$GRD in your DECALC_GRIDS subdirectory.[7]

Move the cursor to box D5 and type 25 <RETURN>. Notice that you have displayed $25.00. You are seeing the result of your formatting work. Try some of the other columns that you formatted with a dollar sign to see that things are as you want them. Now restore the grid by typing /SRCHECK <RETURN> Y. The Y tells DECalc to overwrite the current grid with your previously saved CHECK grid.

We next define the relations between the boxes so that, when we enter a deposit or check, DECalc will compute the balance accurately. Move the cursor to box F6 and type F5+D6-E6 <RETURN>. Notice that $.00 appears in box F6. This is as we intended from our FORMAT commands (/FZ). If you have not done the /FZ commands, you will get an error message (ERR) in the affected boxes. Now save the grid so you can experiment with your work.

Enter $2,500 as your initial deposit by moving the cursor to box D5 and typing 2500 <RETURN>. (2500 will also register automatically in box F5.) Move to box E6 and type 25 <RETURN>. You can see that the formula you entered for box F6 has come into action. DECalc calculated F5 + D6 – E6 ($2,500.00 + $0.00 – $25.00) to give you a balance of $2,475.00 in box F6.

We could now (very laboriously) type the appropriate formulas all the way down column F, from row 7 to row 18. However, let's use a variation of the REPRODUCE command that we encountered earlier. Type /RF6:F6 F7:F18 <RETURN>, which tells DECalc to Reproduce the contents of range F6 through F6 to the target range of F7 through F18, and adjust for the position in the case of each of the entries in box F6. Move the cursor to box F7 and you will see that the calculations are as they should be, namely, F6 + D7 – E7. Your data should be correct, down to box F18.

We end this interactive session by defining the totals in row 20. Move the cursor to box D20 and type SUM(D5:D18) <RETURN>, which calculates the

7. Or, for version 4.0 (or higher), in your current directory in CHECK.CALC$DTR.

sum of the deposits. Similarly, enter `SUM(E5:E18)` <RETURN> for box E20, and simply enter `F18` for box F20. (Can you tell why?)

There is one loose end that we can take care of by moving to F5 and typing `D5-E5` <RETURN>. Why is this reasonable?

Now save your grid. However, before leaving this session, you might enter some deposit or check amounts to verify that your grid is working properly.

In the next section, we discuss how to use the code column to keep track of spending in certain categories, using the `IF` function.

## 8.4 Interactive Session 4: Checkbook Revisited

Suppose you wish to link your home budget with your new electronic checkbook. You have already created a column called Code (box C3) into which you can enter a code for each type of check expense; for example, a 2 might indicate groceries. Now let's build a simple table to the right of the checkbook (Figure 8.4 shows a section of the completed grid) so that if the code associated with the check is 2, then the amount of the check will be entered in the table. If the code is not 2, a 0 will be entered. In this way, you can keep track of how much you spend on this category.

Retrieve your checkbook grid. Move the cursor to box H2. Type `Expenses` in H2 and `in Code 2:` in box I2. Type `No.`, `Amount`, and hyphens in boxes H3, I3, and H4 and I4, respectively. Also put hyphens in boxes H19 and I19.

Now move the cursor to cell H5 and type `IF (C5=2,A5,0)` <RETURN>. This sequence of phrases, called an `IF` statement, tells DECalc that if C5 (the code entry for the check or deposit for this row) is 2 (if C5 = 2 is true), then the value of the check number (box A5) will be displayed in cell H5. If C5 is not equal to 2 (if C5 = 2 is false), then a 0 will be displayed in box H5. Reproduce this work down the rest of this column to row 18 by typing `/RH5:H5 H6:H18`. Zeros will appear down this part of column H.

Next, move the cursor to column I and row 5. Since this column will contain the amounts of the checks, these boxes should be formatted with dollar signs. Do this by typing `/FBI5:I18 N $` <RETURN>. Also do the same for box I20, which will contain the totals.

```
I20   \F SUM(I5:I18)
```

| | C | D | E | F | G | H | I |
|---|---|---|---|---|---|---|---|
| 1 | | | | | | | |
| 2 | | | | | | Expenses | in Code 2: |
| 3 | Code | Deposit | Check | Balance | | Type No. | Amount |
| 4 | ---------- | ---------- | ---------- | ---------- | | ---------- | ---------- |
| 5 | | $2,500.00 | | $2,500.00 | | 0 | $.00 |
| 6 | | | $25.00 | $2,475.00 | | 0 | $.00 |
| 7 | | | | $2,475.00 | | 0 | $.00 |
| 8 | | | | $2,475.00 | | 0 | $.00 |
| 9 | | | | $2,475.00 | | 0 | $.00 |
| 10 | | | | $2,475.00 | | 0 | $.00 |
| 11 | | | | $2,475.00 | | 0 | $.00 |
| 12 | | | | $2,475.00 | | 0 | $.00 |
| 13 | | | | $2,475.00 | | 0 | $.00 |
| 14 | | | | $2,475.00 | | 0 | $.00 |
| 15 | | | | $2,475.00 | | 0 | $.00 |
| 16 | | | | $2,475.00 | | 0 | $.00 |
| 17 | | | | $2,475.00 | | 0 | $.00 |
| 18 | | | | $2,475.00 | | 0 | $.00 |
| 19 | ---------- | ---------- | ---------- | ---------- | | ---------- | ---------- |
| 20 | | $2,500.00 | $25.00 | $2,475.00 | | | $.00 |
| . | | | | | | | |
| . | | | | | | | |

**Figure 8.4 Adding a Check Category**

Next, make certain that if the check is code 2, then its amount is posted in column I. Do so for box I5 by typing `IF(C5=2,E5,0)`. This will cause the amount (box E5) of a code 2 check to be entered in box I5. Otherwise, the value in I5 will be zero. Then reproduce this work down the column by typing `/RI5:I5 I6:I18`. Finally, allow for the calculation of the total amount of code 2 checks by moving the cursor to box I20 and entering `SUM(I5:I18)` <RETURN>.

Save your grid, then make some entries to see if everything is functioning as it should be. If it is not, go back over your work and redo the parts related to the boxes that are malfunctioning.

It should not be too difficult to see how you could set up several tables to keep track of any number of codes in your checkbook. See if you can use the REPRODUCE option to make another table for code 1.

## 8.5 A Few Tips on DECalc

This section contains a few tips that you may find helpful as you use DECalc. One is to be aware that DECalc supports a limited amount of windowing. In DECalc, this means that you can divide the display portion of your screen into two windows, either horizontal or vertical, but not both (at least in version 3.0 of DECalc). For instance, you might use the window option with the gradebook grid to specify two horizontal windows, where the upper window contains the column headings. This way, when the number of students exceeds the number of lines in the display area, you can still see what the entries represent. For more information on windows, enter DECalc and type /W <PF2>. Similar to the WINDOWS command is the TITLES command. For more information on the TITLES command, type /T <PF2>.

You have probably already noticed that when you placed hyphens in different boxes for marking divisions in your grid, a blank space was left between adjacent columns. If you want this blank space to contain a hyphen too, you could achieve this in one of at least two ways. One method is to use continuous labels; the other is to use repeating labels. With continuous labels, you are asked to give *all* the characters for a particular set of boxes, which you specify. This includes the blanks between columns. For more information on continuous labels, enter DECalc and type /L <PF2>.

With repeating labels, you can specify a single character (or a string of characters) that is to be repeated over a range of boxes. This will also cause the blank between the columns to be filled. For more information on repeating labels, enter DECalc and type /- (the hyphen character) followed by <PF2>.

If you intend arithmetic calculations to be done in the manner that you learned in your algebra classes, rather than strictly left to right within grouping symbols, it is advisable to use the /GMMA command (as discussed earlier). For more information on mathematical operations, enter DECalc and type /GM <PF2>.

It is also advisable not to forget that the grids you save using the /SS command are saved in the subdirectory DECALC_GRIDS (for versions earlier than 4.0). One of the implications of this fact is that when you are near the limit of your disk quota (which you can find out by issuing the SHOW QUOTA command at the operating system prompt), you might still have very few files in your root directory. The largest part of your quota might be allocated to the grids that you have saved and later forgotten. So, when getting rid of old files, do not forget the DECalc subdirectory in your deleting and purging.

One way of purging multiple versions of your grid files in the DECALC_GRIDS directory is to insert the following line in your LOGIN.COM file:

```
$ DPU*RGE == "PURGE [.DECALC_GRIDS]*.*"
```

After any subsequent log-in, you can purge multiple versions of your grid files from the DECALC_GRIDS directory by typing DPU at the operating system prompt while in the root directory.

## 8.6 Simple Graphics with DECalc

DECalc can be used to construct line graphs, bar graphs, and pie charts. In order to do the work in this section, you must have access to a graphics terminal and a graphics printer. Specifically, you need a terminal and printer that can display and print REGIS (REmote Graphics Instruction Set) output. Check with your instructor or local user services staff to find out if these facilities exist at your site and which commands are necessary to print to the appropriate printer.

Our example in this section concerns another gradebook, available in the TEXTFILES directory: GRAPHS.CALC$COM. It uses a few concepts not covered in this book, like assigning letter grades using numeric averages. However, you need not understand these concepts in order to draw the graphs. If you do not have access to a TEXTFILES directory, you should be able to replicate enough of the grid displayed in the following figures to generate your own graphs.

```
A18   "X. JUAN


         A      | B |  C |  D |  E |  F |  G |  H   |  I   |  J   |  K   |  L  |  M
 1  Course 1:         Hwk  Hwk  Hwk  Hwk  Hwk  Exam  Exam  Exam  Final Final Grade
 2  Name        No.     1    2    3    4    5     1     2     3  Exam   Avg  Num.
 3  -----------------------------------------------------------------------------
 4  C. Siva       1   8.7  3.2  9.5   10  7.5    65    77    96     90 81.16 85
 5  J. Toggle     2    10  5.5  4.4    7   10    50    66    95     66 70.16 75
 6  B. Unger      3    10   10  9.5  7.8    2    95    80    70     42 73.12 75
 7  A. Zonk       4   2.5  5.5  9.5    6    4    66    88    78     65  70.4 75
 8  -----------------------------------------------------------------------------
 9  Averages          7.8 6.05 8.23  7.7 5.88    69 77.75 84.75 65.75 73.71
10  -----------------------------------------------------------------------------
11  -----------------------------------------------------------------------------
12  Course 2:         Hwk  Hwk  Hwk  Hwk  Hwk  Exam  Exam  Exam  Final Final Grade
13  Name        No.     1    2    3    4    5     1     2     3  Exam   Avg  Num.
14  -----------------------------------------------------------------------------
15  J. Albert     1   5.5  8.8  9.4    6  8.9    55    87    90     66 75.04 75
16  Q. Jacks      2   6.6  9.8  8.7    4  7.4    45    84    87     75  72.8 75
17  D. Lump       3    10   10   10  9.7  1.5    88    80    90     80 84.08 85
18  X. Juan       4   9.7  9.6  9.5   10   10    89    90    96     95 93.52 95
19  -----------------------------------------------------------------------------
20  Averages         7.95 9.55  9.4 7.43 6.95 69.25 85.25 90.75     79 81.36
 .
 .
```

**Figure 8.5 Left Part of the GRAPHS Grid**

Once you have copied `GRAPHS.CALC$COM` into your own directory, load it into DECalc via `/SCGRAPHS` <RETURN>. You should be able to examine the grid displayed in two parts in Figures 8.5 and 8.6. As you can see, this grid contains a set of grades for two courses with four students each.

### 8.6.1 *Generating a Line Graph*

First we discuss how to generate a line graph. The goal here is to draw two lines. One line will connect the homework averages for the five assignments in course 1, and the other will connect the homework averages for the five assignments in course 2.

```
017    IF (M17="A",1,0)


     E | F | G |  H  |  I  |  J  |  K  |  L  |  M  | N | O | P | Q | R | S
 1 Hwk  Hwk  Hwk  Exam  Exam  Exam  Final Final Grade     No. No. No. No. No.
 2    3    4    5     1     2     3 Exam  Avg   Num.      A's B's C's D's F's
 3 -----------------------------------------------------  --- --- --- --- ---
 4  9.5   10  7.5    65    77    96    90 81.16 B           0   1   0   0   0
 5  4.4    7   10    50    66    95    66 70.16 C           0   0   1   0   0
 6  9.5  7.8    2    95    80    70    42 73.12 C           0   0   1   0   0
 7  9.5    6    4    66    88    78    65  70.4 C           0   0   1   0   0
 8 -----------------------------------------------------  --- --- --- --- ---
 9 8.23  7.7 5.88    69 77.75 84.75 65.75 73.71             0   1   3   0   0
10 ---------------------------------------------------------------------------
11 ---------------------------------------------------------------------------
12 Hwk  Hwk  Hwk  Exam  Exam  Exam  Final Final Grade     No. No. No. No. No.
13    3    4    5     1     2     3 Exam  Avg   Num.      A's B's C's D's F's
14 -----------------------------------------------------  --- --- --- --- ---
15  9.4    6  8.9    55    87    90    66 75.04 C           0   0   1   0   0
16  8.7    4  7.4    45    84    87    75  72.8 C           0   0   1   0   0
17   10  9.7  1.5    88    80    90    80 84.08 B           0   1   0   0   0
18  9.5   10   10    89    90    96    95 93.52 A           1   0   0   0   0
19 -----------------------------------------------------  --- --- --- --- ---
20  9.4 7.43 6.95 69.25 85.25 90.75    79 81.36             1   1   2   0   0
 .
 .
```

**Figure 8.6 Right Part of the GRAPHS Grid**

Start the process by typing `/XGLINE1 S`. This specifies that you want to use a program external (`X`) to DECalc (in this case, DECgraph). The `G` picks the Graph option and `LINE1` names a file in your directory (`LINE1.CALC$DGR`) that will contain the specifications you are about to give. The `S` indicates that you want to specify the characteristics of the graph. Once you type the `S`, your screen will reconstruct as shown in Figure 8.7. Fill in the fields as shown in the figure by typing the colored text following `Title:`, `Subtitle:`, etc.

As you can see, we have picked the contents of C2 through G2 for the *X* values. This will cause 1, 2, 3, 4, 5 to be displayed along the *X* (horizontal) axis. The *Y* values for line 1 and line 2 are chosen from the appropriate cells containing the homework averages for course 1 and course 2 (C9 through G9, and C20 through G20, respectively).

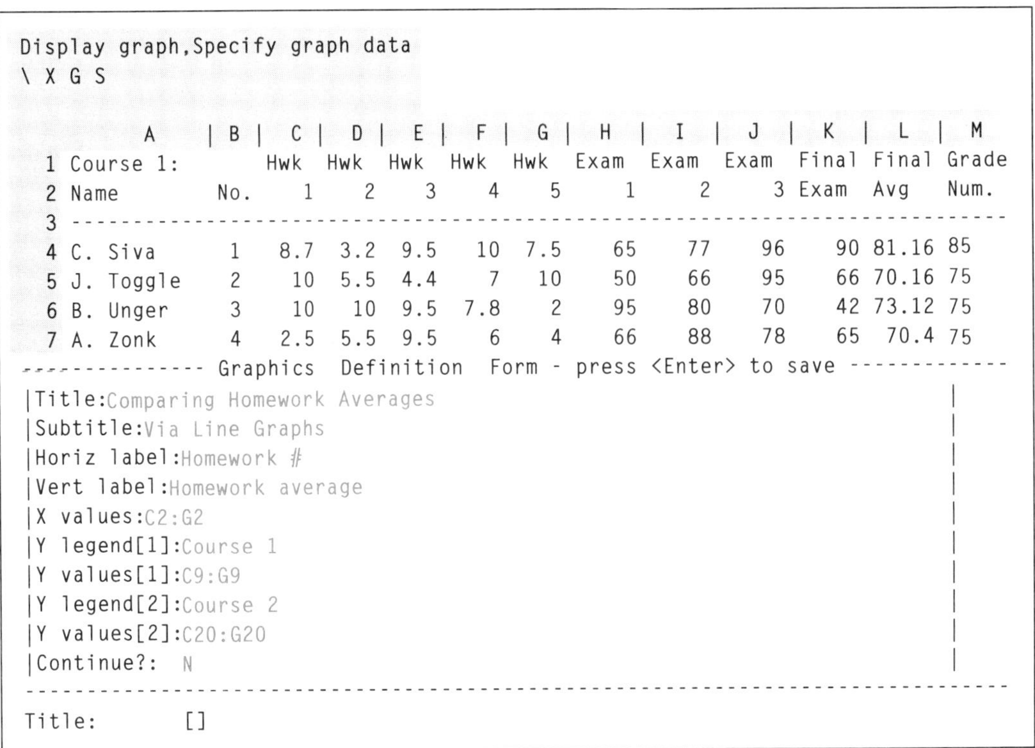

```
Display graph,Specify graph data
\ X G S

          A       | B |  C |  D |  E |  F |  G |  H   |  I   |  J   |  K   |  L   | M
  1 Course 1:          Hwk  Hwk  Hwk  Hwk  Hwk  Exam  Exam  Exam  Final Final Grade
  2 Name          No.    1    2    3    4    5     1     2     3 Exam   Avg   Num.
  3 ------------------------------------------------------------------------------
  4 C. Siva        1   8.7  3.2  9.5   10  7.5    65    77    96    90 81.16 85
  5 J. Toggle      2    10  5.5  4.4    7   10    50    66    95    66 70.16 75
  6 B. Unger       3    10   10  9.5  7.8    2    95    80    70    42 73.12 75
  7 A. Zonk        4   2.5  5.5  9.5    6    4    66    88    78    65  70.4 75
--------------- Graphics Definition Form - press <Enter> to save ------------
|Title:Comparing Homework Averages                                          |
|Subtitle:Via Line Graphs                                                   |
|Horiz label:Homework #                                                     |
|Vert label:Homework average                                                |
|X values:C2:G2                                                             |
|Y legend[1]:Course 1                                                       |
|Y values[1]:C9:G9                                                          |
|Y legend[2]:Course 2                                                       |
|Y values[2]:C20:G20                                                        |
|Continue?: N                                                               |
------------------------------------------------------------------------------
Title:      []
```

**Figure 8.7 Specifying a Line Graph**

Once you have typed `N` at the `Continue?:` prompt, your cursor will return to the command line and you can finish what you have been typing, `XGLINE1 S`, by typing `LOLINE1` <RETURN>. This picks the Line graph option and specifies that you want your Output to be printed to a file. The name of this output file, `LINE1.GRO`, is specified by `LINE1`. (Choosing the `D` (Display) option instead of `O` will cause the results to be displayed on your screen if your terminal can display REGIS output.)

Now exit DECalc with `/EY`, and check to see what new files have been created. You should find the following files:

| | |
|---|---|
| `LINE1.CALC$DGR` | Created to hold your specifications. |
| `LINE1.GRO` | Contains your graph, which can now be printed on an appropriate printer. |

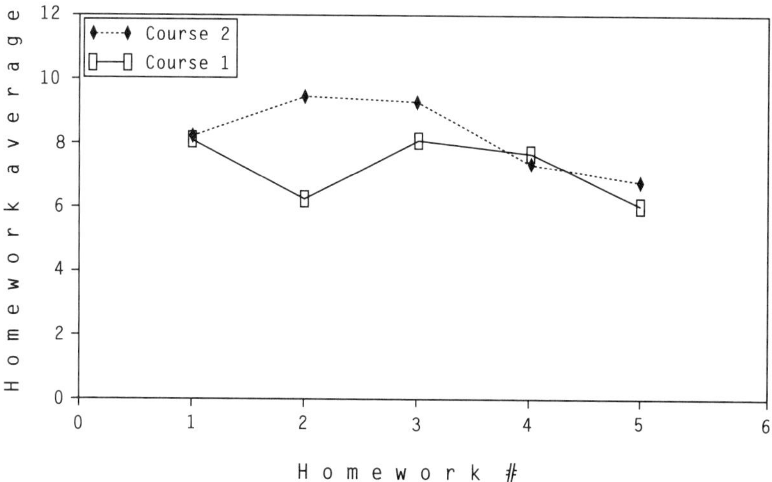


**Figure 8.8 Result of Printing LINE1.GRO**

| | |
|---|---|
| `LINE.GRD` | Holds the data for DECgraph. You would need to study DECgraph to fully understand the purpose of this file. |
| `LINE.GRI` | Holds the identification information for DECgraph. You would need to study DECgraph to fully understand the purpose of this file. |

Figure 8.8 shows the resulting line graph when the `LINE1.GRO` file is printed.

### 8.6.2 *Generating a Bar Graph*

The procedure for generating a bar graph is similar to that demonstrated in the previous section with a line graph. We take the same set of data, the homework averages for the two courses, and display them in a bar graph format.

Re-enter DECalc and reload the `GRAPHS` grid. Then type `/XGBAR1 S`. As before, you ask for the External (`X`) option so that you can access the program DECgraph. Then you pick the Graph option and give the file name `BAR1` for the specification file (the one with the file type `.CALC$DGR`). By typing `S`, for Specify, you get the same specification form as before, and this time fill it with the colored input as shown in Figure 8.9.

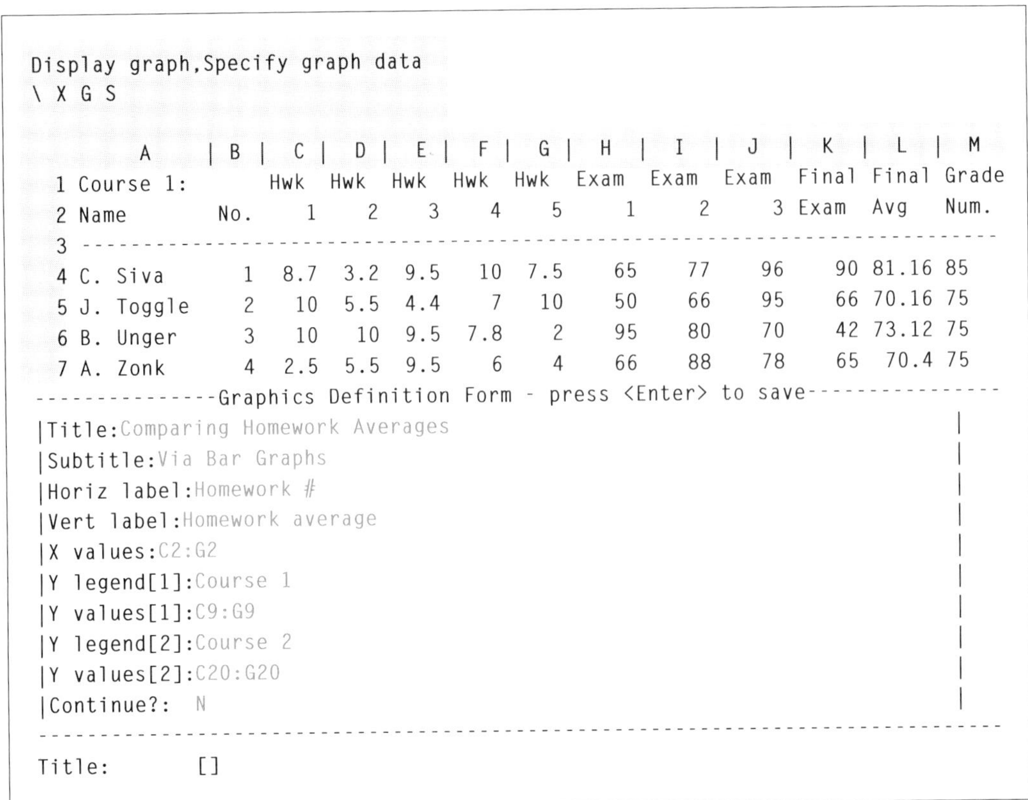

```
Display graph,Specify graph data
\ X G S
         A     | B | C | D | E | F | G | H | I | J | K | L | M
  1 Course 1:        Hwk  Hwk  Hwk  Hwk  Hwk  Exam  Exam  Exam  Final Final Grade
  2 Name        No.    1    2    3    4    5     1     2     3  Exam  Avg   Num.
  3 -----------------------------------------------------------------------------
  4 C. Siva       1  8.7  3.2  9.5   10  7.5    65    77    96    90 81.16 85
  5 J. Toggle     2   10  5.5  4.4    7   10    50    66    95    66 70.16 75
  6 B. Unger      3   10   10  9.5  7.8    2    95    80    70    42 73.12 75
  7 A. Zonk       4  2.5  5.5  9.5    6    4    66    88    78    65  70.4 75
--------------Graphics Definition Form - press <Enter> to save---------------
|Title:Comparing Homework Averages                                           |
|Subtitle:Via Bar Graphs                                                     |
|Horiz label:Homework #                                                      |
|Vert label:Homework average                                                 |
|X values:C2:G2                                                              |
|Y legend[1]:Course 1                                                        |
|Y values[1]:C9:G9                                                           |
|Y legend[2]:Course 2                                                        |
|Y values[2]:C20:G20                                                         |
|Continue?:  N                                                               |
-----------------------------------------------------------------------------
Title:        []
```

**Figure 8.9 Specifying a Bar Graph**

Once you have responded with `N` at the `Continue?:` prompt, complete the entries on the command line, currently `/XGBAR1 S`, by typing `BOBAR1` <RETURN>. This chooses the Bar graph option with Output to be sent to a file with the file name `BAR1` (and file type `.GRO`). Again, if you are at an appropriate graphics (REGIS) terminal, typing `D` (Display) instead of `O` (Output) will cause the bar graph to be displayed on your terminal screen.

Exit DECalc with `/EY`, and as in the case of the line graph, you have four files, `BAR1.CALC$DGR`, `BAR1.GRD`, `BAR1.GRI`, and `BAR1.GRO`. `BAR1.GRO` is the file to be printed on the graphics (REGIS) printer. Figure 8.10 shows the resulting graph.

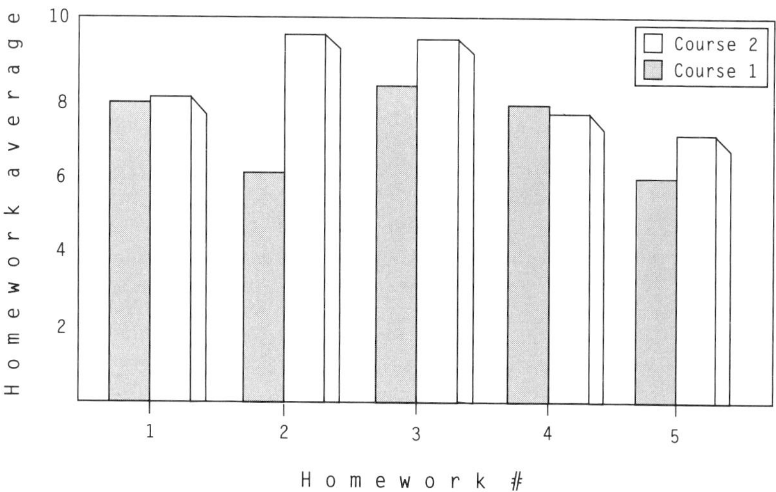


**Figure 8.10 Result of Printing BAR1.GRO**

```
Display graph,Specify graph data
\ X G S

          A      | B |  C |  D |  E |  F |  G |   H  |   I  |   J  |  K  |  L  |  M
  1 Course 1:          Hwk  Hwk  Hwk  Hwk  Hwk  Exam   Exam   Exam  Final Final Grade
  2 Name         No.     1    2    3    4    5     1      2      3 Exam  Avg   Num.
  3 --------------------------------------------------------------------------------
  4 C. Siva        1   8.7  3.2  9.5   10  7.5    65     77     96    90 81.16 85
  5 J. Toggle      2    10  5.5  4.4    7   10    50     66     95    66 70.16 75
  6 B. Unger       3    10   10  9.5  7.8    2    95     80     70    42 73.12 75
  7 A. Zonk        4   2.5  5.5  9.5    6    4    66     88     78    65  70.4 75
-------------- Graphics  Definition  Form - press <Enter> to save ------------
|Title:Grade Distribution                                                    |
|Subtitle:in Course 2                                                        |
|Horiz label:Grades                                                          |
|Vert label:                                                                 |
|X values:02:S2                                                              |
|Y legend[1]:                                                                |
|Y values[1]:020:S20                                                         |
|Y legend[2]:                                                                |
|Y values[2]:                                                                |
|Continue?:  N                                                               |
--------------------------------------------------------------------------------
Title:        []
```

**Figure 8.11 Specifying a Pie Chart**

### 8.6.3 *Generating a Pie Chart*

We conclude our discussion of generating graphs with DECalc by using the same gradebook example to generate a pie chart showing the percentages of A's, B's, and so on, in course 2. There will be only one set of *X* values and one set of *Y* values.

Let's begin by loading the `GRAPHS.CALC$COM` grid back into DECalc. Once this is done, type `/XGPIE1 S`. By now you can recognize that you have asked for the External (`X`) use of the Graph option, thus calling the DECgraph program. You have named the specification file `PIE1.CALC$DGR` by giving the file name `PIE1`, and have indicated that you wish to specify the chart's characteristics by typing `S`. As before, the specification form appears. Complete it as indicated by the colored text in Figure 8.11.

When you have completed the specification form by typing `N` at the `Continue?:` prompt, finish the command currently on the command line, `/XGPIE1 S`, by typing `POPIE1` <RETURN>. In so doing, you have chosen the Pie graph option to be saved (Output) to a file named `PIE1.GRO`. As before, choosing the `D` (Display) option rather than `O` (Output) will cause the chart to be displayed on the screen of a REGIS terminal.

After exiting DECalc with `/EY`, you will find the following four files: `PIE1.CALC$DGR`, `PIE1.GRD`, `PIE1.GRI`, `PIE1.GRO`. The file `PIE1.GRO` can now be printed on the appropriate printer. Figure 8.12 shows the resulting chart.

### 8.6.4 *Additional Options*

If you have already specified a graph and just want to change a few specifications, you can proceed as discussed earlier except that you will be starting with your original specifications already entered on the form rather than from scratch. For example, once you are in DECalc with the grid loaded, to change some specifications on the line graph, type `/XGLINE1 S`, and when asked if you want to change some specifications, reply with `Y`.

If you are at a REGIS terminal, you can also display any `.GRO` file that you printed out by typing `TY` *filename*`.GRO` <RETURN>. For example, if you want to look at the results in `LINE1.GRO` before printing it, simply type `TY LINE1.GRO` <RETURN>.

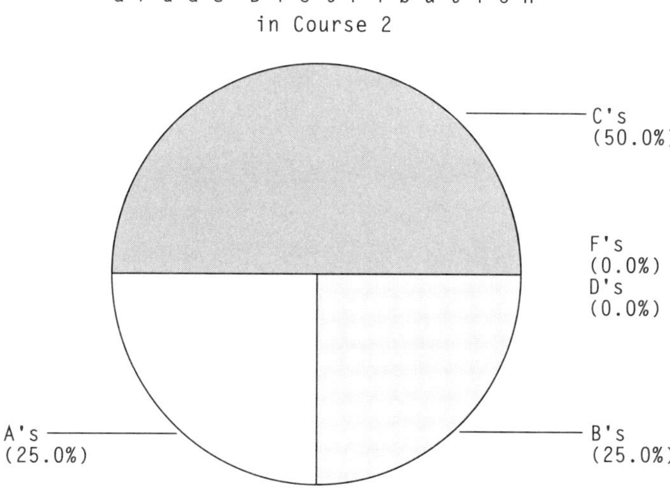


**Figure 8.12 Result of Printing PIE1.GRO**

## 8.7 Importing a DATATRIEVE Domain into DECalc

For this section, we assume that you have already studied the sample domains in Chapter 7 (DATATRIEVE). Now, you will learn how to import the PERSONNEL domain into a DECalc grid. One of the uses for such an action is that calculations can be made easily on both rows and columns. Although this can be done on columns (fields) in DATATRIEVE, explaining how is beyond the scope of this book. However, it can be easily accomplished in DECalc.

Once you get into DECalc, type /XDPERSONNEL S. This calls an External (X) program, specifically the Database program (DATATRIEVE in this case). The specification file that DECalc uses is given the file name PERSONNEL, and the file type will be .CALC$DTR by default. The S requests a specification form. Once the Specify option is chosen, the specification form appears at the bottom of your DECalc screen. Figure 8.13 shows the form; the text you fill in is in color.

```
A1
Retrieve Only,Specify,Interactive
\ X D S
         A   |    B    |    C    |    D    |    E    |    F    |    G
  1
  2
  3
  4
  5
  6
  7
  8
-------------- Database  Definition  Form - press <Enter> to save ----------
|Dictionary:CDD$TOP.DTR$NEWUSER                                            |
|Domain name:PERSONNEL                                                     |
|RSE:PERSONNEL                                                             |
|                                                                          |
|                                                                          |
|Field [optional]:                                                         |
|Row, Column [R/C]:C                                                       |
|Headings [Y/N]:Y                                                          |
|Starting Box:A1 <RETURN>                                                  |
----------------------------------------------------------------------------
Dictionary:   []
```

**Figure 8.13 Specifying a DATATRIEVE Domain**

All entries except the first line should be self-explanatory. The first line is site-specific and might be different from the line shown here. If this line does not work, consult your instructor or local user services staff for the appropriate specification for the NEWUSER domain in the Common Data Dictionary.

If your specifications are correct, your screen should reconstruct to resemble the screen in Figure 8.14. You will discover that there is also one more column containing data that is not shown in Figure 8.14. Column H contains the SUP_ID numbers. Notice that the entries in the START_DATE column are *>*. This means that the column is not wide enough. You can easily fix this with the /FC command. The SALARY column needs to be given a $ format with an /FB command. You will also find that you need to widen column G after you have reformatted it to the $ format.

```
A1        "ID
23 database records were imported

        A       |    B      |    C      |    D      |     E     |     F     |  G
 1  ID          STATUS      FIRST_NAME  LAST_NAME   DEPT        START_DATE  SALARY
 2          12  EXPERIENCE  CHARLOTTE   SPIVA       TOP         *>*          75892
 3         891  EXPERIENCE  FRED        HOWL        F11         *>*          59594
 4        2943  EXPERIENCE  CASS        TERRY       D98         *>*          29908
 5       12643  TRAINEE     JEFF        TASHKENT    C82         *>*          32918
 6       32432  TRAINEE     THOMAS      SCHWEIK     F11         *>*          26723
 7       34456  TRAINEE     HANK        MORRISON    T32         *>*          30000
 8       38462  EXPERIENCE  BILL        SWAY        T32         *>*          54000
 9       38465  EXPERIENCE  JOANNE      FREIBURG    E46         *>*          23908
10       39485  EXPERIENCE  DEE         TERRICK     D98         *>*          55829
11       48475  EXPERIENCE  GAIL        CASSIDY     E46         *>*          55407
12       48573  TRAINEE     SY          KELLER      T32         *>*          31546
13       49001  EXPERIENCE  DAN         ROBERTS     C82         *>*          41395
14       49843  TRAINEE     BART        HAMMER      D98         *>*          26392
15       78923  EXPERIENCE  LYDIA       HARRISON    F11         *>*          40747
16       83764  EXPERIENCE  JIM         MEADER      T32         *>*          41029
17       84375  EXPERIENCE  MARY        NALEVO      D98         *>*          56847
18       87289  EXPERIENCE  LOUISE      DEPALMA     G20         *>*          57598
19       87465  EXPERIENCE  ANTHONY     IACOBONE    C82         *>*          58462
20       87701  TRAINEE     NATHANIEL   CHONTZ      F11         *>*          24502
 .
 .
```

**Figure 8.14 First Screen after Importing the PERSONNEL Domain**

Once you have reformatted the grid as you think appropriate, use what you have learned up to this point to perform such calculations as obtaining the average salary of all employees.

## 8.8 Sorting a DATATRIEVE Domain in DECalc

One useful item that we have not yet discussed is how to sort data in a DECalc grid. In this section, we describe how to sort the data in the PERSONNEL grid by salary and, after that, by last name.

First, to sort the data in the grid by salary, type the following command:

```
/O A2:H27 A2 G <RETURN><RETURN>
```

This picks the Order option and specifies that, as a particular column is used for sorting, the entire spreadsheet (A2:H27) will be rewritten. Had we specified G2:G27 instead of A2:H27, the salaries would have been sorted but the names and all other column entries would have stayed the same.

The second A2 specifies that we want the target (where the sorted data will be written) to begin at box A2. Had we wanted to keep the current grid and place the sorted grid below it, we could have specified something on the order of box A30. The G specifies that we want the ordering to be done on the data in column G (SALARY). The two <RETURN>s specify that there is no secondary key for sorting and that the Ascending order (default) is to be used for the sort. DECalc then does the sorting for you.

Another sorting example is one where we sort the data in the grid by LAST_NAME (primary key) and FIRST_NAME (secondary key). The command is

```
/O A2:H27 A2 D C A
```

Everything to the first A2 is the same as in the first example. Column D (LAST_NAME) is taken as the primary key for sorting, and column C (FIRST_NAME) is taken as the secondary key for sorting. A (Ascending) order is chosen for the direction of the sort. After you have typed this last A, DECalc performs the sorting.

## Quick Reference: DECalc Commands and Functions

*See Bibliography [6] for more details.*

### Entering and Exiting DECalc

| *Command* | *Description* |
|---|---|
| `CALC` | Issued at the operating system `MYNODE$` prompt, this command executes DECalc. |
| `/E` or `/EY` | Exits DECalc. |

### DECalc Commands

The following commands are issued while in the DECalc program.

| *Command* | *Description* |
|---|---|
| <PF2> | Enters DECalc's on-line help system. |
| <PF3> | Begins editing contents of current box. |
| \|*box-number* | Moves the cursor to the specified *box-number*. |
| `/GMMA` | Sets globally the mathematics (calculations) to be algebraic rather than the left-to-right default. |
| `/R ...` | `REPRODUCE` option. |

`/R`*source-range target-range*

Reproduces *source-range* to *target-range*. If a formula is involved, you will need to decide how variables are to be reproduced, and reply accordingly to prompts on the `DIRECTIONS` line.

`/R`*source-range target-box*

Reproduces *source-range* beginning at *target-box*.

| | |
|---|---|
| `/F ...` | `FORMAT` option. |

`/FC`*column* `N` *column-width* <RETURN>

Formats Column with a New width of *column-width*.

`/FB`*box-range* `N C` <RETURN>

Formats Boxes in *box-range* with a New format of Centering.

`/FB`*box-range* `N $` <RETURN>

Formats Boxes in *box-range* with a New format of $.

/FZ*box-range* <RETURN>

Formats *box-range* so that any blank in *box-range* is assumed to be zero.

---

/S ... STORAGE option.

/SS*grid-name* <RETURN><RETURN>

Saves current grid to *grid-name*.

/SR*grid-name* <RETURN>

Restores specified grid to spreadsheet. A Y (for YES) will be required if grid is not empty.

/SL Lists directory.

/SC*file*.CALC$COM <RETURN>

Retrieves *file*.CALC$COM as a Command file.

---

/P ... PRINT option.

/PS*grid-range file* <RETURN><RETURN>

Prints Selected *grid-range* to the specified file. Creates file *file*.LIS, useful for obtaining hard copy of grid. *Note*: This file cannot be retrieved properly by DECalc.

/PD*grid-range file* <RETURN>

Prints *grid-range* to a DUMP file. This creates a file *file*.CALC$COM, which can be retrieved using the /SC command.

---

/B ... BLANK option.

/BS*grid-range* B Y Blanks out contents of *grid-range*, of Both values and formats, after confirming YES.

---

/D ... DELETE option.

/DR*begin-row end-row* Y

Deletes Rows from *begin-row* to *end-row* after confirming YES.

/DC*begin-col end-col* Y

Deletes Columns from *begin-col* to *end-col* after confirming YES.

/IC*col-name no-cols* <RETURN>

Inserts number of Columns specified by *no-cols* before *col-name*.

/MR*begin-row end-row new-row* <RETURN>

Moves Rows from *begin-row* to *end-row* to a position before *new-row*.

/O *range target primary-key secondary-key sort-direction*

Orders (sorts) the specified range to be written, starting at *target*. The columns specified as *primary-key* and *secondary-key* determine the ordering. The direction of the sort is Ascending or Descending.

### DECalc Functions

*Function* — *Description*

SUM(*begin-box*:*end-box*) <RETURN>

Calculates sum of boxes from *begin-box* to *end-box*.

AVE(*begin-box*:*end-box*) <RETURN>

Calculates average of boxes from *begin-box* to *end-box*.

IF (*logical-expression,value-1,value-2*) <RETURN>

If logical expression is *true*, then box will take on value of *value-1*; otherwise, it will take on value of *value-2*.

### DECalc Graphics Commands

*Command* — *Description*

/XG*filespec-1* S ... *graph-type* O *filespec-2*

Requests the External (X) program option, calling DECgraph, specifying a specification file (*filespec-1*), requesting the Specification form. Fill out the Specification form, then choose the type of graph (Line, Bar, Pie), writing the Output to *filespec-2*.

/XG*filespec-1* RY ... *graph-type* O *filespec-2*

Same as preceding comm and except retrieves a specification file (*filespec-1*) that has already been created.

/XG*filespec-1* S ... *graph-type* D

Same as first command except Displays graph to your graphics (REGIS) terminal.

### Manipulating DATATRIEVE Domains in DECalc

| *Command* | *Description* |
|---|---|
| `/XD`*filespec* `S ...` | Requests the External (`X`) program option, importing DATATRIEVE, specifying a specification file (*filespec*), requesting the Specification form. Fill out the Specification form, and as much of the DATATRIEVE domain as can be loaded into DECalc will be loaded. |
| `/XD`*filespec* `RY ...` | Same as preceding command except retrieves a specification file (*filespec*) that has already been created. |

## 8.10 Exercises

1. Generate a file containing all the on-line help outside of DECalc by typing the following commands at the operating system prompt:

```
HELP/OUTPUT=CALC.HLP DECALC...
PRINT/DELETE/NOTIFY DECALC1.HLP
```

2. Using the `LIBRARY` command discussed in Chapter 2, Exercise 9, and keeping in mind that the `HELP` within DECalc is on the file named `SYS$HELP:CALC.HLB`, print out a copy of the complete on-line help available from within the DECalc program.

3. Construct a gradebook similar to the one discussed in this chapter. The first two rows should contain column headings, and the third row hyphens. Your gradebook should have these columns and widths, *in this order*:

| Column | Width |
|---|---|
| Name | 15 |
| Homework 1 | 10 |
| Homework 2 | 10 |
| Homework 3 | 10 |
| Homework 4 | 10 |
| Homework 5 | 10 |
| Homework Average | 10 |
| Exam 1 | 10 |
| Exam 2 | 10 |
| Final Exam | 10 |
| Final Average | 10 |

Construct the relations between boxes so that your grid calculates the average. All exams should count the same in the average *and* the homework average should count as one exam in the average.

Put in five sets of names and grades. Be sure to use the /GMMA command on your grid.

Now generate .CALC$COM and .LIS files.

4. Construct a checkbook grid using the procedure discussed in Sections 8.3 and 8.4. Fill in all the spaces with sample transactions. Be sure to include several deposits and checks (no checks and deposits on the same line). Include at least five code 2 items.

   Generate .CALC$COM and .LIS files.

5. Using the grid that you produced in Exercise 4, allow for three categories of expenses, and generate two more summary tables to the right of the summary table that already exists.

   Generate .CALC$COM and .LIS files. Will you be able to print out your entire display using one .LIS file and printer paper having 132 columns? If not, how should you proceed to get a complete and clear display?

6. You are a new sales manager for a small computer store. Construct a grid that will summarize the total daily profit from selling several types of personal computers. Your grid should have the following columns appropriately labeled and centered:

| Column | Width |
|---|---|
| Type of Computer | 10 |
| Selling Price | 10 |
| Number Sold | 7 |
| Percent Profit/Unit (Based on Selling Price) | 10 |
| Total Profit | 15 |

   Format the columns appropriately so that no ERR messages occur. Define box relations so that you can update the grid each day by simply typing the total number of each computer type sold that day. Include the following computer types and accompanying relations:

| Computer Type | Selling Price | Percent Profit/Unit |
|---|---|---|
| Big Green PC | $ 950 | 10 |
| Big Green PC/YT | $1,250 | 10 |
| Big Green PC/BT | $1,975 | 15 |
| Jack | $1,750 | 15 |
| Jack Plus | $2,449 | 20 |
| Fruit IID | $1,219 | 5 |
| Meager | $1,459 | 12 |
| Safari | $1,179 | 20 |

Also provide entries that summarize the total number of computers sold each day, along with the total daily profit.

Generate `.CALC$COM` and `.LIS` files.

7. Repeat the gradebook session discussed in Section 8.1, except supplement the discussion of inserting hyphens with what you learn about continuous labels from the DECalc on-line help (obtained by typing `/L` <PF2>). Similarly, apply what you learn about repeated labels from the DECalc on-line help (obtained by typing `/-` <PF2>). Which of the two options, continuous or repeated labels, do you prefer? Why?

8. Using what you learn from the DECalc on-line help obtained by typing `/W` <PF2>, split your gradebook grid into two horizontal windows so that the top window includes the column headers. Applying the same information, split the checkbook grid into two vertical windows so that the left window includes only the check numbers. Discuss the advantages and disadvantages of such windows.

9. If you have studied Chapter 5, which discusses the KERMIT program, how would you back up your DECalc grids to diskettes? Would you download the `.CALC$GRD` or the `.CALC$COM` files? Why?

10. Using the gradebook grid you constructed in Exercise 3, format the Average columns so that only two digits before and after the decimal point will be displayed. This can be done by typing `/FB`*box-range* `N D` <RETURN>, which tells DECalc to Format the Boxes in *box-range* (you supply the appropriate box range) with a New format, using a specified Description. At the point where you are prompted for descriptors, type `zz.zz` <RETURN>.

11. Create the following graphs using DECalc and the `/XG` option:

    a. A line graph for the Exam 1, 2, and 3 grades of J. Toggle. Include the following:

       Title: J. Toggle's Exam Performance
       Horiz label: Exam #
       Vert label: Exam Grades
       Y legend(1): J. Toggle

    b. A bar graph comparing the exam averages for Exams 1, 2, and 3 of courses 1 and 2. Include the following:

       Title: Exam Grades for
       Subtitle: Courses 1 & 2
       Horiz label: Exam #
       Vert label: Exam Grades
       Y legend(1): Course 1
       Y legend(2): Course 2

    c. A pie chart comparing the grade distribution (A's, B's, C's only) for course 1. Include the following:

       Title: Grade Distribution
       Subtitle: for Course 1

12. Import the `YACHTS` domain into DECalc and do the following:

    a. Widen the columns as necessary to display the data.

    b. Format the columns that contain dollar amounts to display appropriately.

    c. Place a continuous label (using `/-`) at the bottom of the data and between the column labels.

    d. At the bottom of the following columns after the continuous label, calculate the averages (formatting appropriately for dollar values):

       ```
       LENGTH_OVER_ALL
       DISPLACEMENT
       BEAM
       PRICE
       ```

    e. Turn in your `.CALC$COM` and `.LIS` files, the latter set to be 80 columns wide. Turn in these files on narrow forms printed by the line printer.

Chapter 9

# Some Notes on VAX BASIC

As the title of this chapter implies, its purpose is not to teach BASIC programming or to give an exhaustive discussion of VAX BASIC. Rather, the intention is to point out some of VAX BASIC's features and to give you a few tips that might prove useful in programming BASIC on VAX/VMS systems.

You could use this chapter to supplement a "generic" BASIC programming text or a computer literacy text, such as Spencer [20] or Owens and Edwards [16], which contain appendixes on BASIC. For a much more extensive treatment of VAX BASIC, refer to any of several programming texts that are directed specifically to VAX BASIC (see Bibliography [8, 14, 24]).

If the TEXTFILES directory has been set up on your system as discussed in Chapter 1, then all the files mentioned in this chapter should be available by way of the COPY command, in the form

COPY TEXTFILES:*chapter-filename your-filename*

## 9.1 In and Out of VAX BASIC for On-line Help

Once you are logged in to the VAX and obtain the operating system prompt, simply type BASIC <RETURN>. You will be greeted by VAX BASIC and the

```
MYNODE$ BASIC

VAX BASIC V3.2

Ready
HELP COMMANDS

COMMANDS

   In the BASIC environment, commands let you perform
operations on your program, such as merging,
compiling and running. They cannot appear in a program and do
not need line numbers. You can type commands in response to
the Ready prompt, along with any valid arguments.

   Additional information available:

APPEND  ASSIGN    COMPILE  CONTINUE  DELETE      EDIT  EXIT
HELP    IDENTIFY  INQUIRE  LIST      LISTNH      LOAD  LOCK
NEW     OLD       RENAME   REPLACE   RESEQUENCE  RUN   RUNNH
SAVE    SCALE     SCRATCH  SEQUENCE  SET         SHOW  UNSAVE

COMMANDS Subtopic? <RETURN>

Topic? <RETURN>

Ready
EXIT <RETURN>

MYNODE$
```

**Figure 9.1 HELP on BASIC Programming Commands**

Ready prompt, with the cursor on the next line. To leave VAX BASIC, type EXIT <RETURN>.

As you should know from other sources, there are two types of commands, or statements, in BASIC. System commands, such as EXIT and RUN, get you out of BASIC and execute your program, respectively. You use BASIC programming commands, such as LET, INPUT, and READ, to tell the program what functions to perform. You can get on-line help concerning BASIC system commands by typing HELP COMMANDS <RETURN> while in BASIC. Figure 9.1 shows approximately what your screen will look like after such a command. Try your hand at getting help on BASIC system commands that you already know, for example, RUN or NEW. One thing to notice among these commands is that you use the OLD *filename* command to load an existing

```
MYNODE$ BASIC

VAX BASIC V3.2

Ready
HELP LET

LET

  The LET statement assigns a value to one or more variables.
    Examples

    LET A = 3.1415926535
    A$ = "ABCDEFG"

    Additional information available:

Syntax

LET Subtopic? <RETURN>

Topic? <RETURN>

Ready
EXIT <RETURN>

MYNODE$
```

**Figure 9.2 HELP on a BASIC Statement**

file into BASIC, and *not* the LOAD command, as is done in some dialects of BASIC. LOAD is used for something else in VAX BASIC.

You can get help on BASIC programming commands (statements) while in BASIC by typing HELP, followed by the appropriate statement, and pressing <RETURN>.[1] Figure 9.2 shows the approximate result of entering BASIC and issuing the HELP LET command. Look at some of the other commands.

## 9.2 Some Useful Syntax Variations of VAX BASIC

The syntax of VAX BASIC differs from more limited dialects of the language. The first variation is the convention for naming variables.

1. On some earlier versions of VAX BASIC, you would have to use HELP STATEMENTS followed by the appropriate statement.

Some dialects of BASIC only allow for numeric and string variables, where numeric variable names may consist of a letter or a letter followed by a single digit; string variable names may consist of the same items with the additional qualification that the variable designation must end with a dollar sign ($).

VAX BASIC has several more *types* of variables. (For more information on variable types, see on-line help in BASIC by typing `HELP VARIABLES` <RETURN> while in BASIC.) However, numeric and string variable names may consist of up to thirty-one alphanumeric characters. The only qualification for string variables is that the first character must be alphabetic and the last must be a $. The underscore _ is also allowed in variable names. These additional features related to variable names can often prove quite useful for naming variables in a mnemonic fashion; for example, `FIRST_NAME$`.

Another characteristic of VAX BASIC syntax is that, in assignment statements, the `LET` part is *not* required. For example,

```
10 LET NAME$ = "JOHN JONES"
```

and

```
10 NAME$ = "JOHN JONES"
```

are both valid in VAX BASIC. For more information, you can get BASIC on-line help (while in BASIC) by typing `HELP LET`, as illustrated in Figure 9.2.

Another useful feature in VAX BASIC that is not available in all BASIC dialects can be found in the `INPUT` statement. The `INPUT` statement in VAX BASIC allows character strings to be printed along with input variable lists. This ability can be particularly useful in prompting the user for input. For example, we may use

```
30 INPUT "What is your name and average"; NAME$, AVG
```

rather than

```
25 PRINT "What is your name and average";
30 INPUT NAME$, AVG
```

## 9.3 Saving an Interactive Session to a File

Since BASIC is intended for writing highly interactive programs, much of the program input and output is from and to your terminal. A problem arises from this fact when you want to save your interactive BASIC session to a file—for example, when you want to demonstrate that you have done a homework assignment or to show what is going wrong if you seek help in debugging your BASIC program.

It turns out that VAX/VMS systems offer such assistance[2] by way of the SET HOST command. While at the operating system prompt, issue the command HELP SET HOST <RETURN> and browse through the subtopics. Essentially, the SET HOST command allows you to connect to another computer (a "host" or "node") while being logged into your current node. For example, if you were on MYNODE and wanted to log into NODE2 (assuming that MYNODE and NODE2 are properly networked), you would simply type SET HOST NODE2 <RETURN> at the operating system prompt. You would be greeted with the Username: log-in prompt from NODE2. You could then proceed to log in as usual and conduct your business on NODE2. When you logged out from NODE2, you would still be logged into MYNODE, from which you would need to log out separately.

So, what does this have to do with saving an interactive session with a BASIC program to a file in your directory? The answer is that if you type the command SET HOST 0/LOG <RETURN>, you can log in *again* to the *same* node (that is the "0" part of the command). Everything that occurs is then saved to a file named SETHOST.LOG in your directory. After logging in a second time, you have a *second* job on the same node and can proceed as you please. For example, you could enter BASIC, load and run your program, and so on. When you log out of this second job on the VAX, you can print out the SETHOST.LOG file for a hard copy of your interactive session.

This sounds easy. However, you must keep in mind some important things. First, you will probably want to use the SET HOST 0/LOG command only for short sessions—for instance, for demonstrating successful completion of an assignment or demonstrating a problem with your program that you cannot figure out by yourself. The reason for keeping things short on your second session is that the file SETHOST.LOG *grows* as you proceed. If you do not keep your sessions short, you could exceed your disk quota and might have to delete some files in order to proceed. Guess which file you *cannot* delete because it is being used by another job? You guessed it! It is the SETHOST.LOG file.

---

2. KERMIT offers a similar option with its LOG command. See Chapter 5.

A second thing to keep in mind is that you will need to log out *twice* before leaving. The first log-out is to get out of the session started by the `SET HOST 0/LOG` command; the second log-out is to terminate your initial log-in.

Furthermore, if you use a screen-oriented program such as EVE in your second session, you should *not* print out the `SETHOST.LOG` to a line printer. There are a lot of special characters involved in a screen-oriented program that can cause some rather "interesting" results on the line printer, to say nothing of the wrath of the system operators who have to tend to the line printer when it goes berserk.

Finally, the `$SET NOON` in the `LOGIN.COM` file makes it possible for your second job on the VAX to re-execute your `LOGIN.COM` file without complications. Without this command, you will not get complete execution of the `LOGIN.COM` file. A sure sign of trouble is when your operating system prompt is `$` rather than the node name followed by `$`.

## 9.4 File I/O in VAX BASIC

Before reading this section, you should have mastered (from other sources) the fundamental BASIC programming statements: `INPUT`, `READ`, `DATA`, and `PRINT`. You will then understand that the `INPUT` statement gets data into your program via input from your keyboard, whereas the `READ` statement gets data into your program via `DATA` statements contained in your BASIC program. You will also understand that your results are output to your screen by the `PRINT` statement.

However, you might want your data to come from a file that you have in your directory. You could have originated the file by using a text editor such as EVE, or by running another program. You might also want the output from your program to go to another file in your directory. To do both of these things, you need to learn about the VAX BASIC `OPEN` statement, along with variants of the `INPUT` and `PRINT` statements.

Consider the following partial log of an interactive session on the VAX:

```
MYNODE$ DIR TEAM.*

Directory MYDISK:[MYDIR]

TEAM.BAS;1                    1  1-JAN-1991 09:40
TEAM.INP;1                    1 12-NOV-1990 09:20

Total of 2 files, 2 blocks.

MYNODE$ TY TEAM.BAS
100 REM *** SAMPLE FILE I/O PROGRAM ***
101 OPEN "TEAM.INP" FOR INPUT AS #2
102 OPEN "TEAM.OUT" FOR OUTPUT AS #3
110 INPUT #2, X$, S1
120 INPUT #2, Y$, S2
130 PRINT #3, "TEAM:";X$,"SCORE: ";S1
140 PRINT #3, "TEAM:";Y$,"SCORE: ";S2
160 END
MYNODE$ TY TEAM.INP

DODGERS,4
GIANTS,3
```

Notice that we have two files with the file name TEAM. The TEAM.BAS file is the BASIC program source file, and TEAM.INP is the input data for the program. Entering BASIC, loading, and running the program, we get the following log:

```
MYNODE$ BASIC

VAX BASIC V3.2

Ready
OLD TEAM

Ready
LISTNH

100 REM *** SAMPLE FILE I/O PROGRAM ***
101 OPEN "TEAM.INP" FOR INPUT AS #2
102 OPEN "TEAM.OUT" FOR OUTPUT AS #3
110 INPUT #2, X$, S1
120 INPUT #2, Y$, S2
130 PRINT #3, "TEAM:";X$,"SCORE: ";S1
140 PRINT #3, "TEAM:";Y$,"SCORE: ";S2
160 END

Ready
RUN
```

```
TEAM     1-JAN-1991 09:41

Ready
EXIT

MYNODE$ DIR TEAM.*

Directory MYDISK:[MYDIR]

TEAM.BAS;1                    1   1-JAN-1991 09:40
TEAM.INP;1                    1  12-NOV-1990 09:20
TEAM.OUT;1                    1   1-JAN-1991 09:41

Total of 3 files, 3 blocks.

MYNODE$ TY TEAM.OUT

TEAM:DODGERS SCORE: 4
TEAM:GIANTS SCORE: 3
```

When we ran our program, no program output came to the screen. After exiting BASIC, we see a new file in our directory, `TEAM.OUT`. This is where our program output went.

Let's examine how we accomplished this file I/O. Looking at the BASIC program in Figure 9.3, we see the statement

```
101 OPEN "TEAM.INP" FOR INPUT AS #2
```

This statement tells BASIC that "channel" #2 will refer to the file `TEAM.INP`, which is designated as an `INPUT` file. We tell BASIC to get data from this file by including #2 in our `INPUT` statements. For example,

```
110 INPUT #2, X$, S1
```

```
100 REM *** SAMPLE FILE I/O PROGRAM ***
101 OPEN "TEAM.INP" FOR INPUT AS #2
102 OPEN "TEAM.OUT" FOR OUTPUT AS #3
110 INPUT #2, X$, S1
120 INPUT #2, Y$, S2
130 PRINT #3, "TEAM:";X$,"SCORE: ";S1
140 PRINT #3, "TEAM:";Y$,"SCORE: ";S2
160 END
```

**Figure 9.3 Sample VAX BASIC Program with File I/O**

Similarly, the OPEN statement

```
102 OPEN "TEAM.OUT" FOR OUTPUT AS #3
```

tells BASIC that "channel" #3 will refer to the file TEAM.OUT, which is designated as an OUTPUT file. We then tell BASIC to output its results to this file by including #3 in our PRINT statements. For example,

```
130 PRINT #3, "TEAM:";X$,"SCORE: ";S1
```

## 9.5 Editing Your Program While in VAX BASIC

When you are in BASIC and you detect an error in one line of your program, you can correct the problem by simply retyping the line. BASIC will use the line number of your retyped statement to place it properly. To delete a line in your program, just type its line number and press <RETURN>. BASIC will then delete the line from your program.

But what if you need to make extensive changes in your program? One method would be to exit BASIC, edit your program source file with a text editor such as EVE, re-enter BASIC, and run your program. This is a rather cumbersome method, especially since VAX BASIC can make things so much easier.

Here is how. While in BASIC, type EDIT <RETURN>. Your screen will clear, then fill with the program currently loaded into BASIC. You may then edit your program as though you were in a text editor.[3] When you are finished with your editing, leave the editor as you normally would for either saving your work or aborting the editing session and not saving your work.

This process is identical to using EVE except for one very important thing. While you are in the BASIC editor, exiting as you would to save your work does not save your changes to a file in your directory. The changes are saved

---

3. The default editor is EDT. If you are using EVE and you have the starter LOGIN.COM file, add the following line to your LOGIN.COM file before the $ EXIT: line:

```
$ DEFINE BASIC$EDIT TPU$EDIT
```

If you are using EVE and you have the annotated LOGIN.COM file, remove the ! from a similar line in your LOGIN.COM file.

to a temporary file that exists as long as you remain in BASIC. If you exit BASIC without using the SAVE command, you will lose the editorial work you did while in BASIC. So be sure to SAVE any work you want to keep before exiting BASIC. This proviso also applies to the one-line changes mentioned at the beginning of this section.

After all these dire warnings, we should observe that VAX BASIC does inform you that there are unsaved changes if you try to exit without saving your work. At this point, you may either SAVE your work or go ahead and discard unwanted changes as you EXIT BASIC.

However, there is another way you can lose your edited work while in BASIC. To lose it, you must EDIT your program, then not SAVE it, and then load another program with the OLD *filespec* command. In this case, the current version of VAX BASIC does not warn you, since you are not exiting BASIC.

## 9.6 Some Decision Constructions in VAX BASIC

In the examples that follow, we are not trying to be exhaustive in our discussion of the VAX BASIC extensions, nor are we trying to teach BASIC programming. We are just pointing out some available options by way of a few examples. Furthermore, if you are one who sees BASIC as an easy-to-learn, high-level language but cannot stand the GO TOs that seem to come with BASIC, then VAX BASIC can come to your rescue.

### 9.6.1 An Example of the IF-THEN, ELSE Statement

First, let's look at the IF-THEN, ELSE decision construction. Consider the sample program in Figure 9.4, which is SAMPLE1.BAS in the TEXTFILES directory. In this example, we see a program to which we enter a final average, whereupon the execution of statement 130 causes the appropriate pass/fail message to be printed.

```
100 REM *** SIMPLE GRADE PROGRAM ***
105 REM *** PASS / FAIL ***
120 INPUT "Gimme a final average"; AVG
130 IF AVG = 60
      THEN
        PRINT "You pass!"
      ELSE
        PRINT "You did not pass."
    END IF
140 END
```

**Figure 9.4 A Simple Example of the IF-THEN, ELSE Statement**

The general form of this `IF-THEN, ELSE` statement is

```
line-no IF condition
          THEN
               action-1
          ELSE
               action-2
        END IF
```

where *action-1* is taken if *condition* is true and *action-2* is taken if *condition* is false. For more information, try BASIC's on-line help by typing `HELP IF` <RETURN> while in BASIC.

### 9.6.2 *An Example of the SELECT, CASE Statement*

Consider the BASIC program shown in Figure 9.5, which is `SAMPLE2.BAS` in the `TEXTFILES` directory. In this program, the person's name and average are put into the program by way of the `INPUT` statement, number 30. Then, depending on the value of the average (variable `AVG`), the appropriate grade message is supposed to be printed to the screen.[4]

4. A small warning is appropriate here. The condition in the `CASE 90 TO 100` part of this statement will not work properly if it is written `CASE 100 TO 90`. The phrase `a TO b` requires that a be less than or equal to b.

```
10 REM *** THIS PROGRAM GIVES A GRADE FOR A GIVEN AVERAGE
30 INPUT "What is your name and average";NAME$,AVG
40 SELECT AVG
      CASE 90 TO 100
          PRINT NAME$; " makes an A, with an average of ";AVG
      CASE 80 TO 89
          PRINT NAME$; " makes a B, with an average of ";AVG
      CASE 70 TO 79
          PRINT NAME$; " makes a C, with an average of ";AVG
      CASE 60 TO 69
          PRINT NAME$; " makes a D, with an average of ";AVG
      CASE 0 TO 60
          PRINT NAME$; " makes an F, with an average of ";AVG
      CASE ELSE
          PRINT NAME$; " 's average";AVG;" is out of range."
   END SELECT
50 END
```

**Figure 9.5 A Simple Example of the SELECT, CASE Statement**

The general form of the `SELECT, CASE` statement in VAX BASIC is

```
line-no SELECT expression
            CASE condition-1
               action-1
            CASE condition-2
               action-2
               .
               .
               .
            CASE ELSE
               action-else
         END SELECT
```

where the expression is evaluated and the first of *condition-1, condition-2, . . .* that is true determines which action is taken. If none of the conditions are true, then *action-else* is taken. For more information, try BASIC's on-line help by typing `HELP SELECT` <RETURN> while in BASIC.

Finally, we should point out that the program shown in Figure 9.5 does not quite do what we might expect. For example, type in this program and `RUN` it, trying an average of 89.5, and see what happens. How can this result be corrected?

```
10 REM *** PRINTING THE FIRST N INTEGERS
20 REM *** WITH A FOR -- TO; NEXT LOOP
30 INPUT "How many numbers would you like to print";N
40 PRINT "The first ";N;" integers are as follows:"
50 FOR I = 1 TO N
60   PRINT "I = ";I
70 NEXT I
80 END
```

**Figure 9.6 Using a FOR-TO, NEXT Loop to Print the First N Integers**

```
10 REM *** THIS PROGRAM CALCULATES THE AVERAGE
20 REM *** OF N NUMBERS, USING A FOR -- TO; NEXT LOOP
30 REM ***
40 REM *** INITIALIZE THE SUM AT ZERO
50 LET SUM = 0
60 INPUT "How many numbers are there";N
70 FOR I = 1 TO N
80     IF I = 1 THEN INPUT "What is the first number";NUMBER
90     IF I = 2 THEN INPUT "What is the second number";NUMBER
100    IF I = 3 THEN INPUT "What is the third number";NUMBER
110    IF I > 3 THEN PRINT "What is the ";I;" th number";
         INPUT NUMBER
120    LET SUM = SUM + NUMBER
140 NEXT I
150 REM *** CALCULATE THE AVERAGE AND PRINT IT OUT
160 PRINT "The average of these ";N;" numbers is";SUM/N
170 END
```

**Figure 9.7 Using a FOR-TO, NEXT Loop to Calculate an Average**

## 9.7 Some Loop Constructions in VAX BASIC

### 9.7.1 *Examples of the FOR-TO, NEXT Loop*

You have probably seen plenty of discussions of FOR-TO, NEXT loops in BASIC. Figures 9.6 and 9.7, which use FOR-TO, NEXT loops, are SAMPLE3.BAS and SAMPLE4.BAS in the TEXTFILES directory. We include these figures for comparison with the other loop constructions (discussed later in this section) that perform similar functions.

Figure 9.6 shows a BASIC program that prints the first *N* integers, for a value of *N* given from the terminal. Figure 9.7 shows a BASIC program that calculates the average of *N* values, which are given from the terminal.

```
10 REM *** PRINTING THE FIRST N INTEGERS
20 REM *** WITH A WHILE; NEXT LOOP
30 INPUT "How many numbers would you like to print";N
40 PRINT "The first ";N;" integers are as follows:"
45 LET I = 1
50 WHILE I = < N
     PRINT "I = ";I
     I = I + 1
   NEXT
60 END
```

**Figure 9.8 Using a WHILE, NEXT Loop to Print the First N Integers**

```
10 REM *** THIS PROGRAM CALCULATES THE AVERAGE
20 REM *** OF N NUMBERS, USING A WHILE; NEXT LOOP
30 REM ***
40 REM *** INITIALIZE THE SUM AT ZERO, AND LOOP COUNTER AT 1
50 LET SUM = 0
60 LET I = 1
62 INPUT "What is the first number";NUMBER
65 REM *** NOTE GIVING A NEGATIVE NUMBER WILL CAUSE
66 REM *** LOOP TERMINATION
70 WHILE NUMBER >= 0
        LET I = I + 1
        LET SUM = SUM + NUMBER
        IF I = 2 THEN INPUT "What is the second number";NUMBER
        END IF
        IF I = 3 THEN INPUT "What is the third number";NUMBER
        END IF
        IF I > 3 THEN PRINT "What is the ";I;" th number";
                  INPUT NUMBER
        END IF
    NEXT
150 REM *** CALCULATE THE AVERAGE AND PRINT IT OUT
152 REM *** FIRST REDUCE THE COUNTER, I, BY 1
153 LET I = I - 1
160 PRINT "The average of these ";I;" numbers is";SUM/I
170 END
```

**Figure 9.9 Using a WHILE, NEXT Loop to Calculate an Average**

## 9.7.2 *Examples of the WHILE, NEXT Loop*

Figures 9.8 and 9.9 (SAMPLE5.BAS and SAMPLE6.BAS in the TEXTFILES directory) demonstrate the WHILE, NEXT loop statement of VAX BASIC, performing functions similar to those in Figures 9.6 and 9.7, respectively.

Figure 9.8 shows a VAX BASIC program that prints the first *N* integers, for a value of *N* given from the terminal, and Figure 9.9 shows a VAX BASIC program that calculates the average of *N* values, which are given from the terminal.

The general form of the `WHILE, NEXT` loop is

*line-no* `WHILE` *condition*
*action statement(s)*
`NEXT`

where *action statement(s)* are executed while *condition* is true.

### 9.7.3 Examples of the UNTIL, NEXT Loop

Figures 9.10 and 9.11 (`SAMPLE7.BAS` and `SAMPLE8.BAS` in the `TEXTFILES` directory) demonstrate the `UNTIL, NEXT` loop statement of VAX BASIC, performing functions like those in Figures 9.6 and 9.7. Figure 9.10 shows a VAX BASIC program that prints the first *N* integers, for a value of *N* given from the terminal. Figure 9.11 contains a VAX BASIC program that calculates the average of *N* values, which are given from the terminal.

The general form of the `UNTIL, NEXT` loop is

*line-no* `UNTIL` *condition*
*action statement(s)*
`NEXT`

where *action statement(s)* are executed until *condition* is false.

```
10 REM *** PRINTING THE FIRST N INTEGERS
20 REM *** WITH AN UNTIL; NEXT LOOP
30 INPUT "How many numbers would you like to print";N
40 PRINT "The first ";N;" integers are as follows:"
45 I = 1
50 UNTIL I > N
     PRINT "I = ";I
     I = I + 1
   NEXT
60 END
```

**Figure 9.10 Using an UNTIL, NEXT Loop to Print the First N Integers**

```
10 REM *** THIS PROGRAM CALCULATES THE AVERAGE
20 REM *** OF N NUMBERS, USING AN UNTIL; NEXT LOOP
30 REM ***
40 REM *** INITIALIZE THE SUM AT ZERO, AND LOOP COUNTER AT 1
50 LET SUM = 0
60 LET I = 1
62 INPUT "What is the first number";NUMBER
65 REM *** NOTE GIVING A NEGATIVE NUMBER WILL CAUSE
66 REM *** LOOP TERMINATION
70 UNTIL NUMBER < 0
         LET I = I + 1
         LET SUM = SUM + NUMBER
         IF I = 2 THEN INPUT "What is the second number";NUMBER
         END IF
         IF I = 3 THEN INPUT "What is the third number";NUMBER
         END IF
         IF I > 3 THEN PRINT "What is the ";I;" th number";
                INPUT NUMBER
         END IF
   NEXT
150 REM *** CALCULATE THE AVERAGE AND PRINT IT OUT
155 REM *** DECREASE THE COUNTER, I, BY 1
157 LET I = I - 1
160 PRINT "The average of these ";I;" numbers is";SUM/I
170 END
```

**Figure 9.11 Using an UNTIL, NEXT Loop to Calculate an Average**

## 9.8 Quick Reference: VAX BASIC Commands and Statements

*For more information concerning VAX BASIC, see Bibliography [2].*

### Entering and Exiting VAX BASIC

| *Command* | *Description* |
|---|---|
| `BASIC` | Issued at the `MYNODE$` prompt, this command runs the VAX BASIC interpreter/compiler. |
| `EXIT` | Issued at the `Ready` prompt, this command exits VAX BASIC. |
| `SET HOST 0/LOG` | Issued at the operating system `MYNODE$` prompt, this VAX/VMS command saves a log of your interactive session (after logging in again) on file `SETHOST.LOG`. See also the discussion of the `LOG` command in Chapter 5. |

### VAX BASIC Commands

These VAX BASIC system commands are issued at the `Ready` prompt.

| *Command* | *Description* |
|---|---|
| `EDIT` | Edits current program in same fashion as EVE or EDT. |
| `HELP` | Gets BASIC's on-line help. |
| `LIST` | Prints currently loaded program on screen. |
| `LISTNH` | Same result as `LIST`, except without a header. |
| `NEW` *progname* | Begins a new program *progname*. |
| `OLD` *progname* | Loads an existing program *progname*. |
| `RESEQ` *increment* | Resequences program statement, using *increment*. |
| `RUN` | Executes currently loaded program. |
| `RUNNH` | Same result as `RUN`, except without a header. |
| `SAVE` *progname* | Saves currently loaded program to file in your directory with the name *progname*. |
| `SAVE` | Saves currently loaded program to a file in your directory, using the name it currently has in BASIC. |

### VAX BASIC Program Statements

| *Statement* | *Description* |
|---|---|
| *line-no* `INPUT` "*literal-string*": *variable-list* | Reads *variable-list* from terminal after printing *literal-string* to terminal. |

*line-no* OPEN *"filename"* FOR *mode* AS *#channel*

Specifies (opens) *filename* to be associated with specified channel in *mode* (INPUT/OUTPUT).

*line-no* INPUT *#channel*, *variable-list*

Reads *variable-list* from file associated with *channel*.

*line-no* PRINT *#channel*, *variable-list*

Prints *variable-list* to file associated with *channel*.

```
line-no IF condition
    THEN
        action-1
    ELSE
        action-2
  END IF
```

Takes *action-1* if *condition* is true; takes *action-2* if *condition* is false.

```
line-no SELECT expression
    CASE condition-1
        action-1
    CASE condition-2
        action-2
            .
            .
            .
    CASE ELSE
        action-else
  END SELECT
```

*Expression* is evaluated. The first of *condition-1*, *condition-2*, . . . that is true determines which action is taken. If none of the conditions are true, then *action-else* is taken.

```
line-no WHILE condition
    action statement(s)
  NEXT
```

*Action statement(s)* are executed while *condition* is true.

```
line-no UNTIL condition
    action statement(s)
  NEXT
```

*Action statement(s)* are executed until *condition* is false.

## 9.9 Exercises

We strongly suggest that you use a BASIC text (for example, see Bibliography [8, 14, 16, 20, 24]) for a broader selection of exercises. The following exercises are fairly simple extensions of the material covered in this chapter.

1. Generate a file containing all on-line help outside of BASIC by typing the following commands at the operating system prompt:

   ```
   HELP/OUTPUT=BASIC.HLP BASIC...
   PRINT/DELETE/NOTIFY BASIC1.HLP
   ```

2. How would you save *all* the HELP on the SET HOST command to a file named SETHOST.HLP?

3. Using the LIBRARY command discussed in Chapter 2, Exercise 9, and keeping in mind the fact that the HELP within BASIC is on the file named SYS$HELP:BASICHELP.HLB, print a copy of the complete on-line help available from within BASIC.

4. How would you use what you learned in Exercise 3 to generate a file for printing that contains all on-line help from within BASIC on the PRINT statement? (*Hint*: Look at the EXTRACT part of the command you used in Exercise 3.)

5. Verify the TEAM results discussed in Section 9.4, and rewrite the program so that input comes from the keyboard and output goes to the terminal screen.

6. Rework the simple grade program discussed in Section 9.6.1 so that 70 is the pass/fail point. Alter the program so that the user is asked to specify the student's name as well as his or her average. Also have the pass/fail message include the student's name.

7. Change the program discussed in Exercise 6 so that the inputs and outputs are done by way of files.

8. Correct the grade average program given in Section 9.6.2 so that it will perform properly for averages such as 89.5, 79.5, etc.

9. Using the FOR-TO, NEXT statement and the examples discussed in Section 9.7.1, write a BASIC program that takes as input a student's name and number of grades, followed by all the individual grades, and gives as output the student's name and average.

10. Combine the work you did in Exercises 8 and 9 so that the student's name, average, *and* letter grade are given as output.

11. Repeat Exercise 9 using the `WHILE, NEXT` statement, discussed in Section 9.7.2.

12. Repeat Exercise 10 using the `WHILE, NEXT` statement.

13. Repeat Exercise 9 using the `UNTIL, NEXT` statement, discussed in Section 9.7.3.

14. Repeat Exercise 10 using the `UNTIL, NEXT` statement.

15. Using any one of the loop constructions discussed, enhance the programs discussed in Exercises 9–14 so that the program continues to take students' names until the user enters the string "`DONE`" for the name of a student.

16. Rework Exercise 15 so that the output of each of the students' names, test scores, averages, and letter grades is *also* accumulated in a file that can be printed out later.

Appendix A

# Some Paths to the Username: Prompt

As we indicated in Chapter 1, there are quite a few ways in which you can attach to a particular VAX/VMS system in order to log in. Your particular sequence of steps will depend, in part, on whether you are using the phone lines and a modem, or whether you are using a hard-wired terminal. This sequence of steps will also depend on how your VAX is connected to the outside world and to other computer systems. You should talk to your local user services staff to get the appropriate sequence of steps for your own system. However, in this appendix we try to give you some appreciation for the different arrangements you might encounter.

Figure A.1 gives an example of one of the more involved arrangements. We use Figure A.1 to trace some hypothetical paths to the point of our logging in—that is, to the point of obtaining the `Username:` prompt. The first path is one whereby you use a modem to dial up your system.[1] You are first communicating with a modem at the computer site. Once you are properly attached to a modem, your job or session is put in contact with a port selector, which searches for available lines (ports) to a terminal server. If there are ports available, your job is attached to one of the ports in the terminal server. The terminal server manages the inputs you give to the computer system

1. See Chapter 5 and Appendix G for a discussion of using a modem in conjunction with a microcomputer and a KERMIT communications program.

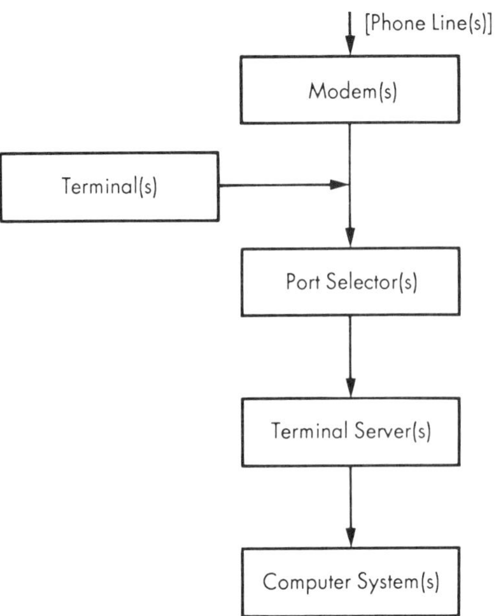


**Figure A.1 A Hypothetical Path to Logging in**

from your terminal and the responses that are sent to you from the computer system. It then attaches your job to a computer system. Finally, you can log in.

With a hard-wired terminal, your job would proceed along the same path as is followed with a modem, except that you do not have to attach to a modem at the beginning of the session. In some arrangements the port selector picks a port attached directly to a computer system, and there is no separate terminal server to deal with. In other arrangements there might be neither a port selector nor a terminal server. In this case, you would attach directly to a computer. (This is often what people mean by calling their terminal hard-wired, although we have not used the term in this way.) Again, check with your local user services staff for the details of your system.

Here is an example drawn from the current arrangement at Southwest Texas State University, in San Marcos, Texas. This system has all the components noted in Figure A.1. This site currently has two VAX 8600 computers, two

```
ENTER CLASS E <RETURN>               ! Tell the port selector
                                     ! to connect your job to
                                     ! the terminal server

GO <RETURN>

Digital Ethernet Terminal Server V2.0 - LAT V5.0
Enter username> RMS <RETURN>         ! "Log in" to the terminal
                                     ! server.

Local> C MENTOR <RETURN>             ! Tell the terminal server to
                                     ! connect to the VAXcluster.

Username: CS1308255 <RETURN>         ! Log in to the VAX node, in the
                                     ! VAXcluster. See Chapter 1
                                     ! for amplification.

Password:               ! No echo for password...
                        ! Note: First-time users might be expected
                        ! to set a new password by issuing
                        ! the command SET PASSWORD,
                        ! and following the prompts ...

      Welcome to VAX/VMS version V4.5 on node NYSSA
   Last interactive login on Wednesday, 24-JUN-1991 08:48

$ .......               ! $ is the default VMS prompt.
  .                     ! Your terminal session with a VAX 8600.
  .
  .
$ LOGOUT <RETURN>       ! $LO will also work.

CS1308255 logged out at 24-JUN-1991 13:04:53.69
```

**Figure A.2 A Log-in, with a Port Selector and Terminal Server**

DECSystem 10 computers, and a MicroVAX II computer to which a user can attach a job. In our example, you will see the following four prompts:

```
Enter class             ! Prompt from the port selector
Enter username>         ! First prompt from the terminal server
Local>                  ! Second prompt from the terminal server
Username:               ! VMS log-in prompt
```

The example log-in sequence appears in Figure A.2. Recall that what you type appears in color; messages from the computer are in black; and all remarks are preceded by an exclamation point.

Appendix B

# The EDT Screen Editor Program

## B.1 Getting Started

EDT is a general-purpose, screen-oriented editor on VAX/VMS systems.[1] Its job is to help you create and revise text. With EDT, you can also move existing text around within a document. EDT does not perform complete word processing, which requires a combination of EDT and a formatting tool such as SCRIBE (see Appendix C).

Those of you who do not have the annotated `LOGIN.COM` file already available on the VAX and have been directed here from the operating system chapter must use EDT to create your own `LOGIN.COM` file. Follow this appendix through Section B.3.1, "Deleting and Undeleting Lines, Words, and Characters." Once you have mastered the material presented in these few pages, you will know enough about using EDT to create the starter `LOGIN.COM` file shown in Section I.1.2 of Appendix I.

To begin using EDT, you must call it into operation. If you have copied the annotated `LOGIN.COM` file, simply type `EDT` and press <RETURN>. If you do

1. To complete the exercises in this appendix, you must be using at least a Digital Equipment Corporation Video Terminal 52 (VT52) or its compatible. If you are in doubt about the compatibility of your terminal, contact your user services staff or type `SHOW TERMINAL` <RETURN> at the operating system prompt.

not have a LOGIN.COM file, call the editor by typing EDIT/EDT <RETURN>. Because EDT has no way of knowing what file you want to create or change, it asks you.

For our first example, we will create a new file that automates the operation of the editor. This file does the same thing for an editorial session that the LOGIN.COM file does for the beginning of your terminal session: it customizes the editor to suit you. You must be exact when you specify the file name and file type. When the editor asks you for a file, type EDTINI.EDT <RETURN>. EDT gives you the message Input file does not exist. The screen clears and a new screen appears. At the top of the new screen, you will see the string [EOB]. At the bottom, you will then see the blinking cursor just to the right of an asterisk, which is the EDT command prompt. Type C (for CHANGE) <RETURN>. The asterisk disappears and the cursor reappears at the top of the screen. Now type SET WRAP 80. Press <CTRL/z> and observe that the asterisk reappears at the left bottom of the screen. <CTRL/z> tells EDT that you want to stop working on your file. In response to the asterisk, type EXIT <RETURN>. The EXIT command tells the computer to leave EDT and save the file.[2]

Once you get the DCL prompt again, issue the command DIR <RETURN>. There is now a new file in the list: the one you just created. Now type TYPE EDTINI.EDT <RETURN>. The contents of the new file will be displayed on the screen. They are the words SET WRAP 80, just as you typed them when you were using the editor. In EDT's initialization file, these words cause the editor to perform automatic word wrap at column 80. In other words, if the line you are typing into the editor extends past column 80, EDT moves the last word in the line to the start of the next line. You need not be concerned, therefore, about pressing <RETURN> at the end of each line.

Now re-enter EDT, but this time call the editor using the file name you intend to edit. Type EDT EDTINI.EDT <RETURN> if you have the annotated LOGIN.COM file, and EDIT/EDT EDTINI.EDT <RETURN> if you do not. This command tells EDT which file you intend to edit, so it does not ask you which file you want. There is a good reason to call EDT with the file name and type. Remember that the VAX/VMS operating system stores your commands in a stack, which you can retrieve by pressing the <UP ARROW>

2. Be careful not to type QUIT, which takes you out of EDT but does not save the file.

and the <DOWN ARROW> keys. By calling EDT with the file name and type you want, it is easy to leave the editor and save the file; then you can recall EDT and the file by simply pressing <UP ARROW> <RETURN>.

Look at what the editor gives us:

```
1          SET WRAP 80
*
```

The cursor is blinking just after the asterisk. EDT is said to be in *line*, or *command, mode*. If you type EXIT, you exit EDT and save the file. But what if you want to change the text in your file? You need to tell EDT that the characters you are about to type are new text, not commands. Type C (for CHANGE) <RETURN>.

As before, the screen clears and the asterisk as well as the line numbers go away. Immediately under SET WRAP 80 the string [EOB] reappears. These letters are not part of the file. They stand for End of Buffer and indicate that the end of the file is currently on the screen. (It would be possible to have one line full of text followed by thirty blank lines. In that case, the [EOB] warning would appear on the second screen of the file.)

Just to experiment, try to move the cursor past the warning symbol [EOB] using the arrow keys. EDT will remind you that you have made a mistake. Now, using the arrow keys, position the cursor under the S in the word SET. The cursor should appear on top of the left square bracket in the [EOB] warning. Type the words SET MODE CHANGE. Now, in order to get EDT's attention so that you can save your changes, press <CTRL/Z> as you did before. In response to the asterisk, type EXIT <RETURN>. EDT will tell you that you have saved a file named EDTINI.EDT and give you the number of lines in the file (two).

Have a look at the files in your directory using the command DIR <RETURN>.You will see two versions of your file listed: EDTINI.EDT;1 and EDTINI.EDT;2. The second version, EDTINI.EDT;2, is the newer version. At the DCL prompt, type TYPE EDTINI.EDT <RETURN>. Notice that the operating system assumed that you wanted to view the newer file. If you wanted to view the older one, you would have to type TYPE EDTINI.EDT;1. Every time you save a file using the EXIT command, the operating system creates a new version of the file. The operating system keeps a certain number of the latest versions.[3] Once you reach the default number of versions that the system will save, the oldest version (the one with the smallest version number) will vanish each time you leave the editor using the EXIT command. If you are certain that you no longer want the oldest versions of the file you are editing, you may issue the PURGE command (see Chapter 1, Exercise 4). This command does not work within EDT. Instead, it must be issued at the operating system prompt. It deletes *all* versions of *all* files except the most recent. You must be careful not to delete files you do not mean to delete. If you want to be extra careful, use the DELETE command, which asks you to specify the version numbers of the files you wish to delete.

Have a look at the difference that the change in your EDTINI.EDT file made. Use the <UP ARROW> key as you did earlier to retrieve your last few commands. Press the key until you see EDT EDTINI.EDT. Then press <RETURN>. You will see the following:

```
SET WRAP 80
SET MODE CHANGE
[EOB]
```

There is no asterisk on the screen. Any letters you type will be added to the text already there. Place the blinking cursor over any of the letters in your two-line text and type a couple of random letters. Notice that the new letters are inserted and the old ones are shifted to the right. Since you do not want to keep these changes, press <CTRL/Z>, and when the asterisk appears, type QUIT <RETURN>.

The new line (SET MODE CHANGE) in your EDTINI.EDT file causes EDT to begin operating in *full-screen mode*. In other words, SET MODE CHANGE changes EDT from command mode to full-screen mode. Full-screen mode is also known as *keypad mode*. Without the SET MODE CHANGE line, EDT operates in a rather fundamental line-oriented command mode, beginning with the asterisk prompt. You are seeing a bit of history here. EDT was designed at a time when many remote terminals were rather crude. Many printed like typewriters and had no screen at all, so users had to edit line by

---

3. Your system manager usually sets this number, although you can set your own number of versions by using the SET DIRECTORY/VERSION= . . . DCL command.

line. If you must work from such a terminal, you may have to type REN (for RENAME) EDTINI.EDT before you begin to edit. Remember, the file named EDTINI.EDT is special. Its commands to EDT will never be found if you rename it. Both statements in the current EDTINI.EDT file will cause conflicts with a nonscreen terminal.

## B.2 Mapping the Keypad

To further demonstrate EDT, create a file that you can discard later, one that will not change the way the terminal or the editor behaves. If you have a LOGIN.COM file, type COPY LOGIN.COM TRASH.COM <RETURN> at the system prompt. If you do not yet have a LOGIN.COM file, type COPY EDTINI.EDT TRASH.COM <RETURN>. At the next prompt, type EDT TRASH.COM <RETURN> if you have the annotated LOGIN.COM file; otherwise type EDIT/EDT TRASH.COM <RETURN>.

Find the numeric keypad on your terminal and take special notice of the row of keys above the <7> and the <8>. In most cases, the key above the <8> will function as the <HELP> key. This key is sometimes labeled <PF2> or colored red. Press this key. The screen clears and a HELP panel appears, showing the keypad with EDT commands in place of the numbers. The keypad might look like the one displayed in Figure B.1.

You are now in EDT's internal KEYPAD HELP system. In order to remember what keys are associated with each function, draw a grid of squares representing your keypad. Next, press each key and record on your grid what the HELP program says that each key does. Try to find help on every function mentioned in Figure B.1. After you have recorded every key, press the <SPACEBAR> to get out of the KEYPAD HELP system, just as the HELP program instructs you. As you map out all the special keys, keep the notes you have made as an aid to future editing sessions.

## B.3 Some Elementary Editing Commands

Pay special attention to the key just to the left of the <HELP> key. This key, sometimes gold-colored, is referred to as the <GOLD> key. It has the effect of downshifting the special keys so that you can use their alternative

| UP | DOWN | LEFT | RIGHT |
|---|---|---|---|

| | | | |
|---|---|---|---|
| GOLD | HELP | FNDNXT<br>FIND | DEL L<br>UND L |
| PAGE<br>COMMAND | SECT<br>FILL | APPEND<br>REPLACE | DEL W<br>UND W |
| ADVANCE<br>BOTTOM | BACKUP<br>TOP | CUT<br>PASTE | DEL C<br>UND C |
| WORD<br>CHNGCASE | EOL<br>DEL EOL | CHAR<br>SPECINS | ENTER<br>SUBS |
| LINE<br>OPEN LINE | | SELECT<br>RESET | |

**Figure B.1 Part of EDT's Help Screen**

functions. For example, if you press the <FNDNXT/FIND> key, you have issued the FNDNXT command. If you press <GOLD> and then <FNDNXT/FIND>, on the other hand, you have issued the FIND command. Put another way, pressing a key on the keypad without pressing <GOLD> activates the *top* command of the possible two commands associated with that key. Pressing the <GOLD> key first activates the *bottom* command. It is not necessary to hold down the <GOLD> key while pressing the second key.

### B.3.1 Deleting and Undeleting Lines, Words, and Characters

You can demonstrate the actions of the <GOLD> key by deleting a line and then undeleting (restoring) it. Using the arrow keys, place the cursor over the first character of any line. Do not use <RETURN> or you will merely insert blank lines. Now press the <DEL L/UND L> key, often located two keys to the right of <HELP> and sometimes designated the <PF4> key. The line on which the cursor was positioned will vanish. Restore it by pressing the <GOLD> key followed by the key you used to delete the line a few moments ago. The line reappears, as if it had never been deleted. The <DEL W/UND W> and the <DEL C/UND C> keys (the keypad <9> and keypad <6> keys on many terminals) perform the same functions in combination with the <GOLD> key for words and characters, respectively.

Those of you who have been reading this appendix to learn how to create your own initialization file now know enough about EDT to type in the starter `LOGIN.COM` file given in Section I.1.2 of Appendix I. You should turn to Appendix I now and type in the contents of the starter `LOGIN.COM` file exactly as they appear there. Once you have done so, you may return to Chapter 1 and continue where you left off in your study of the operating system. When you return to this appendix, you will have a good head start on learning how to use EDT.

### B.3.2 EDT Buffers

Where is deleted information kept until it is restored? It goes into designated sections of the computer's memory called *buffers*. Among the buffers maintained by EDT are the following:

| Buffer | Description |
|---|---|
| `MAIN` | Contains the current file and all changes made in the current editing session |
| `CHAR` | Contains the last deleted character |
| `WORD` | Contains the last deleted word |
| `LINE` | Contains the last deleted line |
| `PASTE` | Contains the last block of "cut" text[4] |

Notice that only the last line, word, or character deleted is saved in a buffer. Therefore, you can restore only the last line, word, or character deleted. Whenever you exit EDT, the part of the computer's memory reserved for the buffers is released for use by other programs, and the text in the buffers is lost if you have not already saved it.

4. We discuss this buffer in detail in Section B.3.6.

### B.3.3 *Moving the Cursor Around in a File*

There are other ways to move the cursor around in your file. You might have noticed that pressing the <DOWN ARROW> key causes the file to start scrolling upward once you have gone about halfway down the screen. If you were near the top of a large file and wanted to get to the bottom of the file, using <DOWN ARROW> would be quite laborious. However, you can quickly move the cursor to the bottom of the file from anywhere in the file.

If you created your own starter `LOGIN.COM` file from the text given in Appendix I, you need to create a new `TRASH.COM` file that is long enough to illustrate the procedures discussed in the remainder of this chapter. At the system prompt, type `COPY LOGIN.COM TRASH.COM` <RETURN>.

Go back to the keypad display in Figure B.1 and take note of the two keys below the <GOLD> and <HELP> keys. These are the <ADVANCE/ BOTTOM> and the <BACKUP/TOP> keys. By pressing the <GOLD> key followed by the <ADVANCE/BOTTOM> key, you invoke the BOTTOM command. Similarly, you can move the cursor to the top of the file from anywhere in the file by pressing the <GOLD> key followed by the <BACKUP/TOP> key, thus invoking the TOP command. Try these two functions on your `TRASH.COM` file and see what happens.

Sometimes you will want to see part of a screen of text followed or preceded by several lines of adjacent text. You can move the viewing window of your file backward sixteen lines by pressing <BACKUP/TOP> followed by the <SECT/FILL> key. Since there is no <GOLD> key involved, the system executes the top commands on both keys. Similarly, you can move the viewing window of your file forward sixteen lines by pressing <ADVANCE/ BOTTOM> followed by <SECT/FILL>. Again, the system executes the top commands on both keys. Verify these commands on your `TRASH.COM` file.

### B.3.4 *Moving the Cursor by Searching for Character Strings*

Other commands move the cursor more quickly and with greater accuracy. The ADVANCE command sets the direction for cursor movement toward the end of the file or, if you will, toward the bottom of the buffer.[5] The

5. Notice that the `ADVANCE` command is invoked by pressing the <ADVANCE/BOTTOM> key without pressing the <GOLD> key.

BACKUP command reverses the direction of the cursor movement toward the beginning of the file (or the top of the buffer). Thus, all cursor movement commands move the cursor in the direction dictated by the last BACKUP or ADVANCE command.

To demonstrate, move your cursor by whatever method you choose to approximately the middle of the TRASH.COM file. Since the word SET is common in this file, let's ask EDT to find it. Press <GOLD> followed by the <FNDNXT/FIND> key, which issues the FIND command. The words Search for: appear at the bottom of the screen. Type the word SET and end the command by pressing either the keypad <ENTER> or the <GOLD> key.[6] Notice that the cursor has moved to the next occurrence of SET and that the direction of cursor movement is toward the end of the file. This is because the editor starts up with the cursor in ADVANCE mode by default. Press <FNDNXT/FIND> again. This time, because you did not press the <GOLD> key first, you have issued the FNDNXT command. The cursor moves to the next occurrence of the word SET. Now press <BACKUP/TOP> followed by <FNDNXT/FIND>. Notice that the cursor moves to the previous occurrence of the word SET—that is, EDT is now searching backwards for the string SET, toward the beginning of the file.

### B.3.5 Searching for and Substituting Character Strings

Suppose you want to substitute for XXX the word set throughout your file. Press <GOLD> followed by <BACKUP/TOP>. Notice that the cursor has gone to the top of the MAIN buffer. Press <ADVANCE/BOTTOM> to change the direction of your search. Now press <CTRL/Z> and notice that the asterisk has appeared at the bottom of the screen. EDT is now in line mode, waiting for a command. Type SUBSTITUTE/set/XXX/BEGIN THRU END/QUERY <RETURN>.

Notice that EDT takes you forward through the text. Every time the editor finds an occurrence of the string set (without regard to uppercase or lowercase) it asks you if you want to make the change. If you type YES (or

6. The <ADVANCE/BOTTOM> and <BACKUP/TOP> keys also work, explicitly setting the direction of the search. If you use the <GOLD> key, the direction of the search is not altered.

simply Y), EDT makes the substitution, displays the changed line as well as the next line that contains the string set, and asks you if you want to make another change. When the editor reaches the last occurrence of the string set, it tells you how many substitutions you have made and leaves you with the asterisk. Type QUIT <RETURN> if you want to leave EDT without saving your work. If you want to return to full-screen mode, type C (for CHANGE) <RETURN>.

### B.3.6 *Moving Text Around with CUT and PASTE*

Now, using the TRASH.COM file, we explain how to move text around. Position the cursor at the first line of the file by pressing the <GOLD> key and then the <BACKUP/TOP> key. Next, press the <SELECT/RESET> key (often located just below the <3> on the keypad). Now move the cursor down three lines using <DOWN ARROW> to select a range of text to move. Next, you must put this text into the PASTE buffer, which will hold the text in memory until you specify where you want to move it. Press the <CUT/PASTE> key (often the <6> on the keypad). Notice that the text vanishes; it is stored in the PASTE buffer. Using the <DOWN ARROW> key, move the cursor down several lines. Press <GOLD> and then the <CUT/PASTE> key to invoke the PASTE command. EDT pastes the text into the new location at the cursor, where it now reappears.

You will be lucky to get through this sequence without an error message telling you that you have done something out of order. If you sense that you have incorrectly executed a sequence, you will find the RESET command useful. RESET flushes the PASTE buffer so that you can start the cutting and pasting process afresh. You invoke this command by pressing the <GOLD> key and then the <SELECT/RESET> key.

### B.3.7 *Recovering Text after an Abnormal Exit*

QUIT and EXIT typed at the asterisk that appears at the bottom of the screen are considered normal exits from EDT. QUIT aborts the editorial session and discards changes. EXIT saves the latest version of the file with all the changes intact.

There are also abnormal exits from EDT. You can induce one on purpose by pressing <CTRL/y> from within your TRASH.COM file. Abnormal exits can also occur when the connection to the computer is severed, for instance during a thunderstorm or when someone trips over your computer cord. Sometimes you do not lose your work as a result of these disasters. As soon as you can following an abnormal exit, return to the operating system prompt and look for a file that has the same name as the one you were editing followed by the file type `.JOU`. `JOU` stands for a journal file, a temporary file created as needed and deleted by the system when its job is finished. This file saves your work in progress in the event of an abnormal exit from EDT. If you were editing `TRASH.COM` and pressed <CTRL/y>, look for a file called `TRASH.JOU`. If this file exists, your changes should be preserved. To recover them, type `EDT/RECOVER` <RETURN>. EDT will ask you which file you mean to edit. Answer with the original file name. The screen will then mimic your last editorial session, making all your changes one by one. Sometimes the last couple of changes are, for no apparent reason, forgotten.

Once the screen fills and the activity stops, follow the normal procedure for saving the file and leaving EDT. Next, issue the `DIR` command. `TRASH.JOU` should vanish, replaced by a new version of `TRASH.COM`.

## B.4 Fancy Work with Multiple Files

You can do a lot of editing without ever learning about EDT's optional buffers. They become useful when you wish to export text from one file and import it into another file. Buffers are also of great advantage when you wish to draw material from several different files into one final file. Before you pursue this section, you may wish to review the CUT and PASTE commands (see Section B.3.6).

### B.4.1 Moving Text from File to File

To understand how to move text between files, we must return to the concept of buffers. Suppose you are editing `TRASH.COM` with the intention of inserting the contents of `EDTINI.EDT` somewhere in the middle of it. Use <CTRL/Z> to put EDT into command mode. When the asterisk prompt appears, type `SHOW BUFFER` <RETURN>. EDT will tell you that there are currently two buffers that you may edit, `MAIN` and `PASTE`. The other buffers containing your most recent line and character deletions cannot be edited. EDT also tells you the number of lines in each buffer. The `PASTE` buffer should be empty. Note that the equal sign appears next to the buffer that you are currently editing. Now, at the asterisk, type `FIND=PASTE` <RETURN>. The `SHOW BUFFER` command will now cause the equal sign to appear next to the word PASTE. At the asterisk, type INCLUDE EDTINI.EDT <RETURN>. Finally, type C (for CHANGE) and press <RETURN>. Notice that the contents of your EDTINI.EDT file are now displayed on the screen.

Using <CTRL/Z>, cause the asterisk to appear. Type FIND=MAIN <RETURN>. Then type C <RETURN> to resume editing the original TRASH.COM file, which is now in the MAIN buffer. Move the cursor to a place in the file where you might like to move the two lines of the EDTINI.EDT file currently in the PASTE buffer. Next, press <GOLD> followed by the <CUT/PASTE> key. Now the two lines that had been copied (by the INCLUDE command) into your PASTE buffer are also in your TRASH.COM file.

### B.4.2 A More Complicated Text Importation

Imagine that you are an instructor preparing an examination for your students. Since you cannot just give the same exam one semester after another, you might compose your exams from banks of questions on different subjects. For purposes of illustration, use EDT to enter the following two sets of text into two separate files, entitled TOPIC1.TXT and TOPIC2.TXT:

```
QUESTION-1 ON TOPIC ONE
QUESTION-2 ON TOPIC ONE
QUESTION-3 ON TOPIC ONE
QUESTION-4 ON TOPIC ONE
QUESTION-5 ON TOPIC ONE
QUESTION-6 ON TOPIC ONE
```

```
QUESTION-1 ON TOPIC TWO
QUESTION-2 ON TOPIC TWO
QUESTION-3 ON TOPIC TWO
QUESTION-4 ON TOPIC TWO
QUESTION-5 ON TOPIC TWO
QUESTION-6 ON TOPIC TWO
```

Each file might be considered a simple set of questions on different topics covered in your course. You want to use these two sets of questions as raw material for an exam without having to retype them and without breaking up either original topic set. Since each sample question occupies less than a line, the illustration might seem trivial, but the principle applies to paragraphs—even pages—of material.

Once you have created the two source files, create a third file called EXAM1.TXT. Type in a simple header so that you will remember what this file is, for instance SAMPLE EXAM NUMBER ONE followed by one or more blank lines. Using the now familiar <CTRL/z>, cause the asterisk prompt to appear. When it does, issue the command SHOW BUFFER <RETURN> (SHO BUF is an acceptable substitute). Only two editable buffers are present. Now type FIND=TEMP <RETURN>. You have just created a temporary buffer named TEMP.

When the asterisk appears, issue the SHOW BUFFER command again. Notice that there are now three buffers. The equal sign indicates that you are editing the new one, named TEMP. At the asterisk, type INCLUDE TOPIC1.TXT <RETURN>. Typing C <RETURN> will display the contents of the file to the screen. Following the CUT and PASTE instructions you learned in Section B.3.6, CUT the first three questions in the file into the PASTE buffer. They vanish from the screen. To check that you have CUT the correct material into the PASTE buffer, find the PASTE buffer and display the contents to the screen.

Next, skip down and SELECT questions five and six. You cannot CUT these lines into the PASTE buffer because the buffer already has text in it. Instead, you must APPEND the text to the bottom of the PASTE buffer. Press the <APPEND/REPLACE> (rather than the <CUT/PASTE>) key. The selected questions five and six will vanish from the screen. They have been appended to the PASTE buffer. If you wish to check your work, issue the SHOW BUFFER command. The PASTE buffer should now contain five lines.

Now, FIND the MAIN buffer, and display the contents of the file to the screen by typing C <RETURN>. Make sure that the cursor is at the bottom of the file. PASTE the contents of the PASTE buffer at the cursor position by pressing <GOLD> and then <CUT/PASTE>. The five questions you chose from the file called TOPIC1.TXT should appear directly below the header. Use <CTRL/z> to get the asterisk, and type EXIT <RETURN> to save your file.

After a breather, edit EXAM1.TXT again. Set up a temporary buffer and INCLUDE the contents of the file TOPIC2.TXT. As you did moments ago, choose five (not necessarily consecutive) questions for the PASTE buffer. You must use combinations of the SELECT, CUT, and APPEND commands. FIND the PASTE buffer and satisfy yourself that you have selected the questions you intended. If the PASTE buffer has the wrong contents, you have two choices: you can simply issue the QUIT command and lose your work, or at the asterisk prompt you can type CLEAR PASTE <RETURN>.

Once you know that your selection is correct, FIND the MAIN buffer and move the cursor to the bottom of the file. PASTE the contents of the PASTE buffer there and, at the asterisk prompt, EXIT to save your file. At the DCL prompt, TYPE the contents of TOPIC1.TXT, TOPIC2.TXT, and EXAM1.TXT. Notice that these files are unchanged even though you cut lines from them and pasted them into EXAM1.TXT. You did not remove lines from the actual file, you removed them from copies of those files that were held in buffers in the computer's memory. These buffers disappeared when you terminated the editorial session.

### B.4.3 *Destructive Exporting*

Occasionally, you may want to severely alter or wholly dismantle a file that serves as the source for multiple "daughter" files such as EXAM1.TXT. Suppose that, as an instructor, you have resolved never to give the same examination in successive semesters. You want the exam questions to correspond to the material you taught, and you want to discourage cribbing. You decide to use EDT to dismantle each master exam into its various subject areas shortly after you hand the exams back to your students. Begin to edit the sample exam you have just composed by typing EDT EXAM1.TXT <RETURN>. Recall that the contents of EXAM1.TXT are loaded into the MAIN buffer of your editorial session. But you need two buffers, the contents of which will become output files.

Imitating the steps you followed to create the sample exam file, FIND a buffer named TEMP. Now, use the CUT and PASTE procedures to extract all the questions on Topic One, and deposit them in the buffer named TEMP. First, FIND the MAIN buffer and CUT a set of contiguous questions into the PASTE buffer. Next, FIND the TEMP buffer and PASTE the questions you just CUT. Repeat this procedure again if there are more questions on Topic One left in the MAIN buffer.

Once you have removed all the questions on Topic One, you need to write the contents of the TEMP buffer to a file that does not exist yet. While editing the TEMP buffer, get the asterisk prompt by pressing <CTRL/Z>. Then, type

WRITE SUBJ1.TXT <RETURN>. Notice that EDT gives you a message about the file it has created and how many lines it contains, just as it does when you give the EXIT command. However, the text is still in the TEMP buffer. FIND the MAIN buffer, and notice that you have, in fact, removed some of the text that was there. At the asterisk prompt, type EXIT <RETURN>.

At the DCL prompt, use the TYPE command to verify that text once belonging to EXAM1.TXT is now in SUBJ1.TXT. You could edit EXAM1.TXT again, using the process described above, to yield a set of related questions in a file named SUBJ2.TXT.

The underlying utility of buffers should be obvious. Just as a programmer may have written code that is so long and unwieldy that it requires division into a main program and several subprograms, so a businessperson may discover that one memorandum has become so verbose that it really needs to be broken up into several shorter ones. EDT's buffers provide an easy, quick way to combine portions of files, or entire files.

### B.4.4 Saving EDT's Elaborate Buffer Structure

You have noticed, of course, that whenever you begin an editorial session, you can edit only two buffers: MAIN and PASTE. Extra buffers you create with the FIND command vanish whenever you leave EDT. However, there are ways to save your work while preserving the buffers you have created. One method is to use the WRITE command. For example, if you want to save the contents of the MAIN buffer, make the asterisk prompt appear and type WRITE FILE.TYP <RETURN>. This command saves the contents of the MAIN buffer in a file named FILE.TYP. When creating your own buffers, you may choose any legal file name, but you may not use the WRITE command without an explicit file name. In real life, you would probably use the name of the file you are editing.

Another technique is to use the journal file discussed in Section B.3.7. Rather than forcing an abnormal termination with <CTRL/y> as you did earlier, simply type QUIT/SAVE <RETURN> at the asterisk prompt. Because the recovery of a journal file can truncate your last couple of keystrokes, make sure the last keystroke is not of major importance. The safest bet is to use the WRITE command to save a copy of your file to disk, then enter several "garbage" keystrokes that you can undo easily later.

## Quick Reference: EDT Commands

*For more information concerning EDT, see Bibliography [28].*

Remember that the screen-editing state of EDT is *insert mode*: everything you type from the keyboard is inserted into the text at the current cursor position.

### Entering and Exiting EDT

| *Command* | *Description* |
|---|---|
| `EDT` *filespec* | At the `MYNODE$` prompt, calls EDT to edit *filespec*. |
| <CTRL/z> | Within EDT, makes asterisk prompt appear. |
| `EXIT` | At the asterisk prompt, exits and saves changes. |
| `QUIT` | At the asterisk prompt, exits and discards changes. |

### EDT Keypad Commands

These commands are issued from within EDT by pressing keypad keys.

| *Keypad Command* | *Description* |
|---|---|
| <HELP> | Gives help on keypad functions (this key is usually second from the top left on the keypad). |
| <SPACEBAR> | Inserts spaces in `MAIN` buffer to left of cursor. |
| <RETURN> | Inserts blank lines in `MAIN` buffer if cursor is at beginning of line. |
| <DEL C/UND C> | Deletes space or character from `MAIN` buffer. |
| <GOLD><DEL C/UND C> | Undeletes (restores) last deleted character. |
| <DEL L/UND L> | Deletes line from current buffer if cursor is at beginning of line. Otherwise deletes line from cursor position to end of line. |
| <GOLD><DEL L/UND L> | Undeletes (restores) last deleted line. |
| <DEL W/UND W> | Deletes word at current cursor location. If cursor is in middle of word, deletes from cursor to end of word. |
| <GOLD><DEL W/UND W> | Undeletes (restores) last deleted word. |
| <GOLD><FNDNXT/FIND> *string* <ADVANCE/BOTTOM> | Searches from cursor to end of file for first occurrence of *string*. |

| | |
|---|---|
| <FNDNXT/FIND> | Searches for next occurrence of the search string previously entered with FIND command. Direction of search is the current one (ADVANCE or BACKUP). |

<GOLD><FNDNXT/FIND> *string* <BACKUP/TOP>

Searches from cursor to start of file for previous occurrences of *string*.

<ADVANCE/BOTTOM><SECT/FILL>

Moves viewing window forward sixteen lines.

<BACKUP/TOP><SECT/FILL>

Moves viewing window backward sixteen lines.

<GOLD><BACKUP/TOP>

Moves viewing window to top of current buffer.

<GOLD><ADVANCE/BOTTOM>

Moves viewing window to bottom of current buffer.

| | |
|---|---|
| <SELECT/RESET> | Selects a block of one or more lines of text from current buffer for moving. Selected lines show reverse video on many terminals. Selection is terminated by pressing <CUT/PASTE>. |

<GOLD><SELECT/RESET>

Cancels defective SELECT command, letting you select another block of text for moving.

| | |
|---|---|
| <CUT/PASTE> | Moves selected block of text into `PASTE` buffer for relocation. Presumes you have pressed <SELECT/RESET> and moved cursor to include desired range to be CUT. |
| <GOLD><CUT/PASTE> | Moves block of text from `PASTE` buffer to current cursor location in current buffer. |

---

### EDT Asterisk Commands

The following commands are issued from within EDT by typing the command (followed by <RETURN>) at the asterisk prompt.

| *Asterisk Command* | *Description* |
|---|---|
| `C` | Leaves command mode and returns to full-screen, or keypad, mode. (`C` is an abbreviation for `CHANGE`.) |
| `SHOW BUFFER` | Lists buffers that may be edited. The equal sign (=) appears next to current buffer. |
| `FIND=BUF1` | Creates temporary buffer called `BUF1`; makes it the current buffer. |

| | |
|---|---|
| FIND=MAIN | Makes MAIN buffer the current buffer. |
| INCLUDE *filespec* | Copies contents of existing disk file *filespec* into current buffer at cursor position. |
| WRITE *filespec* | Writes contents of current buffer to file *filespec*. |
| EXIT | Writes MAIN buffer to disk file; leaves EDT. |
| EXIT/SAVE | Same as EXIT, but preserves possibility of resuming where you left off. |
| QUIT | Aborts editorial session; discards changes. |
| QUIT/SAVE | Same as QUIT, but preserves possibility of resuming where you left off. |

SUBSTITUTE/*old-string*/*new-string*/*range*/QUERY

Searches for *old-string* and replaces it with *new-string* over the set of lines in range and asks for confirmation at each occurrence (/QUERY). Range specifications take the form "first line THRU second line." For example, range specification of all lines in the MAIN buffer would read BEGIN THRU END.

## B.6 Exercises

1. Use the on-line help library to find out what help is available on EDT by typing HELP EDIT at the operating system prompt and /EDT at the Subtopic? prompt. Next, find help on the subtopic /RECOVER. How does this information relate to what was said in this appendix? What conclusion can you draw concerning other editors on your system by the response given when you type HELP EDIT at the operating system prompt?

2. Generate a file containing HELP on EDT available outside of EDT by issuing the following commands at the operating system level:

```
HELP/OUTPUT=EDT1.HLP EDIT/EDT *
HELP/OUTPUT=EDT2.HLP EDIT *
HELP/OUTPUT=EDT3.HLP EDIT * *
HELP/OUTPUT=EDT4.HLP EDIT. . .
PRINT/DELETE/NOTIFY *.HLP
```

   Examine the files printed. Explain their differences from and similarities to what you get when you type HELP at the operating system prompt, and HELP again at the Subtopic? prompt.

3. There is another HELP library for EDT that you can see from within EDT. Look through the help available by typing HELP @EDTHELP at the operating system prompt, and FIND and/or INCLUDE at the Subtopic? prompt. Now, while editing a file, type <CTRL/Z> to obtain the asterisk prompt. Type HELP and HELP FIND or HELP INCLUDE at subsequent asterisk prompts. Are there any differences between on-line help at the operating system and on-line help within EDT? What conclusion can you draw about using HELP @EDTHELP?

4. Use the HELP @EDTHELP library for EDT to create and print a file containing the help available, along with much more information, by typing the following commands:

```
HELP/OUTPUT=EDT5.HLP @EDTHELP
HELP/OUTPUT=EDT6.HLP @EDTHELP *
HELP/OUTPUT=EDT7.HLP @EDTHELP * *
HELP/OUTPUT=EDT8.HLP @EDTHELP * * *
HELP/OUTPUT=EDT9.HLP @EDTHELP * * * *
HELP/OUTPUT=EDT10.HLP @EDTHELP * * * * *
PRINT/DELETE/NOTIFY *.HLP
```

   Explain the differences and similarities in the printed files, especially between what is given when you type HELP at the operating system prompt and when you type HELP again at the Topic? prompt. For a better means of getting all the on-line help available from within EDT, see Exercise 13 involving the LIBRARY command.

5. Use EDT to personalize the following part of your LOGIN.COM file:

```
$
$WRITE SYS$OUTPUT "     *********************************"
$WRITE SYS$OUTPUT "     *                               *"
$WRITE SYS$OUTPUT "     *   Put Your Own Personalized   *"
$WRITE SYS$OUTPUT "     *          Greeting Here        *"
$WRITE SYS$OUTPUT "     *                               *"
$WRITE SYS$OUTPUT "     *********************************"
$
```

   Also insert the following line just below this part of the file:

```
$SHOW TIME
```

   Once back at the operating system prompt, type @LOGIN, then log out and log in to the system again. What are your conclusions, especially regarding the information you get when you type HELP at the operating system prompt, and then type `@` at the `Topic?` prompt? How would you put together a file containing all the on-line help on the @ symbol?

6. If you have the annotated `LOGIN.COM` file, find the following line:

```
$! SET PROCESS/NAME= "- - - - -"
```

Remove the ! and replace - - - - - with some name by which you would like to be identified. This name will appear under the Process column generated when anyone types the `SHOW USERS` command at the operating system level.

If you have the starter `LOGIN.COM` file, insert the above line in your `LOGIN.COM` file for the same result.

Once you have inserted the indicated line, type the following command at the operating system prompt:

```
@LOGIN
SHOW USERS
```

What conclusions can you draw concerning your process name?

7. As noted earlier, the operating system reads and executes commands in the `LOGIN.COM` file when you log in. The operating system ignores lines in the `LOGIN.COM` file that begin with $! (rather than $ without !). Using on-line help for `DELETE`, determine which line of the `LOGIN.COM` file must have ! inserted after $ in order to avoid being asked if you want to delete a file each time you issue the `DELETE` command at the operating system prompt. If you were not allowed to insert the !, how would you change the line so that you would get the same result?

8. Use EDT to create the following file named `GREETING.COM`:

```
$  CONTEXT= ""
$  START:
$! Obtain and display PIDs, UICs, and Time
$!
$  PID=F$PID(CONTEXT)
$  UIC=F$GETJPI(PID,"UIC")
$  PROCESS=F$PROCESS()
$  IF F$EXTRACT(12,2,F$TIME()) .GES. "12" THEN GOTO AFTERNOON
$  MORNING:
$  WRITE SYS$OUTPUT ""
$  WRITE SYS$OUTPUT "Good Morning, ''PROCESS'."
$! WRITE SYS$OUTPUT "Good Morning, ''UIC'."
$  GOTO MORE
$  AFTERNOON:
```

```
$  IF F$EXTRACT(12,2,F$TIME()) .GES. "18" THEN GOTO EVENING
$  WRITE SYS$OUTPUT ""
$  WRITE SYS$OUTPUT "Good Afternoon, ''PROCESS'."
$! WRITE SYS$OUTPUT "Good Afternoon, ''UIC'."
$  GOTO MORE
$  EVENING:
$  WRITE SYS$OUTPUT ""
$  WRITE SYS$OUTPUT "Good Evening, ''PROCESS."
$! WRITE SYS$OUTPUT "Good Evening, ''UIC'."
$  MORE:
$  WRITE SYS$OUTPUT ""
```

At the operating system level, type `@GREETING`. How would you get this file to execute each time you log in? (For more information concerning `.COM` (command) files, see Bibliography [9] and [19].)

9. If you have the `TEXTFILES` directory, copy the file `PRAYER.ERR` into your directory by issuing the following command:

   ```
   COPY TEXTFILES:PRAYER.ERR PRAYER.ERR
   ```

   If you do not have `TEXTFILES`, create the file from the text given in Section I.2.1 of Appendix I.

   Use EDT to correct all the errors contained therein to obtain an error-free copy of Mark Twain's "War Prayer." Be sure to try the `SUBSTITUTE` command and the <FNDNXT/FIND> keypad functions to help in your task.

10. Follow the instructions for Exercise 9, except apply them to the `TEXTFILES` named `HENRY.PAT`, which contains Patrick Henry's famous "Give me liberty or give me death" speech. Again, if you do not have `TEXTFILES`, create `HENRY.PAT` from the text given in Section I.2.2 of Appendix I.

11. After you have finished your work on Patrick Henry's speech, go back into EDT, editing the `HENRY.PAT` file. Type <CTRL/z> to obtain the asterisk prompt, then type `HELP FILL` <RETURN>. After reading the EDT on-line help, press <FILL> <RETURN>. `EXIT` from EDT, `PRINT` your file, and explain the result. How could this function be helpful? What determines the margins on your printed document?

12. Issue the following commands at the operating system level to copy

SET1.TXT and SET2.TXT into your directory:

```
COPY TEXTFILES:SET1.TXT SET1.TXT
COPY TEXTFILES:SET2.TXT SET2.TXT
```

If you do not have TEXTFILES, create SET1.TXT and SET2.TXT from the text given in Sections I.2.3 and I.2.4 of Appendix I. Assume that these two files represent two test banks of exam questions. You are going to compose an exam that contains questions chosen from both of these files. Using what you have learned about moving text from file to file, create a new file named EXAM.TXT that contains the following header:

```
Computer Literacy Exam I       NAME:__________________

INSTRUCTIONS: Answer the questions in the space provided.
Each numbered question is worth 2 points.
```

*Note*: In the commands given below, we assume that <RETURN> is included where appropriate.

CUT questions 1, 2, 3, 5, and 6 from SET1.TXT (renumbering them 1 through 5), and questions 1, 3, and 5 from SET2.TXT (renumbering them 6 through 8), and PASTE them into the EXAM.TXT file following the header.

13. You have seen that there are at least two sets of on-line help available with EDT. One set of on-line help is available outside EDT by typing HELP at the operating system prompt, typing EDIT at the Topic? prompt, and so on. Previous exercises demonstrate how to store this HELP in a file that you can print out.

    Another set of on-line help is available from within EDT, some of it via keypad commands and some of it by typing HELP at the asterisk prompt. Previous exercises have shown a rather cumbersome means of saving this on-line help to a file that you can also print out.

    There is a much easier way to get this second set of help, via the LIBRARY command. Help available from within programs (not at the operating system prompt) is contained within files at a special location in your system. If, when you type the following command, the operating system responds by saying that there is no such directory or no such files, ask your local user services staff how to get a directory of the HELP LIBRARY files.

To get a listing of the names of these files, type the following command at the operating system level:

```
DIR SYS$HELP:*.HLB
```

The file containing EDT HELP is named EDTHELP.HLB. To get all the help available from within EDT, type the following command at the operating system prompt:

```
LIBRARY/EXTRACT=(*)/OUTPUT=EDTALL.HLP -
SYS$HELP:EDTHELP.HLB
```

The hyphen (-) indicates to the operating system that the line is continued, and is therefore followed by <RETURN>.

Now try the LIBRARY command. Compare the results to those obtained in Exercises 1, 2, 3, 4, and 11.

14. The kinds of printers available at each computer site vary greatly. We give an example of one site and then ask you to construct your own site-specific version.

    Let's say that your site has both a line printer devoted to printing narrow forms (8½ × 11-inch paper) and an LN01 laser printer. In order to print to the narrow forms line printer or the laser printer, you must type the following at the operating system prompt:

```
PRINT/FORMS=NARROW filename        ! For the narrow forms
                                   ! line printer

PRINT/QUEUE=SYS$LN01/NOFEED/FLAG=ONE -
/NOTRAILER/NOBURST filename        ! For the laser printer
```

    Now add the following lines to your LOGIN.COM file. The $LAS*ER line, shown on two lines here, must be added to LOGIN.COM as one continuous line.

```
$ NAR*ROW == "PRINT/FORMS=NARROW"
$ LAS*ER == "PRINT/QUEUE=SYS$LN01/NOFEED/FLAG=ONE
/NOTRAILER/NOBURST"
```

    If you have the annotated LOGIN.COM file, you need only remove the exclamation marks before these lines in your file. If you created your own starter LOGIN.COM file, you need to insert the complete lines exactly as they appear here.

When you finish editing LOGIN.COM, you can either log out and log in, *or* you can type @LOGIN at the operating system prompt. Then type the following DCL commands at the operating system prompt:

```
NARROW/NOTIFY LOGIN.COM
LASER/NOTIFY LOGIN.COM
```

These commands generate copies of the LOGIN.COM file from the narrow forms line printer and the laser printer.

Now check with your local user services staff and see what kinds of printers are available at your site, along with the appropriate DCL commands for sending files to these printers for printing. Using the example given above, edit your LOGIN.COM file appropriately and print out copies of your LOGIN.COM file on the different printers available at your site.

*Note*: The global symbols NARROW and LASER will be in effect at every log-in until the new lines are removed or the dollar sign symbols are augmented by exclamation points. For more information on symbols and DCL, see Bibliography [9]. See also Exercise 13 at the end of Chapter 1.

# Appendix C

# The SCRIBE Text-Formatting Program

## C.1 Basic Terminology and Functioning of SCRIBE

SCRIBE[1] is a text-formatting program that transforms standard ASCII files[2] created by a text editor such as EVE or EDT into neatly formatted text. You can display the text on your terminal or send it to any one of several hard copy printing devices. (Many terminals do not support the graphic displays available on some printers, such as overstriking or underlining, so you will probably need to print your work for the full effect.) If you do not like the results you obtain with SCRIBE, you must go back to the editor, change the SCRIBE source files, and re-SCRIBE those files.

The *source*, or *input*, *file* is called the *manuscript file*; the *formatted*, or *output*, *file* is called the *document file*. SCRIBE source files are usually assigned the type `.MSS`. In most cases, the file type of the document file will reflect the output device for which the document was created. When you do

1. SCRIBE is a product of Unilogic, Ltd., 605 Devonshire St., Pittsburgh, PA 15213.

2. Loosely speaking, ASCII files are those that can be sent to the screen with the TYPE command or to a line printer with the PRINT command. See, for example, Chapter 3 of Spencer, Bibliography [20], or Chapter 5 of Owens and Edwards, Bibliography [16], for more information.

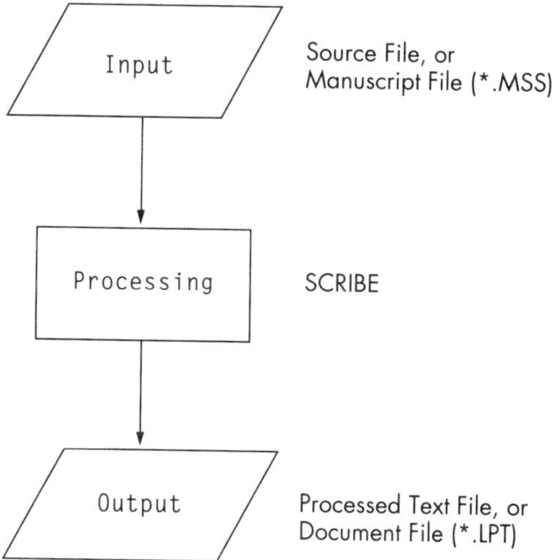


**Figure C.1 The SCRIBE Text-Formatting Process**

not specify an output device, SCRIBE assumes a file type of `.LPT`, meaning that the document was created for a line printer. Figure C.1 gives a graphical characterization of the text-formatting process.

The process of using manuscript and document files may seem tedious to those who advocate microcomputers over systems like, the VAX, but it does have certain advantages. The commands that cause indentation, page breaks, blank spaces for figures, centering, and so forth are composed of ASCII characters, just like the text itself. In other words, as you create your SCRIBE source file, you leave a trail of explicit instructions that tell SCRIBE what to do. These same instructions (which appear in the source document only) can later serve as reminders if you forget the details of how SCRIBE operates. Thus, some users characterize SCRIBE as self-documenting (though it would never appear to be so to someone who had not mastered its fundamentals).

```
The process of using manuscript and document files may seem
tedious to those who advocate microcomputers over systems
like the VAX, but it does have certain advantages. The com-
mands that cause indentation, page breaks, blank spaces for
figures, centering, and so forth are composed of ASCII
characters, just  like the text itself. In other words, as
you create your SCRIBE source file, you leave a trail of
explicit instructions that tell SCRIBE what to do. These same
instructions (which appear in the source document only) can
later serve as reminders if you forget the details of how
SCRIBE operates. Thus, some users characterize SCRIBE as
self-documenting (though it would never appear to be so to
someone who had not mastered its fundamentals).
```

**Figure C.2 TEST.MSS File**

Suppose we want to operate SCRIBE at its most fundamental level. Imagine that the paragraph immediately preceding this one is in a file named TEST.MSS in your directory (see Figure C.2). You could call SCRIBE by typing the following command at the operating system level:[3]

```
MYNODE$ SCRIBE <RETURN>
```

SCRIBE will prompt you with the asterisk. You then type the file name:

```
*TEST.MSS <RETURN>     ! Or simply, TEST, without .MSS
```

SCRIBE will then begin to do its work, informing us of its progress as it goes on:

```
[Processing TEST.MSS
    [Device "LPT"]
    [Document type "TEXT"
]
 1.

**TEST.LPT for device LPT has 1 page.
```

3. To make sure this command works as described, you will need to check with your local user services staff to see what should appear to the right of == in the following command given in the annotated LOGIN.COM file, listed in Section I.1.1 of Appendix I:

```
$!SCR*IBE=="$SYS$EXTERNAL:[SCRIBE.EXE]SCRIBE"
```

Once this is determined, make the appropriate changes in this line, remembering to remove the ! at the beginning of the line in the annotated LOGIN.COM file. For those with the starter LOGIN.COM file, listed in Section I.1.2 of Appendix I, the line described above (without the !) should be inserted just before the $ EXIT: line.

```
The process of using manuscript and document files may seem
tedious to those who advocate microcomputers over systems like
the VAX, but it does have certain advantages. The commands
that cause indentation, page breaks, blank spaces for figures,
centering, and so forth are composed of ASCII characters, just
like the text itself. In other words, as you create your
SCRIBE source file, you leave a trail of explicit instructions
that tell SCRIBE what to do. These same instructions (which
appear in the source document only) can later serve as
reminders if you forget the details of how SCRIBE operates.
Thus, some users characterize SCRIBE as self-documenting
(though it would never appear to be so to someone who had not
mastered its fundamentals).
```

**Figure C.3 TEST.LPT: The Result of Running SCRIBE on TEST.MSS**

After exiting SCRIBE, you will find that a new file, TEST.LPT, exists in your directory. If you send this file to the printer, you will find text with the same words as in the original file. However, there will be a major difference: the right-hand side will be justified, or not ragged (see Figure C.3). SCRIBE made some assumptions without being told anything. It assumed that the output was destined for a line printer, and it assumed that the document was to be TEXT—that is, right-justified. These assumptions are called *default settings*, or simply *defaults*.

SCRIBE can be more creative if you give it explicit instructions, but before you do that, we need to cover some fundamental concepts: *commands*, *environments*, and *delimiters*. Commands tell SCRIBE to forget its assumptions (defaults) and to receive explicit instructions from you. For example, suppose you want to italicize the word "SCRIBE" in your file TEST.LPT. In your manuscript file, you type @i[SCRIBE]; the word emerges italicized, *SCRIBE*, in the formatted, or document, text.

Let's have a look at those odd characters and what they mean. The @ character, called the "at sign," tells SCRIBE that a *command* will immediately follow. The "i" tells SCRIBE to place the following delimited text in an italicized *environment*. The square brackets are the *delimiters*; they tell SCRIBE that we only want to italicize the word or words within the brackets. SCRIBE allows several sets of delimiters, requiring only that there must be

```
@COMMENT(SET THE DOCUMENT TYPE)
@MAKE(MANUAL)
@COMMENT(SET SOME STYLE, ETC. PARAMETERS)
@DEVICE(LPT)
@STYLE(SPACING=2)
@STYLE(INDENT=0)
@STYLE(REFERENCES=STDNUMERIC)
@COMMENT(In order to get the Odd and Even PageHeadings we
@comment(must have DOUBLESIDED=ON, but in order to get no
@comment(extra blank pages at the end of chapters, we must
@comment(have DOUBLESIDED=NO)
@STYLE(DOUBLESIDED=ON)
@Pageheading(Odd,,Left "@B<Applications Programs on the VAX>",
Right "@B<Page @Value(Page)>")
@Pageheading(Even,Left "@B<Page @Value(Page)>",Right
@"@B<@Title(Chapter)>")
@COMMENT(SET UP THE TITLE PAGE)
@BEGIN(TITLEPAGE)
@BEGIN(TITLEBOX)
@B[Applications Programs on the VAX]
@BEGIN(CENTER)

by

Ronald M. Sawey

&

Troy T. Stokes

@B[(DRAFT)]
@END(CENTER)
@COPYRIGHTNOTICE(Digital Press)
@END(TITLEBOX)
@END(TITLEPAGE)
.
.
.
```

**Figure C.4 Lines from a Manuscript File Used to Create This Book**

right and left pairs. Delimiters such as { }, ( ), < >, and some others are all acceptable. SCRIBE can operate in many other environments besides italics. For example, `@b{SCRIBE}` tells the program to place the word enclosed in braces in boldface: **SCRIBE**.

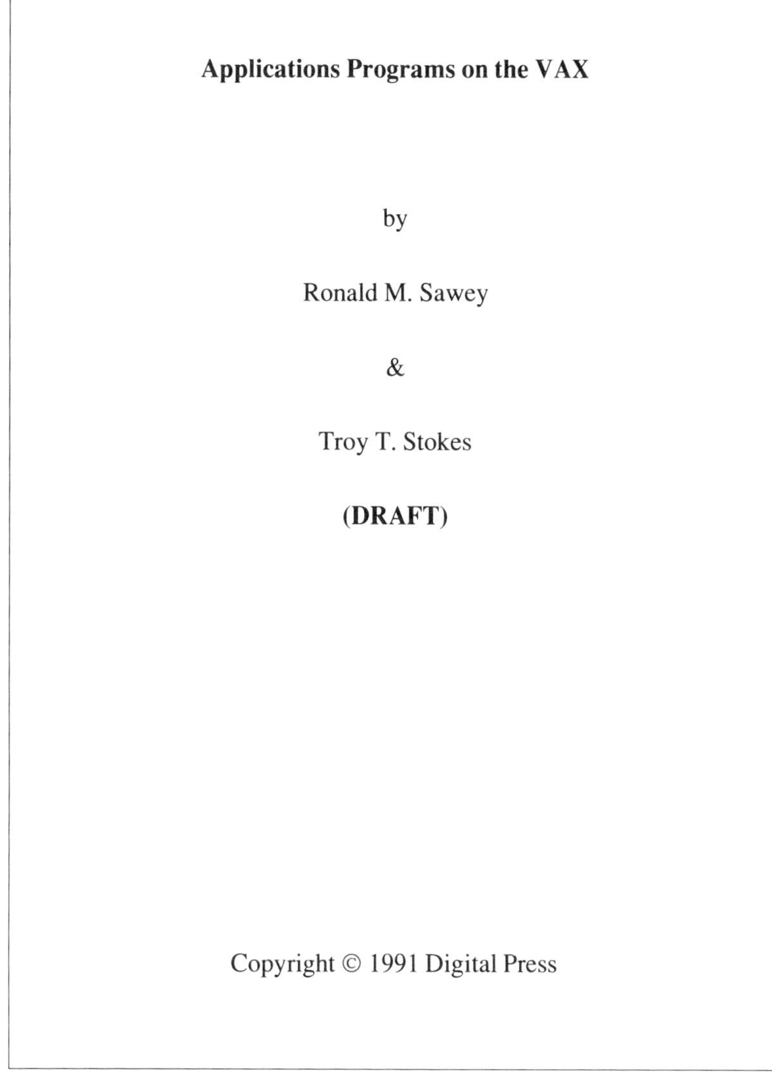
**Applications Programs on the VAX**

by

Ronald M. Sawey

&

Troy T. Stokes

**(DRAFT)**

Copyright © 1991 Digital Press

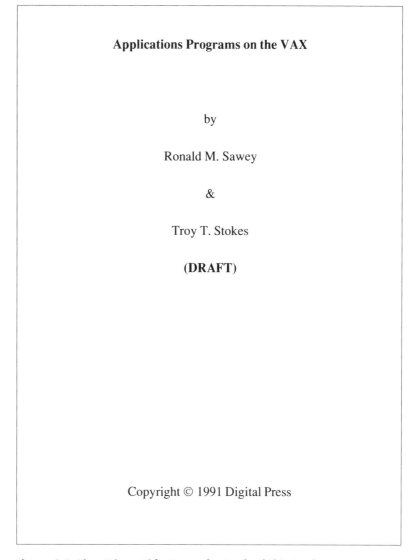

**Figure C.5 Line Printer Title Page of a Draft of This Book**

Like anything else, SCRIBE gets more complicated in real-life examples. After we look at how one draft of this book was put together, our next examples will seem simple indeed! Consider the lines taken from the manuscript file of a draft of this book (see Figure C.4). Figure C.5 shows the title page that results from these SCRIBE commands.

Now, look at what we told SCRIBE to do, and what it actually did. Notice that many of the lines, starting with the first one, are @COMMENT. These lines are optional insofar as the operation of SCRIBE is concerned. They do not affect SCRIBE's operation; their purpose is to help you remember what you told SCRIBE to do. So the first command that actually controls SCRIBE's operation is @MAKE(MANUAL). This command tells the kind of document we intend to produce from our manuscript—a manual, to be precise. A document of this type might have a title page, a table of contents, an introduction, and an index, along with other components.

The next command in Figure C.4 is @DEVICE(LPT), which tells SCRIBE that the final document is to be produced on a line printer. In fact, SCRIBE would have defaulted to this type of printer. Nonetheless, it is a good idea to use an explicit command, because it serves as documentation even when it has the default value. Another good reason to include the device command is that it will be easier to declare a different output device. Changing three letters so that the command reads @DEVICE(CRT) makes the output suitable for display on the screen of a terminal (once you have run SCRIBE again on the manuscript file).

The next two commands, @STYLE(SPACING=2) and @STYLE(INDENT=0), cause SCRIBE to double-space the text in the manual and not to indent for paragraphs. The next command, @STYLE(REFERENCES=STDNUMERIC), concerns keeping track of the references within the manual. The next several lines set up the title page environment. The last line that concerns the title page environment contains the following characters: @END(TITLEPAGE).

Now, look again at the title page in Figure C.5. Notice that all the entries are centered. Some of the lines are printed in boldface, which means that the line printer printed those words twice. The current year has been inserted into the copyright notice. Review the commands in Figure C.4. You will see that the year 1991 is not mentioned anywhere. This information came from preset defaults and assumptions as a consequence of several commands. The @MAKE(MANUAL) and @BEGIN(TITLEPAGE) commands brought about some of the centering. The year 1991 was a consequence of the @COPYRIGHTNOTICE command. By law, notices of copyrights must include the year of publication. The fact that the year in question is 1991 was supplied to SCRIBE by the operating system, which keeps track of the date and time internally.

The point to carry away from all this is that SCRIBE is a very versatile and capable text formatter that can automate many complex tasks. However, it can also perform many simpler tasks, such as the example you will see in the next section.

## C.2 Sample Letter

Call a text editor into operation by typing either `EVE LETTER.MSS` <RETURN> or `EDT LETTER.MSS` <RETURN> at the DCL prompt. Type the following lines into the new file:

```
@device(1pt)
@make(letter)
Your Street Address
Your City, Your State ZIP
@value(date)
@begin(address)
Your Friend
His or Her Street Address
City, State ZIP
@end(address)
@begin(body)
@greeting(Dear Friend:)
```

Substitute your own text here. Insert a blank line to start a new paragraph.

```
@end(body)
Sincerely yours,

Your Name
@begin(notations)
Your capitalized initials/vax
@end(notations)
```

When you are finished, leave the editor and use the proper commands so that your new file will be saved. Now copy `LETTER.MSS` into another file called `FRIEND.MSS`[4] using the DCL copy command at the operating system prompt:

```
MYNODE$ COPY LETTER.MSS FRIEND.MSS <RETURN>
```

Use the DCL command `DIR` to satisfy yourself that two new letter files, `LETTER.MSS` and `FRIEND.MSS`, exist in your directory. Now, using one of the text editors to edit `FRIEND.MSS`, write an actual letter that tells a friend

4. The practice of assigning file names that can be remembered easily is called mnemonic file naming.

something about your experiences over the past several weeks.[5] The usefulness of SCRIBE should be immediately clear. Once you are reasonably sure that the letter is as you want it, SCRIBE it by typing, at the operating system level, `SCRIBE FRIEND` <RETURN>. SCRIBE displays certain information about what it is doing.

Remember, in an earlier example, SCRIBE told you that the document type was `TEXT`. Now, it tells you that the document type is `LETTER`. This categorization is a consequence of the `@MAKE(LETTER)` command in the `FRIEND.MSS` file. That command caused letter defaults to be called into operation, just as the `@MAKE(MANUAL)` command caused manual defaults to operate in the earlier example. Keep the `LETTER.MSS` file in your directory; you might want to use it as a template when you write letters to other people. (See Section C.6.1 for a log of what to expect when you apply SCRIBE to the `LETTER.MSS` file.)

## C.3 Sample Resume

Suppose you are making a career change and want to put together a resume to circulate to prospective employers. You can use SCRIBE to create a resume manuscript file. Copy our example into your own directory at the operating system prompt:

`MYNODE$ COPY TEXTFILES:RES.MSS RES.MSS` <RETURN>

If the `TEXTFILES` directory is not available, you can use a text editor to type in the `RES.MSS` file, shown in Section C.6.2. (In that section, begin typing at the line `@make(text)` and continue through the line `Owners' Association.`)

SCRIBE the `RES.MSS` file just as you did the `FRIEND.MSS` file earlier. Print a copy of the resume by issuing the command `PRINT RES.LPT` <RETURN> at the operating system prompt. (See Section C.6.2 for a log of what to expect when you apply SCRIBE to the `RES.MSS` file.)

Compare the formatted text to the manuscript file to see what SCRIBE has done. `RESUME` is not an official SCRIBE document type, like `LETTER` or `MANUAL`. The document type (declared in the `@MAKE` command) is just `TEXT`, the standard default document type for SCRIBE. For this reason, you have

5. Some sites forbid private use of the computer. Learn the rules for your site from the local user services staff.

explicitly instructed SCRIBE to perform the special spacing and other style effects. The word "RESUME" is centered on the page because of the @HEADING(RESUME) string, which puts the word in a heading environment. The string @i[@u<Born:>] causes the word "Born:" to be underlined and italicized (if the printer you are using can print italics).

Take note of the string @begin(itemize). Looking at the final formatted text, notice that each educational entry begins with a dash and is indented slightly. The @* symbols at the end of each line in the manuscript file cause line breaks in the final formatted text. Had they been omitted, the entire paragraph (item) would have been filled and right-justified—in other words, SCRIBE would have produced a smooth right-hand side because TEXT and ITEMIZE are both environments that are filled and right-justified.

We need to make one other observation. The TEXT environment of SCRIBE recognizes new paragraphs when there is a blank line in the manuscript file. Similarly, the ITEMIZE environment in SCRIBE recognizes new items when it encounters a blank line. You can put several paragraphs under *one* item by grouping them inside an @MULTIPLE environment. See Bibliography [17] for more details.

Next, notice the @begin(enumerate) just after the word "Experience:". This environment works just the same way as the ITEMIZE environment except that each item is *numbered*. Now issue the following command at the operating system prompt:

```
MYNODE$ COPY RES.MSS VITA.MSS <RETURN>
```

The file VITA.MSS is the one you will use to make your own resume. Use a text editor to replace the information about Billy Bob with appropriate data about your own life. When you are confident that your resume is accurate, SCRIBE the manuscript file. Once SCRIBE operates without errors, print the final draft version of the resume by issuing the command PRINT VITA.LPT.

If your resume looks accurate, you may want to get a higher-quality copy on a laser printer, if one is available at your site. (If your site does not have a laser printer, skip to Section C.4.) Recall Chapter 1, Exercise 13, and Chapter 2, Exercise 10. If you have not already done these exercises, do so now.

The example given here assumes the use of an LN01 laser printer. However, once you find out what kind of printers are available at your site, you can probably get sufficient on-line help (by typing HELP SCRIBE at the operating system prompt) to make the necessary adjustments for your own site configuration.

Assuming that you have an LN01 laser printer, go into the VITA.MSS file with a text editor and change the device statement to read @DEVICE(ln01).[6] SCRIBE the file again. When you are finished, notice that a new file, VITA.LNO, exists in your directory. The file type, .LNO, indicates that the file has been formatted for printing on the laser printer known as LN01. To print this new file on the laser printer, do *not* use the PRINT command. Instead, type LASER VITA.LNO <RETURN> at the operating system prompt. (Note that LASER is not a DCL command, even though you issue it at the node prompt, just as you do with the DIR or PRINT commands. In VAX/VMS terms, LASER is a global symbol (alias) as discussed in Chapter 1, Exercise 13, and Chapter 2, Exercise 10.)

## C.4 Writing a Report

SCRIBE is at its best when it tackles some of the more tedious tasks that we were once forced to perform manually. Organizing a research paper or report can be among the most draining tasks a college student or professional person has to face. For instance, if you decide to add one footnote, all the ones after it have to be renumbered. Keeping citations and references straight is just as big a headache. Adding a chapter causes dislocations similar to those of adding a footnote.

To grasp how SCRIBE automates these tasks, look at an example that is very much like this book except that it is much shorter. Issue the following command at the operating system level:

```
MYNODE$ COPY TEXTFILES:DEMO.* DEMO.* <RETURN>
```

If your TEXTFILES directory is not set up, see the listings in Section C.6.3.

With the DIR command, ascertain that there are two new files, DEMO.MSS and DEMO.BIB, in your directory. PRINT both of these files so you can compare

6. This is an example of an item you need to check with your local user services staff. For example, your site might require the designation "postscript" or "ps" in order to use your laser printer.

the input manuscript with the output document files. (Section C.6.3 shows a log of what to expect when you apply SCRIBE to the `DEMO.*` files.)

SCRIBE the file `DEMO.MSS`. Though it does not contain errors, you will see a worrisome warning from SCRIBE indicating that something could be wrong with the references. SCRIBE the file again. Notice that the warning does not appear a second time. Notice, too, that the version number of `DEMO.LPT` is now 2. Print this file with the `/DELETE` option by typing the following command at the operating system prompt:

```
MYNODE$ PRINT DEMO.LPT/DELETE <RETURN>
```

Once you have a printed copy in hand, compare the formatted text with the manuscript and bibliography files you just printed. See if you can figure out how the two input files interact to produce the final formatted text. Notice in the manuscript file the command `@CITE(SPENCER1)`. This command causes the book by Spencer to be cited. The string `SPENCER1` is called the *codeword*, or *keyword*. The reader of your final text never sees this codeword, so it is best to choose a codeword that will help you remember the work you intend to cite. If Spencer had written two books you needed to quote, and you hated the first book and loved the second, you could choose HATE and LOVE for the SCRIBE codewords.

The codeword must also appear just where you see it in the bibliography file `DEMO.BIB`—right after the opening parenthesis (delimiter). The word just before the parenthesis is called the *reference type*. The type of reference (in this case, `@BOOK`) does the same thing for the bibliography entry that the `@MAKE` command does for the manuscript file, that is, it sets the style of the reference. The bibliographic entry for a book is stylistically different from one for a magazine article. The reference type in the `.BIB` file takes care of these differences. SCRIBE is strict about where the type must be placed. It must go exactly where you see it in `DEMO.BIB`—after the @ sign and before the first parenthesis.

SCRIBE uses the `KEY` field of the reference to decide where your reference fits alphabetically in the set of references contained in your formatted output file. The rest of the fields of the `.BIB` file references should be clear from the context.

It is very important to make one more observation about the entries in the .BIB file. Except for the codeword field, *all fields except one* require an equal sign, followed by text contained in double quotation marks, and concluded with a comma. The one exception is the last field, which is concluded by a right parenthesis. Failure to follow this rule can cause substantial grief in getting SCRIBE to process your manuscript files without errors. The fact that SCRIBE is so particular about this rule has caused some wags to call SCRIBE "user-hateful."

An interesting fact about the operation of SCRIBE's bibliographic functions is that you do not have to cite from each work in the bibliography file. For instance, you might be writing several papers or reports on related subjects. You could reduce confusion and work load by using one master bibliography file from which you could draw citations as needed. The only thing you would have to keep straight is renaming the .BIB file so that the part of the file specification before the period is the same as that of the .MSS file. (If you do not do this, be ready to give SCRIBE the name of your .BIB file when you run SCRIBE on your .MSS file.) Keep DEMO.BIB in your directory as a template for a real research paper or report you might do later on.

Bibliography functions are not the only handy functions of DEMO.MSS. This manuscript file makes use of the ITEMIZE and ENUMERATE environments, just as the resume manuscript file did earlier. In addition, you could use it to create figures and tables in a similar way. The lines shown in Figure C.6 are from the manuscript file; they create a figure in the formatted text.

Note the symmetry in the @BEGIN and @END commands. They are like nested delimiters for environments: ({[]}). The order of the @CAPTION and @TAG commands is important. If you reverse the sequence, your figure numbers and their references will be incorrectly numbered. The @CAPTION command gives the figure a title. The only really cryptic command—the @TAG command—allows the figure to be referenced in your text. SCRIBE does not put the figure in exactly the same place in the formatted text as you did in the manuscript file. For this reason you cannot use language such as "shown in the figure at the bottom of the page." You must refer to a figure as a string in your manuscript file; for example, "as shown in @REF[EX]". In the formatted .LPT file, that string would emerge something like "as shown in Figure 1.1". SCRIBE keeps track of the numbering for you automatically.

```
@BEGIN(FIGURE)
@BEGIN(VERBATIM)
X     X
 X   X
  X X
   X
  X X
 X   X
X     X
@END(VERBATIM)
@CAPTION("X" Marks the Spot!)
@tag(ex)
@end(figure)
```

**Figure C.6 Lines from DEMO.MSS File**

With the `@BLANKSPACE` command, SCRIBE can also make room for a more complex figure than it is able to generate. You can then insert professionally drawn or computer-generated artwork in the blank space. The distance SCRIBE leaves for your artwork does not have to be in inches; it can be in centimeters or lines. The empty figure space will have a caption and a tag, just like the others.

SCRIBE handles tables much as it does figures, except that tables are almost always generated by SCRIBE. The two tables in the `DEMO.MSS` file are the same for all practical purposes. However, they achieve their results by relying differently on SCRIBE's tab features. The creator of the first table inserted explicit tab stops by setting them with the @^ characters. The @\ characters have the effect of tabbing to the next stop in the formatted output file.

In the second table SCRIBE inserted the stops by means of the command `@TABDIVIDE(4)`, which sets tab stops so that there are four columns of equal width. Again, the @\ characters have the effect of tabbing to the next stop in the formatted output file. Compare the two tables in the manuscript file and examine the two methods for setting tab stops.

The `@BIBLIOGRAPHY` command causes SCRIBE to print all the references that have been cited in your manuscript file. With this document type, SCRIBE will automatically print out the bibliography at the *end* of your formatted file, even if you do not issue the `@BIBLIOGRAPHY` command.

Keep a copy of DEMO.MSS for use in producing a real research paper or report.

## C.5 A Few Tips on SCRIBE

As you use SCRIBE, keep in mind a few tips we have learned from experience.

- Recall that, in a FIGURE environment, you *must* place the @CAPTION command before the @TAG command if the numbering of figures and tables is to be correct.
- If you have a complicated document containing numerous citations, figures, tables, and the like, and you have made extensive changes in the manuscript file since the last processing by SCRIBE, it is a good idea to delete the .AUX and .OTL files *before* you process your manuscript file through SCRIBE again.
- Do not give SCRIBE a specific version number for a source file, unless you have deleted all related files (such as .AUX and .OTL files) having the same version number. Unless you have become an experienced SCRIBE user, it is best to omit the version number of your source file and let SCRIBE pick the latest version.
- Do not be alarmed if your terminal "springs to life" with errors when you process a new file through SCRIBE. Often a few changes are all that are required. With a little practice, you will find that the error messages usually point the way to the major problems. However, one error message is less than helpful:

```
*Unrecoverable problem; cannot continue this Scribe run*
Error found while processing:
I/O Error while writing file MANUAL.LNO
%SYSTEM-F-ABORT, abort
```

  This message occurs when you have exceeded your disk quota. (For more information, type HELP SHOW QUOTA <RETURN> at the operating system prompt.) Anybody could tell that, right?

## C.6 Some Logs of SCRIBE Sessions

This section contains logs of sessions with SCRIBE, using most of the files discussed previously. The goal is to give you an idea of what to expect when you have your own sessions with SCRIBE. Each session contains a few preliminary remarks, then the session log. Any comments within the session logs are set off in the usual way, with an exclamation point (!).

### C.6.1 A SCRIBE Session Using the Letter Template

The log for this session follows these steps:

- Issue a directory command to show that `LETTER.MSS` exists.
- Type the file to the screen of your terminal.
- Run SCRIBE on the source file, `LETTER.MSS`.
- Check the directory to see that `LETTER.LPT` has been produced.
- Print the formatted (processed) text file, `LETTER.LPT`, to the line printer.

```
MYNODE$ dir letter * <RETURN>

Directory MYDISK:[MYDIR]

LETTER.MSS;1      1      7-JAN-1991 10:35

Total of 1 file, 1 block.

MYNODE$ ty letter.mss <RETURN>
@device(lpt)
@make(letter)
Your Street Address
Your City, Your State ZIP
@value(date)
@begin(address)
Your Friend
His or Her Street Address
City, State ZIP
@end(address)
@begin(body)
@greeting(Dear Friend:)
```

Substitute your own text here. Insert a blank line to start a new paragraph.

```
@end (body)
Sincerely yours,

Your Name
@begin(notations)
Your capitalized initials/vax
@end(notations)

MYNODE$ scribe letter.mss <RETURN>
Scribe 5(1500) Copyright (C) 1981, 1984 UNILOGIC, Ltd.
                                    VAX/VMS
[Processing LETTER.MSS
     [Device "lpt"]
     [Document type "letter"
]
1.

**LETTER.LPT for device lpt has 1 page.
```

```
MYNODE$ dir letter.* <RETURN>

Directory MYDISK:[MYDIR]

LETTER.LPT;1     2      7-JAN-1991 10:36
LETTER.MSS;1     1      7-JAN-1991 10:35

Total of 2 files, 3 blocks.

MYNODE$ pri letter.lpt <RETURN>

Job LETTER (queue SYS$PRINT, entry 756) started on MYNODE_LCA0
```

### C.6.2 A SCRIBE Session Using the Resume Template

The log for this session follows these steps:

- Issue a directory command to show that RES.MSS exists.
- Type the file to the screen of your terminal.
- Run SCRIBE on the source file, RES.MSS.
- Check the directory to see that RES.LPT has been produced.
- Print the formatted (processed) text file, RES.LPT, to the line printer.

```
MYNODE$ dir res.* <RETURN>

Directory MYDISK:[MYDIR]

RES.MSS;4     4     1-OCT-1990 09:45

Total of 1 file, 4 blocks.

MYNODE$ ty res.mss <RETURN>

@make(text)
@device(lpt)
@style(paperwidth=8.5 in, paperlength=11 in)
@style(topmargin=1 in, bottommargin=1 in, leftmargin=1 in,
linewidth=6.5 in)
@style(spacing=1, indent=0)
@heading(RESUME)
@center(Billy Bob Taggart)
2501 The Strand@*
Galveston, TX 78XXX

@i[@u<Born:>]Comfort, Texas, 1933

@i[@u<Education:>]
@begin(itemize)
B.A., Southwest Texas Normal School, 1952@*
Major: Physical Education@*
Minor: Public Speaking and Elocution@*
Honors: Presiding Judge, Luling (Texas) Watermelon Thump 1950,
1951@*
Second String Fullback, SWT Bobcats, 1952
```

```
Graduate, La Grange High School,
La Grange, Texas, 1948@*
Honors: Vice-president, Future Farmers of America@*
Special Award in Chicken Ranching

Mirabeau B. Lamar Elementary School,
Cotulla, Texas, 1942@*
Honors: Captain, English First Hallway Patrol
@end(itemize)

@i[@u<Experience:>]
@begin(enumerate)
1980-present: Chair, English Department, and Football Coach@*
Ball High School, Galveston, Texas.
Duties: Winning at all costs. Instilling attitudes of conven-
tionality and a positive mental attitude among the student
body. Putting the big QT on the subversive notion that varsity
players must maintain a particular grade-point average.

1974-1980: Speech Teacher and Debate Coach@*
Consolidated Middle School, Dime Box, Texas.
Duties: Promoting Western capitalist patriotic values among
the contestants in the University Interscholastic League. Re-
versing disturbing political trends left over from the sixties.
Honors: Fundraising Chair for Burleson County Public Radio.

1953-1973: United States Air Force@*
Job at retirement: Drill Instructor, Lackland Air Force Base,
San Antonio, Texas.
@end(enumerate)

@i[@u<Career Interests:>] Upon completion of my M.Ed. degree,
I hope to advance to the position of principal at the high
school level or perhaps attain the rank of district adminis-
trator for linguistic arts.

@i[@u<Hobbies and Other Interests:>] I am eligible for early
retirement in three years. My hope is that at that time I can
help my brother with what has become the love of his life
since he has embarked on retirement number two: his volunteer
work with the Greater Hidalgo County Recreational Vehicle Park
Owners' Association.

MYNODE$ scribe res <RETURN>      !NOTE: File type .MSS
                                 ! is not required.
Scribe 5(1500) Copyright (C) 1981, 1984 UNILOGIC, Ltd.
                          VAX/VMS
[Processing RES.MSS
     [Device "lpt"]
     [Document type "text"
]
1.
```

```
**RES.LPT for device lpt has 1 page.
MYNODE$ dir res.* <RETURN>

Directory MYDISK:[MYDIR]

RES.LPT;1      5      7-JAN-1991 10:37
RES.MSS;4      4      1-OCT-1990 09:45

Total of 2 files, 9 blocks.

MYNODE$ pri res.lpt <RETURN>

Job RES (queue SYS$PRINT, entry 757) started on MYNODE_LCAO
```

### C.6.3 A SCRIBE Session Using the DEMO Files

The log for this session follows these steps:

- Issue a directory command to show that DEMO.MSS and DEMO.BIB exist.
- Type the two files to the screen of your terminal.
- Run SCRIBE on the source file, DEMO.MSS.
- Check the directory to see what new files with the file name DEMO have been produced.
- Run SCRIBE again on the source file, DEMO.MSS, in order to get the cross-references correct (as discussed previously).
- Print the formatted (processed) text file, DEMO.LPT, to the line printer.
- Purge your directory.

```
MYNODE$ dir demo.* <RETURN>

Directory MYDISK:[MYDIR]

DEMO.BIB;5      1      23-SEP-1990 16:18
DEMO.MSS;8     11       8-OCT-1990 09:59

Total of 2 files, 12 blocks.

MYNODE$ ty demo.mss <RETURN>

@MAKE(REPORT)
@DEVICE(LPT)
@STYLE(PAPERWIDTH=8.5 IN, LINEWIDTH=6.5 IN, PAPERLENGTH=11
IN)
@STYLE(TOPMARGIN=1 IN, BOTTOMMARGIN=1.5 IN)
@STYLE(REFERENCES=STDNUMERIC)
@SET(PAGE=1)
@CHAPTER(Let's Begin)
This is a dummy example of a report you might have to write
sometime. It demonstrates some of the more commonly used fea-
tures of SCRIBE. You might choose to defend certain assertions
at the bottom of the page. @FOOT (Just like your English Com-
position Instructor told you to do.)
```

```
The professor might be impressed if you shared credit for some
of your more stellar discoveries with the author of your text-
book, Donald Spencer. @cite(SPENCER1)

Many papers and reports make use of lists. The ITEMIZE envi-
ronment suspends the normal filling and justification and pro-
duces an un-numbered, itemized list. The following list is an
itemized list:
@begin(itemize)
Item A

Item B

Item D

Item C
@end(itemize)
You might, however, need to refer to your main points in the
order you made them. In this case your rhetoric would be more
compelling if you chose the ENUMERATE environment and created
a numbered list:

@begin(enumerate)
Item A

Item B

Item D

Item C
@end(enumerate)

More text would require more citations as you made reference
perhaps to
Chapter 1 of @U[Introduction to the VAX/VMS at SWTSU]
@cite(VMS1).
You might be inclined to dramatize your points with compelling
illustrations made of ASCII characters entered from the key-
board. Figure @REF(EX) demonstrates this fairly well.
However, more complicated illustrations might require photo-
graphs or drawings. You would need to tell SCRIBE to leave
room as demonstrated by Figure @ref(empty). Notice how SCRIBE
places the figures where it thinks they go best and refers to
them in your text by number.
@BEGIN(FIGURE)
@BEGIN(VERBATIM)
```

```
X     X
 X   X
  X X
   X
  X X
 X   X
X     X

@END(VERBATIM)
@CAPTION("X" Marks the Spot!)
@tag(ex)
@end(figure)
The ability to keep track of figures, footnotes, citations,
and tables and keep track of renumbering, when necessary, is a
powerful feature often omitted from many very popular word-
pro-cessing and text-formatting programs.
@begin(figure)
@blankspace(2 in)
@caption(Nothing Here.)
@tag(empty)
@end(figure)

@NEWPAGE
WORDSTAR, widely used on microcomputers, does not have all
these features. Neither does RUNOFF, another major text pro-
cessor on our VAXclusters.
@chapter(Continuing)
SCRIBE can produce neatly formatted tables. You may explicitly
set the tabs for the columns you need as in Table @ref(first),
which shows the @@^ tab setting option with columns set with
widths of 10,10,15,15; whereas Table @ref(second) shows the
@TABDIVIDE option. You might let SCRIBE set the columns for
you using TABDIVIDE. If the spacing seems odd, you might then
try explicit settings as in Table @ref[first].

@Begin(table,spacing 1)
@begin(verbatim)
@tabclear
         @^        @^              @^            @^
@ux(Column A@\Column B@\Column C@\Column D)

Entry A1@\Entry B1@\Entry C1@\Entry D1
Entry A2@\Entry B2@\Entry C2@\Entry D2
Entry A3@\Entry B3@\Entry C3@\Entry D3

@ux(@\@\@\@\)

TOTAL A@\Total B@\Total C@\Total D

@END(VERBATIM)
@Caption(The @@^ Tab Setting)
@tag(first)
@end(table)
```

Tables and figures are treated very similarly by SCRIBE. The main thing to remember at this elementary level is that they are both interruptions to the standard formatting routine of filling and justification which formats all characters into neat paragraphs with smooth left and right margins. They do not appear in the final text in the same place that you had them in the manuscript file. SCRIBE puts them where they fit and then refers to them by number. Have a look at Table @ref(first), and possibly Table @ref(second) or Figure @ref(ex), and take note of where they appear in the manuscript as well as the formatted text.

```
@Begin(table, spacing 2)
@begin(verbatim)
@tabclear
@tabdivide(4)
@ux(Column A@\Column B@\Column C@\Column D)

Entry A1@\Entry B1@\Entry C1@\Entry D1
Entry A2@\Entry B2@\Entry C2@\Entry D2
Entry A3@\Entry B3@\Entry C3@\Entry D3

@ux(@\@\@\@\)

Total A@\Total B@\Total C@\Total D

@END(VERBATIM)
@Caption(The @@Tabdivide Setting)
@tag(second)
@end(table)

@chapter(Centering)
Lines can be centered,
line by line, using delimiters, as follows:

@center(LINE A)

@CENTER(LINE B)
Or you can declare the environment with BEGIN and END state-
ments similar to the way you used them in verbatim environ-
ments earlier:

@BEGIN(CENTER)
LINE A

LINE B

LINE C
@END(CENTER)

@BEGIN(CENTER)
What might otherwise be a @B(paragraph) can be contained
within a centered environment. And, with skilled application
of @u[delimiters], you can create special effects within that
centered environment.
```

```
It looks dopey in a report, but with the proper spacing and
use of special fonts, you could have a great
@b[WEDDING INVITATION.]
@END(CENTER)
@UNNUMBERED(References)
@bibliography

MYNODE$ ty demo.bib <RETURN>

@BOOK(SPENCER1,
    ,KEY="Spencer"
    ,TITLE="Computers: An Introduction"
    ,AUTHOR="Donald D. Spencer"
    ,YEAR="1986"
    ,ADDRESS="Columbus, Ohio"
    ,PUBLISHER="Merrill Publishing Company"
    )
@MANUAL(VMS1,
    ,KEY="Whiteley"
    ,TITLE="Introduction to the VAX/VMS at SWTSU"
    ,AUTHOR="J. Michael Whiteley and William Bryson, Editors"
    ,YEAR="1986"
    ,MONTH="May"
    ,ADDRESS="San Marcos, Texas"
    ,ORGANIZATION="Academic Computer Center, SWTSU"
    )
MYNODE$ scribe demo <RETURN>
Scribe 5(1500) Copyright (C) 1981, 1984 UNILOGIC, Ltd.
                            VAX/VMS
[Processing DEMO.MSS
    [Device "LPT"]
    [Document type "REPORT"]
(1) 1 2 3 4 (2) 5 6 (3) 7 ()
    [Reference format: STDNUMERIC
      [Subfile DEMO.BIB]
      [Sorted reference list]
    ]
]
8
[CONTENTS]
i
[FIGURECONTENTS]
ii
[TABLECONTENTS]
iii.

Error found while finishing up after the end of the manu-
script: Cross-references to 6 labels are wrong. Run the file
through Scribe again to correct the references.

**DEMO.LPT for device LPT has 11 pages.
```

```
**DEMO.AUX written.
**DEMO.OTL written.
**DEMO.ERR lists 1 error.

MYNODE$ dir demo.* <RETURN>

Directory MYDISK:[MYDIR]

DEMO.AUX;1      1      7-JAN-1991 10:38
DEMO.BIB;5      1     23-SEP-1990 16:18
DEMO.ERR;1      1      7-JAN-1991 10:38
DEMO.LPT;1     17      7-JAN-1991 10:38
DEMO.MSS;8     11      8-OCT-1990 09:56
DEMO.OTL;1      3      7-JAN-1991 10:38

Total of 6 files, 34 blocks.

MYNODE$ scribe demo <RETURN>  ! Run Scribe again to get the
                              ! cross-references correct.
Scribe 5(1500) Copyright (C) 1981, 1984 UNILOGIC, Ltd.
                         VAX/VMS
[Processing DEMO.MSS
     [Device "LPT"]
     [Document type "REPORT"]
     [Subfile DEMO.AUX]
(1) 1 2 3 4 (2) 5 6 (3) 7 ()
     [Reference format: STDNUMERIC
        [Subfile DEMO.BIB]
        [Sorted reference list]
     ]
]
8
[CONTENTS]
i
[FIGURECONTENTS]
ii
[TABLECONTENTS]
iii.

**DEMO.LPT for device LPT has 11 pages.
**DEMO.AUX written.
**DEMO.OTL written.

MYNODE$ dir demo.* <RETURN>

Directory MYDISK:[MYDIR]

DEMO.AUX;2      1      7-JAN-1991 10:38
DEMO.AUX;1      1      7-JAN-1991 10:38
DEMO.BIB;5      1     23-SEP-1990 16:18
DEMO.LPT;2     17      7-JAN-1991 10:38
DEMO.LPT;1     17      7-JAN-1991 10:38
DEMO.MSS;8     11      8-OCT-1990 09:59
DEMO.OTL;2      3      7-JAN-1991 10:38
```

```
DEMO.OTL;1       3     7-JAN-1991 10:38

Total of 8 files, 54 blocks.

MYNODE$ pri demo.lpt <RETURN>

Job DEMO (queue SYS$PRINT, entry 758) started on MYNODE_LCA0

MYNODE$ PURGE <RETURN>

MYNODE$ dir demo.* <RETURN>

Directory MYDISK:[MYDIR]

DEMO.AUX;2       1     7-JAN-1991 10:38
DEMO.BIB;5       1    23-SEP-1990 16:18
DEMO.LPT;2      17     7-JAN-1991 10:38
DEMO.MSS;8      11     8-OCT-1990 09:59
DEMO.OTL;2       3     7-JAN-1991 10:38

Total of 5 files, 33 blocks.
```

## C.7 Quick Reference: SCRIBE Commands

*For a more extensive summary, see Bibliography [18]; for more detailed coverage of SCRIBE see Bibliography [17].*

To run the SCRIBE program on the manuscript file `FILE.MSS`, type `SCRIBE FILE.MSS` <RETURN> at the `MYNODE$` prompt.

### @DEVICE Command and Device Types

Select these device types with the `@DEVICE` command from within SCRIBE.

| *Device Type* | *Description* |
|---|---|
| `LPT` | The default device type, the computer system line printer. |
| `CRT` | Output paginated into 24-line pages suitable for display on a computer terminal screen. No overstriking, underlining, or special effects. |
| `LA36` | LA36 DECwriter II. SCRIBE assumes narrow (8.5-inch) paper is placed on the machine. |
| `LN01` | LN01 laser printer. |

### @STYLE Command and Keywords

The `@STYLE` command specifies the keyword-value pairs that control the appearance of your document. `@STYLE` keywords affecting the overall document definition are restricted to the *beginning* of the manuscript file. Other `@STYLE` keywords can appear *anywhere* in the manuscript file. The `@STYLE` command has the following form:

`@STYLE(`*keyword*$_1$=*value*$_1$, *keyword*$_2$=*value*$_2$`, . . . )`

Some `@STYLE` keywords require *numeric values* (e.g., `1.3 inches`). Others require *keyword values* (e.g., `YES` or `NO`). Others require *delimited string values* (e.g., `"2 April 1991")`. *Do not* use delimiters on keywords or numeric values; for example, do not put quotes around `YES`. The following keyword-value pairs are selected with the `@STYLE` command.

| *Keyword* | *Value* |
|---|---|
| `BOTTOMMARGIN` | Vertical distance between last line of text and bottom of page. Use only at beginning of manuscript file. Numeric value, e.g., 1.3 inches. |
| `DOUBLESIDED` | When set ON, allows for chapters always to begin on a right-hand page. |

| | |
|---|---|
| `INDENT` | Horizontal distance, indicating amount of indenting for each paragraph relative to its left margin. Use only at beginning of manuscript file. Numeric value. |
| `LEFT MARGIN` | Size of the left margin, given in inches, centimeters, or number of spaces. |
| `LINEWIDTH` | Horizontal distance from global left margin to end of line. Use only at beginning of the manuscript file. Numeric value. |
| `PAPERLENGTH` | Vertical distance specifying physical paper dimension. Only meaningful for printing devices on which different lengths of paper can be used. Use only at beginning of manuscript file. Numeric value. |
| `PAPERWIDTH` | Horizontal distance specifying physical paper dimension. Only meaningful for printing devices on which different widths of paper can be used. Use only at beginning of manuscript file. Numeric value. |
| `REFERENCES` | Name of entry in bibliography database specifying reference style and citation style, for example, `@STYLE(REFERENCES=STDNUMERIC)`. With `STDNUMERIC`, SCRIBE will produce numeric citations, such as [7]; open format numerical ordering of references. With `STDALPHABETIC`, SCRIBE will produce alphabetic citations, such as [Smith 86]; open format alphabetical ordering of references. |
| `SPACING` | Specifies spacing in document, for instance, `@STYLE(SPACING=2)`. |
| `TOPMARGIN` | Vertical distance from top of paper to first text line on page. Use only at beginning of the manuscript file. Numeric value. |

***Standard Environments***

The following environments, available in all document types, are specified in either a long form or a short form. The long command form is

`@BEGIN(`*Environment-name*`)`
- - - *Text for body of environment* - - -
`@END(`*Environment-name*`)`

The short command form is

@*Environment-name*`(` - - - *Text for body of environment* - - - `)`

The delimiters used with the short form are ( . . . ), [ . . . ], { . . . }, " . . . ", ' . . . ', or < . . . >.

| *Environment Name* | *Description* |
|---|---|
| `B` | Requests **boldface** printing. |

| | |
|---|---|
| CENTER | Centers each manuscript line in the body of the environment between global margins. |
| DESCRIPTION | Provides paragraphs with header words in widened left margin. Use tab command (@\) to separate header words from rest of each paragraph. |
| ENUMERATE | Numbers each paragraph within body. Sets list off from rest of text with spacing and wider margins. |
| HEADING | Places its body as an un-numbered heading. Breaks lines as in manuscript file. |
| I | Requests *italic* printing. |
| ITEMIZE | Flags each paragraph with special character in margin. Sets list off from rest of text with spacing and wider margins. |
| TEXT | Provides plain running text environment. All formatting normally inside environment TEXT unless specified otherwise. However, you might want, for example, to put text inside figures. |
| U | Requests underlined printing. All nonblank characters will be underlined. |
| UX | Same as @U, except it underlines *all* characters, including spaces. |
| VERBATIM | Breaks lines as in manuscript file. Sets off the body with spacing. Does not adjust margins. |
| FIGURE | Indicates a floating figure. If it contains an @CAPTION command and an @REF command, figure will be assigned a number and listed in the list of figures. *Note*: This environment is available for sectioned document types, including REPORT, ARTICLE, and MANUAL. |

### Punctuation-Character Commands

Most of the punctuation characters are defined as SCRIBE commands. With the exception of @+ and @-, which are synonymous with @PLUS and @MINUS, none of these punctuation-character commands takes an argument.

| *Character* | *Result* |
|---|---|
| @+(*text*) | Prints text as superscript at current cursor position. |
| @-(*text*) | Prints text as subscript at current cursor position. |
| @\ | Tab command. Moves cursor to next tab stop or marks end of text being centered or set flush right. |
| @* | Indicates line to be broken, regardless of the environment. |
| @^ | Sets tab stop at point where typed, relative to current left margin. |

### *Document Types*

To select one of these document types, put the `@MAKE` command in the manuscript file before the first line of text. For example,

```
@MAKE(REPORT)
```

Some document types have variant forms, such as

```
@MAKE(ARTICLE, FORM 2)
```

Each of the basic environments is available in all standard document types. See also the environment summary.

| *Document Type* | *Description* |
| --- | --- |
| `LETTER` | Document type for formal letter. |
| `MANUAL` | A sectioned document similar to `REPORT` but including an index. |
| `TEXT` | Default document type. Unindented, right-justified paragraphs on numbered pages. No table of contents or index. |
| `REPORT` | A sectioned document which provides `CHAPTER`, `SECTION`, `SUBSECTION`, `PARAGRAPH`, `APPENDIX`, and `APPENDIXSEC` sectioning commands. Title page and table of contents, but no index. |

### *Bibliography Database Keywords*

Use keywords in defining bibliography database entries in a `.BIB` file. All take a delimited string or an abbreviation code as a value.

| *Reference Type* | *Description* |
| --- | --- |
| `@ARTICLE` | See Bibliography [17], [18] for a description of Reference Types. |
| `@BOOK` | |
| `@MANUAL` | |

| *Field* | *Meaning* |
| --- | --- |
| `ADDRESS` | Address of publisher, printer, or organization. |
| `AUTHOR` | Name(s) of author(s), in format in which they are to be printed. |
| `KEY` | Sort key for alphabetization purposes. |
| `PUBLISHER` | Name of publishing company. |
| `TITLE` | Title of book, article, thesis, or other document being cited. *Note*: Do not italicize or underline. |
| `YEAR` | Year of publication in four digits; e.g., 1991. |

### Alphabetic List of SCRIBE Commands

These commands work for all devices and document types. See also the environment summary.

| *Command* | *Description* |
|---|---|
| @BEGIN(*environment-name, attribute-value-list*) | Marks beginning of formatting environment of specified kind. See also environment summary and @END. |
| @BIBLIOGRAPHY | Inserts bibliography at this point in document. If command is missing, SCRIBE will put bibliography at end of document. |
| @BLANKSPACE(*vertical distance*) | Inserts blank space (e.g., for a figure). Examples of the vertical distance parameter are 3 inches, 16 cm, 20 lines. |
| @CAPTION(*text of caption*) | Specifies caption for figure or table. *Note*: Any @TAG commands must come *after* @CAPTION. |
| @CITE(*keyword*) | Placed in the manuscript file, this command generates a bibliographic citation to the reference entry identified by keyword, places that citation in the document in place of the @CITE command, and causes that bibliographic entry to be included in the bibliography of the document file. See summary of bibliography database keywords. |
| @COMMENT(*text of message*) | Marks text not to be processed for output document. Delimiter nesting does not work inside @COMMENT. The text may not contain closing delimiter. |
| @DEVICE(*device-type*) | Specifies printing device for output file. See device summary. |
| @END(*environment-name*) | Marks end of formatting environment that was started with @BEGIN. |
| @FOOT(*text of footnote*) | Places and numbers text of footnote, and inserts appropriate footnote numbers in the text. |
| @LABEL(*codeword*) | Makes a place in the document that can be referenced by @REF(*codeword*) or @PAGEREF(*codeword*). |
| @MAKE(*document-type*) | Specifies document type definition. See summary of document types. |

| | |
|---|---|
| `@NEWPAGE` | Breaks current line, then starts at top of new page. If already at top of new page, then nothing is done. |
| `@REF(`*codeword*`)` | Retrieves value of cross-reference marker codeword and places it in document file at that point. To define a cross-reference codeword, see `@LABEL` and `@TAG`. |
| `@TABCLEAR` | Clears all tab stops. |
| `@TABDIVIDE(`*n*`)` | Sets tabs to divide text body into *n* columns. |
| `@TABSET(`$stop_1$`,`$stop_2$`, . . .` | Sets series of tabs at horizontal positions indicated. Distances computed with respect to current left margin. Existing tabs not erased. When stop value is signed (for example, +1 inch), new stop is set relative to preceding stop in list. |
| `@TAG(`*codeword*`)` | Defines codeword as cross-reference label representing position and number of equation, theorem, figure, or table. For use with `@REF`. *Note*: Any `@TAG` commands must come *after* `@CAPTION`. |

## C.8 Exercises

*Note*: If the files mentioned below are not available via the following type of `COPY` command

`COPY TEXTFILES:`*filename your-filename*

you can reproduce the listings in Section C.6 and Appendix I with a text editor.

1. Currently, no on-line help is available from within SCRIBE. See if there is any on-line help outside SCRIBE (at the operating system prompt). If so, use what you learned in doing the exercises of Chapters 1 and 2 to `PRINT` a file containing all the on-line help available on SCRIBE.

2. Run the DECspell spelling checker on the `RES.MSS` file we discussed in this chapter. `ADD` all SCRIBE commands that are flagged as errors. After this DECspell session, `TYPE` the `PERSONAL.LGP` file. What con-

clusions can you draw from this sequence?

3. If you have access to the TEXTFILES directory, issue the following commands at the operating system prompt:

```
COPY TEXTFILES:SCRIBE.LGP SCRIBE.LGP
TY/P SCRIBE.LGP
```

(If you do not have TEXTFILES, see Section I.3.3 of Appendix I.)

For what purpose could you use the file SCRIBE.LGP?

After reading the on-line help (available at the operating system level) on APPEND, use this information to APPEND the SCRIBE.LGP file to your PERSONAL.LGP file. What purpose can you see in doing this? How could you have achieved the same result with a text editor?

4. After doing Exercises 2 and 3, issue the following commands at the operating system prompt:

```
HELP SPELL/FORMAT
HELP SPELL/PACKED
HELP SPELL/LOG
HELP SPELL/OUTPUT
```

After reading the on-line help, issue the following commands at the operating system prompt:

```
SPELL/FORMAT/LOG/OUTPUT=SCRIBE1.LGP PERSONAL.LGP
SPELL/FORMAT/PACKED/OUTPUT=SCRIBE2.LGP PERSONAL.LGP
TY/P PERSONAL.LGP
TY/P SCRIBE1.LGP
TY/P SCRIBE2.LGP
```

What conclusions can you draw from this sequence?

5. At the operating system level, read the on-line help available on DIFFERENCES. Use DIFFERENCES to compare SCRIBE1.LGP and SCRIBE2.LGP, which you obtained in Exercise 4. What conclusions can you draw? Should you RENAME SCRIBE2.LGP to PERSONAL.LGP, and PURGE? If so, what value would there be in this?

6. Articles in your local newspaper or chapters on the subject of computer literacy in texts (see Bibliography [16, 20]) might give you some food for thought. After reading some of this material on the question of computer use and an individual's right to privacy, use the letter template you created in Section C.2 to compose a letter to your congressperson concerning your views on legislation and the privacy issue as it relates to information stored in computers. If your site has a laser printer, print out the final copy of your letter using this device.

7. Using the letter and resume templates you created in Sections C.2 and C.3, use a text editor and SCRIBE to write your own resume and a cover letter in response to an imaginary job that was advertised in an imaginary journal or newspaper. If your site has a laser printer, print out the final copies of your letter and resume using this device.

8. Imagine that you are a student with a full course load. Using `TABLE.MSS` and `TABLE.BIB` as examples (see your `TEXTFILES` directory or Sections I.3.1 and I.3.2 of Appendix I), produce a table that reflects your own schedule. Your table should have the following columns:

   Course—e.g., CS1308
   Section—e.g., .8
   Time—e.g., TTh 2
   Instructor—e.g., Sawey
   Textbook—e.g., [3], referring to Spencer in the Bibliography of `DEMO.BIB`
   (see Exercise 9)

9. Using `DEMO.MSS` and `DEMO.BIB` as examples (see your `TEXTFILES` directory or Section C.6.3), write a five-page paper on the issue of "Computers and Privacy." Include at least five references and at least one table containing statistics related to this issue. If your site has a laser printer, print out your final copy on this device.

# Appendix D

## Directories

A collection of directories might be thought of as a file cabinet that allows you to organize your use of the computer. The cabinet is divided into drawers, each of them a directory, and each drawer contains folders, or files. A directory can be characterized as either a top-level directory or a subdirectory, but the principle is the same: both types of directory (drawers) contain files (folders).

Many users can get by for a long time without ever feeling the need to organize their files into a directory structure, but gradually, as their applications become more sophisticated, most people find they need to organize their work into several directories just to avoid clutter. Some of the applications programs we commonly use actually create their own directories. To describe how VAX/VMS builds directories, we first examine how various applications programs create multiple directories. Then we explain how to create your own directories, and we draw some comparisons to directories in the MS-DOS environment.

### D.1 WPS-PLUS Directories

Regardless of how your particular system is configured, you might want to learn about the directory structure that is used to support WPS-PLUS. You already know about files and the `DIRECTORY` (`DIR`) command from your work in Chapter 1 (the operating system). So, we start from there.

When you first logged in to the VAX computer, any files that you had could be discovered by using the DIR command. At that point, you also learned that a file specification included a file name, a file type, and a file version number. For example, the file specification LOGIN.COM;3 designates a file with name LOGIN, type .COM, and version number ;3. But this is not the whole story of file specification. You might have noticed that when you typed the command DIR LOGIN.COM <RETURN> at the operating system prompt, the results resembled the following:

```
MYNODE$ DIR LOGIN.COM
Directory MYDISK$:[MYDIR]
LOGIN.COM;8      8  28-FEB-1988 18:34
Total of 1 file, 8 blocks.
```

Notice the characters that follow Directory.[1] The string preceding the colon is the name given to the storage device (probably a disk drive) on your system that holds your files. We refer to this as the *device name*.

The string in brackets is referred to as the *directory specification*. This is the part of a file specification that we now discuss in more detail. As indicated, you can think of directories as drawers in a file cabinet that contain files on a particular subject or set of subjects. Thus, if you had files relating to personal correspondence and business correspondence, you might keep them in different drawers in a file cabinet. On a computer system, different sets of files are usually kept in different directories.

The directory of files that you enter when you log in to the VAX computer is referred to as the SYS$LOGIN directory. Some people call this the *root directory*, the *home directory*, or occasionally, the *log-in directory*. It is a top-level directory. Once the system has been set up so that you can use WPS-PLUS, and you issue the DIR command upon logging in, you will discover a "file" named WPSPLUS.DIR in your SYS$LOGIN directory. If you TYPE this "file," you will see that you have something different from a standard text file. Some letters are displayed, but they are not meaningful.

The presence of this "file" indicates that you have a (sub)directory called WPSPLUS at a level below your SYS$LOGIN directory. If you could get to this

---

1. The text on your screen will not read MYDISK$:[MYDIR]; however, you will see a string of characters before a colon (:), followed by another string of characters enclosed in brackets [ ].

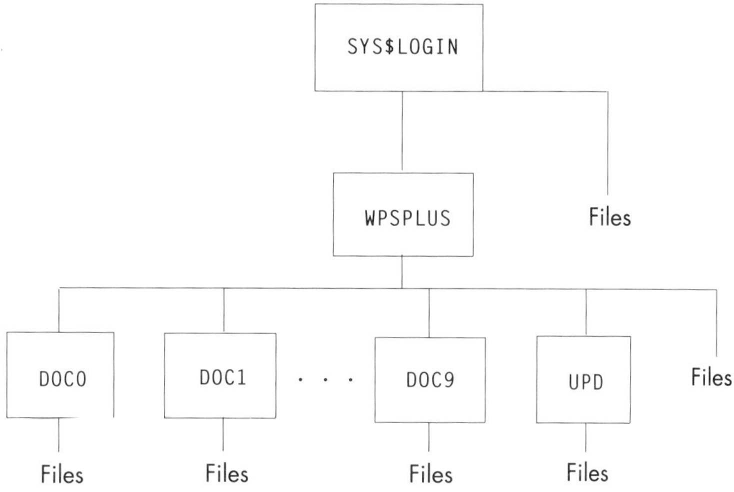


**Figure D.1 WPS-PLUS Directory Structure**

directory, you would see that it contains several files and some more (sub)directories. Figure D.1 shows the tree structure of directories. The directory names are in boxes.

The WPSPLUS directory and the directories below it are used by WPS-PLUS to store the documents that you create as well as to take care of some other WPS-PLUS functions. It is relatively easy to examine these directories, but we caution again that the creation and deletion of WPS-PLUS documents should occur from *within* the WPS-PLUS program. You should not attempt to rename, copy, or delete a WPS-PLUS document from the operating system or VMS level.

So, how can you get to these other directories? Do this by changing your default directory. First, as a precaution, make certain that you are in the SYS$LOGIN directory by typing SET DEFAULT SYS$LOGIN <RETURN>.

Next, determine the name of the SYS$LOGIN directory by typing SHOW DEFAULT <RETURN> (SHO DEF will also work). Take special note of what appears in square brackets. This is the name of your SYS$LOGIN directory. For this discussion, let's say that the SYS$LOGIN directory is named MYDIR. For the rest of this discussion, whenever we tell you to type MYDIR, you should type the name of your particular SYS$LOGIN directory instead. To get one level down in the directory structure (see Figure D.1), type SET DEFAULT [MYDIR.WPSPLUS] <RETURN> at the operating system prompt. If you issued the DIR command now and found that you had a file specified as DAF.DAT;1, and if you wanted to specify this file, including its directory, then the specification would be

```
[MYDIR.WPSPLUS]DAF.DAT;1
```

Notice that the directory part of the specification (in brackets) shows the path down the directory tree. This means that each directory name is included in order, separated by periods. As another example, let's say that the DOC1 directory (see Figure D.1) contains a file ZRZZATFOZ.WPL;1;[2] then the file specification, including the directory, would be

```
[MYDIR.WPSPLUS.DOC1]ZRZZATFOZ.WPL;1
```

Once in the WPSPLUS directory, you can examine the files in it, as discussed earlier in Chapter 1. Issue the DIR command to see what files are in this directory. To get back to your SYS$LOGIN directory, type SET DEFAULT SYS$LOGIN <RETURN>.

In summary, we have done the following:

1. Moved to the SYS$LOGIN directory via

   SET DEFAULT SYS$LOGIN <RETURN>

2. Obtained the name of the SYS$LOGIN directory via

   SHOW DEFAULT <RETURN>

   (In our example, we used the name MYDIR.)

3. Moved to the WPSPLUS directory via

   SET DEFAULT [MYDIR.WPSPLUS] <RETURN>

4. Obtained a list of the files in the WPSPLUS directory via

   DIR <RETURN>

5. Returned to the SYS$LOGIN directory via

   SET DEFAULT SYS$LOGIN <RETURN>

---

2. WPS-PLUS has been criticized because the file names created in its subdirectories bear no resemblance to the names of the documents chosen by the user.

Now check your skills by seeing if the DOC1 directory (see Figure D.1) contains any files; then return to the SYS$LOGIN directory. Do this by typing the following sequence of commands at the operating system prompt. (Remember to substitute the name of your own SYS$LOGIN directory for MYDIR.)

```
SET DEFAULT SYS$LOGIN <RETURN>
SET DEFAULT [MYDIR.WPSPLUS.DOC1] <RETURN>
DIR <RETURN>
SET DEFAULT SYS$LOGIN <RETURN>
```

## D.2 DECalc Directories

As indicated in Chapter 8, the DECalc spreadsheet program creates a subdirectory the first time the program is run. However, in contrast to WPS-PLUS, there is no elaborate tree of subdirectories. There is just one directory. It is always called DECALC_GRIDS. Accordingly, if a user had already accessed WPS-PLUS and DECalc, using the following directory command would produce results similar to those below:

```
MYNODE$
MYNODE$ dir *.dir
Directory MYDISK$:[MYDIR]
DECALC_GRIDS.DIR;1      1  14-MAR-1990 10:57:48.89
WPSPLUS.DIR;1           1  14-MAR-1990 10:58:02.33

Total of 2 files, 2 blocks.
```

The command dir *.dir does not obtain any information about how much disk space has been used to store spreadsheet grids. To find this out, you must follow the instructions in Chapter 8 and type SET DEFAULT [.DECALC_GRIDS]. Then type the DIR command. The results would look similar to the following:

```
TEST1.CALC$GRD;2    4 18-OCT-1989 16:03:53.95
TEST1.CALC$GRD;1    4 18-OCT-1989 16:01:30.29
TRASH.CALC$GRD;2    4 18-OCT-1989 15:48:40.79

Total of 3 files, 12 blocks.
```

Notice that the files all have the type of .CALC$GRD.[3] This was supplied by the DECalc program. We can surmise that the user of this directory saved a

---

3. In versions of DECalc earlier than 4.0. Version 4.0 (and higher) has a file type of .CALC$DTF.

grid by using the /SS command from within DECalc and chose the file name TRASH.

WPS-PLUS users have been cautioned not to delete or rename WPS-PLUS document files from the VMS command prompt. These warnings do not apply to DECalc. Typing the command DEL TRASH.CALC$GRD;* would simply delete the grid named TRASH. See Chapter 8 for a fuller discussion.

## D.3 Creating Your Own Directories

So far, we have looked only at subdirectories that were made automatically by applications programs such as WPS-PLUS. However, you can create your own directories and store your files in them by mastering a few simple VAX/VMS commands. You make a directory by using the CREATE command. Type CREATE/DIR [MYDIR.TEST] <RETURN>. You can then verify that you have created the directory by using the directory command as follows:

```
MYNODE$
MYNODE$ dir t*
Directory MYDISK$:[MYDIR]
TAG.TXT;5       1   28-JUN-1990 11:54:36.48
TOY.TXT;28     56    4-JUN-1990 09:31:56.06
TEST.DIR;1      1    2-JUL-1990 12:06:05.44

Total of 3 files, 58 blocks.
```

Let's review what we did. First we created a new directory called TEST. In the line CREATE/DIR [MYDIR.TEST], we are allowed to choose only TEST. Then, using the directory command, we asked for a list of all files with names starting with the letter T. We found that we had three files. One "file" is, in fact, a directory. It is TEST.DIR, the one we just created. We supplied the file name TEST. The VMS operating system supplied the file extension DIR.[4] TEST.DIR is, of course, not a file like the other two. You cannot type it to the screen like the other two files, which are text files created by a text editor.

4. MYDISK and MYDIR are used for purposes of illustration here. The names of your disk drive and directory will be different.

For the moment, our new directory is empty. Let's put something in it. The first step is to move to the new directory by typing `SET DEFAULT [MYDIR.TEST]` <RETURN>. Now type `EDIT/TPU TEXT.TXT` <RETURN>. When the screen reconstructs, type `This is a line of text` followed by <CTRL/Z>. Using the directory command, verify that you have, in fact, created a new file, `TEXT.TXT`, in your new directory.

You can delete directories, but the procedure is a bit more complicated than the one you already know for deleting files. The first step is to delete the files in the directory. You just verified that one file, named `TEXT.TXT`, exists. Delete it according to the instructions for deletion in Chapter 1. The next step is to return to the directory at the level above `MYDIR.TEST`, that is, to the top-level directory, `SYS$LOGIN`. Do this by typing `SET DEFAULT SYS$LOGIN` <RETURN>. Now type `SET PROTECTION=OWNER:D TEST.DIR` <RETURN>. This command enables you to delete the directory `TEST.DIR` just as though it were a file.

## D.4 Comparison with MS-DOS

VAX/VMS beginners who have arrived via the MS-DOS environment will find remarkable parallels between the two systems. Directories may be created, connected to, filled with and emptied of files, and ultimately deleted. The command grammar is similar but not exactly the same. One important difference is that in MS-DOS there is no need (indeed, no way) to alter the protection of a subdirectory so that it may be deleted. The next section summarizes similar VMS and MS-DOS commands for creating, connecting to, and deleting directories.

## D.5 Quick Reference: Directory Commands in VMS and MS-DOS

### VMS Commands

These commands are issued at the `MYNODE$` operating system prompt.

| *Command* | *Description* |
|---|---|
| `CREATE/DIR [MYDIR.TEST]` | Creates a new directory named `TEST.DIR`. This (sub)directory is just below the root directory. |
| `SET DEFAULT SYS$LOGIN` | Connects to the (top-level) root directory. |
| `SET DEFAULT [MYDIR.TEST]` | Connects to the directory named `TEST.DIR`. |
| `SET PROTECTION=OWNER:D TEST.DIR` | Changes the protection of an empty directory named `TEST.DIR` so that it can be deleted. |

### MS-DOS Commands

Issued at the MS-DOS operating system prompt, the following commands resemble the preceding ones in their actions.

| *Command* | *Description* |
|---|---|
| `MD TEST` | Creates a new directory named `TEST`. This (sub)directory is just below the directory to which you are currently connected. |
| `CD\` | Connects to the (top-level) root directory on any particular disk drive. |
| `CD\TEST` | Connects to the directory named `TEST`. |
| `RD TEST` | Removes or deletes directory named `TEST` *provided that* you are connected to the directory just above `TEST` and that all files in `TEST` have already been deleted. |

# Appendix E

## A Quicky Guide to DOS [1]

Gary Nored

### E.1 Why Should I Learn DOS?

It has been often said that you can do a lot with a computer without ever learning anything about DOS.[2] And that is certainly true. But you can work more efficiently and safely if you do know a little bit about DOS. DOS is really not hard to use—it's just hard to get started with because it's so cryptic. This article is intended to help you get started.

### E.2 What Is DOS?

DOS is really two things. One is a computer program that operates "behind" or "underneath" other programs and that gives your computer its personality. DOS takes care of details like writing files, interpreting what is going on at the keyboard, and putting things on the screen. You need never worry about that part of DOS because it does this part of its work invisibly.

1. Bibliography [15], used with permission. Copyright 1986 by Gary Nored. He is a technical writer living in Austin, Texas, and is an active member of the Society for Technical Communications.

2. The letters stand for Disk Operating System. DOS was written by Microsoft Corporation and is often referred to as MS-DOS.

The other part of DOS is more like a library of programs or a toolkit of computer tricks. As you work on different jobs, DOS saves your work in "files" on the disks. There can be many files on a disk, but DOS helps you keep track of them all. One of the tools in the DOS toolkit is a program that can show you a list of your files at any time. Other tools help you make copies of your work, remove old work from your disks, and assign new or different names to your jobs.

Some of your DOS tools remain in the computer's memory, available for use all the time. The `DIR` command (which means "show me a list of all the files on my disk"), the `DEL` command ("delete this file from the disk"), the `COPY` command ("make a copy of this file"), and the `REN` command ("rename this file") are examples of the tools, or commands, that always reside in the computer's memory.

Most DOS tools, however, are stored as files on a disk. You have to have a copy of them on a disk somewhere in the computer before you can use them.

## E.3 Using DOS

To use DOS, you speak to it using little DOS sentences. The rules, or syntax, for making a DOS sentence are pretty straightforward. The first rule says that you must always separate each word in the sentence with a space. That's a lot like writing in any other language. The second rule says that you must type the words in the proper order. The final rule says to finish each DOS sentence by pressing the <RETURN> key.

**One-word sentences**. The simplest DOS sentence has just one word, a verb. In DOS, verbs are called commands. We'll use "commands" from now on to help you get used to the terms you may later encounter in your DOS manual.

Here's an example of a one-word DOS sentence:

`DIR` <RETURN>

If the bottom line on your computer screen said `A>` when you typed the above sentence, DOS would give you a directory, or list, of the files on the disk located in the disk drive with the name A:.

**Two-word sentences.** Some DOS sentences have two words. The second word in a DOS sentence is the object of the command. The object can be anything the command understands. For example, we can ask for a directory of the files located on any drive in the computer. To see the files on drive B: you would type

DIR B: <RETURN>

Just as many languages have different endings for different words, DOS has different endings for some of its commands. The endings, called switches, usually improve the way the command works in certain situations. For example:

DIR/P <RETURN>

will make very long lists of files stop at the end of each screen so that you have time to read them all. Another:

DIR/W <RETURN>

will put the list into five columns so that you see more file names on the screen. You can even combine endings: DIR/W/P would put the list into five columns *and* stop the listing at each page. The switches are different for each command. To use them you have to learn them—just like any other language. Fortunately, you probably won't need to use very many of them.

**Three-word sentences.** One of the most common DOS sentences is also the longest possible one. It has three words which tell the computer to copy something. It's also the most complex because you have to tell DOS (1) what you want to copy, (2) where you want to put the copy, and (3) what you want to call the copy.

Let's say you've written a letter and saved it to a disk using the file name PAYME. The disk is currently in the A: drive and you want to copy it to a disk in the B: drive. You want to use the same name for the copy as for the original. The last line on your computer says A>. Here's the command:

COPY PAYME B: <RETURN>

In this sentence the first word tells the computer to copy something; the second word tells the computer what to copy; the third word tells the computer where to put the copy and what to call it. If you wanted the copy to have a different name, for example IPAIDYOU, you would put the new name right after the B: like this:

**Table E.1 DOS Punctuation Mark Summary**

| Punctuation Mark | Function |
|---|---|
| Space | Separates words in a DOS sentence.<br>Tells DOS that you intend to use a switch.<br>Separates the drive letter from the file name.<br>Separates the file's first name from its last name. |

`COPY PAYME B:IPAIDYOU` <RETURN>

Notice that there is *no space* between the B: and the new file name. That's because you must use different punctuation to separate parts of file names and their locations. Specifically, use a colon to separate the drive name (usually A:, B:, or C:) from the first part of the file name. Use a period to separate the first part of the file name from the last part.

Here's an example. If the above file was on a disk in the A: drive, its complete name would be `A:IPAIDYOU`. If your file had a last name (called an "extension" in DOS jargon) of `DOC`, its complete name would be `A:IPAIDYOU.DOC`. If the same file was on a disk in the B: drive, its full name would be

`B:IPAIDYOU.DOC.`

Since this is the hardest part about learning to use DOS, the information is summarized in Table E.1.

Let's look at the first copy sentence again.

`COPY PAYME B:` <RETURN>

What will be the name of the new file on drive B:? The answer—`PAYME`. Why? Because whenever you don't tell DOS exactly what you want it to do, it just uses the last thing it heard. In this case, the last file name DOS heard was `PAYME`. So DOS used the name `PAYME` for the new file name when it made the copy.

Let's look at another example. Suppose you wanted to copy a file located on the B: drive, named `PAYME`, onto a disk in the A: drive. The last line on your screen says `A>`. The following sentence will do the job:

`COPY B:PAYME` <RETURN>

What will happen here? Well, DOS will make a copy of `PAYME` on the disk located in the A: drive. Why? DOS put the copy on the A: drive because DOS was looking at the A: drive (that's what the A> on your screen really means) when it started. DOS named the copy PAYME because that's the last file name DOS knew anything about. In fact, any time you leave things out of a DOS sentence, DOS just fills in the blanks. Here's how DOS fills in the missing information in the sentence above.

COPY B:PAYME A:PAYME <RETURN>

Why not just type in the whole sentence? Of course, you could, but the less you type, the fewer errors you're likely to make, right? Letting the computer do it will ensure that the file gets copied under the name you really want.

## E.4 Wild Cards

If DOS allowed only statements like the ones we've been studying, it would take a lot of time and typing to copy all the files on a disk to a backup disk. But DOS has two other tools that help with big jobs like that.

The first tool is "*". Any time you use an asterisk, you tell DOS to match any character or characters it sees for the operation. Put another way, any time you use "*" you're telling DOS that you don't care how many characters are in the file name, or even how the name is spelled. So

COPY A:*.* B: <RETURN>

will copy all the files on the A: drive to the B: drive. Why? Because you've just told DOS to copy all the files, no matter how their names are spelled, from the A: drive to the B: drive.

The instruction

COPY A:*.COM B: <RETURN>

would copy all the files with the last name COM to the B: drive. The instruction will ignore the spelling of all the first names.

There is another wild card, "?", that's similar, except that it matches only one character at a time. Use one question mark for each character in the file name you expect to change. For example,

COPY A:FILE? B: <RETURN>

would copy any file on the A: drive with a name in which the first four letters were FILE and the fifth letter was any character. Using the command above would copy all of the files listed below to the B: drive in one step:

```
FILE0
FILE1
FILE2
FILE3
FILE4
FILE5
FILE6
FILE7
FILE8
FILE9
```

By using the "?" wild card, you've done exactly the same amount of work as if you'd typed the following list of commands:

```
COPY FILE0 B:
COPY FILE1 B:
COPY FILE2 B:
COPY FILE3 B:
COPY FILE4 B:
COPY FILE5 B:
COPY FILE6 B:
COPY FILE7 B:
COPY FILE8 B:
COPY FILE9 B:
```

Just imagine how many mistakes you might have made doing the job that way.

You can also use wild cards to good advantage when removing unwanted files from a disk. For example,

DEL *.BAK <RETURN>

will delete all files with the last name BAK, no matter what their first names. BAK is a popular last name for backup files created automatically by your computer, and sometimes you might want to take some of them off to make more room on a disk.

Try the wild cards with the DIR command for practice. Typing

DIR *.COM <RETURN>

will give you a list of all the files on your disk with the last name COM.

## E.5 Format

One powerful DOS command everyone has to learn how to use is the FORMAT command. You must format each new disk you buy to create data spaces in patterns your particular computer can recognize. The FORMAT command creates these data spaces. If you have two floppy disks, put DOS in the A: drive and a new disk in the B: drive. Make sure that DOS is "logged" (looking at the A: drive) by typing A: <RETURN> before you start. Then type

FORMAT B: <RETURN>

to prepare the disk.

Let's say that you've just bought the latest version of a word processor called Purple Prose. You would like to be able to put your Purple Prose disk into the A: drive, turn on the computer, and start writing—without having to flip a bunch of disks around. What you need is a copy of Purple Prose on a system disk. A system disk contains hidden files the computer needs to put itself together when you first turn it on.

To format a system disk, use the command

FORMAT B:/S <RETURN>

FORMAT will create a disk containing the hidden files it needs for its own system purposes.

FORMAT is the only truly dangerous command in DOS and it's most dangerous to hard-disk owners. Always be careful to specify the drive containing the disk you want to format. If you don't, and you keep answering "yes" to the formatting questions, DOS may just do what you say and format itself out of existence!

## E.6 Conclusion

Now that you know a little more about DOS, try using it. First make a backup copy of a disk you have a lot of data on. Use the COPY *.* instruction to make the backup. Then try making selective directories of your files. Try making selective group copies using the wild cards. Try the DELETE command using different wild cards. (Be sure to use a copy of your disk to practice this command—DEL *.* has caused a lot of DOS owners a lot of grief!)

Try reading about and using the RENAME and other commands in your DOS manual. Most of all, just play with these instructions and find out what they do. Sometime, someday, one of them is going to rescue you from a situation you could never have gotten out of on your own before. And *that* is a great feeling!

Appendix F

# Use of the Instructional Diskette from Digital Press

The instructional diskette is for use by instructors, system support staff, and MS-DOS users working on their own. It has no system files like COMMAND.COM and thus cannot be used to boot the MS-DOS microcomputer. The files at the top level are destined for the beginner's diskette. The files in the subdirectory TEXTFILE will be transferred to the VAX computer into the TEXTFILES directory.

We include instructions on how to transfer certain files to the VAX, but beginners on the MS-DOS microcomputer will probably need help to make sense of these instructions. At the very least, they should consult the DOS manual as well as Chapter 5.

## F.1 Making a Beginner's Diskette

Here are the steps necessary to make a beginner's diskette. Format a blank diskette with the operating system files. When formatting is complete, copy FORMAT.COM and CHKDSK.COM onto the new diskette. Then, using the COPY *.* command, copy all the files from the instructional diskette provided by Digital Press. The MS-DOS command COPY *.* copies only the files at the top-level directory. (Do not worry about the subdirectory called TEXTFILE at this time. Those files will ultimately reside somewhere on the VAX.) To check that you have done your work correctly, issue the DIR command. What you see on the screen should resemble what you see in Figure 5.1 (see Chapter 5). Do not expect all the numbers to match; different versions of MS-DOS have system files of different sizes.

## F.2 Loading TEXTFILES to the VAX

Decide where on your VAX/VMS system you want the TEXTFILES directory to reside. Recall that the TEXTFILES directory is to contain example files for use in demonstrations and exercises in several of the chapters in this book. Once you have decided which directory on the VAX you will be using, review the instructions for transferring files from a microcomputer to a VAX as set forth in Chapter 5, and use the instructional diskette to log in to the VAX. When you are logged in, set your VAX default directory to the TEXTFILES directory.

Use the escape-to-DOS command (<CTRL/]> P) to get back to the microcomputer. Then change to the TEXTFILE subdirectory on the instructional diskette. Notice that the subdirectory on the instructional diskette is called TEXTFILE rather than TEXTFILES as in your VAX directory. This is because MS-DOS only supports directory and file names of up to eight characters. Return to MS-KERMIT via the EXIT command and upload all files via the VAX-KERMIT server and the MS-KERMIT SEND command.

When you have finished sending the files in the TEXTFILE subdirectory on the instructional diskette to the TEXTFILES directory on the VAX, edit the VAX LOGIN.COM file so that the following line defines the correct directory for your local version of TEXTFILES:

```
$! DEFINE TEXTFILES DISK$:[CS1308255]
```

Be sure to remove the exclamation point. You must also be prepared to tell users where this master copy of the LOGIN.COM file resides so that they can follow the COPY instructions in Section 1.2 of Chapter 1.

One final note: The file TEXTFILE.DOC contains a description of all the files that you have just loaded to the VAX.

Appendix G

# Some Remarks for Modem Users

If you are using a Hayes-compatible modem and calling a VAX/VMS computer from a remote site, you must certainly issue a `SET BAUD` command like `SET BAUD 1200` at the `MS-KERMIT>` prompt. To automate this process, a few notes about the sample `MSKERMIT.INI` file (see Appendix H) are probably in order:

- Make certain `SET BAUD 9600` is changed to `SET BAUD 2400` (or some other appropriate baud rate).
- If you are dialing from a pulse phone rather than a touch-tone phone, change ATDT to ATDP.
- If you decide to use the "modem" macro in the `MSKERMIT.INI` file, be sure to change the port setting to 1 if your modem is attached to COM1.
- If you want to make sure that you have set things correctly, type `STATUS` <RETURN> at the `MS-KERMIT>` prompt.
- The <ALT/ p> does not match our actual password.

A frequently made observation about KERMIT is that it does not have the elegant dialing features of many micro-based communications programs, such as QMODEM or PROCOMM. The lack of dialing support is a consequence of the way KERMIT grew to maturity. It was initially a product of

Columbia University, where most of the microcomputers are hard-wired directly to mainframe computers. However, one principal advantage of KERMIT is that it is widely supported at many universities and work sites. This means that someone usually has the job of helping you to make KERMIT work. In addition, KERMIT is distributed by Columbia in its source code form, which allows programmers at your site to improve or alter and reassemble the code.

Appendix H

# Kermit Initialization File

As we mentioned before, in Chapter 5, KERMIT reads a file named MSKERMIT.INI as it loads. This initialization file enables an MS-DOS microcomputer to emulate a VT200 series terminal provided that the keyboard is the IBM AT-style keyboard with function keys horizontally arrayed across the top and a set of six free-standing special keys just above the four cursor movement keys. This arrangement works well with EVE. Just keep in mind that the key labels on the AT-style keyboard will not be exactly right for EVE commands: the <F11> key is <HELP>; <F12> is <DO>; <DELETE> is <SELECT>; <PAGE UP> is <REMOVE>; <HOME> is <INSERT HERE>; <INSERT> is <FIND> ; <PAGE DOWN> is <NEXT PAGE>; and <END> is <PREVIOUS PAGE>.

This MSKERMIT.INI file includes many scan codes. If you want to know the scan code for a series of keystrokes on your microcomputer, simply get to the MS-KERMIT> prompt and type SHOW KEY <RETURN>, followed by the sequence of keystrokes. For more information on KERMIT, see Bibliography [5].

This initialization file is suitable for use with MS-KERMIT version 3.10. If your site has another version of KERMIT, if you are using a specialized application other than EVE, or if you have a different keyboard layout, you should consult with your local user services staff to get the proper MSKERMIT.INI file.

```
;*********************************************************
; MSKERMIT.INI file
;
; Be sure to SET TERM/DEVICE=VT200/NOEIGHT on VAX
;*********************************************************
;
set key \315 \Kpf1
set key \316 \KdecHelp
set key \317 \Kpf3
set key \318 \KdecDo
set key \319 \KdecSelect
set key \320 \KdecRemove
set key \321 \KdecInsert
set key \322 +
;set key \323
set key \324 \Kuparr
set key \389 \KdecHelp
set key \390 \KdecDo
;
set key \852 \Klfarr
set key \853 \Kdnarr
set key \854 \Krtarr
set key \855 \Kkpenter
set key \856 \KdecNext
set key \857 \KdecNext
set key \858 \KdecPrev
set key \859 \Kkpenter
set key \860 \Kkpdot
set key \861 \KdecHelp
;
;
Set the IBM AT-style cursor keypad keys
;
;--------------------
; 4434 ; 4423 ; 4425;
; Find ;Insert;Remov;
;--------------------
; 4435 ; 4431 ; 4433;
;Select; Prev ; Next;
;--------------------
;
SET KEY \4434 \KdecFind    ;Find
SET KEY \4423 \KdecInsert  ;Insert here is an EVE term
SET KEY \4425 \KdecRemove  ;Remove
SET KEY \4435 \KdecSelect  ;End is SELECT
```

```
SET KEY \4431 \KdecPrev    ;Page up is PREV SCREEN
SET KEY \4433 \KdecNext    ;Page down is NEXT SCREEN
;
set key \4399 \Kpf2
set key \311 \Kpf3
set key \330 \Kpf4
set key \327 \Kkp7
set key \328 \Kkp8
set key \329 \Kkp9
set key \334 \Kpf1
set key \331 \Kkp4
set key \332 \Kkp5
set key \333 \Kkp6
set key \335 \Kkp1
set key \336 \Kkp2
set key \337 \Kkp3
set key \338 \Kkp0
set key \339 \Kkpdot
set key \4365 \Kkpenter
;
set key \4937 \kupscn
set key \4945 \kdnscn
set key \5508 \khomscn
set key \5494 \kendscn
set key \4936 \kupone
set key \4944 \kdnone
set key \782 \08
set key \2329 \kdump
;
; Additional DOS commands available from ms-kermit> prompt
define fatal echo error: \%1\13, def \%1, stop

define ren if < argc 2 fatal {rename what?},-
if < argc 3 fatal {rename \%1 to what?},-
run ren \%1 \%2

define copy if < argc 2 fatal {copy what?},-
if < argc 3 fatal {copy \%1 to where?},-
run copy \%1 \%2

define edit if = argc 2 assign \%e \%1,-
if not define \%e fatal {edit what?},-
run edlin \%e
;
set send packet 500
set rece packet 500
set terminal keyclick off
set local-echo on
set com3 \x03E8h
set port com3
set baud 9600
set term vt320
```

```
;
SET TERM COLOR 0,1,37,44
;**********************************************************
; Inserting ALT keys:
;
; The following allow for defining keys to auto-dial with
; a Hayes-compatible modem, along with other items related
; to logging in.
;
; Passwords are not real. They merely serve as examples.
;
; <ALT-D> DIAL the number given below
set key \2336 ATDT4719420\13
;
; <ALT-P> for SWT VAX password
set key \2329 MYPASS\13
;
; <ALT-V> for VAX login
set key \2351 RS01\13
;
; <ALT-I> for San Marcos MICOM
set key \2327 ATDT12452631\13
;
; <ALT-T> for resolution of screen conflict
set key \2324 SET TERM/DEVICE=VT200/NOEIGHT\13
```

# Appendix I

## Listings of Files Discussed in This Book

This appendix contains listings[1] of files discussed in this book. An instructional diskette containing all files is available from Digital Press (see the Introduction for details).

### I.1 Files Used in Chapter 1 (VMS Operating System)

#### I.1.1 The Annotated LOGIN.COM File

```
$! Exclamation points indicate comments in this file.
$!
$! This LOGIN.COM file is broken into the following
$! sections:
$!
$! 1. Those DCL commands that are NOT site-specific and
$! that should work on any VAX/VMS system without changes.
$!
$! 2. DCL commands that ARE site-specific and that need
$! to be changed appropriately in order for everything
$! in the chapters following Chapter 3 (DECspell) to work
$! as described. This will require consulting with your
```

1. Only partial listings are given for particularly long files.

```
$! local user services staff for the specific
$! changes that need to be made.
$!
$! 3. DCL commands that ARE site-specific but that might
$! be changed ONLY if your site has some of the
$! "optional" equipment discussed in subsequent
$! chapters (for example, laser printers).
$!
$! 4. Commands that are to be edited by the user as
$! specified in the body of this text.
$!
$! SECTION 1.
$! "Portable" DCL commands.
$!
$! Allow for not executing the remaining DCL commands
$! if the job executing this file is a batch job.
$! Otherwise, if the job is an interactive one, check
$! to determine the kind of terminal being used, and
$! allow for "line editing" at the DCL level.
$!
$ IF F$MODE() .EQS. "BATCH" THEN GOTO EXIT
$ IF F$MODE() .EQS. "INTERACTIVE" THEN $SET TERMINAL/INQUIRE
$ SET TERMINAL/LINE_EDITING
$!
$! Allow the LOGIN.COM file to be executed, even though
$! a process by the same name is already being executed.
$! This is done so that the SET HOST 0/LOG command will
$! work properly when used for obtaining log files as
$! discussed in the VAX BASIC chapter (Chapter 9).
$ SET NOON
$!
$! Enable (if not already done by system defaults)
$! <CTRL/Y> and <CTRL/T>.
$!
$ SET CONTROL=Y
$ SET CONTROL=T
$!
$! Determine the terminal type. If it is a VT200 series
$! terminal, make its terminal type VT100 so that older
$! versions (before 4.0) of DATATRIEVE's ADT will work
$! properly. Otherwise, leave the terminal alone.
$!
$ CONTEXT=""
$ PID=F$PID(CONTEXT)
$ TERMINAL=F$GETJPI(''PID',"TERMINAL")
$ DEVICE=F$GETDVI(TERMINAL,"DEVTYPE")
$!
```

```
$! Terminal #110 is a VT200 series terminal.
$! Remove the ! if you have a version of
$! DATATRIEVE lower than 4.0.
$!
$! IF DEVICE .EQS. 110 THEN SET TERM/DEVICE=VT100
$!
$! Set up so that the node on which my process is running
$! will be displayed at the operating system level.
$!
$ NODE = F$GETSYI("NODENAME")
$ SET PROMPT =""'NODE'$"
$!
$! Define some system independent global symbols
$! that will:
$! (A) give more than default information with the
$! DIRECTORY command, ask for confirmation when using
$! the DELETE command, and use the "brief"
$! logout procedure.
$!
$ DIR*ECTORY == "DIR/SIZ/DATE"
$ DEL*ETE == "DEL/CONFIRM/LOG"
$ LO*GOUT == "LOGOUT/BRIEF"
$!
$! (B) Purge log files, get back the root directory,
$! and define the NEWUSER command for DATATRIEVE.
$!
$ PU*RGE == "PURGE/LOG"
$ ROOT == "SET DEFAULT SYS$LOGIN"
$ NEWUSER == "@DTR$LIBRARY:NEWUSER"
$!
$! (C) Use "More" to type a file one page at a time,
$! set EDT to call EDT, set EVE to call the default
$! TPU editor, and allow for keypad editing in DECspell.
$!
$ MO*RE == "TYPE/P"
$ EDT == "EDIT/EDT"
$ EVE == "EDIT/TPU"
$ SPE*LL == "SPELL/KEYPAD = EDT"
$!
$!
$! Set up a "Greeting."  You will undoubtedly want to change
$! this when you learn how to use a text editor.
$!
$
```

```
$WRITE SYS$OUTPUT "    ************************************"
$WRITE SYS$OUTPUT "    *                                  *"
$WRITE SYS$OUTPUT "    *     Put Your Own Personalized    *"
$WRITE SYS$OUTPUT "    *          Greeting Here           *"
$WRITE SYS$OUTPUT "    *                                  *"
$WRITE SYS$OUTPUT "    ************************************"
$
$! The remainder of the DCL commands in "Section 1"
$! are "commented out" with !.  Depending on your
$! circumstances, you might find them useful.  For
$! the options you want, simply remove the !.
$!
$! Allow for giving the process a name of your
$! choice by removing the ! and replacing
$! the ----- once text editing has been discussed.
$!
$! SET PROCESS/NAME="-----"
$! Allow for NO PHONE and/or NO MAIL notification
$! if desired (simply remove the !).
$!
$! SET BROADCAST=(NOPHONE)
$! SET BROADCAST=(NOMAIL)
$!
$! Allow (if the ! is removed before MA* ...) for editing (as
$! in EDT) the message you are sending, forwarding, or
$! replying to WHILE in MAIL.
$!
$! MA*IL == "MAIL/EDIT=(SEND,FORWARD,REPLY)"
$!
$! SECTION 2.
$! DCL commands requiring consultation with local user
$! services staff.
$!
$! In the following commands (contained between the rows
$! of *), you will need to check the strings contained
$! in the double quotation marks to the right of the ==.
$! These specifications will be site-specific.  What is
$! given below is only applicable to a particular site.
$! You will also need to remove the !, of course.
$!
$! **************************************************
$! Define global symbols (or logical names) for:
$!
$! Text formatter, SCRIBE
$!
$! SCR*IBE == "$SYS$EXTERNAL:[SCRIBE.EXE]SCRIBE"
$!
$! Micro to VAX/VMS communication, KERMIT
$!
```

```
$! KER*MIT == "$SYS$SYSTEM:KERMIT.EXE"
$!
$! Database Management Program, DATATRIEVE
$!
$! DTR32 == "$SYS$SYSTEM:DTR32.EXE"
$!
$! DECalc (only for version 2.2 and below)
$!
$! DECA*LC == "$SYS$SYSTEM:DECALC.EXE"
$!
$!
$! Specify a logical name for the directory
$! containing the files noted in this text.
$!
$! DEFINE TEXTFILES DISK$:[CS1308255]
$! *************************************************
$!
$! SECTION 3.
$! DCL commands that might be useful, depending on your
$! site's equipment. Consultation with local user
$! services staff will be necessary.  Remember to
$! remove the ! after appropriate editing.
$!
$! Set up global symbols for laser printer output and
$! a line printer that has narrow (8 1/2 x 11) forms:
$!
$! LAS*ER == "PRINT/QUEUE=SYS$LN01/NOFEED/FLAG=DONE/NOTRAILER/NOBURST
$! NAR*ROW == "PRINT/FORMS=NARROW"
$!
$! SECTION 4.
$! Commands that will require editing, as noted in
$! the appropriate sections of the text.
$!
$! Assign a process appropriately so that you will get the
$! correct location in the Common Data Dictionary.
$!
$! ASSIGN/PROCESS/NOLOG "CDD$TOP.DTR$USERS.-----" CDD$DEFAULT
$!
$! Define a global symbol that makes it easier to get to
$! the directory created by DECalc (only for version 2.2
$! and below).
$!
$! DIRC == "SET DEFAULT [.H000100*]
$!
$! Define a global symbol that makes it easier to get to
$! the directory created by DECalc (only for version 3.0
$! and higher).
$!
$ DIRC == "SET DEFAULT [.DECALC_GRIDS]
```

```
$!
$!*****************************************************
$! TPU (EVE)-related logical definitions (remove the !
$! to the right of the $ in order for them to work)
$!
$! DEFINE MAIL$EDIT CALLABLE_TPU ! Allows for using TPU
$!                                  in MAIL
$!
$! DEFINE GMAIL$EDIT GMAILTPU    ! Allows for using TPU
$!                                  in GMAIL
$!
$! DEFINE BASIC$EDIT TPU$EDIT    ! Allows for using TPU
$!                                  in BASIC
$!
$! DEFINE DTR$EDIT TPU           ! Allows for using TPU
$!                                  in DATATRIEVE
$!
$! DEFINE TPUSECINI TPU$SECTION  ! DATATRIEVE (second line
$!                                  necessary after VMS 5.0)
$!
$! EDIT == "EDIT/TPU"            ! Allows for using TPU
$!                                  in DECalc (via /XCE...)
$!
$ EXIT:
```

### I.1.2 The Starter LOGIN.COM File

This file is for those users without access to the annotated LOGIN.COM file. Using your text editor, enter this file *exactly* as it appears here. Spaces, exclamation points, and quote marks are all important.

```
$! Exclamation points indicate comments in this file.
$!
$! This LOGIN.COM file is for those not having
$! access to the files mentioned in the text
$! and who therefore must create their own
$! copies using a text editor.
$!
$! The commands given here should get the reader
$! through the chapters on the operating system,
$! EVE (or EDT appendix), DECspell, electronic
$! communications, and VAX BASIC.
$!
$! The other chapters will require minor additions
$! to this file.
$!
$!
$ IF F$MODE() .EQS. "BATCH" THEN GOTO EXIT
$ IF F$MODE() .EQS. "INTERACTIVE" THEN $SET TERMINAL/INQUIRE
$ SET TERMINAL/LINE_EDITING
```

```
$ SET NOON
$ SET CONTROL=Y
$ SET CONTROL=T
$ NODE=F$GETSYI("NODENAME")
$ SET PROMPT="''NODE'$"
$ DIR*ECTORY == "DIR/SIZ/DATE"
$ DEL*ETE == "DEL/CONFIRM/LOG"
$ LO*GOUT == "LOGOUT/BRIEF"
$ PU*RGE == "PURGE/LOG"
$ MO*RE == "TYPE/P"
$ EDT == "EDIT/EDT"
$ EVE == "EDIT/TPU"
$ SPE*LL == "SPELL/KEYPAD=EDT"
$WRITE SYS$OUTPUT "    *************************************"
$WRITE SYS$OUTPUT "    *                                   *"
$WRITE SYS$OUTPUT "    *     Put Your Own Personalized     *"
$WRITE SYS$OUTPUT "    *           Greeting Here           *"
$WRITE SYS$OUTPUT "    *                                   *"
$WRITE SYS$OUTPUT "    *************************************"
$ EXIT:
```

## I.2 Files Used in Chapters 2, 3, and 4 (EVE, DECspell, and WPS-PLUS)

### I.2.1 The Error-Ridden PRAYER.ERR File

```
                        THE WAR PRAYER
                         by Mark Twain
IT WAS A TIME OF GRATE AND
EXALTING EXCITEMENT.
Teh country was up in armes,
the ware was on,
in every breast
burned the holly fire of patriotism;
the drums weer beating,
the bands were playing,
the toy pistols papping,
the bunched farcrackers
hissing and spluttering;
on every hand adn fer down
the receding and fading spread
of roofs and balconies
a fluttering wilderness of flages
flashed in teh sun;
...............
It was believed afterward
```

```
that the man was a lunatic,
because their was no sense
in wat he saad.
```

### I.2.2 The Error-Ridden HENRY.PAT File

```
No man thinks more highly than I doo of the patriotism, as
well as abilities, of the very worthy gentlemen who have
just addressed the House. But different meen often see the
same subject in different leights; and, therefore, I hope it
will not be thought disrespectful to those gentlemen if,
entertaining as I do opinions of a character very opposite
to theirs, I shall speak forth my sentments freely and
without reserve. This is no time for ceremony. The
questing before the House is one of awfl moment to this
country. For my own part, I consider it as nothing less
than a question of freedom or slavry; and in preportion to
the magnitude of the subject ought to be the freedom of the
debate. It is only in this way that we can hope to arrive
at truth, and fullfill the great responsibility which we hold
to God and our country. Should I keep back my opinions at
such a time, through fear of giving offence, I should
consider myself as guilty of treason towards my country, and
..............
It is in vain, sir, to extenuate the matter. Gentlemen
may cry, Peace, Peace- but there is no peace. The war is
actually begun! The next gale that sweeps from the north
will bring to our ears the clash of resounding arms! Our
brethren are already in the field! Why stand we here idle?
What is it that gentlemen wish? What would they have? Is
life so dear, or peace so sweet, as to be purchased at the
price of chains and slavery? Forbid it, Almighty Gawd! I
know not what course others may take; but as for me, givee me
liberty or give me deth!
Patrick Henry, March 23, 1775.
```

### I.2.3 The SET1.TXT Test Bank

```
1. You want to copy the file RES.MSS from your instructor's
directory into your own directory, where it will be named
RESUME.MSS. Give the one-line command that will do this.

MYNODE$ ______________

2. You decide that you don't like the name of the file that
you obtained in the previous question, and you want to change
its name to DODAH.MSS. Give the one-line command that will do
this.

MYNODE$ _________________

3. How many new files did commands in the previous two
```

questions cause to be in your directory? __________

4. What one-line command do you give if you want to display the file DODAH.MSS to your terminal screen one page at a time?

MYNODE$ _____________

5. What is the name of the file that the operating system reads at the time you log in to the system? _____________

6. What does UIC stand for? __________________

## I.2.4 The SET2.TXT Test Bank

1. You are in EVE and you want EVE's on-line help concerning the FIND key. Which keypad key(s) do you press?

_____________

2. You are in EDT and you have typed PF1-PF3. What will be printed at the bottom of your screen? _______________

3. You are in EVE and the cursor is at the end of the line, and you type <RETURN>. Will a blank line be inserted ABOVE or BELOW the current line? _________________

4. You want to insert the contents of the line buffer at the current cursor position. Which keypad keys do you press?

____________

5. You are in EVE, and you type "Now is the time". Will the text you typed be INSERTED or will you TYPE OVER the current text of that line? _________________

## I.2.5 The Error-Ridden WACO.RCM File

SOURCE: River City Magazine BBS, Austin, TX. AUTHOR: James Arthur Strohm

By now, we've all seen the "Waco Weekend" billboard near Capital Plaza and we've herd Aunt Blabbie mention it...have very many of us really considered all the implicashuns of such a foray into the wilds of IH 35?

Now, the Waco Chamber of Commerce is spending almost a quarter of a millun dollars promoting "the Waco weekend." But have you reelly sat down and axked yoursef "Why Waco?" Well, first you got your Brazos River. It looks like mud and once it's in the city waterworks it tastes like mud too. There's a fake sternwheeler that plies a 3/4 mile stretch of this scenic (read "look at the cute raccoons floating on their backs, mommy") watercourse between the highway and the prototype of the Brooklyn Bridge that is only enches from collapsing. Then you got your Waco zoo--Austin has a zoo just like it--the Humane Society. And you got your Texas

Rangurs museum. Guns, badges, and old maps till ya wanna puke. And last, there is scenic Baylur University.

Now, who wants to go to Waco to see that crap? I'd much rader go to the New Braunfels Snake Farm. Or even to County Jail, if the choice came down to it. No, what I think the CoC is trying to promote is--think about the bill- board now--with the attractive couple in the convertible--"Waco or bust"--is that particular kind of weekend that isn't an outdoor sightseeing weekend, and isn't a huneymoon (well, not exactly), and isn't a go-out-on-the-town (for every bar in Waco, Austin has ten) weeekend. No, it's more like a "Well I want a weekend with my girlfrend but all the motel clerks in Austin know us already" weekend--know what I mean? Why else would somebody drive a hundred miles to the most boreing city in the stat, except to lock the mootel door?

## I.3 Files Used in Appendix C (SCRIBE)

### I.3.1 The TABLE.MSS File

```
@device(1pt)
@make(report)
@style(linewidth 6.5in)
@comment(Setting Tabs Manually)
@begin(table)
@tabclear
          @^          @^          @^
@u(Class@\Section@\Text)
C.S.4338@\01@\@cite(Schrage2,Schrage3)
C.S.3388@\02@\@cite(Gillett)
@end(table)
@blankspace(1in)
@comment(Setting Tabs with the Tabdivide Command)
@begin(table)
@tabclear
@tabdivide(3)
@u(Class@\Section@\Text)
C.S.4338@\01@\@cite(Schrage2,Schrage3)
C.S.3388@\02@\@cite(Gillett)
@end(table)
@comment(Setting Tabs with Tabdivide; Changing Linewidth)
@begin(table,linewidth 9in,spacing 1)
@tabclear
@tabdivide(3)
@u(Class@\Section@\Text)
C.S.4338@\01@\@cite(Schrage2,Schrage3)
C.S.3388@\02@\@cite(Gillett)
@end(table)
@blankspace(2in)
```

```
@heading(References)
@bibliography
```

## I.3.2 The TABLE.BIB File

```
@Book(Schrage2,
    key="Schrage2",
    author="Schrage, L.",
    title="Linear Programming Models with LINDO",
    publisher="Scientific Press, Inc.",
    year="1981",
    address="Palo Alto, California"
    )
@Book(Schrage3,
    key="Schrage3",
    author="Schrage, L.",
    title="User's Manual for LINDO",
    publisher="Scientific Press, Inc.",
    year="1981",
    address="Palo  Alto, California"
    )
@Book(Gillett,
    key="Gillett",
    author="Gillett,B.E.",
    title="Introduction to Operations Research",
    publisher="McGraw-Hill",
    year="1976",
    address="New York"
    )
```

## I.3.3 Partial Listing of the SCRIBE.LGP File[2]

```
@MAKE
DEVICE
LPT
@STYLE
PAPERWIDTH
LINEWIDTH
PAPERLENGTH
TOPMARGIN
BOTTOMMARGIN
STDNUMERIC
@CHAPTER
@FOOT
@cite
@begin
```

2. This listing is the result of running DECspell on all .MSS files related to the SCRIBE appendix, adding all SCRIBE commands to the personal dictionary.

```
@end
....
bottommargin
leftmargin
linewidth
@heading
@i
@value
@greeting
@comment
```

## I.4 The Graphs.Cal File Used in Chapter 8 (DECalc)

```
!DECalc Version 3.0A
! Setting globals for PRIMARY WINDOW
\GC10
\GFLL
\GFVGR
\GFR
\GFU
\GMML
\GMTC
\GMRA
! Restoring individual column widths for PRIMARY WINDOW
\FCB N3
\FCC N4
\FCD N4
\FCE N4
\FCF N4
\FCG N4
\FCH N5
\FCI N5
\FCJ N5
\FCK N5
\FCL N5
\FCM N5
\FCN N3
\FCO N3
\FCP N3
\FCQ N3
\FCR N3
\FCS N3
! Restoring PRIMARY WINDOW box formats and contents
|A1 "Course 1:
!"Course 1:
|C1 "Hwk
!"Hwk
|D1 "Hwk
!"Hwk
```

```
|E1 "Hwk
!"Hwk
|F1 "Hwk
!"Hwk
|G1 "Hwk
!"Hwk
|H1 "Exam
!"Exam
|I1 "Exam
!"Exam
|J1 "Exam
!"Exam
|K1 "Final
!"Final
|L1 "Final
!"Final
|M1 "Grade
!"Grade
|O1 "No.
!"No.
|P1 "No.
!"No.
|Q1 "No.
!"No.
|R1 "No.
!"No.
|S1 "No.
!"No.
|A2 "Name
!"Name
|B2 "No.
!"No.
|C2  1
! 1.00000000000000E+00
|D2  2
! 2.00000000000000E+00
|E2  3
! 3.00000000000000E+00
|F2  4
! 4.00000000000000E+00
|G2  5
! 5.00000000000000E+00
|H2  1
! 1.00000000000000E+00
|I2  2
! 2.00000000000000E+00
|J2  3
! 3.00000000000000E+00
|K2 "Exam
```

```
!"Exam
|L2 "Avg
!"Avg
|M2 "Num.
!"Num.
|O2 "A's
!"A's
|P2 "B's
!"B's
|Q2 "C's
!"C's
|R2 "D's
!"D's
|S2 "F's
!"F's
|A3 \- -
!"-
|B3 \- -
!"-
|C3 \- -
!"-
|D3 \- -
!"-
|E3 \- -
!"-
|F3 \- -
!"-
|G3 \- -
!"-
|H3 \- -
!"-
|I3 \- -
!"-
|J3 \- -
!"-
|K3 \- -
!"-
|L3 \- -
!"-
|M3 \- -
!"
|O3 "---
!"---
|P3 "---
!"---
|Q3 "---
!"---
|R3 "---
!"---
```

```
|S3 "---
!"---
|A4 "C. Siva
!"C. Siva
|B4  1
! 1.00000000000000E+00
|C4  8.7
! 8.70000000000000E+00
|D4  3.2
! 3.20000000000000E+00
|E4  9.5
! 9.50000000000000E+00
|F4  10
! 1.00000000000000E+01
|G4  7.5
! 7.50000000000000E+00
|H4  65
! 6.50000000000000E+01
|I4  77
! 7.70000000000000E+01
|J4  96
! 9.60000000000000E+01
|K4  90
! 9.00000000000000E+01
|L4  ((10*AVE(C4:G4))+H4+I4+J4+K4)/5
! 8.11600000000000E+01
|M4  TAB(L4,$A$26:$G$26,$A$25:$G$25)
!"B
|O4  IF(M4="A",1,0)
! 0.00000000000000E+00
|P4  IF(M4="B",1,0)
! 1.00000000000000E+00
|Q4  IF(M4="C",1,0)
! 0.00000000000000E+00
|R4  IF(M4="D",1,0)
! 0.00000000000000E+00
|S4  IF(M4="F",1,0)
! 0.00000000000000E+00
|A5 "J. Toggle
!"J. Toggle
|B5  2
! 2.00000000000000E+00
|C5  10
! 1.00000000000000E+01
|D5  5.5
! 5.50000000000000E+00
|E5  4.4
! 4.40000000000000E+00
|F5  7
```

```
! 7.00000000000000E+00
|G5  10
! 1.00000000000000E+01
|H5  50
! 5.00000000000000E+01
|I5  66
! 6.60000000000000E+01
|J5  95
! 9.50000000000000E+01
|K5  66
! 6.60000000000000E+01
|L5  ((10*AVE(C5:G5))+H5+I5+J5+K5)/5
! 7.01600000000000E+01
|M5  TAB(L5,$A$26:$G$26,$A$25:$G$25)
!"C
|O5  IF(M5="A",1,0)
! 0.00000000000000E+00
|P5  IF(M5="B",1,0)
! 0.00000000000000E+00
|Q5  IF(M5="C",1,0)
! 1.00000000000000E+00
|R5  IF(M5="D",1,0)
! 0.00000000000000E+00
|S5  IF(M5="F",1,0)
! 0.00000000000000E+00
|A6 "B. Unger
!"B. Unger
|B6  3
! 3.00000000000000E+00
|C6  10
! 1.00000000000000E+01
|D6  10
! 1.00000000000000E+01
|E6  9.5
! 9.50000000000000E+00
|F6  7.8
! 7.80000000000000E+00
|G6  2
! 2.00000000000000E+00
|H6  95
! 9.50000000000000E+01
|I6  80
! 8.00000000000000E+01
|J6  70
! 7.00000000000000E+01
|K6  42
! 4.20000000000000E+01
|L6  ((10*AVE(C6:G6))+H6+I6+J6+K6)/5
```

```
! 7.31200000000000E+01
|M6  TAB(L6,$A$26:$G$26,$A$25:$G$25)
!"C
|O6  IF(M6="A",1,0)
! 0.00000000000000E+00
|P6  IF(M6="B",1,0)
! 0.00000000000000E+00
|Q6  IF(M6="C",1,0)
! 1.00000000000000E+00
|R6  IF(M6="D",1,0)
! 0.00000000000000E+00
|S6  IF(M6="F",1,0)
! 0.00000000000000E+00
|A7 "A. Zonk
!"A. Zonk
|B7  4
! 4.00000000000000E+00
|C7  2.5
! 2.50000000000000E+00
|D7  5.5
! 5.50000000000000E+00
|E7  9.5
! 9.50000000000000E+00
|F7  6
! 6.00000000000000E+00
|G7  4
! 4.00000000000000E+00
|H7  66
! 6.60000000000000E+01
|I7  88
! 8.80000000000000E+01
|J7  78
! 7.80000000000000E+01
|K7  65
! 6.50000000000000E+01
|L7  ((10*AVE(C7:G7))+H7+I7+J7+K7)/5
! 7.04000000000000E+01
|M7  TAB(L7,$A$26:$G$26,$A$25:$G$25)
!"C
|O7  IF(M7="A",1,0)
! 0.00000000000000E+00
|P7  IF(M7="B",1,0)
! 0.00000000000000E+00
|Q7  IF(M7="C",1,0)
! 1.00000000000000E+00
|R7  IF(M7="D",1,0)
```

```
! 0.00000000000000E+00
|S7  IF(M7="F",1,0)
! 0.00000000000000E+00
|A8 \- -
!"-
|B8 \- -
!"-
|C8 \- -
!"-
|D8 \- -
!"-
|E8 \- -
!"-
|F8 \- -
!"-
|G8 \- -
!"-
|H8 \- -
!"-
|I8 \- -
!"-
|J8 \- -
!"-
|K8 \- -
!"-
|L8 \- -
!"-
|M8 \- -
!"-
|O8 "---
!"---
|P8 "---
!"---
|Q8 "---
!"---
|R8 "---
!"---
|S8 "---
!"---
|A9 "Averages
!"Averages
|C9  AVE(C4:C7)
! 7.80000000000000E+00
|D9  AVE(D4:D7)
! 6.05000000000000E+00
|E9  AVE(E4:E7)
! 8.22500000000000E+00
```

```
|F9  AVE(F4:F7)
! 7.70000000000000E+00
|G9  AVE(G4:G7)
! 5.87500000000000E+00
|H9  AVE(H4:H7)
! 6.90000000000000E+01
|I9  AVE(I4:I7)
! 7.77500000000000E+01
|J9  AVE(J4:J7)
! 8.47500000000000E+01
|K9  AVE(K4:K7)
! 6.57500000000000E+01
|L9  AVE(L4:L7)
! 7.37100000000000E+01
|O9  SUM(O4:O7)
! 0.00000000000000E+00
|P9  SUM(P4:P7)
! 1.00000000000000E+00
|Q9  SUM(Q4:Q7)
! 3.00000000000000E+00
|R9  SUM(R4:R7)
! 0.00000000000000E+00
|S9  SUM(S4:S7)
! 0.00000000000000E+00
|A10 \- -
!"-
|B10 \- -
!"-
|C10 \- -
!"-
|D10 \- -
!"-
|E10 \- -
!"-
|F10 \- -
!"-
|G10 \- -
!"-
|H10 \- -
!"-
|I10 \- -
!"-
|J10 \- -
!"-
|K10 \- -
!"-
```

```
|L10 \- -
!"-
|M10 \- -
!"-
|N10 \- -
!"-
|O10 \- -
!"-
|P10 \- -
!"-
|Q10 \- -
!"-
|R10 \- -
!"-
|S10 \- -
!"-
|A11 \- -
!"-
|B11 \- -
!"-
|C11 \- -
!"-
|D11 \- -
!"-
|E11 \- -
!"-
|F11 \- -
!"-
|G11 \- -
!"-
|H11 \- -
!"-
|I11 \- -
!"-
|J11 \- -
!"-
|K11 \- -
!"-
|L11 \- -
!"-
|M11 \- -
!"-
|N11 \- -
!"-
|O11 \- -
!"-
|P11 \- -
```

```
!"-
|Q11 \- -
!"-
|R11 \- -
!"-
|S11 \- -
!"-
|A12 "Course 2:
!"Course 2:
|C12 "Hwk
!"Hwk
|D12 "Hwk
!"Hwk
|E12 "Hwk
!"Hwk
|F12 "Hwk
!"Hwk
|G12 "Hwk
!"Hwk
|H12 "Exam
!"Exam
|I12 "Exam
!"Exam
|J12 "Exam
!"Exam
|K12 "Final
!"Final
|L12 "Final
!"Final
|M12 "Grade
!"Grade
|O12 "No.
!"No.
|P12 "No.
!"No.
|Q12 "No.
!"No.
|R12 "No.
!"No.
|S12 "No.
!"No.
|A13 "Name
!"Name
|B13 "No.
!"No.
|C13  1
! 1.00000000000000E+00
```

```
|D13  2
! 2.00000000000000E+00
|E13  3
! 3.00000000000000E+00
|F13  4
! 4.00000000000000E+00
|G13  5
! 5.00000000000000E+00
|H13  1
! 1.00000000000000E+00
|I13  2
! 2.00000000000000E+00
|J13  3
! 3.00000000000000E+00
|K13 "Exam
!"Exam
|L13 "Avg
!"Avg
|M13 "Num.
!"Num.
|O13 "A's
!"A's
|P13 "B's
!"B's
|Q13 "C's
!"C's
|R13 "D's
!"D's
|S13 "F's
!"F's
|A14 \- -
!"-
|B14 \- -
!"-
|C14 \- -
!"-
|D14 \- -
!"-
|E14 \- -
!"-
|F14 \- -
!"-
|G14 \- -
!"-
|H14 \- -
!"-
|I14 \- -
```

```
!"-
|J14 \- -
!"-
|K14 \- -
!"-
|L14 \- -
!"-
|M14 \- -
!"-
|O14 "---
!"---
|P14 "---
!"---
|Q14 "---
!"---
|R14 "---
!"---
|S14 "---
!"---
|A15 "J. Albert
!"J. Albert
|B15  1
! 1.00000000000000E+00
|C15  5.5
! 5.50000000000000E+00
|D15  8.8
! 8.80000000000000E+00
|E15  9.4
! 9.40000000000000E+00
|F15  6
! 6.00000000000000E+00
|G15  8.9
! 8.90000000000000E+00
|H15  55
! 5.50000000000000E+01
|I15  87
! 8.70000000000000E+01
|J15  90
! 9.00000000000000E+01
|K15  66
! 6.60000000000000E+01
|L15  ((10*AVE(C15:G15))+H15+I15+J15+K15)/5
! 7.50400000000000E+01
|M15  TAB(L15,$A$26:$G$26,$A$25:$G$25)
!"C
|O15  IF(M15="A",1,0)
! 0.00000000000000E+00
```

```
|P15  IF(M15="B",1,0)
! 0.00000000000000E+00
|Q15  IF(M15="C",1,0)
! 1.00000000000000E+00
|R15  IF(M15="D",1,0)
! 0.00000000000000E+00
|S15  IF(M15="F",1,0)
! 0.00000000000000E+00
|A16 "Q. Jacks
!"Q. Jacks
|B16  2
! 2.00000000000000E+00
|C16  6.6
! 6.60000000000000E+00
|D16  9.8
! 9.80000000000000E+00
|E16  8.7
! 8.70000000000000E+00
|F16  4
! 4.00000000000000E+00
|G16  7.4
! 7.40000000000000E+00
|H16  45
! 4.50000000000000E+01
|I16  84
! 8.40000000000000E+01
|J16  87
! 8.70000000000000E+01
|K16  75
! 7.50000000000000E+01
|L16  ((10*AVE(C16:G16))+H16+I16+J16+K16)/5
! 7.28000000000000E+01
|M16  TAB(L16,$A$26:$G$26,$A$25:$G$25)
!"C
|O16  IF(M16="A",1,0)
! 0.00000000000000E+00
|P16  IF(M16="B",1,0)
! 0.00000000000000E+00
|Q16  IF(M16="C",1,0)
! 1.00000000000000E+00
|R16  IF(M16="D",1,0)
! 0.00000000000000E+00
|S16  IF(M16="F",1,0)
! 0.00000000000000E+00
|A17 "D. Lump
!"D. Lump
|B17  3
```

```
! 3.00000000000000E+00
|C17  10
! 1.00000000000000E+01
|D17  10
! 1.00000000000000E+01
|E17  10
! 1.00000000000000E+01
|F17  9.7
! 9.70000000000000E+00
|G17  6/4
! 1.50000000000000E+00
|H17  88
! 8.80000000000000E+01
|I17  80
! 8.00000000000000E+01
|J17  90
! 9.00000000000000E+01
|K17  80
! 8.00000000000000E+01
|L17  ((10*AVE(C17:G17))+H17+I17+J17+K17)/5
! 8.40800000000000E+01
|M17  TAB(L17,$A$26:$G$26,$A$25:$G$25)
!"B
|O17  IF(M17="A",1,0)
! 0.00000000000000E+00
|P17  IF(M17="B",1,0)
! 1.00000000000000E+00
|Q17  IF(M17="C",1,0)
! 0.00000000000000E+00
|R17  IF(M17="D",1,0)
! 0.00000000000000E+00
|S17  IF(M17="F",1,0)
! 0.00000000000000E+00
|A18 "X. Juan
!"X. Juan
|B18  4
! 4.00000000000000E+00
|C18  9.7
! 9.70000000000000E+00
|D18  9.6
! 9.60000000000000E+00
|E18  9.5
! 9.50000000000000E+00
|F18  10
! 1.00000000000000E+01
|G18  10
! 1.00000000000000E+01
```

```
|H18  89
! 8.90000000000000E+01
|I18  90
! 9.00000000000000E+01
|J18  96
! 9.60000000000000E+01
|K18  95
! 9.50000000000000E+01
|L18  ((10*AVE(C18:G18))+H18+I18+J18+K18)/5
! 9.35200000000000E+01
|M18  TAB(L18,$A$26:$G$26,$A$25:$G$25)
!"A
|O18  IF(M18="A",1,0)
! 1.00000000000000E+00
|P18  IF(M18="B",1,0)
! 0.00000000000000E+00
|Q18  IF(M18="C",1,0)
! 0.00000000000000E+00
|R18  IF(M18="D",1,0)
! 0.00000000000000E+00
|S18  IF(M18="F",1,0)
! 0.00000000000000E+00
|A19 \- -
!"-
|B19 \- -
!"-
|C19 \- -
!"-
|D19 \- -
!"-
|E19 \- -
!"-
|F19 \- -
!"-
|G19 \- -
!"-
|H19 \- -
!"-
|I19 \- -
!"-
|J19 \- -
!"-
|K19 \- -
!"-
|L19 \- -
!"-
|M19 \- -
```

```
!"-
|O19 "---
!"---
|P19 "---
!"---
|Q19 "---
!"---
|R19 "---
!"---
|S19 "---
!"---
|A20 "Averages
!"Averages
|C20  AVE(C15:C18)
! 7.95000000000000E+00
|D20  AVE(D15:D18)
! 9.55000000000000E+00
|E20  AVE(E15:E18)
! 9.40000000000000E+00
|F20  AVE(F15:F18)
! 7.42500000000000E+00
|G20  AVE(G15:G18)
! 6.95000000000000E+00
|H20  AVE(H15:H18)
! 6.92500000000000E+01
|I20  AVE(I15:I18)
! 8.52500000000000E+01
|J20  AVE(J15:J18)
! 9.07500000000000E+01
|K20  AVE(K15:K18)
! 7.90000000000000E+01
|L20  AVE(L15:L18)
! 8.13600000000000E+01
|O20  SUM(O15:O18)
! 1.00000000000000E+00
|P20  SUM(P15:P18)
! 1.00000000000000E+00
|Q20  SUM(Q15:Q18)
! 2.00000000000000E+00
|R20  SUM(R15:R18)
! 0.00000000000000E+00
|S20  SUM(S15:S18)
! 0.00000000000000E+00
|A23 "Look-Up
!"Look-Up
|A24 "Table:
!"Table:
```

```
|A25 "F
!"F
|B25 "F
!"F
|C25 "D
!"D
|D25 "C
!"C
|E25 "B
!"B
|F25 "A
!"A
|A26  39.5
! 3.95000000000000E+01
|B26  49.5
! 4.95000000000000E+01
|C26  59.5
! 5.95000000000000E+01
|D26  69.5
! 6.95000000000000E+01
|E26  79.5
! 7.95000000000000E+01
|F26  89.5
! 8.95000000000000E+01
|G26  100
! 1.00000000000000E+02
! Restoring marker to original position
|A1
! End of DECalc Dump file
```

# Bibliography


1. Paul C. Anagnostopoulos. *Writing Real Programs in DCL.* Bedford, Mass.: Digital Press, 1989. Order No. EY-C168E-DP.

2. *BASIC Reference Manual.* Maynard, Mass.: Digital Equipment Corporation, 1984. Order No. AA-HY16B-TE.

3. Fred Beisse. *Using Computer Applications with Introsoftware — IBM.* Edina, Minn.: Burgess Communications, 1986.

4. Ernest S. Colantonio with C. B. Honess and S. A. Bernhardt. *Computers and Applications: Student Software Manual.* Lexington, Mass.: D. C. Heath, 1986.

5. Frank da Cruz. *KERMIT: A File Transfer Protocol.* Bedford, Mass.: Digital Press, 1987. Order No. EY-6705E-DP.

6. *DECalc User's Guide.* Maynard, Mass.: Digital Equipment Corporation, 1985.

7. J. J. Dongarra and E. Grosse. Distribution of Mathematical Software via Electronic Mail. *Communications of the ACM* 30 (May 1987): 403 – 407.

8. E. Joseph Guay. *Programming in VAX BASIC.* Reading, Mass.: Addison-Wesley, 1986.

9. *Guide to Using DCL and Command Procedures on VAX/VMS. 4.0 Edition.* Maynard, Mass.: Digital Equipment Corporation, 1984. Order No. AA-Y501A-TE.

10. *Guide to VAX.* Maynard, Mass.: Digital Equipment Corporation, 1989. Order No. AA-GH98B-TE.

11. *Introduction to VAX DATATRIEVE. 3.0 Edition.* Maynard, Mass.: Digital Equipment Corporation, 1984.

12. *Introduction to VAX/VMS.* Maynard, Mass.: Digital Equipment Corporation, 1984. Order Number AA-Y500A-TE.

13. J. E. Maglitta. Text Processing Thrives. *Digital Review* (September 1988): 75+.

14. Wayne Muller. *Programming Using VAX BASIC.* Sydney, Australia: Prentice-Hall of Australia, 1986.

15. Gary Nored. A Quicky Guide to DOS. *PC Plus 5* (January 1987).

16. Thomas Owens and Perry Edwards. *Principles of Information Processing.* New York: Macmillan, 1987.

17. *SCRIBE Document Production System User Manual,* 4th ed. Pittsburgh, Pa.: Unilogic, 1985.

18. *SCRIBE Pocket Reference.* Pittsburgh, Pa.: Unilogic, 1986.

19. Terry C. Shannon. *Introduction to VAX/VMS.* Spring House, Pa.: Professional Press, 1986.

20. Donald D. Spencer. *Computers: An Introduction.* Columbus, Ohio: Merrill, 1986.

21. Nancy Stern, Robert A. Stern, and Edwin C. Hackleman. *Using Personal Computer Software Notebook.* New York: Wiley, 1985.

22. C. Temple and D. Cordeiro. *Working with WPS-PLUS.* Bedford, Mass.: Digital Press, 1990. Order No. EY-C198E-DP.

23. D. Tobias. Electronic Mail: History and Overview. *Big Blue Disk* 9 (July 1987). Available on computer diskette.

24. Clifford Townsend. *VAX BASIC.* New York: Holt, Rinehart, and Winston, 1986.

25. *VAX Common Data Dictionary. Summary Description.* Maynard, Mass.: Digital Equipment Corporation, 1985.

26. *VAX Common Data Dictionary. User's Guide.* Maynard, Mass.: Digital Equipment Corporation, 1985. Order No. AA-AY81A-TE.

27. *VAX DATATRIEVE Handbook. 5.1 Edition.* Maynard, Mass.: Digital Equipment Corporation, 1989. Order No. AA-W675C-TE.

28. *VAX EDT Reference Manual. 4.0 Edition.* Maynard, Mass.: Digital Equipment Corporation, 1984. Order No. AA-J726A-TC. *5.4 Edition.* 1988. Order No. AA-LA16A-TE.

29. *WPS-PLUS/VMS. Version 4.0 Edition.* Maynard, Mass.: Digital Equipment Corporation, 1991.

30. Eileen Wrigley. *Study Guide and Microcomputer Applications.* Columbus, Ohio: Merrill, 1986.

# Index